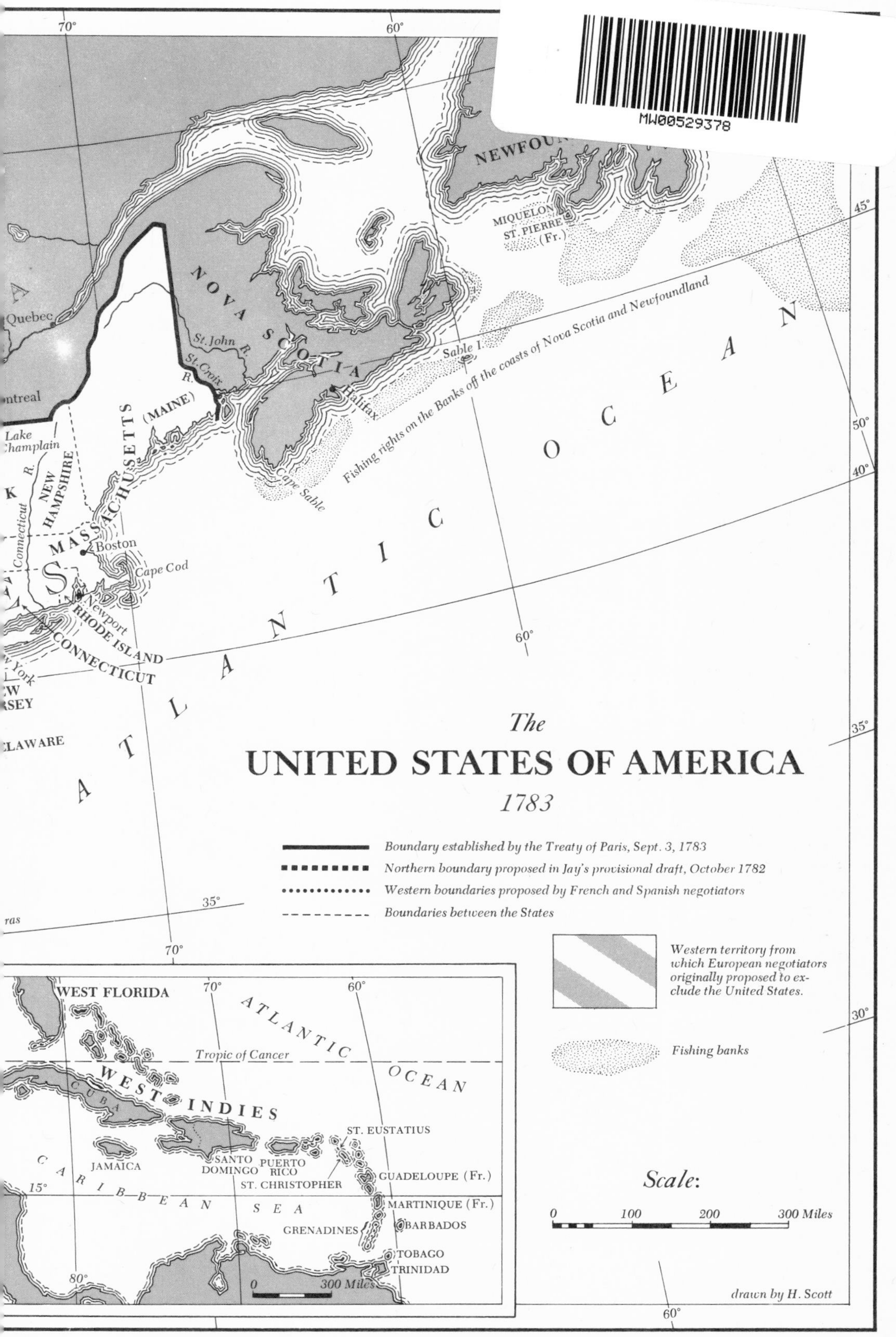
MW00529378
NEWFOUN
MIQUELON
ST. PIERRE (Fr.)
NOVA SCOTIA
Quebec
ntreal
St. John R.
St. Croix R.
Sable I.
Halifax
Cape Sable
Fishing rights on the Banks off the coasts of Nova Scotia and Newfoundland
(MAINE)
MASSACHUSETTS
Lake Champlain
NEW HAMPSHIRE
Connecticut R.
Boston
Cape Cod
Newport
RHODE ISLAND
CONNECTICUT
ATLANTIC OCEAN
The
UNITED STATES OF AMERICA
1783
Boundary established by the Treaty of Paris, Sept. 3, 1783
Northern boundary proposed in Jay's provisional draft, October 1782
Western boundaries proposed by French and Spanish negotiators
Boundaries between the States
Western territory from which European negotiators originally proposed to exclude the United States.
Fishing banks
Scale:
0 100 200 300 Miles
drawn by H. Scott
WEST FLORIDA
ATLANTIC OCEAN
Tropic of Cancer
WEST INDIES
CUBA
JAMAICA
SANTO DOMINGO
PUERTO RICO
ST. EUSTATIUS
ST. CHRISTOPHER
GUADELOUPE (Fr.)
MARTINIQUE (Fr.)
BARBADOS
GRENADINES
TOBAGO
TRINIDAD
CARIBBEAN SEA
0 300 Miles
70°
60°
45°
50°
40°
35°
30°
15°
80°

TRIUMPH IN PARIS

ALSO BY DAVID SCHOENBRUN

As France Goes (1957)

The Three Lives of Charles de Gaulle (1966)

Vietnam: How We Got In, How to Get Out (1968)

The New Israelis (with Robert and Lucy Szekely) (1973)

TRIUMPH IN PARIS

The Exploits of Benjamin Franklin

DAVID SCHOENBRUN

HARPER & ROW, PUBLISHERS

NEW YORK, HAGERSTOWN, SAN FRANCISCO

LONDON

 For information address Harper & Row, Publishers, Inc., 10 East 53rd Street, New York, N.Y. 10022. Published simultaneously in Canada by Fitzhenry & Whiteside Limited, Toronto.

FIRST EDITION

Designed by Sidney Feinberg

Library of Congress Cataloging in Publication Data

Schoenbrun, David
Triumph in Paris.
Bibliography: p.
Includes index.
1. Franklin, Benjamin, 1706–1790. 2. United States—Foreign relations—Revolution, 1775–1783. 3. United States—Foreign relations—France. 4. France—Foreign relations—United States. 5. Paris, Treaty of, 1783.
I. Title.
E302.6.F8S38 1976 973.3'2'0924 [B] 76–9199
ISBN 0–06–013854–8

76 77 78 79 80 10 9 8 7 6 5 4 3 2 1

This book and everything I hold most dear are for

DOROTHY

Contents

PART III

PARIS: *The War*

PART IV

PARIS: *The Peace*

Acknowledgments

Most books, although signed by one name, are the product of many talents. I owe a debt to every archivist and writer in the vast field of Franklin studies. Specific credits may be found in the annotated bibliography following the text.

More closely connected with the production of this book is a team of devoted and talented researchers and editors, foremost of whom is Amy Clampitt, who worked with me for almost two years, perusing and indexing thousands of documents. The completed research file ran to some two thousand single-spaced pages. Amy is a brilliant researcher, accurate, diligent, tireless and creative.

Thanks are due, also, to the cooperative and able staffs of two great French institutions: Les Archives du Ministère des Affaires Etrangères and La Bibliothèque Nationale, in Paris. Special credit accrues to two researchers who worked for me, at those institutions, on the primary documents of the eighteenth century. Lucy Szekely, a co-author, with her husband Robert Szekely, of my book *The New Israelis,* undertook the difficult task of deciphering the handwritten communications of the French Government for the years of Franklin's ambassadorship in Paris, an exceptionally demanding assignment which she accomplished brilliantly. Lucy is also my beloved daughter. Working with equal diligence and skill on the periodicals of the day, Barbara Nagelsmith contributed colorful material on the life of Paris during our Revolutionary War.

Every book I have written has been published and edited by my lifelong friend, Simon Michael Bessie, Senior Vice President of Harper & Row. Mike contributed much personal encouragement and an overall editorial concept. But the hard, page-by-page job of coping with a massive manuscript and cutting it down to manageable size without losing the essential elements was the invaluable contribution of Harper & Row's Sallie Gouverneur. Steady, patient, sensitive, but a strict taskmaster on content and style both, Sallie has made a contribution to every single page of the final manuscript. I am deeply indebted to her. Richard Passmore gave the manuscript a thorough copy editing that was brilliant and dogged. He checked dates, quotes, names and then swept through it for style and rhetoric over and over again. If there are any errors that remain, they are mine, but I don't think he missed anything and I thank him for a remarkable job.

But over and above all these able contributors, there is one who, I can truthfully say, played the major role, for without her love, patience, care and feeding of the author, encouragement during the desperate hours that every writer knows, this book would never have been completed: my wife, Dorothy, to whom the book is dedicated. Ben Franklin would have adored her, as does everyone who has ever known her.

D.S.

PART I

PHILADELPHIA: *A New Mission*

CHAPTER

1

Home, to Rest

The packet bound for Pennsylvania, four sails billowing in a fresh wind, glided out of Portsmouth Harbour under fair skies—rare weather for England on the day that the calendar, but rarely nature, proclaims the first day of spring. Ever the scientist, Benjamin Franklin had brought some simple instruments aboard, so that he could chart the Gulf Stream and observe its particularities. Expecting never to cross the ocean again—he was sixty-nine, in the winter of his life in an era when many men died in their forties—Franklin believed this was his last chance to conclude his maritime observations for a monograph on the subject during the days of rest ahead back home. Full of enthusiasm, the old man rose at dawn, and for hours at a time, until nightfall, he leaned over the ship's rail, dipping his thermometer, at the end of a long rope, into the Gulf Stream waters. He was among the first, perhaps the very first, to note, during night vigils, that those waters are not phosphorescent.

Franklin kept careful records of the temperature of the air as well as of the sea. He discovered, on crossing out of the Stream, a sharp drop in water temperature. From this he inferred the tropical source of the flow, and deduced its cause: the trade winds. He was one of the first to make this discovery, too.

He noted that the Gulf Stream had not only a flow, but a color, of its own, different from that of the surrounding ocean, and he observed a greater density of Gulf weed. He sighted a whale in the Atlantic but none in the Gulf Stream. He thought that, perhaps, the Stream could be considered a kind of river running through the ocean and that if it were so studied, it might be better understood.

He wrote in his journal: "A vessel from Europe to North America may shorten her passage by avoiding to stem the Stream, in which the thermometer will be very useful; and a vessel from America to Europe may do the same by the same means of keeping in it. It may often have happened accidentally that voyages have been shortened by these circumstances. It is well to have command of them."

Franklin the man, like Franklin the scientist, believed in commanding events, avoiding accidents, controlling the environment rather than submitting to it. Above all, he believed in self-control. Early in life, he was aware of dangerous personality traits in himself: he had a quick temper and sharp tongue; a hearty appetite that would result in gluttony if not disciplined; a lust that led him, he confessed in his diaries, to seek to lie with low women, all the while dreading venereal disease. To discipline himself, he invented a personal scorecard, ruled out on a sheet of paper: a horizontal column listing the days of the week and a vertical column, in the margin, listing his faults: temper, gluttony, laziness, vanity and so on. Each day, for years, he would put a black spot in the box next to a fault, to warn him of his errors. He would strive to eliminate that fault the next day, until, finally, he would reach a week without a single black spot on the record. After several years of effort, he did reach that week, but he felt such a surge of pride in the accomplishment that he realized at once the impossibility of controlling his pride. In disgust, he tore up the scorecard and never used it again, although in his diary he insisted that he frequently kept it in mind.

It was this pride that kept him working diligently every waking hour on that voyage in 1775, despite the aches and pains of old age. He suffered from boils, a skin rash that itched maddeningly, and the agony of the gout, but he kept up his studies of the sea by day and then, in the ship's common room, by the poor light of candles, worked until dawn on a long letter to his son William, Royal Governor of New Jersey, a passionate servant of the King. He wanted William to know what had happened in England, that his own career had ended and that he was coming home brokenhearted, fearing that war would inevitably break out between the colonies and the motherland. Later, in an outline for his autobiography, he entitled the letter "Negotiation to Prevent the War." It runs to more than fifty finely printed pages. In his introduction to Franklin's *Autobiographical Writings,* historian Carl Van Doren asserts that with this "masterpiece in the literature of diplomacy," "American diplomatic literature may be said to begin."

The negotiations that Franklin wrote about had been prompted by a series of events beginning in London in the fall of 1773. Franklin, America's principal representative there—he was commercial and political agent of the Massachusetts Bay Colony, New Jersey, Pennsylvania and Georgia—was caught in a cross-fire of conflicts. His mission was to represent the colonies in their commercial relations with London and also to be the advocate in their grievances against unfair laws and edicts of the Parliament and the royal government.

Franklin was profoundly American in his manners, his dress, his love for and faith in his native land. He was just as loyal and patriotic an Englishman and was, in addition, a royal servant, since he held a Crown commission as Postmaster General for the colonies. He had a dream, that he wrote of often and advocated at every opportunity, of a giant British Empire, girdling the globe, based upon a commonwealth of free nations, each with its own laws, its own government and freedoms, but bound together by a compact with the Crown for mutual benefit, mutual defense and the propagation of English freedoms.

Because of his love for America, he had all along advised members of Parliament and the King's Cabinet not to impose onerous taxes upon the Americans unless they were granted the right to representation in the Parliament. He had warned London constantly that Americans had founded a new land, built a society against great odds, and were capable, and determined, to govern themselves. For this, Franklin was denounced as a radical revolutionary, disloyal to his King. Because of his love for England and his vision of an Empire, with America as the greatest jewel in its crown, he just as constantly had counseled Americans not to resist violently, but to be patient and to allow him to negotiate in good faith. He kept writing home to report on the many good friends and freedom-loving Englishmen who were working to correct the grievances, men like Edmund Burke and Lord Chatham, William Pitt the Elder. Because of that, he was denounced by American radicals as a Tory, a valet of the King and disloyal to America.

A friend in London had given Franklin letters from the Royal Governor of the Massachusetts Bay Colony, Thomas Hutchinson—a haughty, arrogant man, much hated in Boston—who had written to London demanding police and army reinforcements to help him put down demonstrations in the colony. Franklin had sent the copies to Boston to prove to his friends there that it was not the Crown, but their very own Governor, who was oppressing them. Franklin begged his correspondents to keep the letters secret, to use them only to prove to the Boston radicals that there was still hope of redress from the Crown. He had miscalculated badly. Sam Adams, one of the leaders of the Sons of Liberty, saw the letters, read them at public meetings and led new demonstrations. He also accused Franklin of trying to save face for the King. But George III felt Franklin had betrayed his trust as Postmaster General by making the letters public and instructed the Solicitor-General to take action against him. Once again, Franklin, the would-be peacemaker, was caught in the middle between warring factions.

The colonial leaders in Boston sent Franklin instructions to petition the removal from office of the hated Governor Hutchinson. Franklin had begun lobbying among his friends, telling them that Hutchinson was now the target of such odium that he could no longer govern efficiently. Hearings on the petition were set for January, 1774.

On January 28, the eve of the hearing before the Privy Council, tea ships returning from Boston brought London news of the infamous Tea Party. Agent of rebellious Massachusetts, the most prominent American at hand, Franklin was the target for all the wrath of the realm.

The hearing was held in the "Cockpit," so called because cockfights had once been staged there. It began quietly enough, he later wrote his Boston friend Thomas Cushing, with Franklin's counsel, Dunning, reading a copy of the Massachusetts petition and resolves, including the demand to remove both Hutchinson and Lieutenant Governor Andrew Oliver from office. But the proceedings flared as Alexander Wedderburn, the fiery and ambitious Solicitor-General, stepped up to the table and launched into a violent attack upon the Massachusetts Assembly. The assemblymen were incorrigible dissidents, he charged. The governors were excellent men with a ten-year record of colonial administration without a single charge of misconduct. The Bostonians simply disliked them and had no real case against them.

Then Wedderburn sailed into his main target, not the petitions or resolves, but Franklin himself:

"They [the governors] owe, therefore, all the ill will which has been raised against them, and the loss of that confidence which the Assembly themselves acknowledge they had hitherto enjoyed, to Dr. Franklin's good offices in sending back these letters to Boston." Wedderburn warmed to the attack. "Nothing then will acquit Dr. Franklin of the charge of obtaining them [the letters] by fraudulent or corrupt means, for the most malignant of purposes; unless he stole them from the person who stole them. This argument is irrefragable."

Wedderburn looked directly at Franklin, and pointing an accusing finger at his victim, shouted: "I hope, my lords, you will mark and brand this man, for the honor of this country, of Europe, and of mankind." Wedderburn, waxing melodramatic, pounded the table and, raising his voice, declaimed: "He has forfeited all the respect of societies and of men. Into what companies will he hereafter go with an unembarrassed face or the honest intrepidity of virtue? Men will watch him with a jealous eye; they will hide their papers from him and lock up their escritoires."

Many of the lords and spectators, particularly those who hated and envied Franklin, laughed, cheered and rapped the table as Wedderburn conducted his scandalous attack on one of the most respected men in the world. Not all, however, joined in. Edmund Burke frowned and grimaced. As he came out of the hearing room, he told friends that the attack was "beyond all bounds and measure." Dr. Joseph Priestley turned his back upon Wedderburn, who had come forward to speak to him, and walked away coldly furious. Ralph Izard, of South Carolina, stated that if he had been so insulted he would have struck back.

Franklin did not strike back.

He sat there, through the entire tirade, never interrupting, never frowning, his head high, immovable, his eyes fixed on the distance, unblinking.

Once before, when under severe attack in London, Franklin had written a friend: "Let us, as we have ever done, uniformly endeavour the Service of our Country, according to the best of our Judgment and Abilities, and Time will do us Justice. Dirt thrown on a Mud-wall may stick and incorporate; but it will not long adhere to polish'd Marble." Now, in the Cockpit, Franklin's was the face of "polish'd Marble" to which, he hoped, the mud would not adhere.

In his letter to his friend Cushing, Franklin said that he was more sorrowful at damage done to principles of government than angry at any insult to himself.

Indeed what I feel on my own account is half lost in what I feel for the public. When I see that all petitions and complaints of grievances are so odious to government that even the mere pipe which conveys them becomes obnoxious, I am at a loss to know how peace and union are to be maintained or restored between the different parts of the Empire. Grievances cannot be redressed until they are known; and they cannot be known but through complaints and petitions. If these are deemed affronts, and the messengers punished as offenders, who will henceforth send petitions? And who will deliver them? It has been thought a dangerous thing in any state to stop up the vent of griefs. Wise governments have therefore generally received petitions with some indulgence, even when but slightly founded. Those who think themselves injured by their rulers are sometimes by a mild and prudent answer, convinced of their error. But where complaining is a crime, hope becomes despair.

Every diplomat, every reporter or editorialist, every leader of a political or civil action group today has voiced these same thoughts, almost with the very same words.

The ax fell on Franklin the very next day, as he had known it would. He was summarily fired from his position as Postmaster General for America. At first he wanted to pack up and go home. But he could not bring himself to leave London in disgrace after almost two decades of service as agent. He had a host of friends to whom he wished to make his farewells and he hoped that, perhaps, after all, one last chance might offer itself to him to prevent the calamity of war, to redeem himself so that he might leave London in triumph, his laurels in bloom.

In the course of his long service to America in London, Franklin had relaxed at the many London clubs of which he was a member. There were dozens of clubs for men of all tastes and backgrounds: for merchants and traders, for wits and for gamblers; for men of letters and of the arts; for men of science and of medicine. Franklin qualified for almost all of them and all of them wanted Franklin as a member. He often appeared at the Royal Society Club, as a guest of the leading host of famous men of the day, Dr. John Pringle, with whom he enjoyed a quiet evening of chess. It was a conversation in that club and his passion for chess that brought him, quite unexpectedly, the chance he had waited for through the long months of humiliation following upon his dismissal as postmaster.

One of the members approached Franklin, early in November, 1774, and said that "there was a certain lady who had a desire of playing with me at chess, fancying she could beat me, and had requested him to bring me to her; it was, he said, a lady with whose acquaintance he was sure I should be pleased, as sister of Lord Howe's, and he hoped I would not refuse the challenge."*

Franklin would certainly not refuse so charming a challenge.

*This opener and the narrative that follows were written by Franklin in his shipboard memoirs.

He loved both chess and ladies. By the end of the month, he had cleared some time, setting the rendezvous for Friday morning, December 2.

"I . . . played a few games with the lady, whom I found of a very sensible conversation and pleasing behaviour, which induced me to agree most readily to another meeting a few days after; though I had not the least apprehension that any political business could have any connection with this new acquaintance."

His last remark could only have been tongue-in-cheek. One of the lady's brothers was General Sir William Howe, who had fought at Quebec, and was rumored to be getting a new command in America. The other, even more important, was Rear Admiral Richard Howe, an earl of the realm and a member of Parliament.

Franklin began to see just who was making the moves in this game when, on the eve of his second chess date, he received a call, at home, from an old friend who was deeply involved in London politics: David Barclay, a Quaker banker and merchant, and a sympathetic supporter of America. Barclay had close ties with an influential peer, Lord Hyde, chancellor of the Duchy of Lancaster, whom Franklin had known when he was in the post office and the diplomatic service, and whom he knew to be a friend of Lord Howe. The chess game had many players.

Barclay, Franklin noted, "spoke of the dangerous situation of American affairs, the hazard that a civil war might be brought on by the present measures, and the great merit that a person would have who could contrive some means of preventing so terrible a calamity and bring about a reconciliation."

These were the words that Franklin had been longing to hear. He almost exploded with excitement when Barclay followed up the meeting with a note informing Franklin that he had "accidentally met our mutual friend, Dr. Fothergill, in my way home, and I intimated to him the subject of our discourse." Immediately thereafter came a note from Dr. John Fothergill, asking Franklin to meet with him and Barclay the following evening "to confer on American affairs."

The name "Fothergill" was all Franklin needed to know that

Barclay had been primed by others higher up. Fothergill was the personal physician of Lord Dartmouth, Secretary of State for America. Franklin did not for a minute believe they had run into each other "accidentally," almost on his doorstep. This was a political chess game for high stakes.

The lady made the first move. After a brief, polite conversation over chess the next morning, Miss Howe got to the point: "And what is to be done with this dispute between Great Britain and the colonies? I hope we are not to have a civil war?"

"They should kiss and be friends," said Franklin. "What can they do better? Quarreling can be of service to neither, but is ruin to both."

"I have often said," she replied, "that I wished government would employ you to settle the dispute for 'em; I am sure nobody could do it so well. Do you not think that the thing is practical?"

"Undoubtedly, madam, if the parties are disposed to reconciliation; for the two countries have really no clashing interests to differ about. 'Tis rather a matter of punctilio which two or three reasonable people might settle in half an hour."

At Dr. Fothergill's that evening, Fothergill told Franklin he hoped he had already "put pen to paper, and formed some plan for consideration, and brought it with me." Franklin, still moving slowly, playing the reluctant mediator, answered that he had formed no plan, for he was convinced that the ministry showed no disposition for accommodation.

Fothergill protested that this was not the case. He said "he had reason, *good reason,* to believe others differently disposed." This was as close as he dared come to saying outright that Dartmouth was of a favorable disposition. He beseeched Franklin to work with the two of them in elaborating a plan and promised it would get attention in the right hands. "And what appeared reasonable to us, two of us being Englishmen, might appear so to them."

Franklin set a date for the following Tuesday evening to bring to them a plan, and worked all through the weekend on a seventeen-point proposal, which he modestly entitled "Hints for Conversation upon the Subject of Terms that might probably produce

Union between Britain and the Colonies."

Article 1 proposed that Boston pay for the tea destroyed, a most generous proposal in the circumstances, establishing Franklin's credentials as a fair negotiator, for the first point went to the ministerial side.

Article 2, balancing the first, proposed repeal of the hated duty on tea.

Article 3 called for re-enactment of the Acts of Navigation, followed by a fourth article proposing the stationing of a Crown naval officer in each colony to supervise the Acts, another gesture of reconciliation with the other side.

Then came a series of demands that had long been put forward by Franklin on behalf of the colonies: repeal of all acts restraining manufactures; all duties to be paid into colonial treasuries; customs officers to be appointed by local governors, not by London; no military requisitions in time of peace; no quartering of troops; an agreement not to build Crown fortresses without consent of the provinces; judges to be appointed and paid by the provinces, not the Crown; finally, Article 17, a vital point: "all powers of internal legislation in the colonies to be disclaimed by Parliament." Franklin noted that Article 17 "could hardly be obtained, but might be tried."

Fothergill and Barclay, upon receiving the plan, finally revealed just who was playing the chess game.

"Suppose," said Mr. Barclay, "I were to show this paper to Lord Hyde; would there be anything amiss in so doing?"

Dr. Fothergill told Franklin what he already knew, that he saw Lord Dartmouth daily and would be pleased to communicate the paper to him as coming from persons who wished the welfare of both countries. Franklin politely told them that he had drawn the paper at their request and "it was now theirs to do with what they pleased."

On December 18, Franklin received a note from Barclay reporting Lord Hyde's "hearty wish that they might be productive," an understandably noncommittal reply, but encouraging nonetheless.

Four days later, a setback: Barclay dined with Franklin and told him that Lord Hyde thought the propositions too hard.

Miss Howe sent a new invitation to Franklin to meet with her on the evening of Christmas Day. It was a cold, bleak Christmas, London at its worst, its famous black snow falling, flakes mixed with soot from the chimneys. Franklin was discouraged, but brightened up when Miss Howe told him that her brother, Lord Howe, "would like to make his acquaintance."

Franklin said he had "always heard a good character of Lord Howe, and should be proud of the honour of being known to him."

To his surprise, she asked if she should not send for him at once, and, Franklin assenting, she wrote a note, dispatched a servant and, in only a few minutes' time, Lord Howe arrived upon the scene.

He wasted no time. He told Franklin he was aware of the "alarming situation of our affairs with America." He knew no one better informed or more qualified to effect a reconciliation than Franklin. He conjectured that Franklin, at this point, would not want direct communications with the ministry, or even acknowledge indirect communication. He assured Franklin of his own discretion and begged him to propose a plan for reconciliation through him.

Franklin assured Lord Howe that his own personal injuries were little compared to the injuries done his country, that he had a sincere desire to heal the breach but saw yet no such disposition on the part of the King or the ministry. But he was ready to try. In a statement of the pure pragmatist, Franklin said that he never allowed his private affairs to interfere with his public duties; "that I could join with my personal enemy in serving the public, or, when it was for its interest, with the public in serving that enemy."

The two men agreed to go on meeting at the sister's house, for it was known that Franklin was now a regular visitor and it would not excite suspicion.

When he came to meet Lord Howe for the second time, Howe told him that events had progressed, that he could now assure him, "of a certainty, that there was a sincere disposition in Lord North [the Prime Minister] and Lord Dartmouth to accommodate the differences with America."

Then Lord Howe, smiling, drew a paper from his pocket and

asked Franklin if it was familiar to him.

It was a copy, in David Barclay's hand, of Franklin's "Hints." Franklin pointed out that it was supposed to have been secret, but he trusted Lord Howe and acknowledged authorship.

Lord Howe expressed his regrets at this, for "there was no likelihood of the admission of those propositions." He hoped Franklin would reconsider and form a more acceptable plan.

Franklin was neither surprised nor dismayed. He had never anticipated a ready acceptance of his admittedly severe terms. But he was angered by Lord Howe's concluding remarks "that he should not think of influencing me by any selfish motive, but certainly I might with reason expect any reward in the power of government to bestow."

It was, unmistakably, indeed crudely, a bribe.

Franklin characterized it: "This to me was what the French vulgarly call *spitting in the soup.*"

However, he kept his temper. He dispatched a paper to Miss Howe for her brother, in which he repeated the Continental Congress' request that all oppressive acts be repealed, promising that in the future Congress would show itself worthy and loyal. This promise, freely made, said Franklin, was more reliable than any made under force.

At the turn of the new year, on January 2, 1775, Lord Howe sent his sister a note for Franklin, promising to forward his propositions but that he was "fearful that the desired accommodation threatens to be attended with much greater difficulty than I had flattered myself . . . there would be reason to apprehend." Miss Howe extended a new invitation to a chess game during that week. There, she showed Franklin a letter from her brother, who was in the country, asking whether it could possibly be arranged that Boston pay for the tea against a sure promise that there would be a redress of their grievances on future petitions. He also wondered whether the proposition in the "Hints" relative to "aids" was still in Franklin's mind.

Franklin sat down and promptly penned a reply confirming that he had not changed his mind on redresses or aids. Parliament had

had no right to tax Americans or extort monies from them on duty Acts, backed up with armed forces, *preceding* the destruction of the tea. Injuries done to America by blocking up the port of Boston as punishment for the Tea Party were twentyfold the injuries done to the tea company. Until this was corrected, and other satisfactions made, there could be no accommodation.

Franklin was cheered at the opening session of Parliament when England's great statesman, Lord Chatham, true to his promises of support, offered a motion to relieve tensions in Boston by ordering General Thomas Gage, who was in charge of the blockade there, to remove his forces. But the majority voted it down. Chatham, not discouraged by the defeat of his motion, began to work on his own plan for reconciliation. Toward the end of January he met with Franklin and showed his plan to him, asking for advice and support. He had gone further than any other leading Englishman by agreeing that only Americans could tax Americans. He approved the Continental Congress and suggested that it be made a permanent institution. Like Franklin he asked Parliament to suspend the acts the Congress complained of, but he still felt that Parliament should legislate for the colonies and bind them to the Empire.

Franklin thought it was far from perfect as a plan but could serve as the basis for a treaty and prevent immediate mischief.

Meanwhile, Howe approached Franklin, this time saying he was planning to go to America and would like to take Franklin with him, as an assistant. Franklin curtly replied that if the propositions to be taken were reasonable he would gladly go and try to persuade his countrymen, but if they were not, there was no point in anyone going. To Franklin's amazement and utter disgust, Lord Howe ignored the rebuff and went on to promise Franklin he would pay him the arrears of his salary as agent, which the ministry had impounded. By a supreme effort, Franklin again held his temper. Howe then asked if Franklin would be willing to meet directly with a minister, with Lord Hyde, for example. Franklin said he would, but Lord Hyde declined to meet with him.

Suddenly, as so often happens in negotiations, when each side is testing the other, a breakthrough appeared. On February 4, at a meeting with Barclay at Dr. Fothergill's, Franklin learned that the "Hints" had been carefully studied and replies prepared on all the seventeen points. Thirteen of the seventeen, in all but minor details, had been approved. Three had been objected to. And the vital article, seventeen, which Franklin knew would be the sticking point, had been rejected as totally inadmissible.

On the face of it, it did not seem a bad first reply, a baker's dozen of seventeen requests approved. But Franklin knew the mind behind the face. The last article was the most meaningful. It had to be read carefully, like the last clause of an insurance policy which canceled all that had gone before.

Franklin told them "that while the Parliament claimed and exercised a power of altering our constitutions at pleasure there could be no agreement; for we were rendered unsafe in every privilege we had a right to, and were secure in nothing."

As he began to lose hope, Franklin's determination to resist at all costs grew. Despite himself, the conciliator was slowly becoming a revolutionary, growing more convinced that war was all but inevitable. His replies to the negotiators and the lords became tarter, shorter, less conciliatory. After a bad session at the House of Lords, Franklin went home "irritated and heated" and hastily dashed off a strongly worded "memorial," or memorandum, to Lord Dartmouth. One last bit of caution remained and he thought to show the document to his friend Thomas Walpole, a member of Commons. As Walpole read it, he looked at Franklin several times, "as if he apprehended me a little out of my senses." Eventually, Walpole responded with a note that said: "I return you the memorial which it is thought might be attended with dangerous consequences to your person, and contribute to exasperate the nation." Franklin began packing all his personal things and voluminous documents. He was finally leaving England.

Franklin, so cool and reasonable, was provoked beyond his talent for self-discipline in those days of March, 1775. He raged about a meeting at Sir John Pringle's where, in his presence, General Clarke boasted that "with a thousand British grenadiers, he would undertake to go from one end of America to the other, and geld all the males, partly by force and partly by a little coaxing."

Franklin made a polite but cool farewell to his charming chess partner and Lord Howe. They would meet again, this time at war. He said farewell to Barclay and Fothergill, bidding them keep up their good efforts. He signed on to take the Pennsylvania packet, leaving for Philadelphia on March 21. The chess game was over, the real game was about to begin.

On his last day in London, ending almost twenty years of faithful service, the old man, crushed in spirit, had made his way to the home of his ever-faithful friend and fellow scientist, Dr. Joseph Priestley, to spend his last hours with him.

Priestley noted those last moments in his journal:

> . . . much of the time was employed in reading American newspapers, especially accounts of the reception which the Boston port bill met with in America; and, as he read the addresses to the inhabitants of Boston, from the places in the neighborhood, the tears trickled down his cheeks. . . .
>
> He urged so much the doctrine of forebearance, that for some time he was unpopular with the Americans on that account, as too much a friend to Great Britain. His advice to them was to bear everything for the present, as they were sure, in time, to outgrow all their grievances; as it could not be in the power of the mother country to oppress them long.
>
> He dreaded the war, and said that, if the difference should come to an open rupture, it would be a war of ten years, and he should not live to see the end of it.

The wise old man, so often right and prophetic, had been wrong this last day in London.

As he got into the post coach for Portsmouth, his eyes were wet, and he was clinging to the hand of his grandson Temple.

Now, on the voyage home, the weather was good. Franklin breathed deeply of the salt air; the sun warmed his old bones, eased his aches. He rubbed oil on his scaling skin and hot poultices on his boils to draw them out. The beautiful days found him at the ship's side, studying the waters. He had designed a primitive odometer to determine its speed. On starry nights, he would take short breaks from his writing and study the skies through his telescope. For the first time in years he was thoroughly indulging himself, thinking of nothing but his maritime studies and his memoirs. He was literally lost at sea without long-distance communication.

The weather in Massachusetts was very different from the calm seas in which Franklin was sailing. The worst political tempests had erupted. General Gage had replaced the hated Governor Hutchinson and things had gone from bad to worse. In the fall of 1774, just as Franklin was beginning his chess game, Gage had dissolved the local Assembly. As soon as they were dismissed, the assemblymen had met promptly at Concord and constituted themselves as a provincial Congress, presided over by John Hancock. Ignoring Gage's existence in Boston, the Assembly of Concord had appointed its own treasurer to collect its own taxes. A Committee of Safety was created to collect arms and munitions and to train a local militia, the embryo of the Minute Men. All through that dismal winter of '74–'75, while Franklin negotiated in vain in London, the forces in Massachusetts had been roaring ahead on a collision course.

Governor Gage, in effect, was the governor of Boston, where his regiments and ships made him master. But he was not the true governor of the Massachusetts Bay Province, which by then was self-governing. The leaders knew that Gage might make a move to dissolve them by force in Concord and try to re-establish British rule throughout the colony. They set up, through the Committee of Safety, not only a militia but an intelligence system to warn them well in advance of any impending British attack.

As one of their intelligence agents in Boston, they chose one of the Sons of Liberty, Paul Revere. Revere and a network of friends kept a close watch on Gage's troops, ready to ride and cry the warning the moment the redcoats packed for a march.

Gage had his own network of informers and observers. In April, he sent one of them, John Howe, on a mission to reconnoiter the countryside, from Boston to Concord, where the Assembly met. Howe interviewed farmers, including one very old man he found cleaning a gun.

"I asked him," wrote Howe, "what he was going to kill, as he was so old. I should not think he could take sight on any game; he said there was a flock of redcoats at Boston which he expected would be here soon; he meant to try and hit some of them, as he expected they would be very good marks. . . . I asked him how old he was and he said: 'Seventy-seven and never was killed yet.' " In the middle of the conversation, the old man turned to his wife and said: "Old woman, put in the bullet pouch a handful of buckshot, as I understand the English like an assortment of plums."

An interview made many years after the war, with a ninety-one-year-old veteran of the Battle of Concord, struck the same chord. Captain Samuel Prescott denied he had taken up arms because of intolerable oppression. Never felt any oppression, he said. "Never saw one of those stamps. I certainly never paid a penny for one of them . . . never drank a drop of the stuff [tea]; the boys threw it all overboard. Never heard of Harington, Sidney or Locke, read only the Bible . . . psalms, the almanach."

He was asked by a puzzled interviewer, "Well, then, what was the matter? And what did you mean in going to the fights?" The veteran replied: "Young man, what we meant in going for those redcoats was this: we always had governed ourselves and we always meant to. They didn't mean we should."

Nothing could more perfectly illustrate how well Franklin understood his fellow Americans, including the simplest of them. He had told British officials that it was not enough to lower duties or cut the price of tea, that Parliament must abandon pretensions to legislate for the colonies. They meant to govern themselves. King George, wrong-minded as he was, guessed correctly when he kept the tea tax on to symbolize Parliament's sovereignty, announcing: "The dye is now cast. The Colonies must either submit or triumph."

General Gage was the man to cast the die. He was unimpressed with the reports of armed men in the countryside. How could mere peasants with antiquated squirrel rifles stand up to the mightiest army on earth with the most modern weapons? He was, however, sufficiently impressed by reports of militia in training, ready to fight, building up arms depots. He did not fear them, but he would not let them grow too big. He decided to pull their teeth by sending Major John Pitcairn out on a raiding expedition to root out arms dumps. They packed to march on the night of the eighteenth of April. Paul Revere and his scouts saw them, saddled up and rode off to warn the countryside that the redcoats were coming.

When Pitcairn and his men reached Lexington, he saw, blocking the way, a determined band of Minute Men lined up, muskets ready. "Disperse, ye rebels, disperse," came the command. Someone, no one knows who, fired a shot. In seconds, flashes came from the muzzles of all the guns facing each other on Lexington Common. As the superior British troops moved forward, bayonets fixed, the Minute Men broke ranks and ran for cover, leaving eight of their fellows dead upon the ground.

The British continued their march to Concord, seat of the Assembly. They meant to wipe out the 'wasps' nest. The farmers were waiting for them there, too, spoiling for a fight, the fight immortalized by Emerson as "the shot heard round the world." Within six days, fast expresses had brought the news to Philadelphia. It was relayed swiftly to Richmond and Charleston. Fighting broke out in Virginia and North Carolina. The news reached London before Gage's official report could give the facts and ran in the British press as an account of a slaughter of peaceful farmers. Parliament rang to the shouts of an enraged opposition. Paris, watching American events closely, thirsting for revenge for the humiliating defeat inflicted on France by Britain in the Seven Years' War, ran screaming headlines, while the Foreign Office made its first plans to keep close to the rebel cause.

It took time, but the shots were eventually heard around the world—everywhere, that is, except aboard the Pennsylvania packet in the mid-Atlantic. There, Ben Franklin was spending his days dipping his thermometer into the waters, his nights poring over the notes of his negotiations and covering sheet after sheet of foolscap with his fine copperplate hand. He was deeply engrossed in the past, a past that was already a dead letter. It no longer mattered—except to future historians—why the war could not be prevented,

or who was responsible; it had already broken out. In a sense, it was symbolically fitting that Franklin was one of the few men in the world who had not heard the shot, for it was a shot he had never wanted to hear, and had labored mightily to forestall.

The Pennsylvania packet sailed into Philadelphia on May 5, under skies as fair as they had left in Portsmouth. But the dark political thunderheads Franklin had deplored in London had moved, he would learn on disembarking, to the colonies. He would find armed men on horseback, militia training in the streets and courtyards, farmers at dawn, before going to their fields, meeting with bankers and clerks to practice military formations.

He could see crowds gathering at the docks waiting for the ship to berth. He expected that, for the arrival of a packet was always a great event. What he did not expect was the presence of a delegation with special news for him. He was home, but he was not going to get any rest.

CHAPTER

2

Benjamin Franklin, Congressman

As Franklin made his unsteady way down the gangplank, he heard cheers breaking out and his name being called. He was startled. For an old man, coming home in disgrace to explain his failure, it was a most unexpected and pleasant greeting.

Men grabbed him and Temple, helping them to the dock and hugging them at the same time, a warm but awkward procedure. When they disentangled and began shaking hands all about, someone shouted to Franklin: "We won the fight, we won, the redcoats broke and ran." Franklin, puzzled, tried to calm them down so they might give him a coherent account of what was going on. He heard the news of Lexington and Concord. It was no more than he had expected and feared, although he kept silent his skepticism about the redcoats breaking ranks and running.

Then came the second news, as important as the first: a Second Continental Congress had been agreed upon, would meet in a few days, and Franklin's friends in Philadelphia wanted him to head up their delegation. Agent Ben Franklin, veteran negotiator and mediator, was now, at sixty-nine, being called upon to assume a new role as a statesman: delegate to a Continental Congress at a time of rebellion.

Franklin did not hesitate a second.

Never a passive or reflective philosopher, always a man of action, he was eager to plunge into the mainstream of events.

Franklin, more than any other American, was ready for the occasion. None had worked so diligently on the question of relations with Britain. None had struggled so long, in the very eye of the storm, to prevent the war, thus none was so free of scruples in waging it. Franklin had nothing for which to reproach himself; he was therefore free to move ahead. Most reluctant, for years, to envisage separation, he had lived with the idea a long time and, the die being cast, was prepared for it. He became one of the most outspoken and ardent advocates for independence among all the congressmen.

But Franklin had no intention of breaking his ties with the many Englishmen with whom he had formed so close a friendship over the years. He knew that if war was coming, a peace would eventually have to be negotiated. He understood that he would have a major role to play in both war and peace, for no other American knew the English so well or was so well known to them. One day his friends would prevail in London, and he meant to stay close to them every step of the way.

The very day after landing, not yet unpacked and besieged by well-wishers and congressional delegates arriving in town, he sat down to write the first of hundreds of letters he would write from Philadelphia and then from Paris in the years ahead, a letter that set the pattern of his future correspondence. It was to one of his closest and most influential friends, David Hartley, a fellow scientist with whom he had conducted experiments on fireproofing homes.

> I arrived last night, and have the pleasure to learn that there is the most perfect unanimity throughout the Colonies; and that even New York, on whose defection the Ministry so confidently rely'd, is as hearty and zealous as any of the rest. I have not yet had time to collect particulars of information for you; and, therefore, the chief intention of this line is to introduce to you the bearer, Capt. Falconer, who is perfectly acquainted with the state of things here, and on whose accounts you may depend.

Franklin was a skilled propagandist. He knew his letters would be passed around and he wanted them to be. It was important that the ministry believe there was perfect unanimity in America, though, in fact, it was considerably less than perfect. New York dragged its feet throughout the Continental Congress, was one of the most Tory, most reluctant of the major colonies. The illusion still persisted there that the King would see the light and that a few more petitions would do the job of restoring legislative liberties. A very few delegates, led by Franklin, were for independence. Most were still loyal to Britain. Lexington and Concord were regarded as acts of self-defense, not of revolution. Franklin, who had had to deal more closely with the ministry than anyone, knew just how futile further petitions would be. But he wanted none of this known in London.

The second characteristic of the letter that set the future pattern was the use of a ship's captain as courier. The mails could no longer be trusted. They would not only be read; they would, Franklin was sure, be seized. Ship's captains were thus the first couriers in what would become the courier system of the U.S. Secret Service.

A week later, Franklin wrote to his friend with the closest ties to ruling circles, the pro-American Bishop of St. Asaph, Jonathan Shipley.

> My Dear Lord,
>
> I arrived here well, the 5th, after a pleasant passage of six weeks. I met with a most cordial reception, I should say from all parties, but that all parties are extinguished here. Britain has found means to unite us. I had not been here a day before I was unanimously elected by our Assembly a delegate to the Congress, which met the 10th, and is now sitting. All the governors have been instructed by the ministry to call their Assemblies and propose to them Lord North's pacific plan. General Gage called his, but, before they could meet, drew the sword; and a war is commenced which the youngest of us may not see the end of. My endeavours will be, if possible, to quench it, as I know yours will be; but the satisfaction of endeavouring to do good is perhaps all we can obtain or effect.

While talking quietly to his fellow delegates about independence, Franklin was more discreet in public and in his letters. For his purposes in London, he still assumed the pose of a man of reconciliation. Had he not done so, his friends there could not have carried on a campaign for him.

Early in the Congress, he drafted a resolution of thanks to Lord Chatham, to Edmund Burke and to Hartley and Shipley, his main correspondents, for their efforts to effect a reconciliation, and he included in the resolution praise to "all the noble Lords and Commoners in both Houses of Parliament who have been pleased to espouse the cause of our much injured and oppressed Country." This resolution does not appear in the official *Journal* of Congress and there is no evidence that Franklin ever introduced it, but copies were sent to London, and, after all, this is what Franklin intended it for.

Meanwhile, Franklin was being feted as a hero in Philadelphia, a new and heart-warming experience for a vain old man who yearned for love and honors.

Christopher Marshall, a retired druggist, kept a diary and noted on May 7 the enthusiastic reception for Ben Franklin, "the long exiled chief of the liberals, to the satisfaction of his friends and the lovers of liberty." On May 9, crowds gathered again at the docks to cheer the arrival of four delegates from South Carolina on the Charleston packet. Marshall, in the crowd that day, noted: "The officers of all the city companies, and nearly every gentleman who could get a horse, five hundred mounted men in all, rode six miles out of town to meet the coming members and escort them to the city. All Philadelphia gathered in the streets, at the windows, on the housetops, to see the procession pass and salute the delegate with cheers." On the tenth arrived the delegates from New England, New York and New Jersey. That night all the assembled congressmen met to dine together. Franklin proposed a toast to Edmund Burke and promptly sent him a note: "Your health was among the foremost."

John Dickinson, a Pennsylvania lawyer, with whom Franklin had clashed many years earlier in a quarrel over the colony's constitution, favored a second petition to the King. Franklin opposed such a move, not only as futile but because it would be read by George III as a sign of weakness, reducing the shock wave of Lexington and Concord. But he did not press his opposition, letting it merely ride for the record. It was more important, Franklin thought, to maintain a united front, so he humored Dickinson and his group. So reasonable was Franklin that, when the motion passed, he was named to a committee of five to prepare the draft of the petition to the King.

This was only one of ten committees to which Franklin was named: to investigate the sources of saltpeter, to negotiate with the Indians, to get Continental money engraved and printed, to consider a conciliatory proposal from Lord North, to serve on the salt and lead committee and the regulation of commerce committee. The most important, after that on drafting the Declaration of Independence, was the Committee of Secret Correspondence, charged with relations with foreign countries. It was the origin of the U.S. Department of State, and Ben Franklin, when he left in the fall of 1776 on his mission to Paris, would become America's first ambassador abroad.

In addition to all those duties, Franklin was elected chairman of the Committee of Safety of Pennsylvania and put in charge of organizing the colony's means of defense. He also served on a committee to draft a resolution appointing George Washington commander in chief of the Continental Armies. The appointment that delighted him most, however, was his own appointment as the first Postmaster General of the United States (although they were still referred to as the united colonies). It was, essentially, the same post he had held in London, but this time by appointment of his fellows, not the Crown.

Franklin laid down a system of procedures that solidly established the postal department down to our own day. He changed the franking stamp he had used in London, which had read "Free, Ben Franklin," to read "B. free Franklin."

He had thought to come home to rest. Instead, the year from the summer of 1775 to the summer of 1776 was one of the busiest of his life. He was up at dawn supervising the training of the Pennsylvania militia, planning arms dumps and caches, scouting out sources of saltpeter, studying various chemical formulae for gunpowder. The committee asked him to design a new model of pike for infantry use against a British bayonet charge. He helped design a river obstruction of iron and logs on the model of the French chevaux de frise. Placed in the channel leading to the harbor, these obstructions later kept the British fleet out of range of Philadelphia for almost two months.

Gone were the leisure months at the London clubs, the long dinners in taverns or at the homes of friends. Gone the graceful English country estates. None of these was available in colonial America girding for war. Franklin went out little, went to bed early to prepare for a day that would exhaust any man, let alone one moving into his seventieth year. He was most pleased when one of the first of the American armed boats constructed on a design he had helped oversee was named the *Franklin.*

When, on July 21, the Congress resolved itself into a committee of the whole to undertake a study of "the state of America," Franklin drafted and presented a remarkable document, called "The Articles of Confederation and Perpetual Union." It was a somewhat revised version of the plan for union he had first drafted for the Albany Congress in 1753, and the precursor to the federal Constitution.

Franklin's plan for "confederation and perpetual union" came as close to a declaration of independence as one could come without actually proclaiming the act. He softened it only by adding the qualification that the union was to remain in effect until the King accepted the petition of Congress, repealed restraining acts, made reparations for the injuries to Boston and the burning of neighboring Charlestown, and withdrew all British troops from America. In other words, never, for Franklin did not expect any of his conditions to be met. It was his way of pushing the Congress toward independence without actually saying so.

Thomas Jefferson, who admired the old man tremendously, was becoming his fast friend. He liked the Articles and was ready to vote for them. But most of the delegates were still too loyal, still hopeful of reconciliation, and the motion could not carry. Instead, Franklin was asked to join with Jefferson and Richard Henry Lee to propose a reply to Lord North's so-called peace offer. They judged it was not serious, for it contained no important concessions. They reported against it and the Congress voted to reject it.

Franklin, aware of his lack of skill as an orator, in Congress followed the method that he had used in London, of speaking little but saying something meaningful when he did speak, counting on his extraordinary prestige to carry him through his long silences.

John Adams never did quite understand the tremendous success Franklin had in the Congress. He noted that Franklin almost never spoke and, when he did, not very well, yet, like Jefferson and Washington, two other strong and silent men, Franklin kept getting appointed to the most important committees, while Adams, who fancied himself an eloquent orator, was appointed to but a few minor posts.

One member of Congress, Benjamin Rush, sent a letter to his wife in Princeton, to tell her of his role. "I spoke for the first time today, about ten minutes, upon a question that proved successful. I felt I was not thundering like Cato in the Utica of our committee of inspection. The audience is truly respectable. Dr. Franklin, alone, is enough to confound with his presence a thousand such men as myself."

Franklin suffered two bitter personal disappointments at this time, in the final defection from the Congress and the American cause of his blood son, William, still Royal Governor of New Jersey, and his spiritual son, Joseph Galloway, a Philadelphia lawyer and politician to whom Franklin had been almost a father in years past. He went to see both of them, pleading with them to join the Congress. Both were adamant in rejecting the cause. Franklin had counted on them to work closely with him and he was dejected when he left them.

In all letters to England, Franklin kept his spirits high.

On July 7, he sent a long letter to Jonathan Shipley, relating the state of affairs, and warning of dire consequences to Britain. It was clearly the letter of a man who had thrown off the cloak of conciliation to draw the sword of revolution.

He began by telling Shipley how the tradesmen of the city were in the field twice a day, at military exercises. He boasted that Philadelphia alone had three battalions, a troop of light horse and a company of artillery. The Continental Army, he claimed, was already twenty thousand strong.

He spoke with indignation of the behavior of Gage's troops who, "without the least necessity, barbarously plundered a fine, undefended town opposite to Boston, called Charlestown, consisting of about four hundred houses, many of them elegantly built; some sick, aged and decrepit poor persons, who could not be carried off in time, perishing in the flames." Franklin railed that "we never received so much damage from the Indian savages as in this one day there." Lest the ministers think this a way to force reconciliation, let them be warned that "I am not half so reconcilable now as I was a month ago."

Franklin thought that England had neither the temper nor wisdom "of recovering our affections." He foresaw the war going on with "an end to all commerce between us." Blockade would do England no good, for America had all the resources it needed to live on, within its own lands. We buy from you, wrote Franklin, mainly luxuries and superfluities to the extent of four to five millions per year. A blockade would only help America to save that money and pay for the war, leaving England, eventually, with, at the most, some fortified places, "as the Spaniards on the coast of Africa, but can penetrate as little into the country."

"In this ministerial war against us, all Europe is conjured not to sell us arms or ammunition, that we may be found defenseless and more easily murdered. . . . You see I am warm; and, if a temper naturally cool and phlegmatic can, in old age, which often cools the warmest, be thus heated, you will judge by that of the general temper here, which is now little short of madness."

Shortly after writing to Shipley, he took up his pen for a note to another old friend, his landlady, Margaret Stevenson of Craven Street, London. Her daughter, Polly, had sent Franklin a cash donation for the victims of Lexington and Concord, for which he had thanked her. Now he wanted to do a good turn for the family, with some financial advice. Franklin, born poor and self-made, was always concerned about money and investments, particularly since his family was a severe drain on his resources. He was always watching stock markets, studying land schemes, and would continue those pursuits all through the war and the peace negotiations in Paris.

"My dear, dear friend," he wrote. "All Trade and Business, Building, Improving etc., being at a Stand here, and nothing thought of but arms, I find no Convenience at present of putting out your money in this country." He went on to advise her to hold it liquid for the time being.

Franklin kept busy with the practical work of his important committees and avoided taking much part in the long and, he thought, boring debates in Congress, an attitude which continued to bother John Adams. Adams wrote home to his wife, who, like most Americans, was fascinated by Franklin and wanted to know all about him:

> You have more than once, in your letters, mentioned Dr. Franklin, and, in one, intimated a desire that I should write you something concerning him. . . .
>
> His conduct has been composed and grave. . . . He has not assumed anything, nor affected to take the lead. . . . Yet he has not been backward, has been very useful on many occasions and discovered a disposition entirely American. He does not hesitate at our boldest measures, but rather seems to think us irresolute and backward. He thinks us at present in an odd state, neither in peace nor in war, neither dependent nor independent; but he thinks that we shall soon assume a character more decisive . . . and set up a separate state.

Franklin, the oldest member of the Congress—more than half of the members were under forty—was one of the most determined on the issue of independence. Boston radicals had accused him, when he was playing the role of conciliator in London, of dragging his feet, if not actually favoring the British side. Now he was far ahead of most of them, once having made up his mind that independence was ineluctable.

Franklin worked hard to set up reserves of saltpeter, salt, lead, arms and munitions, interspersing his duties with visits to friends and family. In the fall he made a last visit to his son at the governor's mansion in Perth Amboy, where they broke irreparably, and a visit to General Washington's headquarters in Cambridge, close to British power, massed in Boston. General Sir William Howe, his former chess partner's brother, was now in command.

British troops, showing their strength and determination, burned down Falmouth, a major port for trips to Europe. There were rumbles of a possible attack upon Philadelphia. Franklin kept a brave face through all this, writing, as always, to London to warn them that none of these operations would force America to give up the struggle for its basic liberties.

To Jonathan Shipley, on September 13, he wrote: ". . . We have given up our commerce; our best ships, thirty-four sail, left this port on the 9th inst. And, in our minds, we give up the seacoast, though part may be a little disputed, to the barbarous ravages of your ships of war; but the internal country we shall defend. It is a good one and fruitful. It is, with our liberties, worth defending and it will, itself, by its own fertility, enable us to defend it." He warned Shipley, and through him the ministry, that the war "will not be a short one."

Franklin received letters constantly from London. One of his correspondents, the printer William Strahan, who had worked on so many of Franklin's pamphlets and articles, sent him the favorite conservative argument of the day: a warning to men of property that it was dangerous to put arms into the hands of the lower classes, for fear that they would use them, not against Britain, but to seize property and power for themselves.

Franklin always sent polite and well-reasoned answers to such letters, but one from Strahan angered him so that he penned a furious reply:

> You are a Member of Parliament, one of that majority which has doomed my country to destruction. You have begun to burn our towns and murder our people. Look upon your hands! They are stained with the blood of your relations. You and I were long friends. You are now my enemy, and I am
>
> Yours,
> Ben Franklin

He knew it was the wrong thing to say, in too harsh terms, but he could not resist writing it. He could, however, resist mailing it. And so he did. But, typical of Franklin, he did not tear it up. He liked it so much he left it in his file for posterity.

With his prodigious energy, he kept up an activity that tired, even killed, men almost half his age. The first President of the Congress, Peyton Randolph, collapsed and died, and was replaced by John Hancock. But Franklin could not continue all his manifold duties. At the turn of the year, 1776, he resigned from the Pennsylvania Committee of Safety and the Assembly, spent little time in Congress, concentrating on continent-wide defense plans, on correspondence with London and with a new kind of correspondence that would change his life and change the course of the war.

On the twenty-ninth of November, 1775, Congress decided, after long deliberation on the issue, to set up a Committee of Secret Correspondence, "for the sole purpose of corresponding with our friends in Great Britain, Ireland, and other parts of the world." It was the beginning of an American diplomatic service, the first step toward seeking foreign aid against Great Britain, a portentous step. Five men were named to the committee: Benjamin Harrison, Thomas Johnson, John Dickinson, John Jay and Franklin. Of them all, Franklin was the only one with broad and deep experience overseas. He soon became the leading member.

CHAPTER

3

Benjamin Franklin, Secret Agent

Secret agents of foreign countries were already at work in America. A great many nations were curious about events in the colonies, wondering just how they might eventually affect the unstable European balance of power. The nation most concerned was France.

France had been badly beaten in the Seven Years' War and had lost almost all her most precious colonial possessions to the British. At the Peace Treaty of 1763, the British, wishing to seem generous in victory, decided to leave France some crumbs from the colonial pie. At first, it was thought, in London, to leave Canada to the French. It was a cold, bleak land, overrun with Indians. Some wanted to get rid of Canada and keep, instead, the sunny, sugar-rich islands, Martinique and Guadeloupe. But Ben Franklin campaigned vigorously to keep Canada. He foresaw a great expansion through its huge spaces and profitable trade in furs, wood pulp, construction logs and minerals. His arguments won out. Britain kept Canada and let France keep the sugar islands, plus two minuscule fishing islands, St. Pierre and Miquelon, off the coast of Canada.

France fumed in helpless humiliation at the debate over which crumbs it would get. One Frenchman, who would play the definitive role in the American Revolution—far greater than Lafayette's, although American historians have long overlooked his importance

—was a young man, then in the foreign service, Charles Gravier, the Comte de Vergennes. He spent years in a difficult post in Turkey, concerned with French interests in an always threatening conflict between the Turkish Porte and Russia. But, as a fervently patriotic Frenchman, he never took his eyes off the rivalry with Britain, and swore vengeance one day. When he became Foreign Minister of Louis XVI, Vergennes's opportunity was there and he took it.

He dispatched to Philadelphia a secret agent, Achard de Bonvouloir.

The very first man he was instructed to contact was Benjamin Franklin. Franklin's works were not only well known and widely praised in France, but he had charmed the French personally in short visits in the sixties. Louis may have been King of France, but for French intellectuals, a power in the realm, philosophers were the real kings and Dr. Franklin ranked with Voltaire and Rousseau, his contemporaries.

Bonvouloir went to a French bookseller in Philadelphia, certain that he would have had dealings with Franklin. He was right. Franklin bought French treatises on science, particularly electricity, and sent many of his own papers to France. The bookseller discreetly told Franklin of Bonvouloir's desire to meet with him and Franklin agreed to the meeting.

America desperately needed foreign trade and arms. Franklin had urged Congress to maintain the existing nonimportation restrictions to provoke British merchants, and he often boasted of American self-sufficiency. His boast was highly exaggerated. America could feed herself but, for a long war, could not arm or clothe herself. Trade was needed to prevent a general economic depression that might weaken America's resolve to hold out. Yet he did not want to admit this. Centuries later, Charles de Gaulle, exiled leader in London of the Free French, was to tell Anthony Eden, who protested his intransigence: "Sir, I am too weak to yield." Franklin could have said the same: America was too weak to seek aid from a strong power for fear of becoming dependent on it. He had to maneuver that power to press aid upon him. Then he could, without embarrassment, generously accept what, in truth, he desperately needed.

He was also faced with a seemingly hopeless dilemma.

France, not yet strong enough to face England, dared not goad the British bulldog by entering into commerce with a rebellious colony. There could be no diplomatic excuse for such action, as Vergennes, a brilliant diplomat, knew well. However, should the colonies declare their independence and break all ties with Britain, why, then, much as it might anger the British, the French had every right under existing maritime law to enter into free and mutual trade with such an independent state. It might infuriate the British, but it was not a casus belli.

The majority of the Congress, however, though moving toward the idea of independence, were still nervous and unsure. Unless they had assurances of outside help, they were afraid to take the fatal step. So they could not get foreign aid without declaring independence, yet could not declare independence without foreign aid.

Franklin met alone and surreptitiously with Bonvouloir until he judged the time had come to arrange a clandestine meeting with his four colleagues of the Secret Committee. They all assured Bonvouloir that Congress had decided to declare independence but had, as he might well understand, a number of undertakings to carry out before this could be made public. Franklin's stature, his great prestige in America, which Bonvouloir noted, and the affirmations of four other important congressmen finally persuaded Bonvouloir, and he reported to Vergennes, in a dispatch at the end of December, 1775, that independence was assured for 1776.

On December 12, the committee wrote to Arthur Lee, who had served in London with Franklin as his subagent, and who had returned there from the Continent, to take over Franklin's agency —too late, for war had started. They sent him expense money and told him to sound out, as secretly as possible, the sentiments of foreign powers in the European embassies in London.

On that same day, Franklin wrote a letter to Don Gabriel de Bourbon, with whom he had earlier set up a literary correspondence. The Prince of Spain had sent Franklin, through his London Ambassador, a fine edition of Sallust. Franklin seized the occasion not only to thank him but to send him, in return, a copy of the proceedings of the American Congress, apologizing, in a way to delight the Spaniard, by saying that the literary Muses "have scarcely visited these remote regions." Europe has long nourished itself on the thought that its civilization was superior to America's, and Franklin did not mind in the least flattering the European ego.

Not content to let it go at that, Franklin added the thought: "I see a powerful dominion growing up here, whose interest it will be to form a close and firm alliance with Spain (their territories bordering) and who, being united, will be able not only to preserve their own people in peace but to repel the force of all the other powers in Europe."

This was a most outrageous and, at the time, almost lunatic boast. Little, unarmed, backward America was telling one of the world's powers that it ought to ally with the United States, for together they would be strong enough to challenge all the great powers in the world. It may be thought that Don Gabriel was more startled than flattered. Perhaps, being a Spaniard, he understood the nature of fighting cocks.

Franklin also opened up correspondence with a literary friend in The Hague, Charles Dumas, and resumed that with his constant correspondent of years, Dr. Barbeu Dubourg in Paris, asking them to let him know everything they heard about European opinion and what was being said about relations with the rebellious colonies. He did not overtly seek aid and was chary about the word "alliance" except in the phrase "commercial alliance." Indeed, while he actively fished for alliances, he continually denied that he sought them and even recommended in Congress that America not overtly seek them out. In his colorful language, Franklin did not feel it proper "for a virgin to go suitoring."

A commercial agent, a M. Penet, was dispatched to France to seek contracts for munitions, with congressional commitments to pay for them with exports, since America had no gold or reliable currency. Later, in March, 1776, Silas Deane, delegate from Connecticut, was sent over on the recommendation of and with instructions by Franklin, armed with letters to all Franklin's friends in Paris. He was instructed to report to Robert Morris, head of the Commerce Committee of the Congress. To mask his mission, he was told to assume the guise of a merchant seeking goods for the Indian trade. He was to see Vergennes and repeat the affirmations on independence given to Bonvouloir.

Deane was also given vials of invisible ink, while John Jay, his "control officer," was given vials of a chemical solvent that would make the ink appear. Since he could not send blank letters, he was instructed, probably by Franklin, who thoroughly enjoyed the cloak-and-dagger plan, to write on large paper, with widely spaced lines, leaving the end of the letter, following the signature, blank.

Later, in Paris, agents and spies went through this rather primitive and ineffective nonsense—ineffective for, by then, everyone knew that secret ink was being used by all sides, and most of the solvents were available to everyone.

It was at that moment, when Deane was sent to Paris, in March, 1776, that Franklin was dispatched as an agent on an almost farcical mission that came close to ending his life. He was asked to go to Canada, to win the colonists there to the American side. He was most enthusiastic, for he had always highly estimated the importance of Canada, and was willing to take the risks of an extremely hazardous journey in one of the worst months of the year for travel north. March featured squalls and blizzards and much of the journey would be over water or through dense forests. Congressmen Samuel Chase and John Carroll, both Catholics, educated in France, were assigned to accompany Franklin. It was believed that they might get through to the French Catholics of Canada, who had no sympathy for the American cause.

The commissioners went first to New York, then took a sloop for Albany and anchored overnight en route. The next morning a March squall split their mainsail and they had to wait two days for the wind to die and the crew to repair the damage. They struggled on, finally reaching Albany, where they were made welcome by the commander of Continental forces there, General Philip Schuyler.

They noted that most of the people in Albany still spoke Dutch. From Albany they took a carriage overland to Saratoga, traveling all day to cover a bit more than thirty miles.

Saratoga was snowed in and kept them bottled up a week.

Franklin, exhausted—he was now seventy—wrote to his friend Josiah Quincy of Massachusetts: "I begin to apprehend that I have undertaken a fatigue that at my time of life may prove too much for me; so I sit down to write to a few friends by way of farewell. . . ."

They rowed in a small boat up the Hudson, had to fight their way through ice on Lake George, landing frequently on shore to light fires and heat tea. They slept in the forest at night, two in the woods, Franklin on the boat. They had forgotten to bring camp cots with them. To get to Lake Champlain, they had to go through the woods by portage. It was agony for the gout-ridden septuagenarian. They had set out in March and arrived in Montreal at the end of April.

There they were greeted by General Benedict Arnold, who had spent the winter leading an unsuccessful siege of Quebec and who told them that nothing could be done with the French Catholics. Arnold also said he had run out of funds and his soldiers were threatening to march home. Poor Franklin had to advance them more than three hundred pounds in gold, out of his personal account. His legs swollen, afflicted with an outbreak of boils, the old man left Montreal on May 11, painfully making his way home. The trip had been a disaster.

Back in Philadelphia, more dead than alive, Franklin was cheered by news that Congress was quietly considering drafting a declaration of independence. It was June, 1776.

On June 7, Richard Henry Lee introduced a resolution declaring "these United Colonies are, and of right ought to be, free and independent States." Governor William Franklin was arrested at that time by resolution of Congress, at a session probably attended by Ben Franklin.

On the committee to prepare the declaration were Jefferson, Adams, Franklin, Robert Livingston and Roger Sherman. The committeemen elected Jefferson to draw up the first draft. He worked closely with them, showing work in progress often to both Adams and Franklin. Franklin told him not to bother submitting each sentence but to go ahead and write it himself. Masterpieces, Franklin observed, are not written by committees. Franklin himself made several minor but only one significant change in Jefferson's text. Where Jefferson had written: "We hold these truths to be sacred and undeniable," Franklin had changed it to the simpler but much more effective "to be self-evident."

From the moment America declared her independence, Franklin busied himself with plans to deal with foreign nations, particularly France and Spain. He drafted proposals for a treaty of friendship and commerce, and, both foresighted and practical, even drafted terms for peace with England. He wisely thought that envoys might carry such papers as protection, showing their willingness to make peace. He also thought this might worry the French enough to keep them faithful to the alliance. It was a tactic he would come to use repeatedly in Paris.

Meanwhile, the British, alarmed by the move from rebellion to revolution, had finally acceded to Lord Howe's proposal that he be sent as a peace emissary to America. Naturally, his first thought was to see Franklin and pick up where the London chess game had ended. As soon as his flagship anchored off Sandy Hook, he sent a friendly note to Franklin asking to see him, assuring him he was ready to pardon the rebels. Franklin sharply replied that injured parties did not seek pardon from those who had injured them but rather an end to the injuries. As for Howe's hints of peace proposals, Franklin sternly suggested that he would entertain peace proposals between two independent states at war but not between a motherland and a colony. He added that America would prefer to enter into foreign alliances before talking peace with Britain. Howe's proposal, as offered, stood rebuffed.

Unfortunately for Franklin's brave words, the war went badly for the poorly organized, ill-armed, inexperienced American mixture of regulars and irregulars, who, if they had chores or troubles back at the farm, simply took off for home. Washington, who had asked Congress to enact a law providing regular pay for firm, one-year enlistments, was trounced by the British on Long Island at the end of August, and just barely managed to beat a ragged retreat to temporary quarters in Manhattan.

Rear Admiral Lord Richard Howe, sensing an opportunity, paroled General John Sullivan, whom British troops had captured, and sent him to Philadelphia carrying proposals for a peace parley. Congress decided to send in return a delegation, not to negotiate peace, but to find out what Howe had in mind and what authority he had from London. Named to the commission with Franklin were John Adams and Edward Rutledge of South Carolina.

Howe met them on the beach at Staten Island, with a strong guard of Hessians behind him. Franklin noted the presence of foreign mercenaries. He had complained to friends in London about this and used it as additional justification of America's right to seek foreign assistance.

The parley consisted of a series of long harangues on each side. Howe had no authority to treat with the colonies as states independent of the Crown, and he regretted that the delegation had come so far to no avail. That was the postscript to the London chess game.

The two Howe brothers, Admiral and General, threw their powerful combined forces against Washington, driving him out of Manhattan to Harlem Heights, out of Harlem to White Plains. Nathan Hale, captured behind the British lines, was hanged as a spy. New York caught fire and a third of the city burned down. The die had been definitely cast.

At this low point, a letter from his close friend Dr. Barbeu Dubourg arrived to lift Franklin's spirits. It was long and detailed, in the flowery style of eighteenth-century French prose, yet wonderfully precise, as the French language is. It presented a prototype of the maddening situation that Franklin would find in Paris later: everyone willing and friendly, all goods and materials available, contracts set and details stipulated, and yet, somehow, nothing done. Anyone who has ever dealt with the French will readily understand the difficulties. Franklin had yet to learn this, so the letter was a tonic for a low spirit.

It was dated June 10, addressed, as many French were accustomed to addressing Franklin, to "My dear Master." Dubourg began by telling Franklin that he had just met with the commercial agent Penet, with whom Franklin had made arrangements in Philadelphia to procure arms and material in France. Penet had told Dubourg he had a letter for him from Franklin and a number of papers, but that he had left everything in Rotterdam, for fear of being searched by police or customs officers, coming through Holland into France. This bothered Dubourg, who had no proof that Penet was what he said he was. However, after questioning him sharply, Dubourg decided he probably was legitimate and not some kind of agent provocateur.

He took Penet out to Versailles to introduce him to officials of the government, established there at the King's palace. They met with a financial authority, a M. Dupont, who told them of the government's sympathy for America and fears that its struggle might fail for lack of funds. The government, he said, was studying plans to open credits for America in some way that would not be readily apparent to the British, but these plans had not yet materialized.

Penet said he would go to his company offices in Nantes and then begin visiting the ports and merchants, looking for the goods that the Secret Committee had commissioned. Meanwhile, he asked Dubourg to be Franklin's representative in Paris and Versailles. Dubourg was reluctant to make definite moves until Penet had shown his credentials from Philadelphia. He was worried, too, that the work might interfere with, if not ruin, his medical practice, his experiments and writings. He argued with himself throughout the letter, finally giving in to his pro-American passion and agreeing to become the Secret Committee's man in Paris, all this without the slightest accreditation, on the word of a commercial agent he had never heard of or met before.

Dubourg described how he made the rounds, knocking at all doors, "speaking vaguely to some, enigmatically to others, half-confidences to several and what had to be said to the Ministers of the King. I had the satisfaction of being warmly received by all. On the other hand, you would hardly believe the mess of contradictory information and misinformation offered me. A Minister, full of goodwill, told me where I could find saltpeter, guns and powder magazines, but when I checked his source, the saltpeter was far too expensive and the guns defective."

Dubourg described his six trips to Versailles, checking and rechecking his sources, until he finally found what was wanted in the King's own arsenals. Adopting the cover name of M. de La Tuillerie, Dr. Dubourg negotiated the "loan" of fifteen thousand rifles, of the 1763 model, on the promise that he would later replace them in the arsenal with new ones. The rifles had already been shipped to Penet in Nantes, awaiting the arrival of ships which, Penet said, the Secret Committee had promised to send to pick up their precious cargo.

"I hope your brave warriors will like these rifles. I must warn you not to trust the ordinary commercial rifle being sold here. They are as dangerous to friends as to enemies."

Dubourg said he could also get some splendid bronze cannons. Unfortunately, they bore the royal coat of arms and the King's initials. "We could, of course, file off the L. L. and the fleur de lis but all that costs money and who will advance it?" His friends at court were all so busy with "plots and cabals, trying just to keep their jobs" that he could not count on them to arrange credits.

There were some excellent engineers available for service, asking only free passage to America, Dubourg wrote. One was the son of the Chevalier de St. Louis, the other in the service of the Duc d'Orléans. He had finally had a letter from Nantes and knew now that Penet's firm was called Pliarne, Penet, and well reputed, but six weeks had gone by, and Penet had still not sent the letter of accreditation, nor the maps and brochures that Franklin had given him for Dubourg.

Dubourg plunged right ahead nonetheless, apparently, in his love for Franklin and passion for America, quite ready to brave personal ruin. He took the considerable risk of negotiating tobacco contracts with the Farmers-General, the royal tax collection agency, for a year's supply of the best Virginia. He also took the political risk of bringing Penet to Versailles to meet with the Foreign Minister, Vergennes, who questioned him long and closely on the situation in America.

Dubourg heard that the Secret Committee had already ordered cannon from a Belgian foundry in Liège. He admonished Franklin, telling him that French cannon were far superior and could be had on better terms.

In the absence of any communication from across the Atlantic, Dubourg thought things might work much faster across the Channel, so he had the unhappy idea, which he would later rue, of getting in touch with the temperamental Arthur Lee, who had replaced Franklin in London.

He closed the letter with a postscript saying he was worried about mail interception by the British Navy, so he was sending copies on several ships. He also attached to the letter a coded, numbered alphabet for their secret communications.

The letter, carefully read, was larded with booby traps, but Franklin, who expected hazards, was less troubled by the dangers than exhilarated by the thought that, at last, help was being organized.

Dubourg's letter was followed by one from Silas Deane. Deane had met with Dubourg and had finally given him his copy of Franklin's letter to his friends in Paris. He said the Frenchman glowed with delight. He also met a certain young gentleman named Dr. Bancroft, who had come over from England, claiming to be a supporter of the American cause. These gentlemen told Deane that money—solid credit—was a serious problem. Poor Deane, not knowing what he was getting into, replied, "I would certify to the merchants that the Congress would pay for whatever stores they would credit them with."

Dubourg told Deane the French ministers did not yet dare meet with him as a representative of America. His arrival had already been reported by spies to London. The British Ambassador to Paris, Lord Stormont, a brilliant and zealous diplomat who did not miss a trick, had rushed to the court at Versailles to protest Deane's presence.

Deane showed his letter of accreditation by the Congress and pointed out that America had already declared its independence. Dubourg relayed this to the court and Vergennes agreed to let him come for an audience, but most quietly and confidentially. At Versailles, Deane met Vergennes and Vergennes's First Secretary, Conrad Alexandre Gérard. Deane was delighted to discover that Gérard spoke fluent English and was most favorable to the American cause.

Vergennes told him, Deane wrote, that

> Considering the good understanding between the two courts of Versailles and London, they could not *openly* encourage the shipping of warlike stores, but no obstruction of any kind would be given. . . . That I was under his immediate protection and, should I meet with any difficulty, either from their police, with the rules of which he supposed me unacquainted, or from any other quarter, I had but to apply to him. . . . That as to independency, it was an event in the womb of time, and it would be highly improper for him to say anything on the subject until it had actually taken place.

The French apparently felt there was a gap to be filled between a declaration of independence and the real winning of it. They might be able to engage in peaceable trade with America, but not yet, openly, in military arms.

Vergennes told Deane to leave his address with his secretary, to keep in touch with him only through his secretary, to arrange secret meetings away from the Foreign Minister's too-public office and, above all, to keep away from Englishmen in Paris. They all were Stormont's informers.

Future storms showed their first clouds in this letter from Deane, for he told Franklin he had met with a certain Beaumarchais, who was in a muddle with Dubourg. He was Caron de Beaumarchais, the playwright who would win literary immortality as the author of *Le Mariage de Figaro* and *Le Barbier de Séville,* a notorious playboy, a man of fashion and flair. Given his personality, Beaumarchais's passion for the American cause was lyrical, but, unfortunately, as is often the case, his head was so high in the air that he rarely touched solid ground in his transactions.

Deane explained that Beaumarchais was known to be careless in money matters; that he claimed to have from the court a monopoly on dealing with America, and could supply anything and everything the Americans wanted. His promises were so lavish, his style so flamboyant, that Dubourg did not believe half he said, Deane reported.

Worried, they had gone out to Versailles to see Vergennes, and, to their surprise, heard the Foreign Minister say that "I might rely on whatever Mons. Beaumarchais should engage in the commercial way of supplies."

Deane was enthusiastic about the help he had received from Dubourg and from Dr. Edward Bancroft, whom Franklin knew and thought well of, as did Deane. Neither could guess how treacherous a double agent he would turn out to be.

Franklin may or may not have seen the dangers, but he was encouraged by the progress of his representatives and by the excellent reception they had been afforded by Vergennes. He felt the time had come for action.

On September 26, in secret session, Congress appointed three commissioners to the court of France: Silas Deane, secret agent of the Committee of Commerce but still posing as an Indian trader, although Vergennes now knew better; Thomas Jefferson and Benjamin Franklin.

Jefferson's wife was ill and his personal affairs demanded his presence, so he bowed out. The cantankerous Arthur Lee was named in his place and instructions sent for him to leave London for Paris. Franklin would have two unsteady crutches in Lee and Deane, themselves to be crippled and twisted by their own quarrels and machinations.

Franklin gave little thought to anything but the dramatic new challenge in his life.

PART II

PARIS: *The Alliance*

CHAPTER

4

Aboard the "Reprisal," Paris Bound

On October 25, 1776, Benjamin Franklin went quietly around to see his friends and fellow congressmen, wishing them a discreet farewell, and enjoining them to secrecy about his departure the next day for Paris. British spies abounded in the new American capital and his injunction was in vain. Lord Stormont in Paris already knew all about his mission.

He dined quietly at home with his daughter, Sarah ("Sally") Bache, and her family in Market Street, in the new house he had had built for his wife, Deborah, but had not seen until his return after her death, in December, 1774. He was fond of his son-in-law, Richard, who became a son to replace the disgraced William. He adored Sally, and thanked her for letting him take his beloved seven-year-old grandson, Benjamin Franklin Bache, to Paris with him, along with his most adored older grandson, William Temple Franklin, whom he called "Temple," aged seventeen. Temple had been a comfort to him in London, in his failure; he meant him now to share in what he was sure would be success in Paris, as his trusted personal secretary, his salary to be paid by Congress.

He had been shopping surreptitiously for weeks, so that no suspicion would be aroused by a great volume of purchases. Remembering his sufferings in Canada and knowing the ship's facilities would be austere, he bought the best bedding he could find. He laid in sea stores, linens, drugs, and jams and jawbreakers for the boys. In all, he sent to the docks three trunks, luggage cases and a sea chest.

A detail of Marines guarded the ship at the docks to keep the sailors on board. Desertions were frequent in those days and the crew of the *Reprisal* was in an ugly mood. On an earlier trip to Martinique, they had captured three enemy vessels and had not yet been paid their share of the prize money.

Captain Lambert Wickes was in command; an intelligent, able seaman, aged only twenty-four, he had sealed orders he was to read only when at sea. When he opened them, he was informed:

> You are not to delay time on this outward passage for the sake of cruising; but, if you are beset with contrary winds, or, during the passage, be so circumstances that Doctor Franklin may approve of your speaking any vessel you may see, do therein as he shall direct . . . it is equally so that you keep totally secret where you are bound . . . or what is your business.

To throw spies off the scent, Franklin hired a coach and horses and took off with his grandsons, as though for a picnic in the countryside. They rode to Chester, where they dined at an inn and spent the night. The next morning they rode on to Marcus Hook, where they were to rendezvous with the *Reprisal.*

Wickes and his officers, in bright new uniforms, designed in September by the Marine Committee, were lined on deck to pipe the old and young men aboard. The complement of the *Reprisal* totaled 130 men, including a company of Marines, a captain, two sergeants and twenty-four troopers. The American flag had not yet been adopted and the *Reprisal* was flying an approved flag of the Grand Union: red and white stripes with a British union next to the staff. It was the same flag Washington had hoisted when he opened his first headquarters in Cambridge at the start of that extraordinary year, 1776.

The old gentleman, knowing too well the rigors of the Atlantic in November and December, came aboard wearing a heavy coat and a fur hat. Captain Wickes wore a blue uniform with red lapels and red facing on his stiff, stand-up collar; slash cuffs over his wrists;

and flat yellow buttons. Marine Captain Miles Pennington wore a coat, skirted and folded back, green faced with white, sleeves and pockets slashed, and silver epaulets upon his shoulders. The young American Navy meant to put on a good show for its great passenger.

With the important passengers aboard, along with a cargo of thirty-five barrels of indigo—Robert Morris of the Commerce Committee, who would be the financial captain of the Revolution, wanted to turn a profit, even from a diplomatic mission—the *Reprisal* set sail. By noon, the twenty-seventh, it was abreast of Wilmington; by nightfall, almost to Bombay Hook; and by Tuesday, under full sail, the *Reprisal* passed out of coastal waters, around Cape Henlopen, heading into the Atlantic.

As they passed the cape, the old British lighthouse, the last familiar sight for some six weeks, fell behind. Almost immediately an Atlantic gale hit the ship and it rolled dangerously. Happily, Franklin was not at the rail with his thermometer. He did continue his observations, insofar as he could, through the voyage, but it was rough all the way, with heavy seas and high winds.

Wickes spread all the canvas he dared upon the tall masts, which bent beneath the howling force of almost continual gales. More than once Franklin remembered, with a sickly smile, his promise to his sister, Jane Mecom, not ever to sail the Atlantic again. There was little to eat except game, fowl and salt beef, which Franklin could barely chew. And the poor old man was again afflicted, as he had been on the journey to Canada; he noted in his journal: "Boils continued to vex me, and the scurff extending all the small of my back, of my sides, my arms, besides what continued under my hair."

Most of the time, the vast ocean was empty, but in the second week of the journey they spied two British men-of-war. Wickes went into evasive action and soon left them behind. Franklin admired the young captain's seamanship and the discipline of his well-trained crew, finding them the "equal to anything of the kind in the best ships of the King's fleet."

Wickes and Franklin had long talks about the Gulf Stream and pored over maps together to chart the best and shortest route to

Nantes, their port of disembarkation. Wickes navigated his rakish, black ship with consummate skill, trying to ease the tossing and pitching in the gales, seeking always smoother waters. But despite his every effort, the ship continued to roll and pitch in the foul weather. Franklin tossed about, subsisting on a poor diet, unable to sleep well because of his afflictions, growing weaker and weaker. Unless the weather improved, he would arrive in Paris in a lamentable condition that would not help the launching of his mission.

While Franklin was dreaming of better times ahead, and suffering in the Atlantic storms, Lord Stormont, the British Ambassador in Paris, was preparing a hostile reception for him. All through November, Stormont besieged Vergennes, mixing threats with news of British victories in Long Island and New York. He carried on a daily correspondence with Lord Weymouth, charged with foreign affairs in the London government, giving him spy reports and bombarding him with suggestions for intercepting American agents' mail.

Stormont told him that Deane used a mail drop in London, at the address of a respectable trading firm, Germany and Giraudot, and proposed that their mail be checked. On his list as undercover correspondents and American mail drops were: Thomas Walpole; Sam Wharton of Lisle Street; Leicester, Fields and Hammersmith; and Thomas Boylston of Bristol. Stormont was indefatigable, his spies legion. He would be a more than worthy opponent for Franklin.

The Ambassador was elated when the news of the Howe brothers' victories in New York was finally confirmed by French dispatches. He wrote Weymouth:

> The Concern which all of the people of this country feel upon the occasion and which few, except the ministers, attempt to conceal, heightens my Joy and increases my Impatience for such a decisive blow as may utterly confound their hopes. As I think it of importance to raise in M. de Vergennes a suspicion and Mistrust of Deane, I contrived this morning to drop some obscure hints of a Negotiation, begun by Lord Howe. . . . I shall continue to wear the same appearance and never betray the least suspicion of the secret machinations of this Court.

Stormont, able as he was, was fooling himself. Vergennes knew exactly what he was up to and, with his own army of spies everywhere, was perfectly informed of the "secret machinations" of the British court. Obscure hints about peace negotiations simply made him more anxious to help the American revolutionaries so that they not be forced to submit to a dictated peace.

Franklin knew none of this and would not have been concerned had he known. He was too experienced, knew the British too well, to have any illusions about their attitude toward his mission. This was Vergennes's worry, not his. Later, when Lee or Deane fretted about Stormont's activities, Franklin would admonish them to mind their own affairs. He had not only an old man's wisdom but an old man's need to conserve his strength, and he limited his efforts to what was strictly necessary for his mission.

After a terrible voyage, the *Reprisal* approached the coast of France. On the morning of November 27, sail was sighted and, about noon of that day, a small British brigantine, sailing north, crossed their route.

Wickes had had strict instructions not to cruise or seek to capture prizes. But this tempting little prize showed up right under his bows. He rushed to consult Franklin, who proved nervous about engaging in privateering off the coast of France. It might anger Vergennes. But Franklin had suffered many indignities from the British and had had so miserable a voyage that he could not resist the chance for revenge and adventure. He gave his consent.

The young captain, laying on sail and drawing abreast of the brigantine, hailed it and issued a sharp order to heave to. Down came the brigantine's sails, while American Marines prepared to board and seize it. It was the brigantine *George,* and Franklin smiled at the name.

A few hours later another vessel, apparently unfamiliar with the new American flag, imprudently approached: it was the brigantine *La Vigne,* a vessel of 150 tons, its holds filled with valuable cargo it had just loaded in France, bound for Hull. Wickes hailed it, seized it and brought its master aboard to join the unlucky captain of the *George.*

Both captains made proposals to ransom their ships. Franklin almost accepted. He was not at all sure that the French would permit them to sell the ships and cargo in France, for it would be a violation of French treaties with England. Wickes thought he could arrange a sale without revealing the source of the prizes. The captain and crew stood to earn a good share and Franklin could not refuse them, so he agreed to let them be taken in.

As they came upon the French coast, still a distance from Nantes, in Brittany, the winds turned contrary and Wickes had to throw his anchor to wait for a shift that would carry him north.

Day after day, the winds blew the wrong way.

After four days, Franklin, weak and ill, eager to be off the accursed ship, could no longer stand the delay. He ordered Wickes to put him ashore in a small boat. He would make his way to Nantes, thence to Paris, by land.

On December 3, a fishing boat, hailed by Wickes, picked up Franklin, his grandsons and luggage and took them ashore at the village of Auray.

Franklin was so weak he could hardly walk. He had to be helped to an inn and all but carried up to a bed.

But he had survived; he was in France. He had a powerful constitution and an incredible will to carry on. He would rest a bit, then on to Paris, where he yearned to meet old friends and make new ones for America.

CHAPTER

5

The First Time He Saw Paris

General de Gaulle once said, "A statesman has no friends, only interests." Franklin would have put it quite differently: friends *are* interests.

On taking up his mission in Paris, he would lean heavily on old friends, who shared many interests with him—philosophy, science, economics and devotion to human liberties. Several of them, particularly Barbeu Dubourg, would devote their lives, give up their careers, to help Franklin and his cause.

It was to Dubourg in Paris that he wrote first from the "wretched" inn in Auray, where he briefly recuperated from the exhausting voyage. Franklin had first corresponded with Dr. Dubourg more than a decade earlier, when the latter had begun translating Franklin's works into French and brought them to the attention of the great naturalist Buffon, whose own encyclopedic and universal studies he had sent on to Franklin in London. They had, at last, met, during two brief trips Franklin made to Paris in 1767 and 1769, visits that, fortuitously, laid the groundwork for the mission he was about to undertake. When he reached Paris, just before Christmas, 1776, he was not merely a famous scientist but a dear old friend. The French do not open their homes and hearts easily to strangers, but once friendship is won from a Frenchman it is deep and almost unbreakable.

Franklin had had no impulse himself to visit France in 1767. The invitation came from M. Durand, the French Minister in London, in the late spring of that year. Durand first invited Franklin to dine at the French Embassy, and, at dinner, spoke at length about the great potential of America, while praising Franklin for his brilliant works, assuring him that he was as well known in France as in England. He kept urging Franklin to visit France and meet his fellow scientists.

Franklin was pleased but not fooled. The French government would have little reason to send an invitation for scientists to meet. The French Academy would be more likely to do that on its own if it wished. The day that Franklin set out from London for Dover, en route to Paris, he noted that Durand "pretends to have a great esteem for me, on account of the abilities shown in my examination; has desired to have all my political writings, invited me to dine with him, was very inquisitive, treated me with great civility, makes me visits, etc. I fancy that intriguing nation would like very well to meddle on occasion, and blow up the coals between Britain and her colonies; but I hope we shall give them no opportunity."

In 1767 Franklin was still pursuing his dream of a great, imperial British commonwealth. He had cheered Britain's great victory in the Seven Years' War, and the virtual destruction of the French Empire by the Treaty of Utrecht ending that war in 1763. The Duc de Choiseul, leading minister of Louis XV, was smarting for revenge and thought America might be a weapon for it, just as Vergennes later conceived the same policy for Louis XVI.

Franklin was merely eager to visit the Continent and meet French scientists and economists, particularly the King's physician, Dr. François Quesnay, leader of a school of economic theory whose followers became known as the physiocrats. Franklin had evolved no theory of economics of his own but had written pieces on the subject and was fascinated by demographic trends. His writings were later praised by Malthus, and Adam Smith spoke highly of Franklin's books, which he had in his library. Franklin chose as traveling companion his good friend and chess partner Sir John Pringle, and the British press noted Sir John's departure for holidays in Paris. But there was not a word about Franklin's leaving. He felt it necessary to keep his own plans tightly secret, for the British government would instantly suspect what Franklin had surmised. He did write his son William of his plans but cautioned him to "Communicate nothing of this letter."

As so often was the case, the only full account of this trip, aside from scraps in the Paris press, was a letter by Franklin. It was to Polly Stevenson, daughter of his landlady at his home in Craven Street, London:

> At Dover . . . we embarked for Calais. . . . We got to Calais that Evening. Various impositions we suffer'd from Boat-men, Porters, etc., on both Sides of the Water. I know not which are the most rapacious, the English or French; but the latter have, with their Knavery, the most Politeness.
>
> The Roads we found equally good with ours in England, in some Places pav'd with smooth stone like our new streets for many miles together, and Rows of trees on each Side and yet there are no Turnpikes. But then the poor Peasants complain'd to us grievously, that they were oblig'd to work upon the Roads full two Months in the Year without being paid for their labours. Whether this is truth, or whether, like Englishmen, they grumble Cause or no Cause, I have not yet been able fully to inform myself.
>
> The women we saw at Calais, on the Road, at Boulogne and in the Inns and Villages, were generally of dark complexions; but, arriving at Abbeville, we found a sudden change, a Multitude both of Women and Men in that Place appearing remarkably fair.

On all his travels Franklin had an eye for female beauty and always most admired those of white skin and pink cheeks. It was a question not of race but of taste. Franklin would not have considered himself a racist. He disapproved of slavery and bitterly criticized the slave trade.

Franklin was puzzled by the fairness of the people of Abbeville, particularly since he noted that as soon as he left the town, "the Swarthiness returned." He guessed that, perhaps, they were so confined to the woolen mills there that they were never exposed to the sun.

I speak generally, for there are some fair women in Paris, who I think are not whiten'd by Art. As to Rouge, they don't pretend to imitate Nature in laying it on. There is no gradual diminution of the Color from the full Bloom in the Middle of the Cheek to the faint Tint near the sides, nor does it show itself differently in different Faces. I have not had the honour of being at any Lady's Toylette to see how it is laid on, but I fancy I can tell you how it is or may be done; Cut a Hole of 3 inches diameter, in such a manner as the top of the Hole may be just under your eye; then with a brush dipt in the colour paint Face and Paper together; so when the Paper is taken off there will remain a round Patch of Red exactly the form of the hole. This is the Mode, from the Actresses on the Stage upwards thro' all Ranks of Ladies to the Princesses of the Blood, but it stops there, the Queen not using it, having the Serenity, Complacence and Benignity that shine so eminently in or rather through her countenance, sufficient Beauty, tho' now an old Woman, to do extremely well without it.

You see, I speak of the Queen as if I had seen her, and so I have; for you must know I have been at Court. We went to Versailles last Sunday, and had the Honour of being presented to the King, he spoke to both of us very graciously and cheerfully, is a handsome Man, and has a very lively Look, and appears younger than he is.

The King, Louis XV, reigned through 1774. His Queen, whom Franklin admired, was Maria Leszczyńska, in the last year of her life.

In the evening Franklin was invited to the "Grand Couvert," the banquet in which the royal family supped in public. The King chatted a bit with Franklin, he told Polly, adding: "That's saying enough, for I would not have you think me so pleas'd with this King and Queen as to have a Whit less Regard than I us'd to have for ours. No Frenchman shall go beyond me in thinking my own King and Queen the very best in the world and the most amiable."

Franklin was impressed with the world's most beautiful palace, Versailles, but was concerned about how much it had cost to build it. He said some had estimated eighty million pounds sterling. He marveled at the range of buildings, the gardens, the statues, figures, urns, the marble and bronze "of exquisite workmanship," finding it "beyond conception." But, like all Americans, he complained that "the Waterworks are out of Repair . . . there is, in short, both at Versailles and Paris a prodigious mixture of Magnificence and Negligence, with every kind of Elegance, except that of Cleanliness, and what we call Tydyness."

He did feel that Paris had certain advantages over London. The drinking water came from fresh springs and was filtered through sand. The streets, by constant sweeping, were fit to walk in and the people did walk, instead of being conveyed in carriages or chaises. Pedestrians took up less room than carriages and cabs, Franklin noted, so the streets, though narrower, were less encumbered. He was favorably impressed by Paris' cubed paving stones, which, "when worn on one side, may be turn'd and become new."

> The Civilities we everywhere receive give us the strongest Impressions of the French Politeness. . . . At the Church of Notre Dame, when we went to see a Magnificent Illumination . . . we found an immense Crowd who were kept out by the Guards; but the Officer being told that we were Strangers from England, he immediately admitted us. . . . Why don't we practice this Urbanity to Frenchmen? Why should they be allow'd to outdo us in anything?

Franklin ended his letter by telling Polly that his tailor and his wigmaker "had transformed me into a Frenchman. Only think what a figure I make in a little Bag Wig and naked Ears! They told me I was become twenty years younger, and look'd very galante; so being in Paris where the Mode is to be sacredly follow'd, I was once very near to making Love to my Friend's Wife."

The last line is vintage Franklin. He loved the ladies, flirted outrageously, talked and wrote at length about love affairs. There is no documentary evidence, no memoir, no spy report, nothing to prove that he was, in his old age, the agile lover he may well have been in his younger days, though, of course, there is no definitive evidence that he was not. In any case, his "affairs" in 1776 were more of the heart and mind than the body, very much in tune with the spirit of the eighteenth century in France, a time of gallantry, of extravagant and often naughty rather than lecherous behavior. He genuinely liked women, well beyond sexual attraction, enjoying their warmth and grace and the fine minds of many he would meet in Paris. They would all adore Franklin and play an important role in his mission, for women were skillful courtiers and their salons were excellent lobbies for foreign and secret agents.

The circle of physiocrats in Paris all knew Franklin's reputation and his works. A few months before he arrived, they had published in their journal, *Ephemerides,* a letter Franklin had written "On the Price of Corn." They were developing a theory of economics in which agriculture was viewed as the basis of national prosperity and argued that taxes on farmers should be kept low to encourage their production. They feared the too rapid growth of industrialization and were strongly opposed to public welfare projects, such as those, including a social security system and a dole, which had been launched in London, where there was a miserably depressed, unemployed mass of poverty-stricken citizens. Franklin had also long opposed these "welfare schemes," warning his fellow Americans not to adopt them in the colonies, for they encouraged sloth and idleness. "Jobs" Franklin called for; "work" is what man needs, not government handouts. He was convinced that there was work enough for everyone in the vast, undeveloped and yet to be explored lands of continental America.

Franklin had been strongly impressed by the physiocratic theories and, on his return to London, wrote a number of pieces in their style, adopting it as his own. In a letter to Philadelphia he wrote: "There seem to be but three ways for a nation to acquire wealth. The first is by war, as the Romans did, in plundering their conquered neighbors. This is robbery. The second by commerce, which is generally cheating. The third by agriculture, the only honest way, wherein man receives a real increase of the seed thrown into the ground in a kind of continual miracle."

Franklin was swimming in the mainstream of his day. He was a philosopher, not as the term is used today to denote a particular capacity for philosophic thought, but in the eighteenth-century sense, a lover of all the sciences; and it was mainly as a scientist that Franklin had won the title. A few months before his reception by the physiocrats, Adam Smith had come to discuss these same theories with these same men, out of which grew his thesis on *The Wealth of Nations.* Love of the land and of nature was being preached by Rousseau. But Franklin was ever practical in his theorizing, for he knew that America's greatest wealth was her boundless land, whereas the narrow and cramped British Isles had no choice but to develop industry and commerce. As early as 1767 he had realized how these important factors, which went beyond the political, tended to the separation of the colonies and the mother country.

He met of course with fellow scientists at the Academy, gave lectures on lightning, measures for protecting oneself in storms, means of fireproofing homes. He met physicist Joseph-Etienne Berthier, who proclaimed himself to be a "Franklinist." He was wined, dined and praised and had the time of his life.

On his return to London, he wrote letters of thanks which were widely circulated and increased the love already felt for him in Paris. To the Abbé d'Alibard he wrote: "The time I spent in Paris, in the inspiring conversation and agreeable society of so many ingenious and learned men, seems now like a pleasing dream, from which I was only to be awakened by finding myself in London." This was shameless flattery, designed to enchant the French with the thought that Paris was his dream city. Even more shameless was his letter to one of the leaders of the physiocrats and of French society, Pierre Dupont de Nemours: "There is such a freedom from local and national Prejudice and Partialities, so much Benevolence to Mankind in general, so much Goodness mixt with the Wisdom, in the principles of your new Philosophy, that I am perfectly charmed with them and wish I could have studied at your School, that I might by conversing with its Founders have made myself quite a Master of that Philosophy."

To hear that Franklin, one of the world's most respected philosophers, would have wanted to study under them was a joy to his friends in Paris and made them respect him even more for thus respecting them. He kept up his correspondence with Dupont de Nemours and others, telling them how much he would like to bring them to America with him one day: "I purpose returning to America in the ensuing summer, if our disputes should be adjusted as I hope they will be in the next session of Parliament. Would to God I could have with me Messrs Dupont, Dubourg and some other French friends with their good Ladies! I might then, by mixing them with my friends in Philadelphia, form a happy little Society." (Pierre Dupont did indeed later emigrate to America, with Franklin's encouragement, and founded one of America's greatest and most powerful family dynasties. He was, along with a young Englishman whom Franklin had helped emigrate, Tom Paine, one of the good Doctor's most eminent recruits for our country.)

Berthier, the physicist, in a letter answering Franklin's thanks, waxed lyrical: "To crown your work, you should again make a journey to France. It is your country as much as is England. You should be here in the midst of Franklinists, a father in his own country, where the country is inhabited by his children. I was a Franklinist without knowing it; now that I do know it, I shall not fail to name the founder of my sect."

This love and praise had inspired Franklin to make another trip in July of 1769. It was the same triumph again, his circle of friends expanding, along with his future correspondence with them all. The time would surely come when this would furnish more than personal pleasure. It came in 1776, as the old man, now rested in Auray, began the last lap of his third and last trip to Paris.

CHAPTER

6

Christmas in Paris and Trenton

After a French breakfast of thick country bread, fresh butter—the first in six weeks—and a soup bowl of coffee and hot milk, Franklin felt very much better on the morning of December 4, and sat down to take care of his correspondence with Paris.

First, a letter to the devoted Dr. Dubourg:

> My dear, good friend will be much surprised to receive a letter from me dated in France, when neither of us had been expecting such a thing. . . . Learning that the post leaves here this evening, I seize the opportunity to salute you. . . .
>
> I suppose that Messrs. Deane and Morris have the honour of being known to you, and as I do not know their address, I take the liberty of addressing each of them a word under your cover, and beg you to transmit it to them. I shall see to the reimbursement of your expenses.
>
> I see that you have had bad news of our affairs in America, but they are not true. . . . In different skirmishes which had occurred lately, between parties of five hundred and a thousand men on each side, we have always had the advantage, and have driven them from the field with loss, our fire being more destructive than theirs. On the sea we have seriously molested their commerce, taking large numbers of their ships in the West Indies, which are daily brought to our ports. But I do not care to dwell upon these subjects until I shall have the pleasure of seeing you.

The most comforting line in the letter for Dubourg was the promise to reimburse his expenses. He was already thousands of livres out of pocket. It was also good to hear from Franklin that the bad news of American defeats was untrue. Unfortunately, Dubourg had no way of knowing how exaggerated Franklin's assurances were. The Americans had been beaten back from Long Island, Manhattan and Connecticut; Benedict Arnold had been forced to retreat from Canada; American losses were very high, enlistments unstable and insufficient. But Franklin, from the very first day he landed in France, determined to put a brave face on the war. He never doubted that America would hold out and saw no reason to yield to gloomy reports, however true they might be.

He did not like to admit to Dubourg that he did not know Deane's address. Deane was his man in Paris, had been there for more than half a year. Where had his dispatches to Franklin, with his address on them, gone? Obviously to British naval interception. This was very bad news to be giving a French agent who was shipping material to America, but Franklin had to get word to Deane of his arrival and he trusted Dubourg enough to risk letting him know.

To Deane he wrote of the arrival on the *Reprisal,* the good news of the capture of two British vessels, worth about four thousand pounds, plus cargo of indigo which he hoped to sell at current market prices totaling another three thousand sterling, and the act of Congress appropriating seven thousand more, the whole to be used by the commissioners for their expenses. At the same time, he informed Deane of his appointment as one of the three commissioners of the Congress and asked him in turn to inform Arthur Lee. Franklin was about to take the post to Nantes and would be three or four days en route to Paris; he begged Deane to find lodgings for the Franklins to be ready for their arrival in Paris.

Meanwhile, Deane, in Paris, was suffering nervous depression from hard, dangerous and costly work, without a word from home to reassure him. While Franklin was in Auray writing to him, on December 4, Deane was writing to Robert Morris, head of the Commerce Committee of Congress, complaining: "Eight months with but two letters, when so much depended on the exact and constant correspondence, has been by much the most trying scene of my life." Deane, deeply unhappy, had to inform Morris that the latter's younger brother, Thomas, a dipsomaniac, who had been sent to Paris in the hope that new challenges might help him break off drinking, had gone on to London, where he was disgracing himself and the American cause. "A respectable friend of mine wrote me that the company he dipp'd into at once was so dissolute and expensive that it very essentially injured the reputation of your House."

Deane bemoaned the fact that "Our credit with individuals since the affair on Long Island and New York, has been most wrecked, and, having no intelligence from you, by which to counteract the reports exaggerated and spread by British emissaries, it has completed the triumph." Deane, clearly, could not cope and Franklin's steadiness was urgently needed.

Despite his nervousness, Deane had done a most commendable job for the Congress. He had bought forty tons of saltpeter, at a unit price of ten sous, just before the market jumped to fourteen sous. He had purchased two hundred thousandweight of powder at three sous below the market rate. The purchases of gunpowder that Franklin and his associates made in Europe were a major factor in staving off defeat and eventually forcing the British to sue for peace. In fact, 90 percent of all the gunpowder used by Washington's army was sent by the Paris commissioners.

On December 3, Deane had dashed off a nervous letter to John Jay, describing his situation: "Without intelligence, without orders, and without remittances, yet plunging boldly into contracts, engagements, and negotiations hourly, hoping that something will arrive from America." He had already been irritated to learn from an American Captain Leavey, to whom he had entrusted letters to Morris, that the letters had been delivered but Morris had not sent back any reply. The congressional leaders were either incredibly negligent or harassed to distraction. Communication between Paris and Philadelphia was all but nonexistent.

Meanwhile, Deane had already contracted, mainly through Beaumarchais, to send thirty thousand rifles, two hundred pieces of brass, thirty mortars, four thousand tents, and clothing for thirty thousand men, along with two hundred tons of powder, lead and balls, all involving enormous credits. This matter of credits would prove to be one of the most vexatious of Franklin's problems in Paris.

The Beaumarchais affair began in the summer of 1776. Beaumarchais was close to the King, who sent him to London on some business. There he sensed the seriousness of the crisis and that the war would be a long struggle. There, too, he met Arthur Lee to discuss what France might do to help. On his return to Paris, Beaumarchais, transported by his own zeal and playwright's penchant for drama, addressed a long, excited memorial to the King:

To the King alone:

The King of England, the ministry, the Parliament, the Opposition, the nation, the English people, the parties which tear asunder the state, agree in giving us all hope of bringing back the American colonies without a severe struggle. . . .

Now, Mr. Arthur Lee, secret deputy of the Colonies at London, is discouraged by the uselessness of his applications to France for assistance. He offers a Secret Treaty of Commerce in exchange for secret help.

Consider everything, Sire. You will see that—

1⁰ If England triumphs, they will seek to make up the cost necessary for such a struggle by seizing our West Indian sugar islands.

2⁰ If America conquers, the English will try to make up the loss of some of their American colonies by acquiring all of ours.

3⁰ If England gives up the Colonies without a blow, the result is the same, save that England will be stronger and the better able to make war.

4⁰ If America and England are reconciled, the Americans, enraged against France by her present refusal to aid them, threaten to join the English in the attack.

What to do? We can preserve peace only by giving aid to the Americans; two or three millions may save us our sugar islands, worth three hundred.

Beaumarchais, despite his ardent prose, was no fool. His arguments were cogent, and would be used by Franklin, even by Vergennes himself, to persuade a reluctant young King—Louis XVI was only twenty-two—who did not want to go to war with mighty England. Vergennes had wanted to press the idea of aid to America upon the King and was pleased to find support from so famous a figure as Beaumarchais, who was in the King's confidence. He accordingly worked out a scheme with Beaumarchais that would aid the colonies but quiet the fears of the young King, a cover operation carried out by a supposedly commercial company. They created the fictitious Roderigue, Hortalez et cie, and gave it all the physical attributes of a trading house. It would be run by Beaumarchais, but financed by France and Spain. The court would deny any connection with it and turn away the British Ambassador's complaints, saying it was difficult to prevent merchants from carrying out free trade.

Vergennes laid down the rules for Beaumarchais:

> The operation must have essentially, in the eyes of the English government, and even in the eyes of the Americans, the aspect of an individual speculation, to which we are strangers. That it may be so in appearance, it must be so to a certain extent, in reality. We will give you secretly a million. We will endeavour to persuade the Court of Spain to unite in giving you another. With these two millions you shall found a great commercial establishment, and, at your own risk and peril, you shall furnish to America arms and everything else necessary to sustain war. Our arsenals will deliver to you arms and munitions, but you shall pay for them. You will not demand money of the Americans for they have none; but you can ask return in their staple products.

It was a daring and clever plan and the King finally assented to it.

Not knowing or caring that Arthur Lee was in no way authorized to offer secret treaties or enter into contracts with him—Silas Deane was the only accredited representative in the summer of 1776—Beaumarchais wrote to Lee as soon as Vergennes gave the green light. Shortly afterward, he discovered the existence of Silas Deane and was told by Vergennes to deal with him. He broke off connections with Lee, who was furious at being suddenly excluded.

Deane, delighted, wrote Congress, explaining that the secret aid would be paid for in American products. Lee, angry, wrote Congress that the King was giving aid freely and that Deane and Beaumarchais were trying to make personal profit. Lee insisted that Congress did not have to pay, Deane kept pleading for payments. This nasty quarrel was waiting to break upon Franklin, then making his way slowly through Brittany.

Franklin noted in his diary some details of his trip from Auray to Nantes: "The carriage was a miserable one, with tired horses, the evening dark, scarce a traveler but ourselves on the road; and, to make it more comfortable, the driver stopped near a wood we were to pass through, to tell us that a gang of eighteen robbers infested that wood, who but two weeks ago had murdered some travelers on that very spot." Things began to look brighter when they got past the woods without incident. Franklin noted the next day: "We met six or seven country women in company, on horseback and Astride; they were all of fair white and red complexions but one among them was the fairest woman I ever beheld." His eyes were as keen and roving as ever.

The party arrived at Nantes on the seventh of December. The town leaders had been watching the road for days, awaiting his arrival, and promptly held a banquet in his honor. After all his sufferings, it was a grand occasion and Franklin ate heartily and drank his fill. He loved French wines, and in Paris his household accounts would run high for the cost of his cellar. It was not the best cure for gout and he paid the price of his self-indulgence.

He had been given the address of one of the partners of the commercial agent Penet, whose headquarters were in Nantes. It was a fine house and Franklin was made comfortable there. He was to have no peace and quiet, though, for all the dignitaries and social leaders of Nantes flocked to the house to see the famous man. The French, like most people, love heroes and here was one for history, bearing high the banner of liberty.

The news of Franklin's arrival in Nantes was carried swiftly to Paris, exciting speculation as to his mission. He blandly informed everyone, with a straight face, that he had come to France, which he loved, to end his days in reading, experimenting and working with the great scientists of France, a cover story that no one, least of all the British Ambassador, would believe for an instant.

While Franklin was still in Nantes, on December 11, Lord Stormont reported on his arrival to Lord Weymouth, the Foreign Secretary in London:

> My Lord,
>
> I learned yesterday evening that the famous Dr. Franklin is arrived at Nantes with his two grandchildren; they came on board an American Privateer, which took several English vessels in her Passage. Some People think that either some private Dissatisfaction or Despair of success have brought him to this Country. I cannot but suspect that he comes charged with a secret Commission from the Congress, and as he is a subtle, artful Man, and void of all Truth, he will, in that Case, use every means to deceive. . . . He has the advantage of several intimate connexions here, and stands high in the general opinion. . . . I accidentally met a particular friend of his this Evening and the Manner in which that friend, who certainly has heard from him, endeavoured to make me believe that he is probably here upon some Quarrel with the Congress, confirms me in my suspicion that he is charged with a secret and, I doubt not, very important Commission.

All Paris was buzzing about the arrival of the famous Dr. Franklin and in the cafés dozens of men asserted that they had seen him that very day. That he was still in Nantes did not stop the rumors. Military officers boasted in loud voices that they had been recruited by Franklin and were about to sail to America to help the colonials beat "les sales Anglais."

Stormont rushed out to Versailles to complain to Vergennes about the recruiting of French officers. Vergennes stoutly denied that any officers were being sent to America. He admitted that there were many volunteers among the civilians, but he told Stormont that it was impossible to stop Frenchmen from traveling as they wished, and "that there will ever be such men in all countries who are ready to run every risk as they have nothing to lose." But he was alarmed by the indiscretions, which endangered his plans for secret aid, and sent a note to the Lieutenant of Police of Paris, Lenoir, asking him to take action against the rumormongers.

"It is reported on all sides, Sir, that several private persons, calling themselves officers, give out in the cafés, the theaters, and other public places that they are sent by the Government to the insurgents, and that they receive encouragement for that purpose." He asked Lenoir to send out patrols of police officers, and "where they may meet persons who announce themselves as appointed to America, to arrest them." He added that these arrests should be carried out with maximum publicity and severity, meaning to impress Stormont with his sincerity.

While Franklin continued to enjoy himself in Nantes, Stormont ran around in a kind of frenzy, querying everyone, fellow ambassadors, writers, his own spies, about Franklin's activities. He amassed a great deal of accurate information, made some shrewd guesses, but also collected wild and inaccurate gossip which he failed to distinguish from the truth.

On December 12, he sent an urgent message to the Foreign Office in London, announcing that Franklin had been received by Vergennes at Versailles the night before, and had immediately demanded to be recognized "as the Minister from the Independent Colonies." He also had "learned" that bankers had advanced the Americans ten million livres of credit. Three days later, he told London that Franklin had offered France the exclusive trade of North America, and that France was ready "to pull off the Mask" and give open aid to the rebels. On December 18, the Ambassador wrote an embarrassed letter, admitting that the troublesome Dr. Franklin was still joyfully making the rounds of dinner parties and banquets in Nantes and had not yet reached Paris.

Franklin finally made it to Versailles by the twentieth, but he was much tired by the journey and sent Deane a note to meet him at an inn, and he would then go on to his lodgings in Paris the next day. Deane made the necessary arrangements, met Franklin at Versailles and on the twenty-first escorted him to his new lodgings at the Hôtel d'Hambourg in the Rue de l'Université, nor far from the

Church of St. Germain, in the heart of the old Latin Quarter.

Unfortunately, on the day of his arrival in Paris to take up his duties, a mail packet had arrived, with detailed official news for Vergennes about Washington's crushing defeats in Long Island and New York. The battles were long over, the military situation already changing, but as far as Vergennes could see, the Americans were losing, and this cooled his ardor for moves that might induce England to make war on France. It certainly was no time for his own cherished plans for declaring war on England unless the Americans could successfully tie up the bulk of the British Army and fleet.

The Spanish were watching events closely, too. Bound to France by the Family Compact between the related Bourbons, Spain's main interest was not in American independence—Spain viewed the rebels with distaste—but in a chance to profit from a successful war with England by conquering Portugal, Gibraltar and Minorca and making a deal with the American rebels for keeping Spanish colonies in America. At the slightest hint of bad news, the Spaniards would shy away and Vergennes had a difficult time keeping them in line with his policy.

By the time Franklin arrived in Paris, Arthur Lee had come from London, so all three of the commissioners were at last in place, ready to begin their mission. Although they were technically equal in rank, Franklin, by his age, his prestige and his knowledge of French, was clearly head of the delegation. All communications to the French Foreign Ministry were signed with his name first, Deane's second and Lee's last.

The very first of these was sent on December 23, 1776:

Sir:

We beg leave to acquaint your Excellency that we are appointed and fully empowered by the Congress of the United States to propose and negotiate a treaty of amity and commerce between France and the United States. The just and generous treatment their trading ships have received by a free admission into the ports of this kingdom, and other considerations of respect, has induced the Congress to make this offer first to France. We request an audience of your Excellency, where we may have an opportunity of presenting our credentials, and we flatter ourselves that the propositions we are authorized to make are such as will not be found unacceptable.

The cool, sly phrase "to make this offer first to France" was a Franklin touch. He was no longer playing the role of the shy virgin; this time he was deliberately going suitoring for help and did not want the French to think they were the only ones he might have to lean upon. Congress had decided to seek help from Prussia—Frederick at first seemed well disposed—and from Tuscany, as well as Spain, perhaps even from Catherine of Russia. Franklin had little hope of all this; he knew France would be the mainstay, but he did not intend to admit it.

The day after the commissioners' note marked the beginning of the Christmas holiday and Franklin knew there would be no audience granted for a few days. He needed those few days to sit down with Deane and Lee and let them read the plan for the treaties and their instructions from the Congress, of which Franklin had been the principal draftsman.

The plan called for a fairly innocuous and general treaty of amity and the outline for a treaty of commerce. There was no mention at this point, nor ever specifically so ordered by the Congress, of the negotiation of a far more important treaty for a political and military alliance. That would develop slowly over the months ahead, carefully and discreetly nurtured and manipulated by Franklin and Vergennes.

Articles 1 and 2 provided for equal treatment at the countries' respective ports as regards duties and so forth. Article 3 dealt with fishery rights and confirmed to the King of France the same rights that the British had granted him in the Treaty of Paris in 1763. Four and 5 dealt with measures of protection for each other's vessels and persons in the respective dominions. Article 6 promised joint action against pirates. In Article 7 the King would accept responsibility for action against the Barbary pirates in the Mediterranean, where the French had a strong fleet.

Article 8 was the major concession that America was ready to offer France: "If, in consequence of this treaty the King of Great

Britain should declare war against the Most Christian King, the said United States shall not assist Great Britain in such a war, with men, money, ships or any of the articles in this treaty denominated contraband." This was an important offer to remain a nonbelligerent in any Anglo-French war. It was, of course, a two-sided offer, the second not being expressed: if France did not conclude this treaty, then America might well throw her forces and materials behind the British. One of Franklin's techniques was, rather than to threaten explicitly, to dangle an offer that was tempting, its reverse effect being obvious to an experienced diplomat.

The next article, the ninth, grew out of Franklin's strong convictions about the future expansion of continental America, and really did not belong in a treaty of friendship and commerce. It bound the King of France never to invade New Britain, Nova Scotia, Canada, Florida, Newfoundland, Cape Breton and St. Johns, stating that it was the future destiny of the United States to extend over the whole continent. When he was a loyal Englishman, Franklin was an imperialist; as a loyal American he pursued the same views and was one of the first, if not the very first, to lay down the principle of America's manifest destiny.

Article 10 forbade fishing by any party in the waters of the other, the boundaries to be defined by existing international laws. The eleventh and twelfth articles dealt with rights and tariffs regarding any West Indian islands the French might conquer. The thirteenth, important to New England, stipulated no tax on molasses from the Indies. Fourteen exempted American citizens resident in France from certain French taxes. The articles from 15 to 30 dealt with the rights of neutrals at sea, definitions of contraband, right of search, an agreement not to accept commissions as privateers from a third power against each other, or to allow hostile privateers to use each other's ports. Finally, there was an annex affixing forms of sea letters and passports to be used in case of war. In all, it was a straightforward treaty generally advantageous to both sides, perhaps favoring America a bit. But America was a small, weak nation and France a mighty power. France could be generous since its aims were to weaken England as well as to win American commerce.

Accompanying the draft of the treaty was a long list of instructions to the commissioners, including authorization to make whatever changes they might have to. Congress knew how difficult communications were. It trusted Franklin, who was, after all, the architect of the plan, to know as well as anyone in Philadelphia how to handle or shift the terms of the negotiations.

Some of the possible changes were specified in advance in the instructions. The first two clauses might be dropped completely if the King did not want to grant reciprocal most-favored-nation rights. Article 3 was unimportant, granting France what it already had. Four, Congress insisted, could not be changed or dropped, for French naval protection was essential to the outnumbered American trading ships and fleet. Seven, on the Barbary pirates, could be waived if it held up the treaty. A lot of maneuvering was anticipated on the most important article, 8.

It could be strengthened, if the French so demanded, by promising never to grant England any more privileges in trade than to France and reaffirming America's solemn vow never to pay allegiance or obedience to the British King. Further, no peace treaty would be entered into with the British until all parties had been notified and given an opportunity of being included in the peace, if they thought it proper. This would include any war that might possibly break out between Britain and France as a consequence of this treaty. The articles on West Indian trade could be waived if the French objected, the same with that on taxes on American residents of France. Only very minor points were raised regarding the balance of the articles.

Added to these instructions were important requests for aid: the immediate solicitation from France of twenty to thirty thousand muskets and bayonets, and a large supply of ammunition and brass field pieces, to be sent under convoy by France. This was a demand almost certain to lead to war with England, if the French Navy were to convoy arms to a belligerent. Congress undertook to guarantee payment for the arms, artillery and ammunition and to indemnify France for the expense of the convoy. The commissioners were asked to recruit engineers for American service.

Spain was to be told that there would be no molestation of its colonies in America or South America. Of course, without being stated, the thought was conveyed that Spain might be concerned about the consequences if it did not aid the United States. Finally, the commissioners were summoned to make every effort to get France to acknowledge publicly its recognition of American independence. The instructions were signed by John Hancock, President of the Congress.

Most of Christmas in Paris was spent going over these papers, with a break for a Christmas party for Franklin's grandsons and attendance at Mass at Notre Dame. Franklin went to sleep that Christmas night well satisfied with the briefing session, looking ahead to the negotiations, certain of success, equally certain that there would be better news from the military fronts back home.

While Franklin had been at sea and then in Brittany, George Washington was embarked upon a campaign fraught with peril. He had reorganized his forces after the disastrous defeats in New York and had gathered together an army of five thousand men, winning a race to get to New Jersey before Cornwallis could catch up with them. Early in December, Sir William Howe crossed into Jersey and took personal command of Cornwallis' forces, with a plan to pin Washington into a corner and make him fight a decisive action.

Washington was outraged by the conduct of the men of New Jersey. In a letter to his brother, he wrote: "The conduct of the Jerseys has been most infamous . . . they are making their submissions as fast as they can." He trudged his way across New Jersey, keeping a step ahead of Howe. On December 8, when Franklin was greeted with cheers in Nantes, Washington's little band was preparing to cross the Delaware for the first time to take up defensive positions on the Pennsylvania side of the river. General William Alexander delayed Howe at Princeton, made a forced march to Trenton and got his last man on board to cross the river, just as the Hessians, brass bands playing at the head of their troops, entered the city.

Washington, with foresight, had sent out patrols to gather up all the boats up and down the river. Howe had none to use.

General Howe decided on December 13 that he could not then force Washington into an open fight. The weather was frightful, his men were cold and so was he. He had a warm home, a mistress waiting for him in New York, and he doubted that Washington could keep his volunteers with him through the cold winter months. He had seen the desertions and defections throughout Jersey. Why bother to camp out? By spring the American Army would have faded away and they would realize they could not fight the mighty British Army. So Sir William packed up and left.

Howe's suspicion that Washington could not hold an army together camped out on the banks of the ice-packed Delaware was entertained by Washington himself. He knew he had to take some action or he would have no army left. The enlistments of more than half his troops would expire on the thirty-first of December, some two weeks thence.

He decided to gamble.

Washington took half his troops, about 2,500 men, and led them about ten miles upriver to a ferry station where the boats had been cached. By early evening, Christmas Day, when Franklin and the commissioners were sleeping off their holiday feast in Paris, Washington began crossing the Delaware. By three in the morning all the men and field pieces had crossed through the ice floes. Washington reformed his regiments and, under a heavy snow and biting winds, started to advance toward Trenton.

At sunrise, they began their attack on the town. To their surprise and relief, the Hessians were sleeping off their Christmas celebrations, and in minutes it was all over. American artillery raked the main streets, the Hessian barracks were surrounded by fierce-looking snowmen, the German officers gave the order to surrender. With only four men wounded, two frozen to death, but no other casualties, General Washington captured more than nine hundred prisoners, twelve hundred small arms, brass cannon and the Hessian standards. It was the first great American victory of the war.

Unfortunately, no one in Paris, not Franklin, not Vergennes, not Lord Stormont—none of the principal actors—would know of this event for many, many weeks. Franklin would begin negotiations under the grim clouds of Long Island, not the triumph of Trenton.

CHAPTER

7

The Negotiations Begin

On December 28, Vergennes received the commissioners for the first time. He greeted them all politely but addressed his warmest remarks to Franklin, whom he welcomed to France as a true friend of the nation, respected and beloved by French savants and the entire French people. He told him he wanted to be in close touch with him through his First Secretary, Gérard, but that the meetings must often be secret and confidential because of spies and the constant complaints of Lord Stormont. He asked Franklin to be discreet about his public statements. Franklin assured him that this was his own intention.

Franklin understood from the very opening talks of the negotiations that Vergennes's goals and those of the Americans coincided, that it was not necessary to push and prod him unduly but that he should do everything possible to cooperate and help Vergennes carry out his policy, which depended upon his being able to persuade the King to make war upon another powerful king on behalf of rebels. Talk of revolution and liberties by French and American intellectuals did not at all please the absolute ruler of the French kingdom.

Franklin knew he could help Vergennes and the common cause most by rallying the leaders of French society, the great families and the savants of France, to his side. If the noblest families declared themselves for America, along with France's leading writers and scientists, this would go far toward calming the King's anxieties. On the very next night after meeting Vergennes, Franklin tried his luck with a remarkable old lady, a determined Tory with no sympathy whatever for the insurgents' cause: the aged Marquise du Deffand, once one of the beauties of France, now a blind, caustic, social dictator who presided over the most prestigious salon of Parisian society.

He did not win her over. She wrote a note highly critical of the Americans to her old friend Horace Walpole in London. But at her salon Franklin made his first important social contacts and had his first success. A brilliant company was gathered to meet the famous Dr. Franklin. The Duc de Choiseul, former Prime Minister to the King, was there. He hoped to win back royal favor through Franklin and became a good friend and co-conspirator. The Abbé de Barthélemy, the King's librarian, spoke to Franklin about his collected works in French. Franklin was warmly greeted by the Comte de Guines, former Ambassador to London, who conversed at length with him about British politics.

They had all just heard the disastrous news of Washington's defeats in Long Island and New York. Madame du Deffand made pointed remarks about the power and the glory of England. Franklin was very much on the spot, but the man who had kept his head in the Cockpit was not to be tripped up by a sharp-tongued old lady in a Paris salon. He agreed that England was powerful and glorious. He merely thought that even the highest and mightiest were capable of error, while the poorest and meekest could rise to the occasion to defend their most precious rights and liberties. He made these remarks in a low tone of voice with a smile on his lips. He would enter into no arguments with the old lady, for if he won, he would lose. He sought goodwill, not polemics.

He listened politely to everyone. When questions were raised, he would nod his head, rub his chin and lean forward listening, until the questioner would fill the pause by rushing on with the conversation. His successes in London and in Congress, where he spoke only when he had something just right to say, had prepared him well for the salons of the garrulous French. He did not seek to compete with them in wit but rather let them see how much he enjoyed their brilliance. Since they respected him as one of the most learned men in the world, he had nothing to prove and could make them love him just by admiring them. He walked out of the salon in triumph, most of the noble company asking him please to reserve evenings and dinners for them.

Franklin arranged to get all the Paris periodicals to keep up with the latest developments in arts, letters, science and—one of his delights—the gossip and scandal involving high society and the court, the circles in which he was operating. He began his day by reading *Le Journal de Paris, Le Mercure, La Correspondance Secrète, Les Mémoires Secrets* and others.

One day he noted that puce was no longer a fashionable color —the latest rage was buff, or chamois. When, two years later, Queen Marie Antoinette had a baby, he would be convulsed with laughter to learn that the new chic color was "caca-brown." There is only one Paris in the world, and Franklin thoroughly enjoyed his life there.

On another day he read with great interest about a new system that had just been invented by the Lieutenant General of Police. It was called a "Public Street Cleaning Service." Municipal workers would clean all places designated as "public," distinguished from the walks bordering on private property, which had to be cleaned by the owners or tenants. The new "street cleaners" would be responsible for snow removal, sanding icy bridges and walks, sprinkling the public places with water during hot spells. For a modest fee proprietors and tenants could also hire the cleaners to keep their own properties clean. The new system not only kept Paris clean but provided work for the unemployed.

A few days later Franklin learned that platinum, or "white gold," had been classified as a perfect metal, like gold and silver, and that the King of Spain had closed his platinum mines, creating a scarcity and forcing prices up in the metal market. However, the French government had put aside a quantity of platinum for use by scientists, particularly members of the Royal Academy. Franklin noted the name of the agent; he wanted to experiment with platinum's conductivity of electricity.

Franklin read, rested, attended to correspondence and received mail from America. The news was old, not much different from what he already knew, and he was disappointed. He had hoped for some good news, knowing how cautious Vergennes was about going too far with what might be a loser. He was still busy unpacking, breaking Tempe into his secretarial duties, answering questions from Lee and Deane on the treaty plans and instructions. And the New Year holidays, important in Catholic France, brought him a round of invitations to keep him occupied and distract him.

On January 3, the New Year really began with excellent news: Vergennes informed him of the granting of a subsidy of two million livres, with only the vaguest references to repayment. This encouraged him to request another audience and to put an audacious request to the Foreign Minister. In an official memorial, dated January 5, 1777, Franklin and the other two commissioners submitted the following proposal:

Sir,

The Congress, the better to defend their coasts, protect their trade and drive off the enemy, have instructed us to apply to France for eight ships of the line, completely manned, the expense of which they will undertake to pay. As other princes of Europe are lending or hiring their troops to Britain against America, it is apprehended that France may, if she thinks fit, afford our independent States the same kind of aid, without giving England any first cause of complaint. But if England should on that account declare war, we conceive that by the united force of France, Spain and America, she will lose all her possessions in the West Indies, much the greatest part of that commerce which has rendered her so opulent, and be reduced to that state of weakness and humiliation which she has, by her perfidy, her insolence and her cruelty, both in the east and in the west, so justly merited.

This was not just an opening bid in a delicate negotiation; it was a dealing of all the cards face up on the table. The instructions from Congress did not propose what amounted to a triple alliance of America, France and Spain, as a "united force" should England "declare war." The proposal went well beyond a treaty of amity and commerce. Although Franklin had decided not to push and prod Vergennes tactically, he had made a strategic decision to begin negotiations by asking for the utmost possible, hoping to get as much as he could.

He went on in that memorial to request, as Congress had stipulated, twenty to thirty thousand muskets and bayonets, large quantities of ammunition and brass fieldpieces, all to be shipped under French convoy. He pointed out that this was all the more necessary since he had learned that Mr. Deane's purchase of this material had not been granted an export license.

Stormont had heard about the Deane-Beaumarchais contract, and his spies at the port had spotted the deliveries. He had gone to protest vehemently to Vergennes, who proclaimed his innocence and said he would block the deal for export. Vergennes did this over and over again, encouraging Franklin in private, granting him subsidies and ships, then reversing himself when Stormont caught him out—for he was not yet ready for war, particularly not when the colonies were losing the battle.

Franklin concluded the memorial by offering France and Spain America's "amity and commerce" and guarantees for their West Indies possessions, saying that, in time, this commerce would be immense, an opportunity which, "if neglected, may never again return; and we cannot help suggesting that a considerable delay may be attended with fatal consequences." This last phrase was much more than a push or a prod. From a diplomat, such language sounded very much like a threat. It was a bold beginning.

Vergennes had not anticipated this opening ploy. Only the day before, he had sent a note to the Marquis d'Ossun, French Ambassador to Spain, asking him to inform the Spanish King that Franklin had arrived and had in mind a treaty of commerce. He instructed the Ambassador to tell the King of Spain that his nephew, the King of France, had taken no firm position yet on this issue. He had already informed Franklin, he wrote, that there must be "the most perfect identity of sentiments and principles and views between Their Most Christian Majesties." Vergennes added that he was most pleasantly surprised by the "modesty of the American stance, for they seem only to be asking what France has already, in part, granted them."

Experienced diplomat that he was, cunning and Machiavellian, Vergennes did not rule out the possibility that the Americans "might be hiding something in their pockets." He dryly commented that he did not intend to dig into their pockets to find out. Knowing Spain's reluctance, he assured the Ambassador that he did not seek to make war on England at this time and would never be the first to declare war, but immediately pointed out that "The Two Crowns cannot allow America to be subjugated by the mother country." He concluded that, at that time, France and Spain were the equal of Britain in numbers but admitted that the British were far more skilled and powerful at sea and in military sciences. However, appealing to the pride of the Spaniards, he added: "We surpass them by the nobility and disinterestedness of our views."

It was the very next morning that Vergennes discovered, as he had half-suspected, that the apparently modest Americans did, indeed, have something hidden in their pockets.

One of the French diplomatic techniques, which was to baffle and irritate American diplomats nearly two centuries later, in the course of creating an Atlantic alliance, was first used on Franklin. When a note does not please a French Foreign Minister, and when an answer might make things worse, the French simply do not send a reply. They call this, in a very French phrase, "une fin de non-recevoir," that is, "a conclusion by nonreceipt"; they simply do not acknowledge the note, at least in writing.

The answer was given, negatively, a few days later, not by Vergennes, who always stepped aside when the going was rough, or when he wanted to put importunate diplomats in their place, but by Gérard. There is no record of it, other than a strong hint, in a letter from Franklin to Gérard on January 14, protesting that they did not mean to force the King's hand:

> We thank M. Gérard for the polite and explicit manner in which he has communicated His Majesty's message.

We beg to return our most grateful sense of the gracious intentions which His Majesty has had the goodness to signify to our States and to assure His Majesty that we shall ever retain the warmest gratitude for the substantial proofs he has given us of his regard. . . .

We feel the strength of the reasons His Majesty has been pleased to assign for the conduct he means to hold, and the magnanimity of his motives. We beg leave to assure His Majesty that we shall at all times and in all things endeavor to conform ourselves to the views he has opened for us, as nothing is further from our intentions than to precipitate His Majesty into any measures which his royal wisdom and justice may disapprove. And if in any thing we should contravene those purposes we shall always be happy and ready to amend it according to the advice and direction of the government.

This was really crawling on one's hands and knees. The answer to their bold proposal must have been a very sharp reprimand for Franklin to lay on balm as thickly as this. Deane and Lee and, above all, John Adams, when he came, would never for a moment assume such a posture. But there was nothing that Franklin was not prepared to do for the good of his country, and he was sufficiently self-confident and assured of his own merit not to be ashamed to bend himself in two if occasion demanded, as this one so clearly did. His flexibility, his real desire to do everything the French wanted, endeared him to Vergennes and the court.

Vergennes's reasons for turning down the memorial of the Americans were summarized in a document now in the files of the French Foreign Ministry, in the form of "Minutes presented to the King in the Presence of the First Minister, the Comte de Maurepas."

In this document, dated January 9, 1777, Vergennes argues that the sending of eight vessels of the line would not radically help America's situation because England, with vast reserves, would merely increase Lord Howe's American fleet. Further, such an act on France's part would "compromise her openly" and be a "legitimate motive of war," as would the sending of armed French convoys with American supplies. These, he felt, should be "the consequence and not the preliminary of war. War, still far off, may draw near," he estimated, but France must await, not force, events. The right policy was to assist America secretly, offer facilities of ports and purchases, but no warships or armed convoys.

Busy Lord Stormont had already gotten wind of all this and informed London that France did not intend "to take the Americans by the Hand, till they appear able to defend themselves better." Vergennes had persuaded Stormont of his strict neutrality and explained his audiences with Franklin as merely being in line with the tradition of French hospitality to strangers. A minister's house, he said, is an open house. Stormont noted with satisfaction that Franklin had come back from Versailles much dissatisfied.

Stormont would have felt less smug had he read another secret document in the Foreign Ministry files, an exposé of the importance of America, unsigned, but written by an official of high station for the King's Council.

> This is a people already civilized by its understanding and which, having acquired its political independence, is about to choose for itself the legislation that is to establish its identity for all time. The history of the world, perhaps, shows no spectacle more interesting, and the political stage has never, perhaps, presented an event, the consequences of which are more important and widespread in the general condition of this globe.

Despite memoranda of this kind and the enthusiastic support of the Duc de Choiseul and other nobles, Vergennes was moving slowly. When Stormont protested that a shipment arranged by Beaumarchais and Deane was a violation of treaties, Vergennes passed the buck to his colleague, Antoine Sartine, the Minister of the Navy, who refused to issue an export permit, blocking the ship in port.

Franklin, as yet unaware of these duplicitous moves, impressed by Vergennes's assurances of friendship and, above all, by the very concrete arrangement of a two-million-livres loan, without repayment date or guarantees, sent a highly optimistic letter to the Committee of Secret Correspondence on January 17:

> The hearts of the French are universally for us, and the cries are strong for immediate war with Britain. . . . They have already a fleet of twenty-six

sail of the line manned and fitted for sea. Spain has seventeen sail in the same state.

This was all technically correct, save that the cry for war was coming from public not governmental sources and the sails of the line were hardly being prepared to take to sea against the British.

The letter told of the importance of the organization called the Farmers-General, "the most efficient part of government here and the absolute part in all commercial or moneyed concerns." Franklin had entered into contracts with them for the purchase of Maryland and Virginia tobacco at the below-market price of three sous. Franklin felt that the importance of the Farmers-General in French politics was such that it would be worthwhile cutting prices to win their favor and support. He was pleased to tell the committee that the first five hundred thousand livres of the promised loan of two millions had just been paid to their banker and that the rest would be paid in quarterly half-million installments.

In a postscript, he admitted that the agreement with the Farmers-General had not yet been signed and that there might be small changes made but that the Americans must not delay taking immediate steps to purchase the tobacco. In true Franklin style, he promised his colleagues that all would go well and the aid would be received, but appended the admonition that "America should exert herself as if she had no aid to expect but from God and her own valor." Franklin never quite trusted the French government and did not want America to develop a psychological dependency on foreign powers. America could win better and faster with aid but must be prepared to win without it.

Franklin, the other commissioners and a network of agents, both American and foreign friends of Franklin, were busy elsewhere in Europe, bargaining with American tobacco, rice, indigo and sugar for gunpowder, cannon, clothing and medical supplies. Charles Dumas, in The Hague, had reported on the Dutch gunpowder industry, the biggest in Europe—Dutch mills could turn out 150,000 pounds of powder a month.

There were complications in Holland, but they could be circumvented. Holland was an ally of Great Britain, and after Lexington and Concord the States-General imposed an embargo on the export of arms and munitions, either from the United Provinces themselves or from their West Indian colonies. This embargo was reissued with stricter terms after America's declaration of independence.

But nothing could stop merchants from turning a big profit. Gunpowder shipped from Holland doubled in price when it reached the West Indian port of St. Eustatius, and then went up another 20 to 30 percent when resold to the American colonies. The British Ambassador to Holland, Sir Joseph Yorke, complained to the States-General that "Munitions have been loaded in Dutch ports as publicly as if you had never issued a prohibitory order." At the same time, Dutch merchants, short of seamen and ships, were paying top prices on the international market and hiring a great number of British sailors and vessels. Sir Joseph stormed, "We run the risk of seeing half the merchant marine of Great Britain employed to make war on the other half." Big business, in the eighteenth century, put profits well ahead of patriotism.

Dutch ships carried sailing orders to Lisbon, in Portugal, and Santander or Bilbao in Spain, with bills made out to merchants there, although the contraband was intended for reshipment to America. The Americans further confounded the British and their allies, the Portuguese, who had also imposed an embargo, by sailing into harbors flying the British flag and wearing British uniforms. Since Americans were, ethnically and culturally, Englishmen, they had no trouble masquerading as such.

The British Navy may have been the most powerful in the world, but it had not enough ships to patrol the entire North and South Atlantic. Nor was it empowered to stop and search European vessels, particularly of allied nations. Gunrunning became the most profitable business in Europe.

Spain was at odds with Portugal, its main rival in South America. It also coveted Minorca and Gibraltar, so the British kept close watch on Spanish activities. Spanish ports gave free access to American privateers, who preyed on British shipping. Many of the so-called "Americans" were, in fact, Spanish, with false papers and dummy crews. This led the British to believe that the court of Spain was, like the French, actively intervening on the side of the rebels. It was not true, since most of the undercover work was being carried out by merchants; but it was true that the Spanish Foreign Minister, the Marqués de Grimaldi, like Vergennes, knew about it and denied everything. Security would be tightened when Grimaldi was replaced by the Conde de Floridablanca, a more cautious man with no enthusiasm for the American cause.

Although the British were worried about American successes in purchasing arms throughout Europe, the situation was different on the American side of the ocean. Robert Morris sent a pessimistic report to his agent, Deane, early in 1777. Several American ships, loaded with cargo to Europe, to pay for purchases already made, had been intercepted and captured by the British blockade fleet. "Our Ports were shut the greatest part of the summer, and now, again, when we expected them certainly to be open, the enemy are cruising at the mouths of our Bays, and along the Coast with more industry than ever." Morris lamented the fact that the Eastern states could not produce enough of what Europe wanted. The British prevented New England fishermen from reaching their favorite waters. There was only small production of masts and spars in New Hampshire and a little beeswax and flaxseed in Connecticut and Rhode Island. There was good news from Maryland and Virginia, where there were rich tobacco crops, but ships were lacking and the British blockade tight. Morris pleaded for French naval aid, particularly battle ships and convoys, at the very moment that Vergennes was letting Franklin and Deane know that it was impossible. The only hope was to get French ships with false bills of lading to sail for the French West Indies, and then to run the cargo by small ships, at night, into American harbors.

Meanwhile, Arthur Lee's brother William, in London, wrote to Dr. Dubourg to explain why he had invited a representative of the Farmers-General to meet him at Dieppe to discuss contracts, when Dubourg had already arranged for Deane and Franklin to work this out. Lee complained to Dubourg that the people dealing with the

Farmers-General "neither know the country nor the people of Virginia and Maryland, without which knowledge it is impossible to succeed." In other words, a Southerner was needed, obviously one of the Lee brothers, who more and more resented the preeminence of Deane and Franklin. Throughout the difficult negotiations, Franklin had as much trouble with his own colleagues as with the French or the British.

The British were closely following the contract deals with the Farmers-General. Lord Stormont reported to London that Franklin's commercial projects were "a great and tempting Lure" to the French. His spies had reported that Franklin and Deane had made a contract for very large quantities of tobacco at very low prices. He proposed direct action by London to "prevent the Execution" of Franklin's plans, "either by getting immediately possession of Virginia and Maryland, or by stationing our cruisers in such a manner to intercept the trade of those Colonies with France and the French West Indies."

The London War Ministry was already working on plans to invade the Southern tobacco lands. In these early weeks of 1777, however, Howe had his hands full in New England and New Jersey, with no troops to spare for the South. It would have helped Franklin's cause tremendously had he known that Cornwallis had been savaged by American troops at Princeton on January 3. More than a hundred British troops had surrendered to Washington, who also captured a great amount of stores, particularly badly needed shoes and blankets for his snow-frozen, raggedy band. Cornwallis had attacked with eight thousand British regulars, compared with Washington's five thousand. Later, Cornwallis would call Princeton "Washington's brightest laurel." But there were no laurel wreaths in Paris in January, 1777, where Franklin had to suffer bickering, double-dealing, espionage and disappointments, created by crossed wires throughout the political, diplomatic and commercial networks.

Beaumarchais, already in trouble with Vergennes for his indiscreet and inefficient handling of affairs, was angered to receive a letter from an intermediary, M. Durival. It was the first time that

Vergennes had not dealt with him directly. He wrote to protest to Vergennes in his usual extravagant language, which no one else would have dared employ in addressing the King's powerful Foreign Minister: "It will not be long before you come out of the cloud, and are more convinced than ever that I am your devoted Servant. . . ." Vergennes was not pleased at being told that his head was in a cloud.

Beaumarchais himself was not only under a cloud but in the middle of the disastrous wreckage of his plans, with grave consequences for Deane and the Americans. He had made contact with an artillery officer, Sieur Phillipus-Charles Jean-Baptiste Tronson du Coudray, a man as pompous and arrogant as his name. He had introduced him to Deane, who contracted with him to become a major general in Washington's army, in charge of artillery and engineers. Du Coudray had also agreed to recruit a large contingent of men and munitions and to sail with them for America aboard the *Amphitrite,* a ship that Beaumarchais and Deane had chartered in Le Havre.

Beaumarchais went to Le Havre to supervise the loading and departure of the ship, working frantically to get it loaded and off before an order, which he knew was being drafted in Paris, would arrive to cancel its export and sailing licenses. He wrote: "I employed more than a hundred men, working them throughout two nights, and three-fourths of the goods were carried to the bay in lighters amid the wildest confusion." Cargo destined for another ship was loaded by the *Amphitrite,* while some of its own cargo was misdirected to the other ship. Two other ships that he had bought were impounded by officials and unloaded while he was trying to get the *Amphitrite* dispatched.

Du Coudray infuriated Beaumarchais by delaying departure until he could finish writing what he called important letters, losing hours of favorable winds. Beaumarchais was in tears and near hysterics by the time the *Amphitrite,* his first major shipment to America, finally sailed out of Le Havre.

At that moment new complications were developing.

Franklin, when he was in Nantes, had received very good reports on Congress' agent, Penet, and had been told that the House of Penet, Pliarne was of the highest integrity. Suddenly, Franklin was told that they had expanded their activities by a merger with the House of Gruel, one of the principal merchants of France, and had sent out a circular letter to all the principal merchants, claiming to be the exclusive agents for the Congress, for all American transactions, and instructing all merchants and tradesmen to do business through them. Deane was apoplectic when Franklin asked him about this peculiar affair. He wrote to Penet demanding recall and retraction of his letter. Penet was hardly contrite, claiming that Congress had hired him to accomplish this mission. To make matters worse, his house began writing vicious letters attacking a rival house, with whom Deane had done business in Bordeaux, as "an Irish-Jew house." Franklin wanted to cancel all arrangements with Penet, but that was difficult, for they had many contracts of value for supplies needed in the states. The ancient rule which held that if anything could go wrong, it would, prevailed as Franklin struggled to bring order into the tangled affairs of the American mission.

At this low point, a master spy came to Paris to weave his web around Franklin.

Paul Wentworth, an American, had been colonial agent for New Hampshire but had remained loyal to the Crown. He was recruited by William Eden, an ambitious undersecretary, who was organizing a secret service, and had been given a salary, a generous expense account, even promised honors and jobs in England once the war was won. Wentworth had similarly recruited an American who had won Franklin's friendship in London, Dr. Edward Bancroft. Bancroft, who had worked with Franklin in the Massachusetts agency and had been present during the terrible moment in the Cockpit, was sure to worm his way into Franklin's most intimate circles.

When Deane arrived in Paris in the summer of '76, he had brought with him a letter of introduction to Bancroft from Franklin, and the offer of a job, at a good salary, as Deane's secretary and right-hand man. Wentworth offered Bancroft an even bigger salary and told him he might keep both if he would spy upon his colleagues. Bancroft eagerly agreed. To allay suspicions, Bancroft would visit London and bring back secret information furnished him by Wentworth. He even had himself arrested on trumped-up charges to prove he was not a British spy.

Arthur Lee took an instant dislike to Bancroft and told Franklin that he was a spy. (Lee suspected everyone, except his own personal and trusted secretary, Major John Thornton—who was, of course, another spy.) Franklin knew that Paris was swarming with spies but refused to believe that Bancroft was one of them. He had been warned by a friend that he was surrounded by spies in Paris. He acknowledged this in a letter on January 19, arguing that it hardly mattered:

> As it is impossible to discover in every case the falsity of pretended friends who would know our affairs; and more so to prevent being watched by spies when interested people may think proper to place them for that purpose; I have long observed one rule which prevents any inconvenience from such practices. It is simply this: to be concerned in no affairs that I should blush to have made public, and to do nothing but what spies may see and welcome. . . . If I was sure, therefore, that my valet de place was a spy, as he probably is, I think I should not discharge him for that, if, in other respects, I liked him.

Franklin could and did cunningly plant misinformation for spies, but it is difficult to accept, as some biographers have done, the wisdom of this attitude. Bancroft and other spies were able to gather much accurate information for Stormont to relay to the British fleet, and some shipments for America may well have been intercepted because of Franklin's refusal to take spies seriously.

Early in January, when Bancroft accompanied Franklin to a meeting with Vergennes, he met secretly in Paris with Paul Wentworth, and filled him in on all Franklin's negotiations. Wentworth used the code name "Mr. Edwards" in his dispatches to London on Bancroft's reports. He had a full and accurate rundown on the memorial of January 5 and Vergennes's rejection of it. He knew all the details of contract negotiations with the Farmers-General. Stormont knew, down to the last hogshead of powder, the cargo and plans of the *Amphitrite.*

Then came disastrous news.

The voyage of the *Amphitrite* to America did not make it beyond the English Channel. The *Amphitrite,* loaded "in the wildest confusion," was tossed about by Channel storms. The officers, packed eighteen to a cabin, sleeping and eating on the floor, were violently ill. The provisions went bad, animals died and were tossed overboard, depriving the crew of fresh food and milk. Sails that might have been British men-of-war were sighted on the western horizon, frightening the captain. And so du Coudray declared himself to be the master of the ship and ordered the captain to turn about and make his way back to the port of Lorient.

Stormont, exulting in a dispatch to London, commented: "This freak will cost France 100,000 crowns and more, and such exploits cannot fail to debase her and make her ridiculous in the eyes of foreigners."

Deane, laid up in bed with a cold and fever, received a note telling him of the *Amphitrite* fiasco. It made him sicker still, particularly the news that, on arrival in Lorient, the *Amphitrite,* with its cargo, had been impounded and forbidden to sail to America. Deane wrote Beaumarchais that they would have to make every effort to get the imposition lifted, for the American armies, destitute, badly needed the supplies.

Then he made a capital error for which he would pay dearly. Deane told Beaumarchais that his own commission with Franklin and Lee to work on a treaty of amity and commerce did not supersede his earlier commission from Congress to be the representative of the Committee of Commerce, and that he, Deane, was fully responsible for all purchases of stores and merchandise. Franklin's mission was political, Deane's commercial. And, he added, there must be no "inter-meddling by my colleagues."

He told this to Franklin, who was pleased to leave Deane that onerous responsibility, for it gave him an excellent excuse to keep his hands clean of the entire Beaumarchais-Deane-Lee mess. Franklin liked Deane, was sorry about his troubles, but knew they were of his own making. Now Deane himself had told Franklin—and Lee—to keep hands off. Franklin happily did. Lee, a born meddler, ignored Deane's injunction. All their work overlapped, however. Deane was foolish to take upon himself a responsibility that he could not fully carry out. Franklin had to deal with the Farmers-General and with all kinds of purchases and supplies. His nephew, Jonathan Williams, was shuttling back and forth between Paris and Nantes, handling affairs for the old man. William Carmichael, a friend of Arthur Lee, traveled throughout France and Holland, writing sometimes to Deane, sometimes to Franklin. Arthur Lee pushed himself into every affair and could not be kept out. Franklin, so brilliant in so many fields, was a poor administrator and never straightened out the affairs of his mission. He conserved his energy for the most important affairs, including his social life, which was as important as it was pleasurable. He simply had no time or temper to play ringmaster to his fellow commissioners.

His good friend Captain Wickes was busy working for him, checking out ships and crews for possible use in the American mission. He kept sending reports to Franklin about ships to be purchased, asking for credits to do so. Franklin was busy morning and night on a multitude of bewildering, complex, devious transactions.

There were, to his delight, lighter moments that brought warmth and cheer to his heart.

Free concerts were open to the public in the Château des Tuileries, and in the gardens when weather permitted. The Comédie-Française and the Comédie-Italienne played to overflow crowds. Franklin saw an opera based on Corneille's *Horace.* At one performance of *Alceste,* the soprano slid off a high note on the phrase "and he is breaking my heart." A critic in the audience cried out: "And you are breaking my ears." One of her admirers reached out for him and shouted: "Good, now I'll give you a new set!"

Whenever Franklin wandered out into the streets of Paris, people would spot him instantly and begin to cheer. He gave them a spectacle, so dear to the French, for Paris is more than just a city;

it was then and has remained a living theater.

Rousseau had popularized a return to nature, the simple life, and Franklin fitted into that role as the French took him to be a great, simple, backwoods philosopher. Voltaire had praised the Quakers of Philadelphia; Franklin was from Philadelphia; so, ipso facto, he became, for Paris, a beloved, tolerant Quaker.

Franklin encouraged this belief by wearing the simplest garments, without lace or frills. Old and self-indulgent, he kept his glasses on at all times, an uncommon practice then. Since they were bifocals, of his own invention and unknown in France, people took them to be cracked, and admired him all the more for his thrift and poverty—none of which had any resemblance to the truth, all of which Franklin of course thoroughly enjoyed. In his youth just under six feet, with a broad frame, he was now stooped by age to about five ten, and running to fat, but was nonetheless a commanding figure. He wore the round fur hat that had kept him warm aboard the *Reprisal* far down on his forehead, his long, silver locks flowing out from under it. It completed the picture of the rustic philosopher and became the rage of Paris. All the ladies rushed to their milliners to get fur hats "à la Franklin."

The police, who followed him wherever he went, took careful notes on his appearance. In the French archives one finds their description:

> Doctor Franklin . . . is very much run after and feted, not only by the savants, his confreres, but by all people who can get hold of him; for he is very difficult to be approached and lives in a reserve which is supposed to be directed by the government. This Quaker wears the full costume of his sect. He has an agreeable physiognomy. . . . He wears no powder but a neat air; linen very white, a brown coat make his dress. His only defense is a stick in his hand.

Despite his fatigue after all his daily efforts and vexations, and the bad winter weather, Franklin was out every night, making important friends and enjoying himself at sumptuous French banquets. He was seventy-one years old and apparently indestructible.

He dined with one of the first peers of France, the Duc de La

Rochefoucauld, a great admirer of America, who had set himself the task of translating into French the constitutions of the thirteen colonies. He met a most attractive young nobleman, only nineteen years old, the Marquis de Lafayette, who was charmed by Franklin and revered him. Lafayette, whose wife was a Noailles, introduced Franklin into the powerful Noailles family. The Prince de Broglie startled Franklin by generously offering to be a benevolent dictator of America to help it win its independence. Despite this occasional high-flown nonsense, most of the men and women he met were powerful, serious and able to help his cause and plead it at the court, for the great nobles were more influential with the young King than the government ministers.

Franklin's mission in Paris had been launched successfully despite all the difficulties and disappointments. He understood Vergennes's dilemma, his desire to help but his fear that Stormont might provoke war prematurely. Franklin was patient; he knew the struggle would be a long one. He might as well enjoy it as long as possible.

His fun would not be cut off, but his stay in Paris would be.

CHAPTER 8

Hideout in Passy

Early in his social rounds in Paris, Franklin had met a man of great wealth and influence with many ties to America. He was Jacques-Donatien Leray de Chaumont, a contractor for the French government, named by Vergennes to help facilitate the secret aid to America and put in charge of selling American prizes captured at sea through dummy fronts, so that Stormont would not know the French were guilty of breaking their treaty with England. His true family name was Leray, but when he made his fortune, he purchased the magnificent Château de Chaumont and tagged "de Chaumont" to this name. He was one of the superintendents of the Hôtel des Invalides, Overseer of the King's Forest and Quartermaster of the French Army, in charge of procuring uniforms—all in all a most important contact for Franklin.

Best of all, Chaumont owned a beautiful and spacious estate in the fashionable village of Passy, then midway between Paris and Versailles. It was still called the Hôtel de Valentinois, after the Duchesse de Valentinois, who had sold it to Chaumont. It had two dwellings on its grounds, "le grand" and "le petit" hôtels, both of them spacious mansions. The large house was occupied by the Chaumont family, his wife, son and three daughters. Franklin, with his old man's liberties, charm and love for ladies, soon took over the family as he had in Craven Street, London. One of the daughters became the overseer of his household and keeper of his household accounts. One daughter he soon began calling, jokingly, "my wife," another "my child" and a third "my dear friend." All three girls were delighted with their titles.

The house is no longer standing today and there is only one sketch of it, made in the 1860s by Victor Hugo, who had visited the house where Franklin spent the rest of his sojourn in France. Chaumont commissioned the King's painter, Joseph Duplessis, to do an oil of Franklin, which the old man considered to be his official portrait. (It hangs today in the Metropolitan Museum in New York.)

Chaumont's offer of his home must certainly have been inspired by Vergennes. The French Foreign Minister knew how easy it was for spies to enter and leave Franklin's hotel rooms in Paris. The very center of Paris was exactly where he did not want Franklin to live. He was far too visible to Stormont's observers, and every time he took a horse and carriage for the trip to Versailles he was easily followed. It was, moreover, a tiring trip for the old man.

Vergennes wanted him near at hand, hidden out in a vast estate, behind linden trees and shrubs, where it would be easy for Vergennes or Gérard or Franklin himself to slip in and out unnoticed. It was a convenient arrangement for both of them, and Franklin, short of funds, was delighted to receive Chaumont's generous offer to be his guest. Franklin may have had qualms about accepting anything free, knowing that sooner or later gifts are paid for by favors asked. Perhaps he felt that Chaumont would be paid by the French. In any case, Chaumont was making rich commissions on his American business.

Franklin had many socially eminent neighbors in Passy: the Marquis de Bougainvilliers, Provost of Paris and Lord of Passy, Princesse de Lamballe and Maréchal d'Estaing, who would play an important role in the war with England, and is an ancestor of the President of France, Valéry Giscard d'Estaing. It was on the estate of Chaumont that Franklin erected more of his famous lightning rods, and, at a nearby laboratory, in the village of La Muette, that he conducted experiments in electricity and the weight of air with his friends of the French Academy of Sciences Jean-Baptiste Le Roy and the Abbé La Roche.

The Passy hideout was to change Franklin's mode of life in France from the early hectic concentration on politics and aid to a much broader social and intellectual activity, which played its part in his campaign. Not that he stopped his meetings with all his agents; they were stepped up, but more secret, while he continued to cope with the complex business of procuring ships and supplies and refereeing the fights inside his own camp. In all this Chaumont was most helpful. He went to see Sartine, Minister of the Navy, to support Franklin's pleas for lifting the ban on American shipments. He outfitted most of the ships that did get export licenses. He sold prizes for Captain Wickes of the *Reprisal,* who became the terror of the French and Spanish coasts to British merchant ships and, later, for Captain John Paul Jones, the scourge of Scottish and English waters.

This multiringed circus was in full swing as Franklin, early in 1777, began packing in Paris for the move to Passy. He offered to take Silas Deane with him and Deane gratefully accepted. Lee, always the loner, suspicious and jealous of the other two, decided to maintain his own lodgings. But he grumbled constantly about "one always having to go to see two," although admitting that, out of deference for Franklin's age, infirmities and fame, it was fitting that he should be the one to call upon him. Yet he resented the intimacy of the other two commissioners and was constantly hurt by being excluded from their conferences and trips.

Bad news continued to arrive from America. It truly was a time to try men's souls. Franklin received a letter from his congressional committee, datelined Baltimore, December 21. It was a low point in the Revolution, before Washington's victory at Trenton. British troops were chasing him through the Jerseys, others were camping not far from Philadelphia, while the British fleet was patrolling the bay and approaches of the Delaware. A nervous Congress had hastily picked up its papers and fled to Baltimore. The letter was so hopelessly out of date that it referred to Franklin's conferences with Lord Howe on his so-called peace proposals and added that it was necessary for Deane to know the truth about this, in the event "of Dr. Franklin's not arriving." The old man did not know whether to laugh or cry at that last plaintive note. After his frenetic two months of work, Congress still did not know that he was in Paris.

Unaware of the French loan that had been accorded, Congress had decided to raise a loan of its own from its own citizens, to the amount of two millions sterling, offering to pay 6 percent interest. It had also resolved to raise ninety-four battalions of infantry, some with cavalry support, thirteen frigates, and from twenty-four to thirty-six guns, which had already been launched and were fitting. To pay for all this and supply the munitions needed, Congress pleaded for intensive action by the commissioners (which, of course, was already their principal preoccupation). They all groaned to read a paragraph instructing them to work closely with Thomas Morris, the representative of the Commerce Committee in France, that same dissolute brother about whom they had already reported to Robert Morris. The lack of communications drove them to despair.

A second letter from Baltimore, written on December 30, had arrived with the same packet. It informed them that, in the haste of packing up in Philadelphia, some papers had been misplaced, including additional instructions for their conduct in negotiations. The committee warned that the papers might have fallen into the wrong hands. They also chided Deane for having sent "open dispatches" to the committee through a Mr. Bingham; they thought Bingham reputable but too young to handle such business. The committee also announced that new commissioners were being named, and would soon be dispatched, to carry on its business in the courts of Vienna, Russia, Spain and the Grand Duchy of Tuscany. Franklin and his colleagues groaned again when they read this news. Franklin was already in close touch with the Spanish Ambassador in Paris. Arthur Lee was preparing a trip to Spain. The Grand Duke of Tuscany, an amateur scientist, was in regular correspondence with Franklin. Franklin could see only more crossed wires to tangle up his life. And he was nervous about getting ambushed in the forests of eighteenth-century European politics, with Prussia, Austria and Russia so many wolves at each other's throats and Vergennes leading his own wolfpack. In Europe, throughout that century, treaties and alliances were made, broken, remade, betrayed and reversed with regularity.

In 1755 Britain had signed the Treaty of St. Petersburg, which guaranteed a Russian diversionary attack should Prussia attack Hanover, but later signed a treaty with Frederick of Prussia, while Russia allied herself with Austria in the Seven Years' War. Still later Britain sought a treaty with Catherine of Russia against France, but Catherine refused unless Britain would agree to support her policies on Turkey, in the south, and her "Northern System" of alliances with Norway and Denmark. Frederick of Prussia was outspokenly contemptuous of the British King, who, he said, "changes his ministers as he changes his shirts."

Catherine of Russia was equally contemptuous of George III. She did not see how the English King could possibly have let things get so out of hand as to allow his serfs in America to rebel against him. She never quite understood that the colonists were not serfs, but free Englishmen. In a letter written in September, 1776, Catherine asked derisively: "What can one say of colonies that arise and say farewell forever to England? It's enough to line up everyone with the opposition."

The British, not knowing her feelings, thought she might help out, particularly because of the excellent relations which existed between the British and Russian fleets. The British Ambassador in St. Petersburg applied to Catherine for the "loan" of twenty thousand Russian troops for service in Canada. Catherine said she did not want to get involved in what might become a war with France and Spain. She asked, to the embarrassment of the British, what the consequences would be for the dignity of the two great powers if they had to combine forces simply to calm down a rebellion that had no foreign troops in its own support.

England and Russia agreed on one thing: the dangerous enemy was France. France was supporting the Porte of Turkey, which was intriguing to overthrow Catherine's puppet, the Khan of Crimea. These complications made it impossible for Franklin to try to open negotiations with Russia, as Congress had naïvely asked. He would have enough trouble seeking good relations with Prussia, Austria and Spain, each of whom was suspicious of the others, and whose reigning monarchs mistrusted the rebels. Even Holland, a republic, had little sympathy for America.

Most versions of American history lead one to believe that the American Revolution was the most important event in French minds at the time. It was not, by far. Later, when France took the fatal step that led to war with England, the American Revolution would become the French obsession and would lead, eventually, to the weakening and collapse of the Ancien Régime, and the French Revolution. But the future was not clear in the early days of 1777, except to one farsighted man, out of favor with the King, the great financier Turgot, who predicted that the American affair would wreck the kingdom.

Meanwhile, French dilatory tactics were threatening to let the Americans down. Washington, despite his successes at Trenton and Princeton, was having the greatest difficulties holding his army together. When enlistments ran out at the end of the year, there was no rush to sign on again. When, after Princeton, he withdrew to defensive positions around Morristown, his enlisted strength had dropped to a low of a thousand men, with another two thousand highly unreliable and unstable irregulars who could not be counted on to stay from week to week.

In Paris, feeling lonely, disappointed and frustrated, Deane and Lee poured out their woes to Franklin. The old man had worries and fears of his own, but knew he had to be their rock of strength. He tried to stir their spirits first by submitting a strong resolution to Vergennes, hoping for a cheering reply. The resolution, dated February 2, 1777, read:

> We, the Commissioners plenipotentiary from the Congress of the United States of America, are unanimously of the opinion, that if France or Spain should conclude a Treaty of Amity and Commerce with our

States, and enter into a war with Great Britain in consequence of that, or of open aid given to our States; it will be right and proper for us, or in the absence of any of the others, for any one of us, to stipulate and agree that the United States shall not separately conclude a Peace, nor aid Great Britain against France or Spain, nor intermit their best exertions against Great Britain during the continuance of such war. Provided always that France and Spain do, on their part, enter into a similar stipulation with our states.

The silence with which this resolution was greeted at the French Foreign Office and Spanish Embassy was an emphatic, clear answer. Two, three days went by without a murmur. The commissioners huddled together but had little comfort. When there still was no reply, on February 5 the three lonely men met again in joint conference to draft another resolution, more for themselves than anyone. It is one of the most poignant documents in all American history, perfectly mirroring their mood of despair, yet defiance:

> It is farther considered, that in the present peril of the liberties of our Country, it is our duty to hazard every thing in their support and defence.
>
> Therefore, Resolved unanimously—
>
> That, if it should be necessary, for the attainment of any thing, in our best judgment, material to the defence and support of the public cause; that we should pledge our persons or hazard the censure of the Congress by exceeding our Instructions—we will, for such purpose, most cheerfully risque our personal liberty or life. B. Franklin, Silas Deane, Arthur Lee.

One can see vividly the scene in Franklin's rooms in the Rue de l'Université, bags and papers half packed, ready for a move into isolation in the countryside, no word from home, no clearance from Vergennes for their ships, the Congress having fled to Baltimore, General Washington, so far as they knew, defeated and on the run, lacking the powder and guns they had bought but could not ship. That they could make such a resolve, persevere in their efforts, continue with contracts and entreaties, harassed by Stormont and their own quarrels, was some kind of human miracle of steadfastness and courage, particularly for an ailing man in his seventies. It is hard to understand how, with all this, Franklin could make his sorties into society, predicting, smiling and confident, the eventual American victory.

Beaumarchais did not make things better. He came around to see them, utterly dispirited, and furious to learn from Deane that Arthur Lee claimed assurances from Vergennes that there was no obstacle to the ships' leaving Le Havre (it is doubtful that Vergennes told this to Lee). Furthermore, Lee, the troublemaker, had added that if Beaumarchais still claimed he was blocked it was only because of some cheating or crookedness on his own part.

Beaumarchais, livid, had sent off a rocket to Vergennes in stronger language than even he had ever dared use: "I beg leave to say, M. le Comte, . . . after having swallowed so many other disgusting things without complaint, this one simply sticks in my gorge and is strangling me on the way down." He enclosed, in his letter, four original letters from Minister Sartine, imposing embargoes on his ships, and he demanded to know just who was guilty of low play. Now, were his ships cleared or weren't they?

Vergennes was not offended by the language of the note. He understood Beaumarchais's desperation and frustration. He knew he had been playing a double game and realized that he would have to make a move or the whole affair he was so carefully nursing would explode. America might lose out and all Vergennes's hopes for a test with England explode with it. He hastily sent a message to Beaumarchais promising immediate action to clear his ships.

Franklin was bitter about human nature but resolute in putting a brave face on everything, as he demonstrated at that bad moment by two letters to his friends in London, one to Dr. Priestley, the other to his beloved Polly Stevenson (now Mrs. Hewson).

To Priestley he wrote:

I believe in my conscience, that Mankind are wicked enough to continue slaughtering one another, as long as they can find Money to pay the Butchers. But, of all the Wars in my time, this on the part of England appears to me to be the wickedest; having no Cause but Malice against Liberty, and the Jealousy of Commerce. And I think the Crime seems likely to meet with its proper punishment; a total loss of her own Liberty, and the Destruction of her own Commerce.

I suppose you would like to know something of the state of Affairs in America. [Then, despite all the accumulated bad news, he had the audacity to claim:] In all Probability we shall be much stronger the next campaign than we were in the last . . . this War must end in our favour, and in the Ruin of Britain. . . . Do not believe the reports you hear of our internal Divisions. We are, I believe, as much united as any People ever were, and as firmly.

To Polly, the indomitable old man gave no sign of his miseries, but sent her a light fashion note on Paris coiffures:

[Temple] took notice that at the ball in Nantes, there were no heads less than 5 and a few 7 lengths of the Face above the top of the forehead. . . . Yesterday we din'd at the Duke de Rochefoucauld's, where there were three Duchesses and a Countess, and no Head higher than a Face and a half. So, it seems the farther from Court, the more extravagant the Mode.

Still smiling and confident, Franklin made the rounds of French society and the intellectual set. He was entertained by Prince Gallitzin, Russia's Minister to The Hague, on visit in Paris, and, like Franklin, a member of the Masons, whose lodges would play a major role in helping Franklin's mission. He was called on by Baron Blume, Minister of Denmark in Paris, one of the best-informed and wisest diplomats in Europe. Everyone of high rank and reputation rushed to meet Franklin, and police spies reported every visit and party back to the French government, which was highly impressed.

Franklin's colleagues, particularly Arthur Lee, and later John Adams, looked down their Puritan noses at the old man's "cavorting in high style," never quite understanding not only its advantage for his mission but what it did for his morale in his darkest hours.

It was not doing much for Stormont's morale. He was alarmed at Franklin's success with all the European diplomats, and particularly upset when he learned that Franklin had been invited to meet with two men Stormont counted on to hold him in check: the Minister of the Navy, Sartine, and the Lieutenant of Police, Lenoir. Stormont reported to London that Wickes was cruising off the coast of Nantes and that two ships were being readied to sail to America. Franklin would have been pleased to have had Stormont's "information."

But Franklin was cheered when his friend Wickes did have a great success on his privateering cruise. In the *Reprisal* he captured the British packet from Falmouth and four English merchantmen. Stormont rushed out to Versailles to protest to Vergennes, asking that the ships be returned instantly to Britain. The slippery Vergennes smiled his regrets and said he was so much a friend of Britain that as soon as he heard the news he had sent out an order to prevent Wickes from bringing his prizes into a French port, ordering him back to sea. Of course, this was to enable Wickes to get his prizes to Spain, or to slip back into a southern French port when the heat was off. Vergennes also swore to Stormont that he had seen Franklin only once and had sternly read to him the clauses of the Treaty of Utrecht. Stormont knew he was lying, but how does an ambassador call a foreign minister a liar?

Stormont's spies were busy sending him reports. Some of them, who could not afford to be seen near his house, such as the treacherous Dr. Bancroft, delivered secrets by depositing them in a sealed bottle in the hollow of a tree on the south side of the Tuileries gardens, to be picked up by a Stormont courier.

Meanwhile, Edward Bancroft, on a mission to London, was feeding back scare news to depress Deane. He wrote him that transports were being readied "to carry out additional British and German troops" by the beginning of March, to launch a major spring campaign to destroy the New England rebels, then to turn south to mop up the rest of the colonies by summer. He also said that Lord Weymouth was talking openly about declaring war on France.

The letter was bad news, but nothing so depressing as the letter the commissioners then received from Robert Morris. It was dated Philadelphia, December 31, 1776. Washington had already won his great victory at Trenton, but Morris, not far away in Philadelphia, knew nothing about it. Instead, he wrote sadly about the much earlier defeat at Fort Washington and the loss of 2,700 prisoners to the British. He rocked the commissioners by saying that, by some act of treachery, Washington's dispatches to the Congress had been intercepted, revealing to the enemy that his army's enlistments were running out, that his troops were fatigued and underarmed, and his situation desperate. The British, elated, had attacked, said Morris, driving Washington all through the Jerseys and he was now "forced across the Delaware, where he still remains."

Morris went on to tell them that, by another act of betrayal, General Charles Lee had been captured by the British, and that General Henry Clinton had invaded and conquered Rhode Island. To make matters worse, Morris wrote, the cause was threatened with instant and total ruin by the collapse in the value of Continental currency.

"The enormous pay of our army, the immense expenses at which they are supplied provisions, clothing and other necessities, and, in short, the extravagance that has prevailed in most departments of the public service, have called forth prodigious emissions of paper money, both continental and colonial." Inflation was rampant. Shoes cost three dollars, a hat twelve dollars, and a common laborer demanded two dollars a day, "and idles half the time." Help must come from France, Morris pleaded, and urgently or all would be lost. Despite the currency problems, America still was rich in tobacco, rice, indigo, deerskins, furs, wheat, flour, iron, beeswax, pot and pearl ashes and could pay, by trade, anything the commissioners could buy in France. Our fate is in your hands, Morris wrote the shocked commissioners in Paris.

On March 4, the day before receiving Morris' gloomy letter, the three Americans, steeped in their own gloom, had dispatched a letter to the Congress pointing out that they had been "Deprived of any intelligence from you since the 1st of last November." They had no remittances from the Congress and were virtually out of funds. "We are really unable to account for this silence, and, while we are affected with the unhappy consequences of it, must entreat the honorable Congress to devise some method for giving us the earliest and most certain intelligence of what passes in America."

They must have regretted their request for up-to-date intelligence when they received Morris' depressing and inaccurate letter the next day.

The situation could not have seemed worse as Franklin moved out of Paris to the hideout in Passy.

CHAPTER

9

Franklin in War and Love

There would be no early escape from reality in Passy. Merchants, tradesmen, engineers and officers, seeking commissions for or in America, besieged Franklin throughout the day. "These are my perpetual torment," Franklin wrote. No one would believe that he was not commissioned by the Congress to recruit officers for the army and navy. Franklin's friends were entreated by friends of friends to recommend worthy officers to Washington. "Great officers of all ranks, in all departments; ladies, great and small, besides professed solicitors, worry me from morning to night. The noise of every coach now that enters my court terrifies me."

Franklin's sense of humor was, fortunately, intact and he vented his vexation by drawing up a model letter for all recommendations:

> The bearer of this, who is going to America, presses me to give him a letter of recommendation, though I know nothing of him, not even his name. This may seem extraordinary, but I assure you it is not uncommon here. Sometimes, indeed, one unknown person brings another, equally unknown, to recommend him; and sometimes they recommend one another. As to this gentleman, I must refer you to himself for his character and merits, with which he is certainly better acquainted than I can possibly be. I recommend him, however, to those civilities which every stranger of whom one knows no harm has a right to; and I request you will do him all good offices.

At last there was good news to cheer him up. The *Amphitrite,* with the dilatory du Coudray aboard, had finally set sail for Santo Domingo, bearing precious cargo for Washington, who needed powder, guns, brass and uniforms. It was important, too, to Beaumarchais, who had been spending money lavishly and needed a return cargo of American products to get his money back. He was rapidly running through the earlier French and Spanish advances which had financed the House of Hortalez.

The ubiquitous, indefatigable Lord Stormont went raging through the French government, from Vergennes to the Prime Minister, the Comte de Maurepas. It was Maurepas who told him that du Coudray was aboard the *Amphitrite,* having deceived the ministry and eluded its watch. Stormont did not believe him any more than he believed Vergennes.

In addition to the *Amphitrite,* a number of other vessels were already at sea: *L'Amélie, Le Mercure, Le Marquis de Chalotais, La Seine, La Concorde,* two Bermudian vessels about to take sail and, finally, a ship that Franklin's nephew, Jonathan Williams, had chartered in Nantes, named the *Comte de Vergennes.* Beaumarchais nervously informed Vergennes of the name of the ship, pointing out that he had nothing to do with naming it and asking for permission to let it sail under his name, or, if it were compromising, to order a new name. He expressed his delight and gratitude to the Foreign Minister for making these voyages possible.

Beaumarchais also gave him good news from America, news that Franklin had not yet officially received and was only rumored by visitors from London, where events in America were reported much sooner than in Paris, since the London mail was free of blockade or interception. Beaumarchais had heard that the British "had been thrashed" in three major and twenty minor encounters. "The Americans have recaptured the whole of the Jersies, a band of 6000 men from Connecticut has seized Kingsbridge," and "everyone's courage in that country is rekindled by these successes." He did not yet have the real stories of the victories at Trenton and Princeton, but he was getting close to the truth and it was the very first good news from America that Vergennes had received. It seemed to him to reaffirm his judgment in risking British wrath by letting Beaumarchais's ships "slip away."

Beaumarchais, characteristically, also had something to complain about. This time, with the good news, he told Vergennes he was having trouble with both the Farmers-General and the Comptroller-General over goods being brought over by American privateers. They had been sent on their way to unload in Bilbao, Spain, where it would cost a lot of money to ship back to France. The Comptroller-General would do nothing, he said, without fresh orders to clear the American cargo. Since Beaumarchais was expecting heavily laden ships, with American products for him, he urgently needed these new orders and pleaded with Vergennes to help clear the way.

Poor Vergennes! He had no sooner finished reading Beaumarchais's latest report than another letter arrived by special messenger, bearing more Beaumarchais "news." Beaumarchais, knowing full well how intrusive he was, began the letter by saying: "Another letter, you will say! He is never done. How, indeed, can I finish, M. le Comte, when fresh matters incessantly excite my attention and my vigilance? You must know everything!"

The "everything," this time, was a choice morsel. Vergennes did not know whether it was true or not, for Beaumarchais was both well informed and misinformed, but it worried him, for it might just be true. The news was of an emissary from London to Franklin, bearing "proposals of peace." Beaumarchais had been told by a London source that "the offers of England to America are such that a deputy may send them to Philadelphia with honour."

The news was not true; it was a rumor, which might well have been launched by Franklin himself. The canny Doctor played a carrot-and-stick game with Vergennes, offering him the profits of American commerce plus the humiliation of England, or, if he did not help America sufficiently, the threat of a peace with England that would frustrate all Vergennes's plans.

Vergennes received that rocket at home on a Sunday morning, March 8. The very next morning, at his office in Versailles, another messenger arrived from the irrepressible Beaumarchais. To show

Vergennes how much he knew, Beaumarchais had the gall to begin by telling him that someone had informed him that Vergennes or Gérard had just had an important meeting at Versailles with Silas Deane. He then went on with his peace rumors. "England's proposals are fine, acceptable. People in America have been flattered too much with hopes of an alliance with France." He warned Vergennes that, if he did not soon conclude such an alliance, "peace will be decided on with England." Beaumarchais, incredibly arrogant, told the Foreign Minister that "I have several proposals to make to you in the matter and to M. de Maurepas." Vergennes, nervous and enraged, wrote to his embassy in London to check this "information." His nerves relaxed but not his anger with Beaumarchais when the report was firmly denied.

Franklin was busy trying to mollify Vergennes about the activities of Captain Wickes and his captured prizes. Franklin played the same game with Vergennes that Vergennes played with Stormont, denying knowledge of every infraction and promising to put everything right. Vergennes knew exactly what he was doing and approved of it, just so he had documents to show Stormont that the affair was being put right. It was necessary to maintain face and form, then do what you please.

In a memorandum to Vergennes, Franklin insisted that "We have ordered no Prizes into the Ports of France, nor do we know of any that have entered, for any other purpose but to provide themselves with necessaries, until they could sail for America, or some Port in Europe." This, Franklin said, was not inconsistent with France's treaty with England. He further argued that, while the *Reprisal* was cruising in the open sea, well off the coast of France, "British Men of War are, at this instant, cruising near the coast of France for intercepting the Commerce with America." He promised Vergennes that he would reconfirm his orders to the *Reprisal* not "to take a Station offensive to France."

While Franklin was corresponding with Vergennes and trying to fight off importunate recruits at Passy, cases of munitions arrived from Nantes, sent by Jonathan Williams. That young man, to show his care and zeal, had extracted from each cargo of guns and other munitions samples for Franklin to examine, to be sure that the goods were proper. This task excited the scientist's curiosity and consumed a lot of his time needlessly, for, despite his scientific acumen, Franklin was no expert on guns and munitions. But he could not resist playing expert.

Franklin also took time to keep up his correspondence with influential friends in other capitals where America might seek aid. One of his oldest friends was a Dutch-born doctor of medicine and a physicist, Jan Ingenhousz, who had achieved an important role as doctor to the Emperor of Austria, in Vienna, in 1769. He had met Franklin earlier in London, during residency there, and kept up a correspondence mainly on scientific experiments. Since Congress now wanted efforts to be made in Vienna, Ingenhousz had to be contacted and won over to the cause.

Franklin informed Ingenhousz that he had been ordered by the Congress "to procure such Aids from European Powers for enabling us to defend our Freedom and Independence, as it is certainly their interest to grant, as by that means the great and rapidly growing Trade of America will be open to them all and not a Monopoly to Britain as heretofore."

Using an argument that he used with Vergennes, and with friends in all the important capitals of Europe, Franklin warned Ingenhousz, and, through him, the Emperor of Austria, that, if England could restore this monopoly, there would be "such an Increase of her Strength by Sea, and if she can reduce us again to Submission, she will have thereby so great an Addition to her Strength by Sea and Land, as will together make her the most formidable power the World has yet seen, and, from her natural Pride and Insolence in Prosperity, of all others the most intolerable."

This argument proved to be Franklin's most powerful in Paris. Vergennes accepted it willingly, for he believed it himself, and used it to bully the reluctant young Louis XVI.

Franklin went on to thank Ingenhousz for a report the latter had sent him on Volta's latest experiments in electricity. He observed that, to him, it seemed quite similar to the experiments with the

Leyden jar, and explicable by the same principles. Franklin was the world's leading electrical scientist at the time. He had been the first to expound the theory of single-fluid electricity, correctly identifying negative and positive forces within a current. Historians of science rank him among the greats, just below Newton. Franklin was a theoretical scientist of first rank and at the same time a tireless, imaginative inventor and tinkerer, a kind of combination Edison and Newton. The scope and depth of his accomplishments are incredible, particularly for a grade-school dropout who was completely self-educated.

He thought the time had now come to open up a delicate correspondence with his principal adversary, Lord Stormont. Franklin was convinced that Britain would eventually sue for peace and that there ought to be a channel established to ease the way. He hit upon the question of war prisoners as the proper humanitarian issue, with equal interests on both sides. Toward the end of February, Franklin sent the following note to Stormont:

My Lord

Captain Wickes, of the Reprisal frigate, belonging to the United States of America, has now in his hands near 100 British seamen, prisoners. He desires to know whether an exchange may be made with him for an equal number of American seamen, now prisoners in England. We take the liberty of proposing this matter to your lordship and of requesting your opinion, if there is no impropriety in your giving it, whether such an exchange will probably be agreed by your Court. If your people cannot soon be exchanged here, they will be sent to America.

Stormont was indignant at receiving a message from a rebel. Not too indignant to open and read it, he made a copy of it, then resealed it and sent it back to Franklin as though unread. He sent the copy to Lord Weymouth in London:

My Lord

I send your Lordship a Copy of a very Extraordinary and Insolent Letter, that has just been left at my house by a Person who called himself an English Gentleman; I thought it by no means proper to appear to have received and kept such a Letter, and, therefore, My Lord, instantly sent it back, by a Savoyard, seemingly unopened, under cover to Mr. Carmichael, who, I discovered to be the person that had brought the letter. I added the following short, unsigned note: "The King's Ambassador receives no letters from rebels but when they come to implore His Majesty's Mercy."

Franklin laughed heartily at Stormont's haughty reply. He knew him to be a diligent, professional diplomat but a bit of a pompous ass, as were so many of his government fellows in London. Undaunted, Franklin continued to send messages about prisoners, not only to Stormont, for the record, but to members of Parliament who were opposed to the war. As to Stormont, Franklin harried him with his wit. When asked at a dinner party about Stormont's reports of British victories, Franklin replied: "Truth is one thing; Stormont another." The phrase was instantly picked up by Parisians, who converted the name "Stormont" into a new verb, "stormonter," meaning to distort or to lie. Stormont was livid.

Franklin decided the time had also come to sound out the courts in Holland and Spain. He asked Deane if he would undertake the mission to Holland and Lee that to Spain. Deane said he was too busy with his purchases in France at the moment but would go as soon as was practical. Lee was delighted to go at once. At last, weary of the dominance of the other two men, he would have the chance to show what he could do on his own.

He set out in February for Madrid, full of his mission. Unfortunately, the Spanish Foreign Minister, Grimaldi, fearful of British pressures and serving a most unsympathetic King, did not want Lee in Madrid, and to abort his mission went to meet him in Burgos. To sweeten the bitter pill, he gave Lee a modest draft on a bank for the purchase of supplies, promising to try to do better later. Lee wrote to Franklin asking whether he should stay on in Burgos and try, eventually, to get to Madrid, or whether he should make his way to Berlin or Tuscany. He was eager to complete a successful mission.

By the time his letter reached Franklin, news, great news, had at last arrived from America: the victories at Trenton and Princeton, Cornwallis' retreat to Brunswick and the decimation of two of his regiments. Washington had turned his flank to Newark and Elizabeth Town, forcing him to fall back farther and retreat to New York. Howe had pulled his garrisons out of Fort Lee and Fort Constitution, now back in American hands. Forts Washington and Independence had also been retaken and the British troops in Rhode Island had been recalled to bolster the defenses of New York.

This was just what Franklin had hoped for, had expected and was ready to use on Vergennes.

There was a good deal more in the letter from Congress, for it, too, was eager to move ahead on all fronts: Franklin was appointed commissioner to Spain as well as to Paris. This was another blow to poor Lee. Franklin softened it by writing him that he was too old and tired to undertake such a journey and that he would excuse himself to Congress, explaining that Lee was already in Spain and just the man for the job.

There were also new and audacious instructions in this latest packet of good news. The commissioners were instructed to tell the French that, if France and Spain entered the war, the United States would help in the conquest of the British sugar islands and of Portugal, the former for France, the latter for Spain. America offered to outfit six frigates, of not less than twenty-four guns each, and provisions up to two million dollars, for this joint war effort, desiring, for America's share, all British possessions on the American continent. It was a most exciting offer to share huge spoils.

Congress also requested an immediate new loan of two million sterling, repayable with interest. Lee was instructed to ask immediately for Spanish permission to bring prizes into Spain's ports and to seek a subsidy or loan.

The British, still riding high on earlier, out-of-date news, had been throwing their weight around Europe, angering their own allies. The court of Holland coldly rejected a British memorial demanding punishment of Dutch traders and of the Governor of St. Eustatius for participating in the gunpowder trade. The city of Amsterdam demanded a British apology and a reprimand of the

Ambassador. The Dutch, to show the British how they felt, promptly commissioned construction of several new battleships. The tide seemed to be turning.

Franklin was elated and admitted that perhaps he had been wrong to advise going slow on alliances. He wrote Lee: "I have never yet chang'd the opinion I gave in Congress, that a Virgin State should preserve the Virgin character, and not go about suitoring for Alliances . . . but I was overrul'd, perhaps for the best." This was a generous statement, but not altogether true. Franklin had already gone very far in suitoring the French, further than Congress had ever asked, anticipating requests long before he received them. His cautious statements may have been destined for history, rather than reality.

Giving way to his pride, he could not help boasting about his foresight: "We are also ordered to build 6 Ships of War. It is a Pleasure to find the things ordered which we were doing without Orders."

On March 18, Franklin sent two memorials to Vergennes, containing the proposals of Congress and the request for the new loan. He went a bit further by asking Vergennes to have French ambassadors throughout Europe protest the dispatch of mercenaries to America and to seek to obtain their recall. There was a typically sly Franklinesque postscript that must have caused Vergennes's eyes to narrow. It suggested that, if France could not produce the requested aid, then the Americans would like to know what the King might think of their making offers of peace to England, or, whether, after all, it was not better to pursue the war. An America talking of peace, after great victories, must have sounded very confident to Vergennes and caused him some anxiety. He certainly did not want a strong America and a strong England reconciled. Franklin was learning to play on all his fears and passions.

Franklin gave urgent orders to recall a letter that he had drafted for Congress on March 12, complaining bitterly that four months had gone by since his departure from Philadelphia without a single line from the Committee of Secret Correspondence. Four months without a word of news or instructions! During this period, Franklin was operating virtually as the President of Congress, even of the United States, in all his dealings in Europe. In our world of jets and communications satellites it is almost impossible to understand the strains and responsibilities of our first envoys to Europe. Luckily, the letter had still not been dispatched. It was brought back to him, and Franklin added a long postscript on April 9.

He told Congress he had received the new instructions and had already delivered new memorials, on all points, to Vergennes. He reported that the court of Spain had intervened with the Germans to obstruct the planned increase of Hessians. Payments on the first two millions of subsidy were coming in, in half-million installments, as promised. Vergennes had told them that the French Treasury was being drained by war preparations, so the new loan of another two millions should be raised from private bankers. He would sound out Amsterdam and The Hague, since the Dutch were angry with the British, and the news of American successes would instantly improve American credit ratings.

He told the Congress of the amazing flood of officers trying to sail to America to fight with Washington. He asked for new orders to handle this recruitment. He reported on Wickes's prizes, which had finally been sold in France, but warned that this was an embarrassment and could not be done too often. He was pleased to announce that he had just completed a contract with the Farmers-General for four hundred thousand hogsheads of tobacco, the biggest such deal ever made. He begged Congress to accept the deal, even though the price was low, and not let the agents in Paris get stuck with the difference in price. He exulted:

> All Europe is for us. . . . Tyranny is so generally established in the rest of the world, that the prospect of an asylum in America, for those who love liberty, gives general joy and our cause is esteemed the cause of all mankind. Slaves naturally become base, as well as wretched. We are fighting for the dignity and happiness of human nature. Glorious is it for the Americans to be called by Providence to this post of honor.

With those words, Franklin affirmed an American credo, an image of ourselves, that was to be the pride of America for nearly two hundred years.

Franklin told Congress that Stormont had gone to warn Vergennes that "if the Americans were permitted to continue to draw supplies of arms, etc., from this kingdom, the peace could not last much longer." Vergennes's icy answer was: "We do not desire war, but we do not fear it." Franklin felt the peace would not endure another year, that "every nation in Europe wishes to see Britain humbled, having all, in their turns, been offended by her insolence."

It was the best moment since Franklin had left America. The Ides of March and the grim winter of despair were behind. Victories had brought a change in the weather, along with the calendar. It was springtime in Paris, and in Paris, more than anywhere, in the springtime a man's fancy turns to love.

Franklin's Passy neighbor and friend, Louis-Guillaume Le Veillard, invited him to a little musicale being held in the home of another neighbor, a wealthy businessman-politician, M. Brillon de Jouy. The artist who would entertain them was Brillon's wife. Her very name, when Franklin heard it, seemed to sound like notes from a harpsichord: Anne-Louise d'Hardancourt Brillon de Jouy. When Le Veillard added that she was a beauty, just entering into the full bloom of her loveliness, in her early thirties, Franklin was intrigued and agreed at once to go.

It was love at first sight for both of them. Franklin, tired by his long labors but on the upswing with the recent good news, yearned for feminine grace, beauty and a new relationship that would bring light and charm into his stormy life. Madame Brillon was bored with a husband twenty-four years her senior, a dull man, not very interested in her (she did not yet know of his mistress). She had two little girls, who also quickly won Franklin's heart, but, being a woman of talent and ambition, she found little challenge in the social life of Passy. She was given to fits of depression, and to her Franklin was a great man of the world. He was much older than her husband, not a man one would choose for a lover, but rather an exciting father figure, the perfect companion and confidant.

Music first brought them together. Franklin was not a man of the arts, but he loved music in an unsophisticated way. His favorite pieces were gay or sentimental Scottish airs; the one he loved most was a popular ballad of the day, "Such Merry As We Have Been." Franklin could play the harpsichord and the violin a bit, without any mastery. He had also perfected a new instrument, invented in Germany, called the harmonica. It was a series of wine glasses, each of a different size and filled with a different amount of water, to produce the various notes that could be drawn from them by rubbing a finger around the brim. He was fascinated by the possibilities of the invention and began to build one of his own design, which he called the armonica. He had special glasses blown and arranged thirty-seven in a pattern, then mounted them on a spindle which was installed in a long case, mounted on four legs, so that it looked something like a harpsichord. Franklin became proficient on the instrument and even composed music for it. He was often invited to musicales and asked to perform, which gave him great pleasure.

Madame Brillon was no amateur, but an artist recognized by leading critics and composers in Europe. Schobert, a famous composer of that time, had been her teacher, and had dedicated works to her. Boccherini dedicated six sonatas to her. Claude Lopez, in her excellent study of Franklin and his French ladies, *Mon Cher Papa,* noted that Beethoven borrowed one of the themes from those sonatas for his First Symphony.

Madame Brillon was acknowledged to be Europe's premier woman artist on the harpsichord. She also played a new instrument then in the process of being perfected: the piano. She owned several models and played with great skill.

She came to play Franklin with great skill, too, doing everything to please him, short of what he wanted most. She would sit on his lap, rumple his long locks, kiss his forehead, calling him "Mon cher papa." From the very first day she met him she determined that she would possess him, in her own way. She wrote Le Veillard, thanking him for having brought Franklin and begging him to find for her the Scottish melodies that Franklin favored, so that she could play them for him and compose new airs in the same style. "I do wish to provide the great man with some moments of relaxation from his occupations, and also have the pleasure of seeing him."

She would see him, from then on, two evenings a week, often for tea, for a game of chess, sometimes in her bathroom while she was soaking in a covered tub.

But Madame Brillon was not the sole object of his affections. There would be other women in his life as a lover, just as there were many people in his life as America's principal envoy abroad. From then on, Ben Franklin was plotting his strategies in two campaigns: in war and in love.

CHAPTER 10

Spies, Profiteers and Privateers

By the spring and summer of 1777 spies outnumbered diplomats in Paris by ten to one. Some were working as secretaries inside the American delegation; others came and went from London spying on their own spies, checking, verifying and, in general, confusing Whitehall, which was swamped by contradictory reports.

Franklin was aware of the activity and continued to treat it with contempt. When he wanted a letter to be surely safe, he entrusted it to the hand of a close friend. For the rest, he felt the tremendous effort it would take to impose tight security was not worth it. What was the point of worrying about shipping information in Paris, important though that information might be, when Le Havre, Lorient, Cherbourg, Nantes and Bordeaux were swarming with spies watching the ships, plying seamen with drink and bribes? French authorities constantly changed orders, confusing everyone, including the spies. Ship captains chose from alternate routes, so no spy could be sure just which route a ship would take or when it would sail. The British blockade was on the prowl beyond the shores of France, and Franklin thought that captains would just have to trust seamanship and luck to get them through.

Franklin also knew that Stormont, armed with accurate information about American privateers and French aid, would rush to Vergennes and accuse him of violating the treaties with England, hoping to make him admit his sympathy for the rebels. This is just what Franklin wanted Stormont to do: overplay his hand and force the break that would make Vergennes take more positive action, provoking Britain to warlike acts.

A British spy, Lieutenant Colonel Edward Smith, alarmed his contacts in London with reports of French aid that went well beyond what France was actually doing. He said that in Havre-de-Grâce "there are twenty-gun ships building, to be ready in June." And added: "Every assistance that Franklin can require is given in the King's Yards, all provisions from his stores, Powder, Cannon and all sorts of ammunition from His Magazines, without any payment." The King's officers, he said, had secret instructions for superintending and forwarding all rebel equipment. "Franklin and his people have but to ask and propose anything, 'tis undertaken largely and expeditiously. I saw this myself." Moreover, Smith claimed, the news from America about the British defeat at Trenton was being fully exploited by Franklin. "The surprising bad behaviour of the Hessians, which is circulated with pains and exaggeration, has persuaded half France that Lord Cornwallis is cut off from Lord William Howe's army . . . this Hessian affair will be a certain foundation for giving credit to every fabricated story that Franklin may choose to put abroad for some Months to come."

He reported that Captain Wickes had sold his prizes for a hundred thousand livres, a very low price, in order to get them off the market before Stormont could stop the sale. Wickes's success had encouraged the Irish and the French to negotiate new deals with American privateers and even to try their own hand at privateering. A shipbuilder had offered Franklin a sixty-gun ship, but he had turned it down, deciding on a policy of smaller, swifter ships to run the British gantlet rather than to challenge the British heavy battleships.

Some of this was true, some of it false, all of it highly exaggerated. Whitehall could not distinguish between the true and the false and was not sure what tactic to adopt to meet the challenge.

Smith told London that Leray de Chaumont, Franklin's landlord, was Vergennes's right-hand man and acted as go-between, so that, in effect, Vergennes was lying when he told Stormont that he had not seen or conducted negotiations with Franklin. Moreover, Franklin's colleague, Deane, was at Versailles early every morning, from seven to nine, closeted with Gérard, Vergennes's First Secretary. "In short, France secretly moves individuals to adventure in every Rebel preparation. . . . France has sent to America 240 pieces of artillery . . . with unlimited credit upon the first hint; officers of rank and Fortune are refused leave to serve but always permitted to go to America, and there is, at this minute of time, one of the first Birth and Fortune . . . upon the eve of his departure."

Smith said he did not know the name of this officer, but he must have been referring to the young Marquis de Lafayette, who certainly fits the phrase "first Birth and Fortune" better than anyone whose departure was being discussed at the time.

Lafayette certainly did not have permission from anyone to go serve in America. Vergennes and Sartine, the appropriate ministers in such matters, were under strict orders from Louis XVI to prevent the departure of any prestigious nobles of France, particularly among those who held royal commissions in the army. Lafayette's in-laws were appalled at the thought of this boy, just growing out of his teens, being thrown into so uncertain and dangerous a struggle. Moreover, his uncle, the Duc de Noailles, was French Ambassador to London, and his position at the court there would be made impossible if his nephew was fighting in the American ranks.

Nonetheless, Lafayette was fired by youthful passion and determined to go despite all opposition. Near the end of '76, before Franklin's arrival, he had entered into negotiations with Deane and had reached agreement with him on a commission in Washington's army. This agreement, when later discovered, would put Deane in disgrace with Vergennes, who reprimanded him severely.

Promised by Deane the rank of major general in the American Army, Lafayette promptly went to different French ports, seeking out shipbuilders and merchants to buy and outfit his own ship and recruit a crew and a contingent of soldiers. He managed to elude all the police spies on his trail and set sail for America. There was an uproar in the court and hysterical demands from the family to send orders to all French and allied naval and port commanders to search for him, arrest him and bring him home. He was caught by the port commander in San Sebastián, Spain, and, protesting bitterly, returned by the first boat to France.

All the details were discovered and correctly reported to Horace Walpole, in London, by the shrewd old Madame du Deffand, who was often better informed than the government or the police. On March 31, she wrote Walpole:

> Of all present departures, the most singular and astonishing is that of M. de la Fayette whom you met when you dined with our ambassador. He is not yet twenty years old; he left recently for America and has taken with him eight or ten of his friends . . . his wife is four months pregnant, his father-in-law and mother-in-law and all the family are much afflicted.

Three weeks later, she sent another note to Walpole, informing him that Lafayette had been caught and brought back to Toulon, where his father-in-law came to escort him home. Her letter helped exonerate the court of France from any complicity in Lafayette's coup, but Deane and Franklin were held responsible.

Deane, on April 2, sent an apologetic note to Gérard, justifying his agreements with Lafayette by saying, "To gain a gallant and amiable Nobleman to espouse our cause and to give to the world a specimen of his native and hereditary bravery, surely cannot be deemed criminal." He insisted that his colleagues had no knowledge of the affair—in truth they did not, and it was important to protect Franklin from Vergennes's wrath.

On April 5, Deane sent Vergennes copies of letters he had exchanged with Lafayette on this scheme, commenting: "No country need be ashamed of him, and I am sure he will one day justify to the world that my early prejudice in his favor was well founded."

It was during this period that Franklin was in conversation with the Polish Ambassador about sending to America a champion of liberty who had already distinguished himself in his own country—Casimir Pulaski—and, in other negotiations, was trying to work out arrangements for Baron Friedrich von Steuben, who had been highly recommended to him. Steuben and Lafayette would eventually play the major foreign roles in helping Washington defeat the British.

An order signed by the King was immediately promulgated, forbidding all French commissioned officers from serving in America. But only one copy of the order was issued by the Minister of the Army and the Minister of the Navy, and the French authorities, as often as not, closed their eyes or looked the other way as the flood of volunteers to America continued. They could not afford to let Lafayette go, but they shrugged off most of the others, showing Stormont their official orders every time he complained.

Lieutenant Colonel Smith reported to London that the French were constantly deceiving Stormont. Minister of the Navy Sartine was letting his representatives work out deals with the Americans despite his every denial. "It is unnatural to think that people like Franklin and Deane are capable of being kept within such rules of propriety as Lord Stormont still supposes they are under." Vergennes, he wrote, was much better at dissimulating his duplicity, for he had a most trustworthy agent in Leray de Chaumont. Obviously, the plan to move Franklin from Paris to Passy was proving a wise one.

Smith reported that he was making good progress recruiting Lee's assistant, William Carmichael, "though his name must never be repeated or anyhow come in a question." He had no doubt that "Carmichael understood me." Smith had been told that Carmichael promised to "tell any little thing that you may wish to know."

Smith's letter was long, rambling and confusing. It annoyed George III, who was shown most of the important spy communications. In a note to Lord North, the King wrote: "The business seems to be properly arranged; but I cannot say that the continuation of Lieut. Col. Smith's narrative is in the least clearer than what I read last night, the whole requires to be methodized to be of the least use."

Deane wrote to Gérard on April 8 that an American captain had just arrived from Baltimore, which he had left on the twenty-seventh of February, having made good time, just about five weeks. He reported no decisive military actions as of that date. Washington was consolidating his armies after the year-end battles. The Congress and the people were of high resolution and good spirit, "relying that they should soon receive large supplies from France, and have relief, by a diversion in their favor." He thanked Vergennes for finally agreeing that his actions in the Lafayette affair were "justly represented."

Deane's secretary, Dr. Edward Bancroft, still operating under his code name "Mr. Edwards"—hardly a brilliant code—kept sending his reports to Wentworth and Eden in London. He said that Franklin was

> prosecuting affairs with Spain (the Department allotted to him) thro' the hands of the Count d'Aranda. The money promised is not yet paid. . . . We are taught to expect, however, that it will be considerable. Other supplies have gone and going from thence for Congress. We received a message from Comte de Maurepas and Vergennes assuring us that there would be no relaxation of their most friendly intentions to save Congress. That Spain was going on fast with her Army and Fleet.

Much of this "inside" information really did come from directly inside Franklin's office, yet the most important part of it, relative to considerable monies and aid from France and Spain, was quite wrong. Not that such promises had not been made, but that they had not been, and for a long time would not be, fully carried out. Not knowing this, London was very worried about the course of events. It would seem to bear out Franklin's contention that spies, in the long run, caused as much mischief to their masters as to their victims, and should not be taken seriously.

Bancroft told Wentworth that "I have papers of the first Consequence and there are now no secrets kept from me." He informed him that Arthur Lee was about to set out for Berlin, accompanied by William Carmichael—this was on April 24—and promised to keep them informed about relations with Prussia. He cautioned Wentworth not to "mention A. Lee's journey for the Present, as it is not talked of out of our House." He urged Wentworth to come to Paris for a secret meeting for there was so much to tell that he dared not hazard committing to paper.

Wentworth, who had spies everywhere, reported the latest news from Antwerp: that the *Amphitrite* and *Mercure,* heavily laden with arms, ammunition and clothing, had successfully run the British blockade and landed in Boston Harbor. His information was correct. The two ships had brought Washington some twenty thousand muskets and much needed powder, balls and lead.

Another spy then active in Paris—Jacobus Van Zandt, alias George Lupton—wrote to London on May 28 that

> I yesterday discovered under what name Mr. Deane receives his letters from England, tho' 'twas attended with some risque. He had occasion to go below for something, in the meanwhile I slipped into his Closet and discovered numbers of letters directed to him under the name of Monsieur Benson, they come to him generally by way of Holland. . . . I hope to pick up much intelligence in particular from Erriers or Nerriers (?) who is at present in Havre and who has almost the whole transacting of the Shipping Business . . . he places the greatest Confidence in me.

George Lupton kept earning his pay with a barrage of information and misinformation for London. He reported, early in June, that four vessels had arrived from America loaded with indigo. An American captain had been told by Franklin to "sink, burn and destroy all that cannot be brought into Port with safety." Ten French vessels were loading at Bordeaux and Nantes for America. Yet, he assured London, Franklin was angry with the French for things were not going well with his negotiations.

Meanwhile, the affairs of American and European merchants were getting more and more entangled, with Robert Morris on one side of the web and Silas Deane on the other. It would lead to the first of the great scandals that recurrently rock the American Republic, in which men are accused of exploiting a sacred public trust for private profit.

Robert Morris had been appointed to the two key Secret Committees: of Commerce and of Correspondence. By the time Franklin left for France, Morris had made himself virtual master of all questions of foreign procurement, with Deane his agent for both committees in Paris. Franklin carefully kept away from the Commerce side of it and was urged to do so by Deane, so it all fell on Deane, who would pay a heavy price for his ambition and indiscretion.

Morris was a patriot with a high sense of public service and mission; he was also a businessman with a keen sense of profit. He could not possibly keep the two motives and the two affairs separate, but he worsened the situation by conducting the committee's business in Europe through his own firm of Willing and Morris. Ostensibly, this was a cover operation to prevent the British from accusing the French of government-to-government operations. The company kept special bookkeeping entries, separating the company's private trade from government operations, but the same agents and commissionaires in a dozen ports worked on both. Morris had an agent and/or partner in all transactions, and everyone took commissions and profits on all deals, including government ones. One should add, in their defense, that this was common practice, and that they took very considerable risks. They received no salaries for their government representation. They purchased ships, signed contracts, laid out in advance considerable sums, incurring debts for which they were personally liable, counting upon reimbursement later by a Congress which had the power to reject their arrangements and refuse to pay. Many enthusiasts in the American cause, in both France and America, were wrecked in this procedure.

Morris made Deane his business partner and delivered himself of a principle questionable on the lips of a high-ranking member of Congress: "Private gain is more our pursuit than Public Good . . . however, I shall continue to discharge my duty faithfully to the Public and pursue my Private Fortune by all such honorable and fair means as the times will admit of." It is impossible to pinpoint just how he would reconcile this private gain and public good, particularly in light of his vague reference to "the times."

A large share of the congressional committee's funds went directly to Willing and Morris and their associates. In the first two years of war, 1775–77, it was more than two million dollars. Some of this government money was used to finance his private ventures, then paid back into the government account when his trades were settled. One scholar of these transactions, James Ferguson, writing in the *William and Mary Quarterly,* has charged that, at one point, Morris "diverted at least $80,000 to his own purposes and did not replace it."

Morris' network ranged throughout Europe, to the West Indies and to New Orleans. His partners or associates supplied the rice, indigo and tobacco bought for exportation to Europe to pay for the supplies other agents were buying there. American warships, the *Reprisal, Hornet, Wasp, Sachem* and *Independence,* sailed back and forth with mixed cargoes of government material and Morris' private goods. There are no records to show that Morris ever paid the government freight charges for the use of public vessels, whose captains sailed under his orders from the Congress. Ships were expensive and freight rates high, so the firm must have profited considerably. Of course, if the British captured the vessels, the loss above the insurance value was Morris'.

Morris contracted partnerships with Leray de Chaumont, as well as with John Holker, who became agent for the French Navy in America, an agency he shared with Morris. Deane, his partner in Paris, was in charge of shipping arrangements for a fleet of vessels. If government cargoes did not fill all the holds, he would add his own private cargo without charging himself. He could delay the sailing of a ship to conform with his commercial contracts, and arrange for warships to convoy private vessels. It was all highly unethical, if not downright crooked, but in the context of the times, considering all the risks involved, none of these men, who considered themselves dedicated and patriotic, seemed to have the slightest doubts or qualms about their operations.

Arthur Lee, a Virginia planter, cared nothing about these commercial transactions. He despised them and considered most merchants to be crooks, particularly his archrival, Silas Deane, who, he kept complaining to Congress, was making private profit out of his commissionership in Paris. Lee apparently was not disturbed by the similar speculations carried on by his brother William.

The shabbiest kind of speculation involved stock market manipulation. Deane, with advance information on the war and on French aid, was able to anticipate stock market movements. He invested heavily on the London Exchange throughout the war, and his books, at one point, showed a twenty-thousand-livres profit on British stocks traded through an Amsterdam firm.

Deane's close relationship with Franklin, and Franklin's own interests in various land speculation schemes, prompted Lee to link Franklin with the unsavory operations. There was no truth to this charge; Franklin had nothing to do with the Morris operation and did not speculate on the London market. This did not stop the jealous Lee, seeking to replace him, from blackening Franklin's name in letters to his influential brother, Richard Henry, in the Continental Congress. Franklin suffered as much, perhaps more, from this backbiting in his own camp as he ever suffered from Stormont and his other adversaries.

Cliques developed in Congress, with the formation of Southern, Middle and Northern blocs of states. John Adams, who never liked Franklin, although he admired his many qualities, joined the Lee-Virginia faction against the Middle-states leaders, principally Morris, Dickinson and Livingston. Franklin, no longer a politician, was nevertheless identified with the Pennsylvania faction and got caught in the cross-fire. The quarrel festered and burned all through 1777, coming to a nasty climax for Deane a year later.

Franklin was marked by it, but was too important and too little involved in the affair for Lee to bring him down. But he was hurt when it was revealed that his own nephew, Jonathan Williams, his agent in Nantes, had been the principal agent of Deane's private trading company. Franklin himself testified that on some of their transactions, involving the sale of prizes, they had made private profits of 8000 percent! Vergennes found out about all this through Chaumont and commented: "In truth Congress has sorry agents. I believe they are more concerned with their private speculations than with the interest of their principals."

Before leaving for Northern Europe and Berlin, Lee heard about Vergennes's comment and dashed off a note to Gérard:

I have just learnt that, during my absence, it was represented to his Excellency, Count Vergennes, that, in conjunction with my brother Commissioners, I had engaged in a scheme of Commerce, Independent of my never having had, nor ever intending to have, any concern in commerce; nothing could be more remote from truth than such a representation. I must, therefore, Sir, so far trespass upon your goodness, as to entreat you to take some opportunity of undeceiving his Excellency.

Lee was not only defending himself; he was delivering a dirty blow to Franklin, particularly in the reference to his "brother Commissioners." This phrase naturally included Franklin, but Vergennes had never himself used the word "commissioners" to designate the guilty parties; he had said "sorry agents," and, with the exception of Deane, they were all agents, not commissioners. Lee, who was a true patriot, with many fine personal qualities, allowed his ambitions and hatreds to poison his character, leading him to commit grievous mischief.

George III heard of these quarrels and of stock market deals by American agents and they disgusted him. He completely lost faith in the double agent Edward Bancroft, who came to London to manage some of Deane's stock dealings. He thought that Bancroft was selling out both England and America, and warned Lord North not to trust his reports: "He certainly is a stock-jobber and is not friendly to England," the King commented in a memorandum to his Prime Minister.

Bancroft, not knowing he was under suspicion, continued to send in his reports, most of them highly accurate, using a primitive numbered code. The letters, with their numbers and ciphers, went on for pages and must have caused considerable irritation in Whitehall. It was quite childish, since anyone with any background in current diplomacy could, with a little effort, break the code.

The British not only had spies but, like the Americans who could disguise themselves as British when entering Spanish ports, also had some tricks of their own. One of these was the subject of an urgent note from Franklin to Vergennes in late June. It referred to the British capture of an American Navy captain, a Captain Burnel, who had taken refuge, with one of his prizes, in the port of Cherbourg, "putting himself under the protection of the King." Franklin wrote:

> That an armed vessel, belonging to the King of England, which, in pursuit of the said Burnel, had cruised some days before the Entrance of the said Port, did at length come in Disguise, and cast Anchor within a half musket-shot of the King's Ports, pretending to be a Smugler, chased in by the British cutter.
>
> The Captain Burnel, deceived by these Pretences, and conceiving himself always Safe under the Command of the King's Ports, did imprudently go on board the pretended Smugler, when immediately the Deck was filled with armed men before concealed, many of them with their Officers in the Uniform of the British Marine, who attempted to seize him. That he broke loose from them and leapt into the Sea, and, swimming, would have got into the French Pilot Boat which brought him on board, the People of which were preparing to receive him, when the English Captain ordered his men to point their guns into the said Pilot Boat and threatened a full Discharge upon the said Boat . . . the English, retaking him, got him again aboard, put him immediately in Irons in the Hold, and, hoisting sail, carried him off.

Franklin told Vergennes that this was clearly a violation of the law of nations and of the King's protection of his ports and requested that steps be taken by Vergennes to force the British to return Captain Burnel, who was not a legitimate war prisoner taken in battle, but the victim of a criminal abduction.

Vergennes was happy to be able to complain about British violations to Stormont and called him in for a dressing down. Stormont could only reply that he was ignorant of the facts and would take up the matter with the Admiralty in London. He did point out to Vergennes that Burnel was an enemy, at war with Britain, and had entered Cherbourg with a British prize, a violation of the Anglo-French treaties.

Each day brought some new crisis to Passy. One of the bad days occurred when a packet arrived with news of an insurrection in Maryland by Tory sympathizers who had to be put down by Virginia militia. It was an act of civil war inside the American camp, and only the first of many. At one point in the war, there were more Southerners fighting on the side of the British than in Washington's army.

Franklin's favorite and most successful captain, Lambert Wickes, also ran into serious trouble in that summer of '77, when the British Navy ruled the waves. As a result of Stormont's constant complaints, Wickes had finally been ordered by Sartine to leave France and never to return as a privateer or on any armed ship. He had set sail in the *Reprisal* to return to America, but en route he had cruised the waters used by Irish "linen ships," a commodity much prized in America. Unfortunately, the Irish ships were protected by deep and sweeping convoys, which intercepted the *Reprisal* and gave chase.

Wickes ran for the nearest port in France. To gain speed he threw all his cannon overboard, and, when he had just made it into the French port, he scuttled his ship by sawing its beams in two so that the British man-of-war could not throw over lines and haul it to sea. In this crippled condition he was laid up in Saint-Malo. At the same time, a Captain Nicholson, in the frigate *Dolphin,* caught in the same chase, sprung his mast and just managed to make port.

Franklin begged Vergennes's permission to allow Wickes and Nicholson to repair their ships and take to sea again. He asked for a safe convoy off the coast of France, so that they might carry urgently needed supplies, and promised Vergennes that Wickes "shall not return to any of the Ports of France, except for the purpose of Commerce."

Vergennes told the commissioners once again what a grave problem they caused him with American privateers but promised to help the captains get home.

By the end of summer Vergennes was thoroughly fed up with Stormont's complaints, and even more by the arrogant demands the British made upon the French King to ban American privateers and armed vessels. If the Americans were to be forbidden any refuge or help in France, it would virtually end all hope of carrying supplies to Washington. The British so far outnumbered the Americans that it seemed to Vergennes undignified of them to attempt to use France to kill off all their chances. He also felt this was a good opportunity to appeal to the pride of Louis XVI. He therefore asked for a special meeting of the King's Council, in the presence of the Prime Minister, so he could deliver a memorial to the King on the subject.

The memorial began with the opinion that an acceptance of British demands to ban American privateers would "express in their ultimate meaning the formal abandonment of the Americans and even wear an aspect of declared hostility towards them." Vergennes argued that the surrender of the prizes would have the effect of removing from Americans the status of belligerents and brand them as common "pirates and sea-robbers." This would infuriate the Americans and tend to make them seek reconciliation with the English, "implanting in the breasts of Americans a hatred and a desire for revenge which the lapse of centuries will perhaps not eradicate."

If the King were to publish special orders on the demand of the British, this would "impose upon him a law too humiliating for us to venture to counsel him to subscribe it." He felt it "very difficult to submit to conditions as haughty as those which are required of us."

Knowing the King's mind, Vergennes was careful to emphasize the importance of keeping the peace with England. He also knew, and referred to, the opinion of the King's uncle, Charles III of Spain, who wanted no war with England at that time and had no sympathy for the American rebellion. He had his own colonies in America and feared uprisings due to the American example. So Vergennes talked of compromise to keep the peace. He proposed to give the Americans minimal help in the most urgent circumstances: that American privateers might enter the ports of France only in distress, according to the ancient traditions of the seas; that they not be permitted "to tarry long"; that they be given only the assistance required to take to sea again and regain their own ports; that the British, in turn, be required to cease all hostile activities in French coastal waters; that they guarantee the liberty and immunity of the French flag and commerce, and that of Spain, and that all disturbances shall cease at once. "The dignity of the King is interested herein."

Vergennes, a cunning man, added this phrase: "The dismissal of the privateers detained within our ports may be agreed on without fixing the date, in order that we may not seem to be delivering them to their enemy." This was just another loophole in the orders he was proposing to offer to the British. Every proposal had a hole in it. Who was to determine how long the Americans would "tarry"? What exactly were the "minimal assistances" to be given them? Who would say how urgent their distress when seeking refuge? In hard fact, Vergennes was giving the British nothing but more diplomatic ambiguity. And he played with skill upon the pride and dignity of the nervous young King. Vergennes was the true French savior of the American Revolution. More than any other statesman, Vergennes singlehandedly, doggedly, if deviously, pursued his goal of aid to America as a necessary step toward the war with England that was his ultimate aim. Lafayette is properly revered by Americans because he believed in our cause, in liberty and independence. For Vergennes, our cause only served his own.

Franklin knew this and counted upon him, not bothering him unnecessarily, letting him do what he intended to do at his own pace. The other commissioners, particularly Lee, and later Adams, never understood this. They thought Franklin lazy, soft and frivolous. They never realized how important were his dinner parties with men and women influential at the court, and how much they helped Vergennes deal with a reluctant King.

Franklin knew what he was doing, enjoyed doing it and would not let his colleagues influence his ways. He would devote himself more and more to the social life of Passy and, in addition to the ladies, to one of the great passions of his life: the printing press, his favorite toy and weapon.

CHAPTER

11

Bagatelles and Billets-Doux

Franklin was eager to begin in Paris the kind of propaganda campaign he had employed so effectively in London, articles in the press and periodicals, satires, essays advancing America's cause. His lack of proficiency in French was a handicap, but he practiced the language daily, beginning with gallant letters to Madame Brillon, who corrected them in red ink and returned them to him—one of the few cases in history where love letters served as grammar lessons.

The enormous success in England of his satirical hoaxes led him to try his hand at the same game in Paris. His target was the Prince of Hesse, who had sent his men, for a considerable fee, to fight as mercenaries in America. Franklin despised both the Hessians and British for their bloody contract and decided to launch his attack as soon as news of the Hessians' defeat at Trenton was well known in Paris.

The article appeared in a Paris periodical, *Correspondance Secrète et Inédite,* purporting to be a letter from a "Count de Schaumbergh," written from Rome to the Baron Hohendorf, commander of the Hessians in America. There was no such person as the Count de Schaumbergh, but there was a Count Schaumburg, agent of King George III, who at the time was trying to hire fresh troops from the Duke of Saxe-Weimar, the famous patron of Goethe and Schiller.

Since the letter was fictitious and the signature false, there was no definite proof that Franklin was its author, but everyone knew he must be. It was in his style, so like his earlier satires, and the subject matter conformed with his attempts at that time to dissuade European princes from sending mercenaries to America.

Datelined Rome, February 18, the letter began by congratulating the Baron on

> the courage of our troops exhibited at Trenton, and you cannot imagine my joy on being told that, of the 1950 Hessians engaged in the fight, but 345 escaped. There were just 1605 men killed and I cannot sufficiently commend your prudence in sending an exact list of the dead to my minister in London.
>
> The Court of London objects that there were a hundred wounded who ought not to be included in the list, nor paid for as dead; but I trust you will not overlook my instructions to you . . . and that you will not have tried by human succor to recall the life of the unfortunate whose days could not be lengthened but by the loss of a leg or an arm . . . a crippled man is a reproach to their profession and there is no wiser course than to let every one of them die when he ceases to be fit to fight.
>
> I am about to send you some new recruits. Don't economize them. Remember glory before all things. Glory is true wealth. There is nothing that degrades the soldier like the love of money. . . . Do you remember that of the 300 Lacedaemonians who defended the defile of Thermopylae, not one returned? How happy should I be could I say the same of my brave Hessians? . . .
>
> I must return to Hesse. It is true grown men are becoming scarce there, but I will send you boys. . . . You did right to send back to Europe that Dr. Crumerus who was so successful in curing dysentery. Don't bother with a man who is subject to looseness of the bowels. That disease makes bad soldiers. . . . Besides you know that they pay me as killed for all who die from disease, and I don't get a farthing for runaways. My trip to Italy, which has cost me enormously, makes it desirable that there should be a great mortality among them.

The letter became the talk of Paris, greatly embarrassing Lord Stormont and all the British diplomats. It was quickly known to be a hoax, with Franklin as the author, and enhanced his reputation as the "American Voltaire."

Some time after his Hessian letter Franklin decided it might be useful to have a printing press of his own. It had been decades since he had practiced the trade of printer, but he had worked closely with printers in London, loved the sound of the presses and the smell of ink. He ordered a small press and installed it in his house at Passy. He built his own foundry and cast his own type, with the help of a foreman and a small staff of three or four.

At first, he used it for the official papers and documents of his mission. But later he began to use it for articles, essays, poems, fables and a series of light writings that he called "Bagatelles"—trifles or frivolities—which he sent to his lady friends and others in Passy, Paris and Versailles. Despite his heavy schedule of meetings and correspondence and his multitudinous duties, he managed to spend several days a week writing and printing his own pieces, enjoying himself hugely and enhancing his reputation as the wit, sage and philosopher of Passy.

Conflicting rumors of victories and defeats kept coming in from London and Gérard kept asking the Americans for clarification, which they received so late that the situation might already have been reversed.

A British expedition of General John Burgoyne's army, feeling out American positions, landed three miles north of Fort Ticonderoga on Lake Champlain. The fort, reputed to be impregnable, was under the command of Major General Arthur St. Clair, who could count on about 2,500 men, including many ill-equipped militia. He saw the British mount heavy guns on Sugar Loaf Hill, and immediately ordered an evacuation of Ticonderoga. His action brought on a storm of abuse and accusations of cowardice, although military scholars describe it as strategically sound. The British moved into Fort Ticonderoga, causing a wave of protest throughout New England.

Some encouragement was provided by the gallant conduct of American troops covering St. Clair's retreat. They stood before the British at Hubbardton and inflicted heavy casualties on Burgoyne's forces. But they finally had to pull back. St. Clair's battered troops made contact with Major General Philip Schuyler's forces at Fort Edward, on the Hudson above Saratoga.

Franklin never for a minute wavered in his complete confidence in eventual American victory. He cheered every scrap of good news, and shrugged off all bad news as merely delaying the inevitable American triumph. His writings and flirtations in Passy were the pressure valves he needed to sustain his morale.

Even ill health was not permitted to depress him. His sense of humor came to the rescue in the most painful moments. Once when he was laid up with a severe attack of gout, he composed his famous "Dialogue Between the Gout and Mr. Franklin." He wrote it as an answer to a fable, in the style of La Fontaine, that Madame Brillon had sent him, called "The Wise Man and the Gout."

In it she chided him for his self-indulgence in pleasures which brought on his attacks: "You like food, you like ladies' sweet talk,/ You play chess when you should take a walk,/You like wine. This may seem good and well,/But your fluids meanwhile rise and swell."

In a letter of reply, Franklin refuted her arguments:

> One of the characters of your fable, Madame La Goutte, seems to me to reason pretty well, except when she supposes that mistresses have had a share in producing this painful malady. I, for one, believe the exact opposite; and here is my argument. When I was a young man, and enjoyed more of the favors of the sex than I do at present, I had no gout. Hence, if the ladies of Passy had shown more of that Christian charity that I have so often recommended to you in vain, I should not be suffering from the gout right now. This seems to me good logic.

In his "Dialogue," Franklin used a character called "Gout" to poke fun at himself for all his bad habits.

> Let us examine your course of life. When the mornings are long and you have plenty of time to go out for a walk, what do you do? Instead of getting up an appetite for breakfast by salutary exercise, you amuse yourself with books, pamphlets and newspapers, most of which are not worth the trouble. Yet you eat an abundant breakfast, not less than four cups of

tea with cream, and one or two slices of buttered toast covered with strips of smoked beef. . . . Immediately afterwards, you sit down to write at your desk. . . . This lasts until an hour after noon, without any kind of bodily exercise. . . . But what do you do after dinner? Instead of walking in the beautiful gardens of your friends with whom you have dined, like a man of sense, you settle down at the chess-board and there you stay for two or three hours.

The Gout is merciless in its description of Franklin's laziness:

> Do not flatter yourself that when you ride for half an hour in your carriage you are taking exercise. Providence has not given carriages to everybody, but it has given everybody a pair of legs.
>
> FRANKLIN: Ah! how tiresome you are. . . . Oh, for heaven's sake leave me! and I promise faithfully that from now on I shall play no more chess but shall take daily exercise and live temperately.
>
> GOUT: I know you too well. You promise beautifully; but, after a few months of good health, you will go back to your old habits. . . . You philosophers are wise men in your maxims and fools in your conduct.

One of Franklin's most popular essays, in his best style, was "The Morals of Chess."

In it he claimed that chess was not "merely an idle Amusement." It sharpened the qualities of the mind. All life is a kind of chess, Franklin wrote: "Points to gain, and Competitors or Adversaries to contend with; and in which there is a vast variety of good and ill events."

By playing chess, one learns: foresight, planning for the future before making a move; circumspection, surveying all possibilities; caution, not to move hastily, important above all in war; lastly, "we learn by Chess the habit of not being discouraged by present bad appearances in the state of our Affairs; the habit of hoping for a favorable Chance and of persevering in the search of resources." In this final point Franklin was mirroring his methods and attitudes in his negotiations.

His friend Dr. Dubourg disagreed with him and sent him a dissenting essay. Chess, he wrote, is "a vain occupation, a painful frivolity, which does not exercise the body, which fatigues the spirit

. . . which dries up and hardens the soul. It is neither a social game, nor a link of friendship; it simulates war . . . feeds the pride of one and mortifies the ego of the other." Dr. Dubourg claimed that chess is a cruel game which snuffs out in the heart of the player every feeling of public virtue. Chess is a thief of time, a game that pits man against man, never to help one another as one is called upon to do in life. In chess one seeks constantly advantage over the other; that may reflect an aspect but not the whole of life. There is no element of luck in chess, as there is in life. In the course of life, Fate plays a role. Chess is a distortion of the worst in life, not the mirror or practice of life as Franklin had claimed.

Dubourg's reply was also widely circulated, and many thought he had won the debate with his philosopher-friend.

Madame Brillon was one of Franklin's favorite chess partners. A game of chess was a good excuse for a visit and the pursuit of his flirtation with her. He beat her easily and did not need to concentrate on his game. She, shrewdly, did not try hard to give him a difficult game. She enjoyed losing to him in chess, rather than in love. She sent him little billets-doux, sometimes daily, teasing him about their relationship. In one she wrote that she was "a little miffed about the six games of chess he won so unhumanly and she warns him that she will spare nothing to get her revenge." In another, she told him that people were gossiping about "the sweet habit I have of sitting in your lap, while you always ask me for what I must always refuse to you."

When Madame Brillon was away on holiday, Franklin wrote her to say that "I often pass your house; it appears desolate now to me. I broke the Commandments by coveting it, along with the wife of my neighbor. Now, I do not covet it any more, so I am a bit less sinful. But, as regards my neighbor's wife, I find the Commandments very inconvenient and I am very sorry they were made. If, in your travels, you happen to see the Holy Father, you might ask him to repeal them, as having been given only to Jews and too hard for good Christians to keep."

Madame Brillon wrote back, admonishing him about the seven sins, absolving him of all but one: "The seventh—I shall not name it." But, she went on to claim, it was the weakness of all great men. "You have been kind and lovable; you have been loved in return! What is so damnable about that? Go on doing great things and loving pretty women; provided that, pretty and lovable though they may be, you never lose sight of my principle: always love God, and America, and me, above all."

Franklin sent back a letter, switching the discussion from the seven sins to the Ten Commandments. He said: "I was brought up to believe that there were Twelve Commandments. The First is: Increase, multiply and fill the earth; the twelfth (a commandment I enjoin you to obey): love one another. Come to think of it, they are a bit misplaced, and shouldn't the last one be first?" He wrote that he had to confess that he always broke the commandment on coveting one's neighbor's wife every time he saw or thought of her; that it was a hopeless case and "I shall never be capable of repenting this sin."

She countered him with the argument that "Perhaps there is no great harm in a man having desires and yielding to them; a woman may have desires, but she must not yield." Then she played a card women often play to keep an importunate suitor in hand: she reminded him that she was married: "My friendship, and a touch of vanity, perhaps, prompt me strongly to pardon you; but I dare not decide the question without consulting that neighbor whose wife you covet, because he is a far better casuist than I am. And, then, too, as Poor Richard would say, In weighty matters, two heads are better than one."

The reference to M. Brillon was not taken seriously by Franklin. He knew him to be a most complaisant husband, preoccupied with his own mistress. So indulgent was he that he once told Franklin: "I know you have come from kissing my wife; let me kiss you, in return."

She in turn openly professed her love for Franklin, leaving out the physical aspect he kept seeking from her: "I want to confess to you in all humility that in the matter of desire, I am as great a sinner as yourself. I have desired to see you, desired to know you, desired your esteem, desired your friendship . . . and now, I desire that you may love me forever; this desire grows day by day in my heart and will last all my life. But, such is the compassion of God, it is said, that I have not the slightest doubt that all our desires will eventually lead us to Paradise." Franklin, seeking a kind of Paradise on earth, like a good Protestant, was offered, by the Catholic lady, only Paradise in the afterlife.

They had a lovers' quarrel when she discovered that she was not, by far, the only lady to whom he was paying court. She wrote him a scolding letter about his sinfulness, saying that he might have only one sin but "it has so many branches, it is repeated so often that it would take infinite calculations to assess its magnitude. . . . The dangerous system you are forever trying to demonstrate, my dear papa, that the friendship a man has for women can be divided ad infinitum—this is something I shall never put up with."

Franklin counterattacked:

> What a difference, my dear friend, between you and me! You find innumerable faults in me, whereas I see only one fault in you (but perhaps it is the fault of my glasses). I mean this kind of avarice which leads you to seek a monopoly on all my affections, and not allow me any for the agreeable ladies of your country. Do you imagine that it is impossible for my affection (or my tenderness) to be divided without being diminished? You deceive yourself. . . . You renounce and totally exclude all that might be of the flesh in our affection, allowing me only some kisses, civil and honest, such as you might grant your little cousins. What am I receiving that is so special as to prevent me from giving the same to others, without taking from what belongs to you? . . .
>
> My poor, little love which you should have cherished, it seems to me, instead of being fat and lively (like those of your elegant paintings) is thin and ready to die of hunger for want of the substantial nourishment that his mother inhumanly refuses. And now, also, she wants to cut his little wings, so that he cannot go to seek it elsewhere.

Franklin, the veteran negotiator and treaty-drafter, then brought these talents to the service of their love, to end the quarrel with a peace treaty, in nine articles:

> Article I There must be peace, friendship and eternal love between Madame B. and Mr. Frank.

Article II In order to maintain this inviolable peace, Madame B. on her side stipulates and agrees that Mr. F. shall come and see her every time she asks him to.

Article III That he shall stay at her house as much and as long as it shall please her.

Article IV That when he is with her, he shall be obliged to take tea, play chess, listen to music or do anything that she may ask him.

Article V And that he shall love no other woman than her.

Article VI And the said Mr. F. on his side stipulates and agrees that he shall go to Madame B.'s as much as he pleases.

Article VII That he shall stay there as long as he pleases.

Article VIII That when he is with her he shall do anything he pleases.

Article IX And that he shall love no other woman as long as he finds her agreeable.

Franklin's draft treaty of love did not advance any more rapidly than his proposed treaty of amity and commerce with France. There was constant haggling with her about the clauses and about his shameless behavior as a septuagenarian Don Juan. She kept up her jealous complaints, as he kept up his own complaints about her refusals to consummate their "affair."

But his quarrels with her were never serious; they were part of the game they were playing, a mannered, eighteenth-century-style love minuet. He enjoyed and valued her friendship, which helped him relieve the pressures of his nerve-straining negotiations with Vergennes.

CHAPTER

12

Climax at Saratoga

Through the summer and fall of 1777, there was good news and bad. Fortunately for Franklin's mission, the good news came swiftly on the heels of the bad before it could do much harm.

The bad news began on the diplomatic front.

The Spanish Foreign Minister, Grimaldi, who had cooperated closely with Vergennes, sharing some of his views, was replaced by a proud chauvinist and royalist, the Conde de Floridablanca. Floridablanca was firmly opposed to American independence, unwilling to make war on England, concerned with his own policies in the Mediterranean and South America.

The Spaniards had fought and bloodied the Portuguese in the Battle of La Plata, which resulted, in June, in an armistice bringing to an end the Portuguese-Spanish conflicts in South America. Floridablanca began to shift Spain's policies toward conciliation based upon his plan for dynastic marriages that would absorb Portugal into the Spanish family without recourse to war. This eliminated one reason for seeking French and American help in the Spanish goal of conquering Portugal.

By doling out secret assistance to America, he went along just far enough with Vergennes to avoid a break with French policy. But his new plan was to persuade Vergennes to join him in a scheme of Franco-Spanish mediation between Britain and the colonies. He sought a long armed truce, with an America neither reconciled to Britain nor totally independent. His plan was sheer fantasy and demonstrated how little he understood the true situation in America or Vergennes's long-range plans. But his obstinacy had the consequence of blocking Vergennes and forcing him to take a stiffer position on aid to America, which France could not and would not carry alone. It was the Spanish response that induced Louis XVI to order Vergennes to take stern measures against American privateers and occasioned his subtle memorial to the King. This satisfied the British and ended a brief war alert.

It was during this unhappy conjuncture of diplomatic shifts that the news arrived in Paris of St. Clair's retreat from Ticonderoga and General Burgoyne's occupation of that key fort. At the same time, General Howe successfully disembarked a huge force of fifteen thousand men at Elkton, near the head of Chesapeake Bay, only fifty miles from Philadelphia. Washington had only ten thousand, five hundred men, including militia, most of them in farmers' clothes, without professional training. While General Sir William Howe's army dominated the land positions, Admiral Richard Howe commanded all sea approaches with the mighty British fleet. The British sensed a chance to break through on all fronts and end the war before the year was out, and they kept sending emissaries to Paris to keep Vergennes and Sartine well informed of their successes.

Franklin never lost his composure, his determined air of confidence. When told that Philadelphia had been taken by Howe, he laughed and said, "No, Howe has been taken by Philadelphia."

He continued his lobbying efforts with all kinds of memoranda and draft plans for the French. Most of them were intercepted by British spies, including one that had been jointly drafted by Franklin and the Abbé Niccoli, one of the eminent Passy coterie.

It was still another argument in favor of France's declaring war on England. In it the authors said it was a mistake to think that America would fight on and tire England out to the point that it would give France and Spain a better opportunity, at a later date, to enter the war. It was true enough that the American war was increasing the British public debt, but Britain's credit was good at home and abroad and she could raise money easily just so long as there was peace in Europe. The war permitted the British government to expend huge sums to build up its land and sea forces, which, the authors pointed out, were being forged under fire into the greatest army and fleet in the world, a danger to Europe if this process was not arrested and reversed.

The British, sensing victory at hand, would launch a massive summer and fall campaign, if not to final victory at least so powerful that it would induce the Americans, left all alone, to seek an accommodation with Britain. America must be conquered by Britain in the current year, the memorandum went on, or Britain would have no chance thereafter, as the colonies, themselves being forged in the heat of battle, would become strong enough to fight on by themselves. Then they would not need Europe and it would be too late for France and Spain. The triumphant Americans might then be more inclined to deal with their English brothers than with the French and Spanish who had let them down.

The great Lord Chatham had already spoken of reconciliation in the House of Peers. If France did not come into the war soon, then America would once again be joined to Britain, either as subject or ally, and France could do nothing to prevent this. France would lose the lucrative American trade and commerce now being offered only as a counterpart to war aid. France would also lose the opportunity of reducing Great Britain, and her own safety and the safety of her remaining colonies in America would be endangered.

The French had already "done too much and too little," the paper argued. France had given enough aid to the Americans to anger the British and determine them to revenge themselves at the first opportunity, but not enough to assure America's successful continuation of the war. If France did not act soon and fully, France would be dangerously exposed and suffer great losses. Franklin and Niccoli quoted a key passage in Lord Chatham's speech, wildly applauded in Parliament: that he fervently wished for peace with America and a war with all the world.

It was a powerfully argued brief, read with the keenest interest in the courts of London and of Paris. Wentworth reported to his superiors that Turgot had said the memoir was being circulated through the whole court, causing much comment.

London was further disquieted by a subsequent report from Wentworth, in mid-September, quoting a confidential dispatch from the spy Bancroft: "Last Sunday Dr. Franklin went to Versailles and was at Court, at the Queen's desire." This was astonishing news, for Marie Antoinette was not known to be a fervent partisan of the American cause and was ever suspicious of the influence of Franklin's disturbing talk of revolution upon her courtiers. If Franklin was truly being received by Their Majesties at court, he was making better progress than Stormont was reporting. It was not, in fact, true. Six months would go by before Franklin was received by the King. But the wily Franklin, setting off for Versailles, quite possibly had announced, for all spies to hear, that he was off to see the Queen.

Bancroft also told Wentworth that it was becoming more difficult to carry out his spying mission. Lord Stormont's accurate information revealed to Vergennes that it was coming from inside Franklin's office. He warned Franklin about this, and, Bancroft said, all important information was now handled verbally and in private by Franklin, Chaumont and Vergennes. Franklin had stopped writing memos on a number of conversations.

Deane was daily engaged in his difficult transactions for goods and ships. Lee had gone on to Berlin, hoping to do better than he had done on his unsuccessful mission to Spain. Alas, poor Lee was as unlucky as he was quarrelsome. Frederick of Prussia did not want to get involved in the American war. His aides did not like Lee's manner or arguments, and, to make things worse, the British Minister in Berlin, Hugh Elliot, had his spies break into his quarters and steal all Lee's papers. This did nothing to improve Lee's disposition upon his return to Paris.

Franklin was receiving his first discreet peace feelers from members of the British Opposition in London. They were brought to him by a young English friend, Benjamin Vaughan. Vaughan was a known British agent, so it was delicate for Franklin to meet openly with him in Paris. Franklin hit upon a safe meeting place: "There is Les Bains de Poitevin, a large white wooden building upon a Boat in the River opposite to the Tuilleries. You may go there in a hackney coach; and you will find me there at Six in the Evening precisely. The People know me only by sight as I go there often to bathe. Ask for an old Englishman with grey hair."

It is hard to believe that Franklin was known in the bathhouse only as an old Englishman with gray hair. With or without his famous fur hat, his was the best-known face in France. His friend Chaumont, at his factory in the Loire, had manufactured a medallion, with a portrait of Franklin, that had been sold by the thousands throughout France. It was inscribed with an epigram in Latin, composed by Turgot: "Eripuit coelo fulmen sceptrumque tyrannis" ("He wrested the lightning from the sky and the scepter from tyrants"). This medallion was sold and worn even at the court of Versailles, to the annoyance of the King, who did not want to hear about scepters being wrested from monarchs, or kings being referred to as tyrants. Louis XVI became so irritated by the adulation of Franklin by one of the ladies of the court, Comtesse Diane de Polignac, that he gave her a New Year's present of a chamberpot in Sèvres porcelain with Franklin's portrait and Turgot's epigram at the bottom of it.

Vaughan and Franklin would meet often from then on. Vaughan had Franklin's works published in London, at some personal risk, and encouraged Franklin to work on his *Autobiography,* which he was then writing episodically in Passy. Later, Franklin had Vaughan elected a member of the American Philosophical Society, which he had established in Philadelphia.

Franklin thought often of his family in Philadelphia, his daughter, Sally, his son-in-law, Richard Bache, and his sister, Jane Mecom, whom he had left with them when she had fled Boston. He was very fond of Jane, was worried about the rumors of Howe's having captured Philadelphia and did not know, when he wrote Jane on October 5, that the city had already fallen and that Jane had left and made her way to Rhode Island. He sent her a cheery letter, without a hint of all his difficulties:

> I enjoy here an exceeding good State of Health. I live in a fine, airy House upon a Hill, which has a large Garden with fine Walks in it, about a half-hour's Drive from the city of Paris. I walk a little every day in the Garden, have a good appetite and sleep well. I think the French cookery agrees with me better than the English—I suppose because there is little or no Butter in their sauces: for, I have never once had the Heart-burn since my being here tho' I eat heartily.

Franklin was not quite telling Jane the truth. French meals were elaborate, particularly at formal parties given for Franklin: eight to ten courses of pâtés, cold and hot fish, game fowl, meats and heaping desserts of puddings, cakes, berries and cream. And he ate too much, drank too much and suffered attacks of indigestion as well as recurring bouts of the gout. The house was as he described it, but he did not take the daily walks he claimed to. The building was not far from the Seine and the hill of Chaillot, where today, on the street that bears his name, at the corner of the Rue Raynouard, Ben Franklin sits eternally in a stone armchair gazing out across the Champs de Mars and the Eiffel Tower.

Despite the bad news from America and the European diplomatic fronts, Franklin, with little leverage, was obliged to go to Versailles again on September 25, and plead with Vergennes for still another loan of two million pounds sterling—some fourteen million French livres, a vast sum. In a memorial he left with the Foreign Minister, he said that Congress had purchased "a great quantity of tobacco, rice, indigo, potassium and other products, which would be sent under convoy as soon as it could overcome the difficulties of recruiting merchant seamen and finding the necessary ships." In return, General Washington urgently needed uniforms, blankets and army and navy munitions. All the money from the loan would be spent in France, Franklin told Vergennes, and greatly profit French merchants and manufacturers. "This will introduce to America French manufactures and products and develop there a taste for French commodities which will be the source of great riches in the future."

Franklin informed Vergennes that Congress was disappointed at the severe restrictions imposed in French and Spanish ports against American ships and exports to America. He further noted a cessation of subsidies previously granted. "America," he claimed, "had done nothing to bring about this change of attitude." It must be due, he politely conjectured, "to other great affairs which occupy your attention," and he hoped that this situation would soon be righted.

It was to the advantage of France and Spain, Franklin argued, to assist America and profit from trade that would provide jobs for their people and weaken Britain at the same time. Above and beyond the advantages of this trade, America was offering her bonds of friendship to the two crowns. He repeated an earlier suggestion that, depending upon events, France and Spain might usefully offer their counsel and influence in a possible peace negotiation with Britain. Franklin constantly played point and counterpoint on the themes of France and Spain declaring war alongside the United States, or playing a consultative role in peace negotiations. And as often as he used these twin arguments, just so often did he deny it, indeed saying the opposite when discussing his policy views with friends and colleagues. Franklin was far more devious than he ever admitted.

Vergennes sat behind his rosewood desk, with its gold-leaf inlays, playing with a silver stiletto letter opener, as he gazed over Franklin's head, out through his double glass doors to the gardens of Versailles, listening patiently and impassively to Franklin's now familiar arguments. When Franklin ended his plea and placed his memorial on the desk, the French Foreign Minister leaned forward and in a quiet voice informed Franklin that he already had received a complete summary of the request and the letter from Congress that had prompted it—from Lord Stormont, the day before.

The commissioners had, of course, been betrayed by the diligent Bancroft. Franklin stubbornly argued that Vergennes was just using the leak as an excuse for refusing to help. If he had wanted to grant the aid, he would have done so, with or without a prior betrayal. Silas Deane rejected the clear evidence of betrayal, claiming that Vergennes was just trying to embarrass them and put them on the defensive. Lee, alone, seized upon it as proof of his charges that their secretaries were traitors and that they negligently left their papers spread around the office, to be read by snoopers day and night. It gave him more ammunition for his campaign in Congress to discredit Franklin and Deane.

Franklin maintained his composure and confidence and worked hard to build the courage of his colleagues. Arthur Lee, despite his jealousy and growing hatred of Franklin, was impressed by the clarity of Franklin's vision and his Olympian certainty about the future. In his journal, he noted a conversation he had with Franklin a month after the embarrassing meeting with Vergennes, which still had not elicited a response from the French and Spanish courts.

Franklin, wrote Lee, felt

> it was well for us that they left us to work out our own salvation; which the efforts we had hitherto made, and the resources we had opened, gave us the fairest reason to hope we should be able to do.
>
> He told me the manner in which the whole of this business had been conducted was such a miracle in human affairs that, if he had not been in the midst of it and seen all the movements, he could not have comprehended how it was effected . . . a whole people for some months without any laws or government at all. In this state their civil governments were to be formed, an army and navy were to be provided for those who had neither a ship of war, a company of soldiers, nor magazines, arms, artillery, or ammunition. Alliances were to be formed, for they had none. All this was to be done, not at leisure nor in a time of tranquility and communication with other nations, but in the face of a most formidable invasion, by the most powerful nation, full provided with armies, fleets, and all the instruments of destruction, powerfully allied and aided.

Franklin had concluded: "The greatest revolution the world ever saw is likely to be effected in a few years; and the power that has for centuries made all Europe tremble, assisted by twenty thousand German mercenaries . . . will be effectually humbled by those whom she insulted and injured, because she conceived they had neither the spirit nor power to resist or revenge it."

No one since has so well described, in so few words, the miracle of the successful American Revolution as did Franklin in that conversation of October 25, 1777, when all his pleas had gone unanswered, British fleets were commanding the seas, and British armies occupying and investing New York and Philadelphia.

Earlier, Captain John Young, of the sloop *Independence,* had arrived in Passy with new dispatches from the Congress, announcing the appointment of Ralph Izard to the court of Tuscany at Florence, of William Lee to Vienna and Berlin, and of Arthur Lee to Madrid. They were not then able to carry out their commissions, for they had been told by the envoys of those courts in Paris that it was not opportune for them to be received. Europe was not willing to make any commitments to the Americans in the expectation that the British would soon crush the Revolution. Franklin was unhappy to have all these temperamental and impatient men on his hands, but there was nothing he could do to rid himself of them.

The dispatches also brought news of Captain Johnson of the *Lexington,* who, Franklin had thought, had successfully run the British gantlet which had earlier caught Wickes. The *Lexington* had been intercepted by a heavily armed British cutter, and a furious battle had ensued in which almost all of the *Lexington*'s officers had been killed, the ship captured and Johnson taken prisoner.

Richard Henry Lee had also sent them a note stating that independence would be gravely endangered if they did not soon conclude the alliance with France and Spain and obtain a considerable loan to purchase arms and ships.

The commissioners called in a good friend, the banker Sir George Grand, who agreed to go see Vergennes to urge action on their request. Grand came back the next day to tell them that Vergennes had not yet laid their memorial before the King. He thought the amount of the loan requested was excessive. Vergennes said an alliance would involve all Europe and help America less than the Americans thought. He repeated that there was a traitor in the American midst, a dangerous business. Grand's report of his talk with Vergennes disheartened all but Franklin, who kept insisting that events would force Vergennes's hand. And, even if not, America would persevere.

There was some sweetening to the bitter cup that Vergennes had handed Grand for delivery to the Americans, as noted by Lee in his journal: "that nothing which we had received or were to receive was lent, but to be considered as given." The limits of Vergennes's generosity were not strictly defined by Grand. He probably was referring to French and Spanish subsidies. Lee took Vergennes literally to mean everything, which confirmed his belief that Deane and Beaumarchais were cheating the Congress by asking for payments for their shipments.

It was during these negotiations that Franklin became the center of another, much more amusing controversy. Word came from London that George III had issued an order for the construction of blunt-tipped lightning rods for his palace and country estates, in contradiction of Dr. Franklin's recommendation that all lightning rods should be sharp-pointed. "We do not follow the designs of rebels," the King was said to have ordered.

In a letter to London, Franklin refused to argue the question.

> I have never entered into any controversy in defence of my philosophical opinions; I leave them to take their chance in the world. If they are *right,* truth and experience will support them; if *wrong* they ought to be refuted and rejected. Disputes are apt to sour one's temper, and disturb one's quiet. . . . The king's changing his pointed conductors for blunt ones is, therefore, a matter of small importance to me. If I had a wish about it, it would be that he had rejected them altogether, as ineffectual. For it is only since he thought himself and family safe from the thunder of Heaven that he dared to use his own thunder in destroying his innocent subjects.

Franklin wrote James Lovell, of the Congress, on October 7, to thank him for communicating a new method of secret writing, and went on to talk of the difficulties involved in handling the torrent of volunteers for America. If Congress thought he was sending over too many, it ought to know how many more he was trying to dissuade from going. He commented: "Poets lose half the Praise they would have got, Were it but known what they discretely blot." He recommended that Congress issue an order forbidding the commissioners in Paris from giving any letters of introduction to further volunteers. However, he added a postscript about his latest recruit, Baron von Steuben, whom he thought would be most helpful.

Friedrich Wilhelm Ludolf Gerhard Augustus von Steuben had been an aide to Frederick the Great, on his General Staff. He had the rank of captain, but, like so many officers who had fought in the Seven Years' War, he was unemployed in a Europe at peace in the summer and fall of 1777. Through an English friend he obtained a letter of introduction to Franklin, who received him at Passy. In a letter to Washington, seeking to impress him, Franklin raised von Steuben's rank impressively, by calling him a lieutenant general and quartermaster general of the King of Prussia.

Washington urgently needed professional officers of high rank and war experience. He accordingly welcomed von Steuben, who was then forty-seven years old, as a senior in the young American Army. He made him a major general and assigned him, at his winter quarters in Valley Forge, to be drillmaster of the American Army. Professional training and coordination, discipline in massed movements—these were Washington's principal headaches, except of course, for supplies. The army had no drill book, no standard manual of arms. Von Steuben wrote one and had every soldier learn it. He himself drilled a model company, and made it the pride of the army in a few weeks' time. Washington, delighted, promoted him to Inspector General of the Army. Von Steuben further took the ragged, uneven American units and reorganized them into battalions of two hundred men each. From then on the American troops were the equal of the best of the British regulars. Of all the European recruits von Steuben was, militarily, the most valuable that Franklin sent.

The one Washington came to like best, valuable not only militarily but politically and diplomatically, was the young Marquis de Lafayette. That determined young man, who had sworn to avenge his father's death in an earlier war with England, had finally outmaneuvered the police, the government and his family and had quietly made his way to America.

Lafayette and some fellow officers, including the Baron de Kalb, did not have a very hospitable first reception, as may be judged by a letter in the French archives, a remarkable document illustrating some of the confusions of the times. The writer, believed to be the Chevalier de Buyson, described how an advance party landed upcoast from the port of Charlestown, fearing British naval patrols outside the harbor.

We preferred carrying arms rather than linen, to defend ourselves against the runaway negroes, so we arrived in Charlestown after three days walking, very much like beggars and brigands. We were received accordingly, and when we said we were French officers, led solely by the desire for glory and to defend their liberty, we were pointed at in scorn by the populace, and treated as adventurers, even by Frenchmen, who are very numerous in Charlestown. Most of these Frenchmen are officers deeply in debt, several discharged from their corps. The French colonies have many such. Governors clear themselves as well as they can of all worthless fellows by giving them letters of recommendation to the Anglo-American generals.

Things looked better when the vessel carrying the Marquis, having successfully evaded the British patrols, arrived in the harbor.

We were now perfectly well received, and the French officers, who had been the first to laugh at us, came in crowds, to basely pay court to the Marquis de Lafayette, and endeavoured to attach themselves to his service. The population of Charlestown, as well as all this part of the continent, detest the French. This is not the case in good society, by whom we have been perfectly well received and feted everywhere.

The party made their way to Philadelphia and went to meet the President of the Congress, to whom they showed their letters from Franklin and dignitaries in France. They were then put in the hands of a man the writer called "Mr. Mouse"—Robert Morris, of the powerful Committees of Commerce and of Foreign Affairs. The next day, Mr. "Mouse" appeared with another Congressman, saying: "This gentleman speaks French very well, and is appointed to deal with all those of your nation, so that it is he, with whom you will deal in the future."

Their new guide, according to the writer, did speak excellent French, but he used it to denounce them all as adventurers and began to scold them about everything that had gone wrong in arrangements with France. "Have you seen Deane's powers? We commissioned him to send us four French engineers. Instead of that, he sent us a M. du Coudray, with some pretended engineers, who are nothing of the sort, and artillerymen who have not served. We have commissioned Mr. Franklin to send us four engineers and they have arrived . . . but this year we have plenty and very experienced ones."

The French contingent were patient. They attributed the affront to the number of schemers and fakers who had preceded them, particularly du Coudray.

> He arrived here with the air of a Lord, giving himself out as one, and as a Brigadier in France, advisor of the French Ministers, and a friend of all the Princes and Dukes, from whom he shows letters. He presented to Congress an agreement signed by Mr. Deane by which he is to have the rank of Major-General, and to be the Commanding Officer of all artillery and engineers, and of all the forts now constructed or to be constructed. . . . He even had the impudence to say and to write to Congress that it was to his ardent and pressing solicitation that they owed the help sent by France.

When the four engineers sent by Franklin arrived, they had confronted du Coudray and unmasked him before the Congress. He was not a brigadier in France, only a lowly "chef de brigade"; not a nobleman, only the son of a wine merchant in Rennes. Lafayette's contingent could understand Congress' anger and suspicion but were offended that they should be put in the same class. They sent a petition to Congress asking to have their expenses paid and return passage arranged. Lafayette and the Baron de Kalb sent memos stating their displeasure at being confounded with adventurers.

Congress sent Committeeman James Lovell to pay its apologies to Lafayette. It had been Lovell who scolded them in the first place. He asked Lafayette to forgive the misunderstanding and to accept the honorary rank of major general, but without pay and without a divisional command, too high a responsibility for a lad just out of his teens. Congress then sent him with an escort to the camp of General Washington.

Lafayette charmed Washington from their first encounter, offering to accept any assignment, any commission, even the lowliest, in order to serve the cause of freedom. Washington gave him a small but independent command, and he acquitted himself well in action.

Two other recruits fared less well. Casimir Pulaski, who had pulled every string to be sent over, although Franklin long hesitated to help him, served in the cavalry, fought bravely and was later killed in action at the head of his troops in the Battle of Savannah. He was not yet thirty when he died. Baron de Kalb, appointed major general, led his troops with great success until he fell, mortally wounded, in the Battle of Camden.

Luckier, and destined for future revolutionary glory in his native Poland, was Thaddeus Kościuszko. A year older than Lafayette, he had come to America shortly after the Declaration of Independence. He was commissioned as an engineer and built the first fortifications at West Point. He fought in the American ranks all through the war, and, when peace was signed, returned to Poland an experienced revolutionary, to fight in one of that unfortunate country's many wars of liberation.

The tides of war were swirling in the Northern and Middle states of America, moving slowly in New York and Pennsylvania, to two contradictory results in the fall of 1777. The bad news would reach Paris at the end of November, when the commissioners had still had no positive reply from Versailles or Madrid to their urgent request of September for a loan and new supplies, and it came from Pennsylvania, where Howe's forces had landed near Philadelphia.

Washington, although dangerously outnumbered, had decided that the capital could not be surrendered without a fight. He made his first stand on Brandywine Creek, twenty-five miles southeast of the city. Howe sent out scouts, located Washington's flanks and weaknesses and moved brilliantly to exploit them, one of the few times in the war that the generally inept British command functioned as professionals and used their superiority to full advantage.

Washington's understrength troops were badly mauled. He lost a thousand men, killed and wounded, and had to retreat. Congress, informed of the British advance, packed up again and moved westward to Lancaster and York, in the wooded Pennsylvania hill country, where small units could mount effective defenses.

Howe, with the road open to Philadelphia, made the mistake of taking the easy and prestigious decision to occupy the American city of independence, instead of the proper military decision to press on and destroy Washington's forces. He occupied Philadelphia on September 26, the day after Franklin had delivered his call for help to Vergennes.

Washington, always a gambler, thought that Howe was so distracted by his occupation of Philadelphia that a surprise attack might catch him off guard. Accordingly, he launched an assault on the British encampments at Germantown, on October 5. The British were not Hessians. They were on the alert, countered Washington's every move and drove him off with another thousand casualties.

In desperate straits, underarmed, virtually without medical supplies or clothing, Washington led his defeated troops into winter quarters at Valley Forge, where his men almost froze and starved to death. Washington wrote that he had "4000 men wanting blankets, near 2000 of which have never had one, altho' some of them have been 12 months in service." Lafayette commented that no European army would have held ranks and endured such suffering and privation as did the Americans.

The news of the fall of Philadelphia and Washington's two defeats was cheered in London and brought a chill to Versailles, where Vergennes feared that all his plans might have to be abandoned. Franklin's stouthearted joke about Philadelphia having taken Howe may have delighted Paris café wits and dilettantes, but it had no effect upon the veteran, coolheaded French Foreign Minister.

Meanwhile, in the North, Burgoyne was running into trouble after his easy occupation of undefended Ticonderoga. He heard that Schuyler had pulled out of Fort Edward and sent a huge, cumbersome wagon train to occupy it. Along with the troops, he sent his officers with their families, wives, children and all their luggage. It took them a month to make the trek through the mountains. He had an almost impossible logistics problem maintaining a supply line from Fort Edward to his main base back in Canada.

While waiting for supplies and reserves to be brought down, he sent out raiding parties, completely underestimating the numbers and fervor of the New England armed farmers and militia. The commander of his expedition, Colonel Barry St. Leger, ran into ambushes every mile of the way, was severely battered, and finally retreated back to Canada. Benedict Arnold was one of the American commanders who harassed his troops and prevented them from capturing Fort Stanwix on the Mohawk River.

Another British raiding party, commanded by Colonel Friedrich Baum, with about seven hundred mixed troops of Germans, Canadians and Indians, went foraging toward Vermont. They never reached the Vermont line, but were overrun by American militia, three to four thousand strong. General John Stark, who had fought the British at Bunker Hill, commanding a force of "Green Mountain Boys," overwhelmed Burgoyne's raiders near Bennington, killing or capturing the whole force. Burgoyne lost more than a thousand men in his raiding parties.

The word spread through New England, and by the hundreds the farmers marched to American camps to join up with the regulars. General Horatio Gates was given the Northern Command by Washington, who sent him reinforcements from New Jersey. Burgoyne moved out of his impossible position in Fort Edward, marched south and cut across the Hudson to rich farmland, where his troops could feed off the countryside and not wait for supplies from Canada. He was dangerously exposed, in hostile country, with only the relatively small expeditionary force under his command, far from his main base in Canada. General Gates's army, swelled by the flood of militiamen, outnumbered him two to one. General Benedict Arnold saw a chance for a strike and begged Gates to give him a brigade of Daniel Morgan's Rifles for a surprise attack.

On September 19, Arnold sprung his assault on a main force of Burgoyne's troops and beat them badly in the Battle of Freeman's Farm. Burgoyne had to pull back to new, defensive positions.

Encouraged by Arnold's success, General Benjamin Lincoln moved to cut off his line of retreat to Canada. Burgoyne was in a trap. His Indian allies and guides quietly slipped away at night and disappeared into the mountains and forests. His foraging parties were ambushed by the skillful guerrilla fighters of New England, who knew their terrain, were deadly marksmen and could move with the stealth of the Indians.

On October 7, Burgoyne, realizing the danger, made a sortie to turn the American lines on the left. Waiting for him to do just that was Benedict Arnold. He led his men on the charge, routed the British and was severely wounded in the action.

Burgoyne was completely cut off on all sides. An original expeditionary force of eight thousand men had been cut down to less than six thousand. General Gates had more than ten thousand troops surrounding the British forces. The campaign for northern New York, centered around Saratoga, had come to a close. Burgoyne knew there was no hope. On October 17, he sent a flag of truce to General Gates. Burgoyne surrendered six generals, three hundred officers and fifty-five hundred enlisted men. Gates accepted their surrender and then generously granted Burgoyne permission to disembark his army, and to return to England on his personal pledge that he would not serve again in America.

The true hero of the campaign, the man who defeated Burgoyne, was Benedict Arnold, but Gates was the man who got all the credit. This infuriated Arnold, already angered by the earlier promotion of junior men over his head, and pushed him further on the road to treason.

Franklin, without the slightest knowledge that Gates had taken thousands of prisoners, was still pursuing the subject of prisoner exchanges. He believed, as other diplomats would come to believe in other wars, that the issue of prisoners, if properly handled, could become the basis for honorable peace talks. He was also genuinely concerned with reports he had received of inhuman treatment of American prisoners.

Stormont's refusal to deal with him did not surprise or dismay him. It merely gave him the opportunity to feed this information to friends in Parliament, members of the liberal and opposition bloc, who would use it to bring pressure upon the North Ministry. The man he chose for this purpose was his friend David Hartley. Franklin wrote to him on October 14, just three days before Burgoyne surrendered his army, and reminded Hartley how often he had predicted that government policy would lead to war and separation, how hard he had tried to prevent it. Even now, in the midst of "this abominable war," Franklin said he would be happy to assist "in any Endeavours for restoring Peace, consistent with the Liberties, the Safety and the Honour of America. As to our submitting again to the government of Britain, 'tis vain to think of it."

Franklin went on to accuse Britain of "barbarities," of bribing slaves to murder their masters, and Indians to massacre American families, of debauching seamen and mistreating prisoners. It had become not just a "ministerial war" but a war by the British people themselves, for a perusal of papers, periodicals, addresses, all accepted by the populace, proved that the people were behind the war. "You are no longer the magnanimous and enlightened Nation we once esteemed."

Despite all this, he was willing to make yet another effort to appeal to the better instincts of the British. "Between nations long exasperated against each other in War, some Act of generosity and kindness towards Prisoners on one side has softened Resentment and abated Animosity on the other, so as to bring on an Accommodation." This, wrote Franklin, was their opportunity. Prisoners had complained of very severe treatment in the British jails. They were "fed scantily on bad provisions, without warm lodging, Clothes or Fire; and not suffered to write or receive visits from their friends, or even from the humane and charitable among their enemies. I can assure you, from my certain knowledge, that your People, Prisoners in America, have been treated with great kindness."

Franklin asked Hartley to request that the Americans be granted the right to send their own representative to take care of their prisoners. He asked him, too, to visit the jails himself, verify the conditions and bring them to the attention of Parliament. He asked for permission to send six hundred pounds to buy food and clothing for the prisoners, and to permit relief to be distributed. He himself had set free two hundred English seamen captured by American privateers, whereas not an American had been released in return. He warned that more severe treatment of British prisoners might result from continued bad treatment of the Americans.

"If a Man naturally cool, and rendered still cooler by Old Age, is so warmed by the treatment of his Country, how much must those People in general be exasperated. . . . Posterity . . . will in all future Ages detest the name of Englishman, as much as the children in Holland now do those of Alva and Spaniard."

Not long after Hartley received this letter and showed it to friends and colleagues in Parliament, London was hit by the news of Burgoyne's surrender and the generous decision of Gates to allow the British to return home instead of being herded into American prison camps. Hartley began an immediate campaign to ease the conditions of American prisoners and to work for their release.

In Paris, Franklin had more vexations to contend with. A zealous American captain had captured a French ship, the *Fortune,* laden with goods for Cádiz, Spain. The French were furious and called Franklin to task. On November 23, he sent an apologetic note to Vergennes, saying he had checked on the incident and discovered that it was all a most regrettable mistake. The ship had come from England and the American captain believed that it was an English merchantman following common practice in disguising itself as a French ship with Spanish goods. Certainly the cargo had been purchased and loaded in Britain.

Franklin said the prize had been taken to Boston and would be sold there, but full restoration of all losses would be made to the French and Spanish, with the most sincere apologies of America. He then proposed that it might be wise, given these circumstances, for France to appoint an agent or consul to be permanently stationed in America as Franklin and his colleagues were in France.

This was a shrewd move by Franklin. The appointment of a consul would, in effect, be a symbol of recognition, the beginning of diplomatic relations in the alliance he had persistently sought in the year he had been in Paris. He could not have guessed how soon this request would be met and the alliance, at long last, drafted and signed. He wrote the memorial at the very worst moment, the day news was confirmed that Howe had taken Philadelphia.

But, on December 4, 1777, a day that Franklin would never forget, the packet from Boston arrived, bearing all the details of the tremendous American victory in the Saratoga campaign. Franklin was in conference with Lee and Deane, in Passy, when the dispatches from General Washington were delivered. The three men cheered and embraced and immediately sat down to compose letters to Versailles and to Madrid.

Vergennes's favorite gardens were enshrouded in early winter gloom, his office cold and in shadows, when a messenger knocked at his door that afternoon, and delivered to him this message from Benjamin Franklin:

> We have the Honour to inform your Excellency that we have just received an Express from Boston, in 30 days, with Advice of the total Reduction of the Force under General Burgoyne, himself and his whole Army having surrendered themselves Prisoners. General Gates was about to send reinforcements to Gen. Washington, who was near Philadelphia with his Army. General Howe was in Possession of this City, but, having no Communication with his Fleet, it was hoped he would soon be reduced to submit to the same terms with Burgoyne, whose Capitulation we enclose; and shall send your Excellency further Particulars of the State of Affairs in America, as soon as we collect them from the Papers.

Appended to the memorial was the following summation:

Acct of Prisoners,	
British troops and	2442
Capitulation of Foreign	2198
troops, Canadians etc.	1100
Staff Officers	12
Total at time of Capitulation	5752

Prisoners taken before	400
Sick and Wounded	518
Deserters	300
Taken at Bennington	1200
Kill'd since Sept. 17	1600
Kill'd, taken, Ticonderoga	413
Total of Burgoyne's Army	10,083

Also taken:	2 Brass	24 pounders
	12 "	18 pdrs
	6 "	4 "
	3 Howitzer	5 Inch
	2 Mortar	8 Inch
	12 pieces	Taken at other times
	37 *pieces taken, along with 4 Members of Parliament*	

It was an exultant letter, even an overly optimistic letter in its references to Howe's situation, but no one would quibble with the fantastic news, least of all Vergennes, who was overjoyed. He knew how the news would be received in Madrid, Vienna and other capitals whose leaders had fought and been beaten by the mighty British. Not only would Europe be delighted with Britain's humiliation but the prestige of his protégés, the Americans, would rise to peak heights. No longer would Frederick or Catherine refer to the Americans as peasants or serfs. They had defeated British troops who had thrashed the best that Europe had. No longer would the nervous young Louis XVI express his doubts. The Americans had confirmed Vergennes's judgment, had perhaps saved his own job for him, had certainly reaffirmed his long-held plans for vengeance on England.

Franklin did not have to be in Vergennes's office that afternoon to know how he received the news. He had been there often enough. He could see the small, stocky Frenchman, his eyes half closed, his poker face betraying no emotion, playing with his silver stiletto, rising to warm himself at the open fire and permit himself a hidden smile. Franklin knew, too, that he would receive a brief note of polite congratulations, cool and measured. Vergennes would now, certainly, push the King toward the alliance, but he would be a tough negotiator and fight for every advantage to France in every clause. Franklin loved the moves in negotiations as he loved chess. He looked forward to the game and was prepared to make the first move.

He made it four days later, on December 8, after receiving the congratulatory message he had expected. He wrote Vergennes:

> The Commissioners from the Congress of the United States of America, beg leave to represent to your Excellency, that it is near a year since they had the Honour of putting into your Hands the propositions of the Congress for a Treaty of Amity and Commerce with this Kingdom, to which, with sundry other Propositions contained in subsequent Memorials, requesting the Aid of Ships of War, and offering Engagements to unite the forces of the said States with those of France and Spain in acting against the Dominions of Great Britain.

Franklin asked for immediate and public action to correct "the ill Impressions on the minds of our People, who, from the Secrecy enjoyned us, cannot be informed of the Friendly and essential Aids that have been so generously but privately offered us." He also expressed his gratitude to the King for a subsidy of three million livres just granted by him, a smaller sum than Franklin had asked back in September, but substantial nonetheless.

Franklin had been informed of the three million by Gérard, who, on December 6, told the commissioners they might expect an additional three million from Spain. He had offered them the congratulations of Vergennes and the Comte de Maurepas, added that since "there appeared no doubt now of the ability and resolution of the States to maintain their independency, he could assure them it was wished they would reassume their former propositions of an alliance," and then further added these most interesting words: "or any new one they might have, and that it could not be done too soon." The court of Spain must be consulted and that would take about three weeks. They must all act in harmony and prepare for war "in a few months."

Gérard had given them Vergennes's signal to move. It was everything that Franklin had worked so hard for, hoped for so faithfully. The climax at Saratoga would produce a triumph at Versailles, as the military and diplomatic fronts of the American Revolution began to interlock. It was appropriate that military victory should spark diplomatic victory, for, as Samuel Eliot Morison noted in his *Oxford History of the American People:* "Military cargoes from France, which slipped through the British blockade, in large measure armed and clothed the American army that forced Burgoyne to surrender."

Franklin's mission had helped stem the British tide. His mission now: to conclude the alliance that would help win the war.

CHAPTER

13

Triumph at Versailles

On the tenth of December, 1777, Benjamin Franklin received a message from Vergennes, proposing a meeting for the morning of the twelfth. Franklin knew it was not to be a routine meeting, for Vergennes requested the tightest security. The commissioners should mention the meeting to no one, proceed by private coach to the east wing of the palace and await further instructions.

When they came to Versailles and sent a footman to notify Gérard of their arrival, he sent back a palace usher, who instructed their coachman to take them to a secluded private house, about a half-mile from Versailles, in the woods. When they reached the house, Vergennes and Gérard were waiting for them.

Vergennes greeted Franklin with both hands outstretched, smiling broadly. He congratulated all three on the great news of victory at Saratoga, but added that what impressed him most was Washington's courage in attacking the main force of Howe's army outside Philadelphia. Saratoga was important, to be sure, but to him it seemed miraculous that a people without an army barely a year ago should have raised one strong enough and daring enough to engage the main force of British regulars. Franklin smiled quietly, nodding his head. This was exactly what he had been telling Vergennes and everyone else for many months.

Vergennes asked Franklin: "Well, Doctor, what do you think of the progress of the war?"*

"We shall succeed. Soon enough the British will tire of it."

Lee interjected: "Your Excellency might judge the progress of the war by noting that the enemy's most signal successes were productive of his greatest misfortunes. For example, Howe's victories in Long Island and New York had raised such a spirit of resistance through the land, that it inspired such actions as Trenton and Princeton. Burgoyne's capture of Ticonderoga and his invasion of New England had brought about a rising of the peoples and his defeat at Saratoga. What hopes could the British now entertain of a war in which the most brilliant success allured them to their ruin?"

Vergennes walked over to a table, picked up a dispatch case and removed the memorial he had received from them on December 8, in which Franklin had pointed out that a full year had gone by and that the time had come to move on the alliance. He read it aloud and then asked: "Well, gentlemen, do you have anything new to offer?"

Franklin said, "No, our goal is what it has always been: the treaty. If there are no objections to the draft we gave you, may we proceed to consider the clauses?"

"We must move," said Vergennes, "but with caution. There must be no terms of which we will later repent. As for our court, be assured that we are resolved to take no advantage of the situation. Whatever we do must be founded upon the basis of mutual interest, as to make it last as long as human institutions will endure."

He paused and added slowly, emphasizing the words: "When we enter into a treaty with you, we will be affirming your independency. Necessarily this will bring about war with England. We cannot do this without consulting Spain, without whose concurrence nothing can be done."

Franklin frowned. He knew that agreement by Spain might still

*This conversation, along with other details of the meeting, was noted down by Arthur Lee in his journal that night.

be long in coming. He wanted no further delays. But this was not the moment to argue that point. It was more useful to hear Vergennes out. He asked quietly whether Vergennes had any first thoughts about the treaty itself.

"Well, to be frank, there are some objectionable articles in the proposed treaty," the Foreign Minister replied. "The twelfth article, for example, granting equality of tariffs between West Indian and French products, was not acceptable. There were also problems about the demand for monopolies of trade in the islands."

Franklin kept a straight face, but he must have been smiling inwardly. He had drafted those articles and had also had a hand in additional instructions from the Congress to waive them if the French objected. He told Vergennes: "Well, perhaps the wording there is not clear enough, and it referred only to islands that might be conquered by unity of French and American forces."

"No, that would not do, either," the Foreign Secretary objected. "We have no interest in conquering any more islands."

Franklin was delighted by the course the conversation was taking. The objections, so far, had been minor, but, even had they been significant, he still would have been overjoyed, for now, instead of arguing about whether there should be an alliance, Count Vergennes had opened clause-by-clause negotiations. The alliance was under way and Franklin vowed to let nothing hinder its conclusion.

Vergennes warned that Spain would not be happy with the lack of precision on boundaries between their colonies and the American states. Virginia, it appeared, ran its boundaries so far that "they might entrench upon California." Franklin replied that a useful boundary might be the Mississippi, which had been used as a boundary in the Treaty of Peace with England in the last war. Vergennes agreed. He also confirmed the clauses on the tobacco trade and on fishery rights. Franklin had insisted that it was a firm principle of America that fishing be "free to all."

Vergennes ended the meeting with his usual cautious warnings. "Your independency must still be considered in the womb. We must not endeavour to hasten its birth prematurely." He promised to send a courier to Spain that day. It would take him about three weeks to return with the Spanish answer. The commissioners were cheered when he lightened his caution by saying that he would recall the strict orders on clearances for American vessels and would speak to his colleague, Navy Minister Sartine, about providing convoys for supplies to America. He was less optimistic about the American request for three ships of the line. "We are having problems in the shipyards and are even buying rather than building our own ships at the moment."

Before parting, Vergennes warned them again about spies. He said that this was the most important moment to be very secretive or the negotiations might be aborted by premature revelation. His own spies in London had told him that the British Secret Service, realizing the potential of Saratoga, was planning a major effort to interfere with negotiations in Paris.

Indeed, the news of Burgoyne's defeat had alerted a number of men to its potential value. Caron de Beaumarchais, knowing that stocks would drop on the London market, rushed to Paris to get full information for his brokers. He drove his carriage so fast that it overturned and he suffered a badly bruised and wrenched arm and shoulder. Edward Bancroft, one of the first to hear the news, left immediately for London to handle his speculations on the market. His employer, Paul Wentworth, crossed the Channel to Paris to direct espionage activities on the spot and to try to feel out Franklin if he could.

Wentworth's mission to Paris had been approved on the highest level, by Lord North. Saratoga had at last convinced George III that a French-American alliance was a reality and that the time had come to sound out the Americans on possible moves toward conciliation before a larger war broke out. Wentworth had received reports from Arthur Lee's secretary, the spy Major Thornton, that Lee was unalterably opposed to anything short of total independence, but that Franklin and Deane seemed more flexible. Thornton had misread Franklin's repeated assurances to English friends that he would never reject an honorable peace.

The French were not quite sure whether Wentworth was a spy or only the speculator and friend of men in high office that he claimed to be. They watched him closely as soon as he arrived in Paris and sent a message to Deane for a meeting the same day the commissioners were closeted in secret with Vergennes in the house near Versailles.

Franklin refused to see Wentworth but encouraged Deane to hear him out. Franklin knew that Vergennes would be suspicious of any meeting with a British agent at that moment, but he also knew that Vergennes would use the occasion to put pressure on Louis XVI, asking him to strike before the British, through a deal, pulled the irons out of the fire. Franklin, playing the honest broker, gave Vergennes a copy of a letter that had been sent from London, asking whether the Americans might not be ready to accept something just a little short of independence. He assured Vergennes that they would not.

Lord Stormont further complicated the intrigue by inviting Wentworth to accompany him to Versailles, where he presented him to Louis XVI. Vergennes, wanting to get a closer look, then invited Wentworth to dine with him. Wentworth's evasiveness at dinner heightened Vergennes's suspicions of him.

To Deane, Wentworth suggested that Britain had never wanted this unfortunate war and wished to correct all old errors. The King, he said, was ready to approve repeal of all the "intolerable acts" of which the Americans had complained. He proposed an armistice to be followed by a general withdrawal of all British land and sea forces, except from New York, which would remain an imperial base. A commission would work on a general reform of all American affairs, on the basis of the Navigation Acts. America, however, would remain a British colony.

Deane told him that no conciliation was possible except on the basis of American independence. He sharply dismissed Wentworth's offer of bribes, in the form of promises of honors and wealth to those who helped bring about the realization of his plan. Independence, said Deane, was the only key to opening the doors to peace.

Wentworth tried again to see Franklin. Once again Franklin refused to meet with him. By then Franklin had received letters from his friends in London, assuring him that they would start a campaign for a genuine reconciliation with America. Opposition to the policies of Lord North and George III was mounting rapidly. Franklin had no reason to listen to any British overtures, the less so since he had just had final word from Gérard that the alliance would be concluded. This word had come on the seventeenth, in a visit by Gérard to Passy. He said they must be patient and wait for word from Madrid, but that the decision had been taken.

On the last day of 1777, word arrived from Madrid: No! The Spaniards were not prepared for war with England. Charles III refused to join his nephew, Louis XVI, and warned him against rash action.

Franklin, undaunted, having expected this answer, coolly told Vergennes that France must then act alone. There must be no turning back at this point. Franklin made no threats, did not point out the consequences of a French refusal. Vergennes had heard the arguments many times. He knew the dangers to France of a sudden American decision to seek reconciliation with England. He asked Franklin for just a bit more patience to permit him to persuade the King.

Now Franklin would play the Wentworth card. It was the moment to press upon French fears. He sent a message to Wentworth that he would see him, but on one condition only: that he not dare repeat a word of the offers of bribery he had made to Deane. He set the appointment for January 6.

"Franklin received me very kindly," Wentworth reported back to London. The spy said he had asked Franklin to inform him of the temper of the Congress, hinting that he understood that the Congress would think as Franklin thought. He wanted to know the terms and means by which reconciliation might be effected, reminding Franklin that he had been one of the earliest proponents of imperial union.

Franklin replied that he held certain opinions under certain circumstances. All that he had proposed might have come about had the government heeded him in his long negotiations with Barclay, Fothergill, Lord Hyde and Lord Howe. But these gentlemen had rejected every proposition he had made, and now circumstances had caused him to advance his opinions. Franklin complained at length, and with some heat, about the British burning of towns and the mistreatment of prisoners. He told Wentworth that, after all that had happened, there was no turning back; the spirit of America was high and would brook no result but absolute independence.

Wentworth was surprised by Franklin's vehemence and discursiveness. "I never knew him so eccentric. . . . Nobody says less, generally, and keeps a point more closely in view, but he was diffuse and unmethodical today."

Wentworth asked Franklin whether he would accept a guarantee of safe-conduct to visit London. Franklin replied he would deal only through a public and official commission, authorized by the Congress. Wentworth soon saw that there was nothing to be done with Franklin. Reports by Thornton and Bancroft about his "flexibility" were obviously inaccurate. The old man was immovable.

Deane came in toward the end of their conversation and stayed on with Bancroft and Wentworth as Franklin's dinner guests. The men joked at dinner and made bets about whether America would become independent. Wentworth went back to London without asking for a second interview with Franklin. His ploy had no chance. Franklin would play no more political chess games with the British.

While these negotiations were going on, Franklin had had to deal with a desperate Beaumarchais, who had recovered from the injuries to his arm but was now suffering more important injuries to his purse. The *Amphitrite,* which he had bought and armed and sent to America, carrying the supplies that had helped win the Battle of Saratoga, had now returned to France, laden with American products. To Beaumarchais's horror, the *Amphitrite* had been consigned not to him but to the American commissioners. Congress, disturbed by Arthur Lee's claims of cheating and his assertions that everything sent was free aid from the King of France, had ordered the captain to deliver the cargo into the hands of Franklin.

Beaumarchais said the entire cargo of the *Amphitrite* had been paid for out of his pocket. He was on the verge of bankruptcy for his zeal and services in the American cause. Everything had been agreed in advance with Deane. He showed Franklin the letter of agreement he had signed with Deane, more than a year before, when Deane was the only American agent in France and the commissioners had not yet been appointed. The agreement stipulated that all remittances would be reimbursed.

Franklin pointed out that Deane had not been authorized to make such an agreement in the name of Congress; that Deane had never shown him a copy of this agreement; that they had understood and had informed Congress that they were not answerable for these supplies. However, Franklin was a fair man and wanted to do justice, particularly to one so zealous in the American cause. As soon as they ascertained the facts of his claim, they would see to it that the cargo was ordered into Beaumarchais's hands. He would take the matter up with Deane as soon as possible. Beaumarchais thanked him and left, somewhat reassured but still nervous.

A few days later, Lee learned of a conversation in London, in which Beaumarchais said he was getting all his munitions from the King's arsenals and said nothing of Congress' having to pay for them. Lee saw to it that Franklin was informed, but Franklin, resting up from a sudden attack of gout, worrying about the last steps to conclude the alliance, was out of patience with the whole affair. It was not his responsibility. His mission was political and diplomatic: to raise money and conclude the treaties of alliance. Deane was solely responsible for contracts and shipments.

Deane, meanwhile, was busy running to and from Gérard's office, carrying to Franklin Gérard's observations on certain clauses. The French were worried about Article 9, which referred to their guarantee to the United States of the territories of Canada, Nova Scotia, Florida and adjacent islands. Franklin and Lee thought it necessary to insist on this, and to make clear that France could not aspire to possession of any of these places. Deane was instructed to insist on the article, but under no conditions to show Gérard the basic briefing paper from Congress on their instructions. He was to refer to them only under pressure, but not reveal them. Franklin did not intend to give Vergennes any leeway, nor pay a price for the alliance. He knew that Vergennes wanted it as much as he did, and he would not be bluffed on any important article, although he was willing to make concessions on lesser points.

On January 7, Franklin heard that the King's Council had met and voted to recommend to the monarch both a treaty of commerce and an alliance, much more than Congress had originally planned and hoped. It was Franklin, all along protesting that he was a shy virgin who would not go asuitoring, who had steered Vergennes, with Vergennes's willing consent, toward a full alliance.

The next day, the eighth, Gérard came in person to meet with the commissioners. He had, he said, some urgent questions to put to them, and would withdraw for an hour or so to give them time to draft their reply. Vergennes was waiting for the answer.

The first question was: What was necessary to give such satisfaction to the American commissioners as to engage them not to listen to any proposition from England for a new connection with that country? Apparently, as Franklin had guessed, his meeting with Wentworth had troubled Vergennes. Franklin, smiling, sharpened a quill, dipped it into a silver inkwell and wrote his reply: The commissioners had long since proposed a treaty of amity and commerce, which was not yet concluded. The immediate conclusion of that treaty would remove all uncertainty with regard to it, and give the Americans such a reliance on the friendship of France as to reject all propositions from the British which did not envision the entire freedom and independence of America, in matters of both government and commerce.

While the commissioners were in the course of reading Franklin's answer, an impatient Gérard walked back in. They showed him the answer and he said it was sufficient. The other questions could wait. This is what Vergennes wanted to know. He then took Franklin's hand and said: "I am at liberty to tell you that the treaty will be concluded."

Franklin had won a diplomatic victory as great as any that would be won on the battlefield, one that would contribute to every military victory thereafter. For soon the supplies from France, which had dribbled rather than flowed, would begin to quicken in pace, and, at critical moments, when all seemed lost, Washington would have the arms to win the day.

From the moment Gérard shook his hand Franklin knew that it was only a matter of back-and-forth dueling on some articles. The issue had been decided. He relaxed, dined out every night, took tea and played chess with his ladies, went to the Opéra and the Comédie-Française, and enjoyed the year-end holidays, to the dismay and disapproval of Arthur Lee. Lee kept coming to Passy to see Franklin, only to be told by his grandson Temple that "Papa" was out and could not be reached.

Franklin knew the French and knew the King. He understood that Vergennes's experts would be going over the treaty clause by clause and that explanations for the King had to be prepared. Now that he had been properly "suitored," he could become again the shy virgin and take his time with the diplomatic trousseau. This was beyond Lee's comprehension. With his jealous eyes, he could only see a vain and self-indulgent old man, neglecting the affairs of his country.

Meanwhile, Vergennes kept hoping for a change of heart in Madrid. Madrid remained silent. It was a full month before the treaties were drafted in final form, all clauses agreed upon and transcribed onto parchment. There were two treaties to be signed: a treaty of amity and commerce and a treaty of defensive alliance. On the evening of February 6, 1778, in the offices of the French Foreign Ministry, at the Hôtel de Lautrec in Paris, the French Plenipotentiary, Gérard, and the three American commissioners signed this historic document, which would then be taken to Versailles for Vergennes to present to the King.

Gérard signed first, then Franklin, then Deane. There was a little trouble when Lee suddenly said he ought to sign twice, since he was commissioner to both France and Spain. They pointed out to him that Spain was not a signatory.

Bancroft and Deane both noted that Franklin, for the occasion, had put on an old coat, of Manchester velvet and British cut. When they asked him about it, Franklin smiled and said: "Well, I would like this coat to have its moment of revenge. I wore it in the Cockpit the day that Wedderburn abused us."

The treaty of amity and commerce followed essentially the guidelines laid down by Franklin's committee in the plan of 1776. Respect for neutral rights, mutual protection of shipping, convoys, rescue from pirates, all these were inserted almost word for word from the American draft. The pledge that the United States would not assist England in any war with France was left out of this treaty but inserted into the treaty of alliance. Instead of the American request that all commerce should grant the same privileges to the nationals of each country, Vergennes insisted on the conventional most-favored-nation clause, which Franklin accepted. France promised free ports in the West Indies and in France. An important clause, proposed earlier by Franklin, was adopted, stipulating the mutual residence of consuls and a consular agreement to be drafted later by specialists. A French guarantee of protection against the Barbary pirates had been weakened to a stipulation of French goodwill on this issue. Overall the treaty was everything that Congress had hoped for and more.

The second treaty, that of alliance, was to come into effect in the eventuality of an outbreak of war between England and France, either by direct hostilities between men-of-war or by Britain's interfering with the commerce and navigation of France.

Article 1 bound the allies to "make common cause and aid each other." Article 2, the truly essential clause and one of vital importance to America, stated that the purpose of the alliance was "to maintain effectually the liberty, sovereignty and independence, absolute and unlimited of the said United States, as well in matters of Government as of commerce." This was recognition, this was what Franklin had been determined to win.

The third and fourth articles dealt with separate and joint war tactics and strategy. The fifth article granted America the option of conquering and possessing North America or the Islands of the Bermudas. In the sixth article, the King of France specifically renounced any claims to the continent of North America, which had been British before the Treaty of 1763. This left the door open to possible French conquest of New Orleans and of Louisiana west of the Mississippi. It also left France an opportunity to strike for inshore fishing rights, on which Vergennes insisted, and which Franklin accepted reluctantly. He felt that since France was making most of the concessions America had to show some generosity.

An important clause for Vergennes, the counterpart to his recognition of American independence, was an agreement binding both parties, but particularly America, not to conclude a separate peace truce with Britain "without the formal consent of the other first obtain'd." France, for its part, agreed not to lay down arms until American independence had been formally assured by conclusion of peace treaties.

A final article stipulated that the treaties must be ratified by both parties within six months, noting that they had been signed in both the French and English languages, but that the original treaty was composed and concluded in French. The French was thus to be considered the official text in the event of any dispute over interpretation.

A secret article reserved the right of the King of Spain to join in the treaties.

The British Secret Service was kept informed step by step by Bancroft, who later boasted that copies of the treaties were delivered in London less than two days after they had been signed in Paris.

This spy alert, plus Wentworth's report on his year-end mission, convinced Lord North that urgent steps had to be taken, at the last minute, to persuade America not to ratify the alliance but to accept generous terms of reconciliation. On February 17, he introduced in Parliament a series of bills repealing all the objectionable legislation passed since 1763. It was almost three years since Franklin had made similar proposals, offering to pay for the loss of tea in Boston himself if Britain would right the wrongs it had imposed upon America. By March 9, 1778, Parliament voted to adopt Lord North's new program, authorizing him to offer peace negotiations with the Americans on the basis of home rule within a British Empire—precisely what Franklin had been proposing for almost twenty years.

Then began a dramatic race across the Atlantic.

The British put their new bills and reforms on a fast sloop, with instructions to the messenger to inform Congress that another ship would soon bring British commissioners, delegated to open peace talks.

The French Ambassador in London correctly called upon the British Foreign Office and informed the government officially on March 13 that the alliance had been concluded. Then the French and Franklin separately put copies of the alliance on mail packets for America.

The British sloop won the race by a large margin and Congress received the peace proposals in mid-April. They caused a sensation and were hailed by many members of Congress. Despite the victory at Saratoga, the British land and sea forces were strong enough to launch a new campaign. Washington had spent a paralyzing winter in Valley Forge. The cost of the war was tremendous and Continental currency had lost its value. A great number of Americans were still opposed to the war and eager for reconciliation. Worst of all, almost impossible to conceive, Congress had not received a single report from Franklin in the entire year that he had been in France, writing to America constantly. Every one of his dispatches had been intercepted, either by double agents before they were dispatched or by the British Navy, which captured the mail packets on the Atlantic. Congress knew nothing about the course of negotiations in Paris, let alone the fact that the alliance had already been successfully concluded. In the absence of any word from Franklin, weighed against the offer of peace and home rule, there was a strong movement for accepting the British terms and opening peace negotiations when the delegates arrived.

But the mail packets from Paris did break through at last, and just in time. On May 2, a few days before the arrival of the British peace delegates, Congress had in hand the full text of the two treaties and Franklin's letter of explanation. Within only two days

Congress moved swiftly to ratify the alliance. When the British delegates arrived, they found an America strengthened by a powerful alliance, determined to fight on for total and absolute independence. Britain's last chance to save the precious colonies for the Crown had been lost.

The British and French withdrew their respective ambassadors. Lord Stormont, defeated by Franklin, packed and left Paris. War against France was decided by England, although hostilities did not break out until the French and British fleets clashed off the coast of Brittany, at Ushant, on the evening of June 17.

The consular pact was drafted and signed, and Vergennes chose his First Secretary Gérard, who had conducted all the negotiations along with him, to be France's first Minister Plenipotentiary to the United States.

Until March 13, when Britain was informed, the alliance was still officially a French state secret. Now the moment had come for it to be publicly recognized by the King, who invited the American commissioners to an audience with him at the Palace of Versailles.

Deane, Lee, Ralph Izard and William Lee all rushed to the tailors to order their official court dress as prescribed by the court chamberlain. Not Franklin. He had successfully played the role of the rustic philosopher, the simple, unpretentious Quaker, and he did not intend to change it for the King. He laid out a plain suit of brown velvet, white hose, buckled shoes and a white hat that he would carry under his arm. He could not quite summon the courage to wear his old fur cap.

For a brief moment, he planned to wear a new wig. One did not appear baldheaded before the King of France. According to Paris periodicals of the day, Franklin called in the most fashionable perruquier of Paris, who scurried about measuring Franklin's head, making a dramatic performance of choosing just the right wig. He placed it on Franklin's head and tugged and pulled, but, to his dismay, the wig would not fit.

Franklin mildly suggested: "Perhaps your wig is too small?"

"No," shouted the temperamental wigmaker. "Your head, sir, is too big!" A Paris reporter commented: "It is true that Franklin does have a fat head. But it is a great head."

Franklin, by now out of patience, dismissed the perruquier and decided to defy custom by appearing before the King uncovered.

When the Americans arrived at Versailles, going first to Vergennes's apartments, the crowd outside set up a rousing cheer and then began to murmur in astonishment when people noted that Franklin was bald and not in court dress. The cheers rose again and they shouted: "The Apostle of Liberty, Citizen Franklin!"

The chamberlain was shocked at the sight of Franklin and a scandal was narrowly averted when Vergennes persuaded him to allow Franklin to enter the King's reception room.

No one paid the slightest attention to Deane, Izard and the Lees. All eyes were on the venerable sage as he walked directly to the King, bowing courteously but not low, as befitted a free man.

Louis XVI, after his first surprise at Franklin's costume, smiled graciously. His words, recorded by the Duc de Croy, were simple yet impressive.

"Firmly assure Congress," said the monarch, "of my friendship."

He spoke generously of Franklin's conduct and behavior in the year he had been in France and thanked him and his colleagues for their efforts.

Franklin spoke for all the commissioners when he told the King: "Your Majesty may count on the gratitude of Congress and its faithful observance of the pledges it now takes."

Breaking court etiquette, the crowd of observers cheered as Franklin and the other Americans crossed the courtyard to be introduced to the Cabinet and the nobles of France.

The five Americans were the guests of honor at a banquet offered by Vergennes and then escorted back to the King and Queen for a more informal meeting. Marie Antoinette, now more sympathetic to the American cause, politely asked Franklin to stand by her side. From time to time she would turn to ask him questions about America.

Late that night, his eyes sparkling, the old man, now seventy-two, left the palace. The morrow would bring new crises, new efforts. But that night Ben Franklin savored his triumph at Versailles.

PART III

PARIS: *The War*

CHAPTER 14

Politics, Women and Money

Before the British attempt to buy off the Americans, the triumph at Versailles was almost wrecked by an unexpected turn in European politics.

On December 30, 1777, when Franklin was enjoying the Christmas and New Year holidays and parties in Passy and in Paris, Maximilian III Joseph, Elector of Bavaria, died without a blood heir, leaving Bavaria, a rich plum in the political orchards of Central Europe, ripe for the plucking by a hungry neighbor, Emperor Joseph II of Austria. Any sudden aggrandizement of Austria would alarm Frederick of Prussia, and upset the delicate balance of power that had kept Europe calm in the decade since the disasters of the Seven Years' War.

Vergennes's policy, which he had finally sold to Louis XVI, was to keep Europe in balance and at peace in order to leave France free for the coming struggle with England. The core of his policy was a defensive alliance with Spain—the Bourbon Family Compact—and with Austria, to balance off Prussia and Russia. One facet of the policy was to encourage and help the Turks, discreetly, to keep the Russians tied up in Southeastern Europe. Frederick of Prussia was old, enjoying a prosperous and secure reign, not seeking adventure unless his hand was forced. He would not help England against France if war was to break out outside of Europe—the high seas and the colonies meant nothing to Frederick. But he would not sit by and let the Austrian Hapsburgs seize one of the largest states of Europe, advancing their frontiers and power near Prussia. He remembered only too clearly his own coup, when he had wrested Silesia from Emperor Joseph II's mother, Maria-Theresa, and he suspected that the Austrian Emperor was seeking to pay him back.

All this Vergennes knew and weighed on the night of January 5, 1778. The treaties with America were to be examined in a final hearing before the King in full ministerial council on January 7. Franklin had received his personal assurances this would be done. Vergennes also knew that Franklin had been receiving new offers from the British, while awaiting his conclusion of the treaties. Any hesitation, any backtracking, now might swing the Americans away from France toward reconciliation with England.

It was the most difficult decision of Vergennes's career, and of vital importance to the United States. Austrian troops were already mobilized and marching toward the border of Bavaria. If Joseph II was not bluffing, Frederick, the military genius of Europe, would surely stir out of his comfortable old age and declare war on Austria. The alliance between Austria and France would give Joseph his chance to call upon Louis XVI for troops and aid. A European war would give France an opportunity to extend its territory to the north, and seize Flanders, demanding of Joseph his provinces in the Netherlands as the price of support. And this could easily have more appeal for Louis XVI than a war with mighty England, which promised no important territorial prizes.

The fate of America was in his hands as Vergennes walked into the King's Council room on January 7 to face the Prime Minister and the Ministers of the Army and the Navy, none of them as enthusiastic about America as Vergennes himself. Yet he did not hesitate; his choice had been made when England had humiliated France in the last war. He presented the proposed texts and argued his case eloquently, warning against the dangers to France's own territory in a European war as against a war on the high seas and in far-off America. His colleagues heard him out, voted to approve his recommendations, and the King assented to conclude the American alliance.

Joseph II carried out his own plans. He forced Charles Theodore, the Elector Palatine, to sign a partition agreement, ceding the major part of Bavaria to Austria, in return for Joseph's guarantee to support his claim to succeed Maximilian. Austrian troops promptly occupied the ceded territories, and Frederick the Great mobilized his troops for war. Joseph immediately appealed to Louis of France for twenty thousand troops should Frederick move to attack. Frederick, on his part, also appealed to France for help against Austria.

Vergennes advised his King to express his sympathy and friendship to both sides, offering to do what he could to end the quarrel, but expressing the strictest neutrality on the part of France. Vergennes's main goal was to keep out of Europe and persuade Spain to join in the war against England.

Floridablanca was determined to prevent Vergennes from bringing the Family Compact into play. France had signed the treaties and provoked war with England without waiting for Spain's agreement. Charles III saw no reason to risk a costly war to save his rash nephew. France's territories in the Americas were limited to a few, relatively unimportant sugar islands, whereas Spain had vast overseas possessions. At the moment, a Spanish treasure fleet was en route home from Mexico, and Floridablanca had no intention of risking its precious cargo against the British Navy. Spain's possessions in South America were more important to her than any profits to be made from commerce with the infant United States. If the Americans and British kept on fighting, they would weaken one another, which suited Floridablanca, who saw no sense in entering the war on either side.

Floridablanca sent strict instructions to his Ambassador in Paris, Conde de Aranda, a friend of Franklin's and an enthusiast for the American cause, to cool his ardor and tell Vergennes that the Spanish court had decided against war with England. He also informed the British Ambassador in Madrid of his decision and added that he had had no hand in France's precipitate decision to sign the treaties. Vergennes, knowing he had acted unilaterally, could not appeal to the terms of the Family Compact, which was a defensive alliance. England had not attacked France; it was France who had forced the issue.

The tough Spanish Foreign Minister did value one prize above all else, above guarantees in Florida and Louisiana, above fishing rights, and above Jamaica, all of which Vergennes offered him. What he wanted, Vergennes did not have. The British had it: Gibraltar. The great rock was and remained through the centuries a Spanish obsession. Floridablanca suggested to Britain that Gibraltar was the best guarantee for his continued neutrality. He wanted it back. He did not say so clearly, for that would have violated diplomatic form, but the British understood that if they did not cede Gibraltar, Spain might change its mind and join France in the war. Floridablanca's strategy on Gibraltar would unfold in the spring of 1778 and play an important role in the outcome of the American Revolution.

Franklin knew what was going on, for stories of the crisis in Central Europe soon appeared in the Paris press. Conde de Aranda was personally as friendly as ever but more reserved in his dealings with Franklin. And Franklin understood European politics well enough to know what was happening. There was nothing he could do about it. This was Vergennes's problem and Franklin had confidence in the wily diplomat.

Franklin continued his round of meetings with personalities in Paris all through the holiday season. During Christmas week he dined with the Comte d'Estaing, an admiral in the fleet, who would, later in the spring, be assigned to challenge the British in American waters. At the dinner, to Franklin's surprise, was the Portuguese Minister, the Duke of Braganza, whose country was allied with England and no friend of America's. Franklin's reputation was so great that even enemies came to him.

He went to the Opéra to hear *Alceste* and to a theater on the boulevards to see a new comedy, a burlesque on Burgoyne's defeat, hastily composed as soon as the news had reached Paris. It was a poor play but excellent propaganda, and Franklin was pleased to be cheered by the audience as soon as it was known that he was in the hall.

Life in Paris was most amusing in that winter of '77–'78. The scandalous transvestite, Mademoiselle La Chevalière d'Eon, who had spent most of her life as a man, was back in Paris, under orders from the King to appear only as a woman. (Years later it was discovered that she was, after all, a man.) She had fought in war, won the Cross of St. Louis, had been prominent in politics and literature, had even attempted to blackmail the King with compromising letters in her possession. Franklin met her at luncheon and listened with fascination as she delivered a tirade against Caron de Beaumarchais, with whom she was having a public quarrel.

The fashions of Paris continued to catch Franklin's eye and he would chuckle at the breakfast table as he read the fashion news. One item that delighted him was a report on a new coiffure, a braid fashioned in the form of a serpent, representing England, with little emerald eyes, twisted in and out of piled-up hair. It was called "Les Insurgents." A meeting was convoked by the Marquise de Narbonnes, who declared that the ornament was too frightening, that ladies had nervous tremors on seeing it, and that it should be sold only to foreign tourists passing through Paris.

Franklin held a party to celebrate the holiday of the Feast of Kings, and had a baker prepare thirteen large brioches, one for each of the American states, with a little flag on each bearing the word "Liberty." The Bishop of Xaintes commented that the flag seemed radical and a provocation. The Chevalière d'Eon thought that it was imprudent to raise the banner of liberty "only three leagues from Versailles, where the word was never used and did not suffer to be known." Franklin himself never referred to such a party in any of his notes. The story appeared in the scandalmongering periodical *Les Mémoirs Secrets,* which was not overscrupulous about the accuracy of its reports. It may never have taken place, but all Paris read about it. Franklin, perpetrator of many journalistic hoaxes, would be the last to complain of one.

He cherished the lighter moments of his life in Paris as an escape from his daily chores and the constant wrangles among his fellow commissioners. Ralph Izard, cooling his heels there because the Grand Duke of Tuscany would not let him come to Florence, thought that Franklin ought to include him in the discussions of the treaty clauses with Gérard. Franklin was having enough trouble with clause-by-clause quibblings by Arthur Lee, in addition to Lee's continual charges that Deane was cheating them.

Lee was a man of considerable intelligence, education, energy, even charm. He was a fervent patriot, and Franklin wanted to like him and work well with him. But his impenetrable self-righteousness and mad jealousies made him an impossible collaborator.

Poor Deane, under attack from Lee, was also in trouble on other grounds back home, and had to come running to Franklin for help. The Congress, out of patience with dozens of adventurers who had come to America bearing army commissions written out by Deane in Paris, had voted to disown agreements with the most incompetent of the volunteers. Franklin hastened to write to James Lovell to explain Deane's difficulties with recruitment.

> I, who am upon the Spot, and know the infinite Difficulty of resisting the powerful Sollicitations here of great Men, who, if disoblig'd might have it in their Power to obstruct the Supplies he was then obtaining, do not wonder that, being then a Stranger to the People, and unacquainted with the Language, he was at first prevailed on to make some such Agreements. . . . You can have no conception how we are still besieged and worried on this head, our Time cut to pieces by personal Applications. . . . I hope, therefore, that favorable Allowance will be made to my worthy colleague. . . . It is my Duty to take this Occasion of giving to his Merit, unask'd, as, considering my great Age, I may probably not live to give it personally in Congress, and I perceive he has enemies.

Deane did have enemies, in the powerful Lee-Adams bloc inside the Congress, who, later in the spring of 1778, ordered Deane home to answer charges that Arthur Lee had leveled, and to testify on whether French shipments were to be free, as Lee averred, or to be paid, as Deane claimed. Franklin could not help him in that controversy; indeed, he was lucky to escape censure himself. Only his world-wide reputation, the respect of the French and the admiration of Jefferson and Washington saved Franklin from sharing

Deane's fate.* When Deane left for America, with Gérard, at the end of March, he took most of the vouchers with him to use in his testimony. But he sailed in such a hurry that he left important papers behind and found himself in difficulty under cross-examination in the Congress. Lee thought he should not have taken the vouchers, and he was angered by not having been consulted by Franklin in the last-minute preparations for Deane's departure. He also argued, to Franklin's astonishment, that he should have been consulted on the French choice of a minister to America. He sent Franklin a bitter note: "Had you studied to deceive the most distrusted and dangerous enemy of the public, you could not have done it more effectually. I trust, Sir, that you will think with me that I have a right to know your reasons for treating me thus." It was the letter of a paranoiac and it broke Franklin's patience.

In one of the angriest letters he ever wrote—Franklin was always careful to be cool and judicious in writing—he replied:

> It is true I have omitted answering some of your letters. I do not like to answer angry letters. I am old, cannot have long to live, have much to do and no time for altercations. If I have often received and borne your magisterial snubbings and rebukes without reply, ascribe it to the right causes: my concern for the honour and success of our mission which would be hurt by our quarreling, my love of peace, my respect for your good qualities and my pity of your sick mind which is for ever tormenting itself with its jealousies, suspicions, and fancies that others mean you ill, wrong you, or fail in respect of you. If you do not cure yourself of this temper it will end in insanity, of which it is a symptomatic forerunner as I have seen in several instances. God preserve you from so terrible an evil; and for His sake pray suffer me to live in quiet.

The situation had become intolerable, and Franklin looked for help to John Adams, who had been named to replace Deane.

Adams arrived on April 8, 1778. A Puritan, Adams took as severe a view of Franklin's social conduct and style of living as Lee

*It did not save his nephew, Jonathan Williams, his agent in Nantes, whose accounts, like practically everyone's, were incomplete and contested. Williams was not disgraced; he was simply moved to other assignments and wound up, some years later, as the first Superintendent at West Point.

had. He thought the commissioners lived too extravagantly for Republicans: Lee had his own house, and Deane had had private lodgings, as well as lodgings that Franklin had given him in the Hôtel Valentinois in Passy—three houses in all for Congress to pay rent on. Franklin pointed out that they paid nothing for the beautiful estate that Chaumont had given them to live in. Adams thought it wrong to accept free gifts from a French contractor to the King; he had moved into a wing of the estate but insisted on paying rent for it.

The difference between Adams and Lee was that Adams' criticisms were forthright, made not in anger, not from fear, and tempered by his own deep respect and admiration for Franklin. Adams was an honest man and knew that Franklin, for all his administrative faults, was the key commissioner, the one whom the French trusted and revered. In his diary he noted: "Franklin's reputation was more universal than that of Leibnitz or Newton, Frederick or Voltaire; and his character more beloved and esteemed than any of them." Adams said that everyone regarded Franklin as "the friend of humankind. . . . His Plans and his example were to abolish monarchy, aristocracy, and hierarchy throughout the world."

These sentiments may well have been part of Franklin's philosophy, but he never gave expression to such radical ideas during his stay in France. Far from seeking to abolish all monarchies and aristocracies, he spent most of his time with the noblemen and -women of France. His mission was to help America defeat the King of England, not to start revolutions everywhere—although that, indeed, became one of the consequences of the American rebellion. Franklin had no contacts with the lower or working classes of France, yet, as Adams correctly reported, they revered him as the philosopher of liberty.

The signing of the treaties and the arrival of Adams, who took some of the administrative work off Franklin's shoulders, released him to enjoy his social life even more. It was during this period that he became enamored of another woman, whom Madame Brillon would come to call "my charming and redoubtable rival": Anne-Catherine de Ligniville d'Autricourt Helvétius.

Madame Helvétius, née de Ligniville, was the tenth of twenty children in a great but impoverished family of Lorraine, distantly related to Queen Marie Antoinette. She had been raised first in a convent, then by an aunt, a novelist who supported herself by her writing and who brought Anne-Catherine to Paris and introduced her to the famous men who met at her salon. Anne-Catherine, bright and beautiful, made an instant hit and received proposals of marriage from distinguished men, including Turgot, the future Comptroller-General of French finances, the man who would warn the King that the American revolutionary war would bankrupt the monarchy. The man she accepted was older and richer, a Farmer-General, Claude-Adrien Helvétius. The marriage was successful for twenty years, until Helvétius' death. In that time, she had established her own political and literary salon on their estate in Auteuil, neighboring on Passy. The leading intellectuals of Europe gathered there on Tuesdays; Condorcet, Turgot, Diderot, the Abbé Galiani and David Hume were among her guests. The writer Fontenelle, in his nineties, looked at her one day, when she was wearing a daringly low-cut gown and sighed: "Oh, to be seventy again!"

By the time Franklin met her, she was well into her fifties, no longer the physical beauty she had once been, but still sexually attractive to men, witty, intelligent and a free spirit, whose independence of life and manners delighted Franklin. A liberated woman, like her aunt, she refused to remarry, had plenty of money to run her estate and receive her friends. Three men lived on her estate with her: a former Benedictine monk, the Abbé de La Roche, in his thirties, who was organizing Helvétius' papers and library; the Abbé Morellet, in his late forties, a scholar and writer; and Pierre-Georges Cabanis, whom Madame Helvétius had taken in and virtually adopted when he was a poor medical student in his twenties. By the time Franklin came to Auteuil, Cabanis was a highly respected medical theorist and writer on science. Her salon soon became so famous that it was dubbed "L'Académie d'Auteuil." And Franklin nicknamed her "Notre Dame d'Auteuil."

Many of the men who frequented the salon were Masons, members of the most influential Paris lodge, the Lodge of the Nine Sisters. Voltaire was a member; Franklin, himself a Mason, was elected to the lodge and later made its "Venerable," that is, Grand Master. The Masons were politically and financially powerful in France and were most useful in Franklin's mission.

Franklin was instantly attracted by this independent woman, with her menage of three men and a dazzling coterie of the leading personalities of Paris. He sent her a letter that tried to analyze her charm, which caused statesmen, philosophers, historians, poets and men of learning "to attach themselves to you as straws to a fine piece of amber." He came to this conclusion: ". . . we find in your sweet society that charming benevolence, that amiable attention to oblige, that disposition to please and be pleased which we do not always find in the society of one another. It springs from you; it has influence on us all; and, in your company, we are not only pleased with you, but better pleased with one another and with ourselves."

Neither John nor Abigail Adams, prim Bostonians, saw Madame Helvétius with the same eyes as Franklin. Shortly after his arrival John Adams met Madame Brillon, Franklin's first love, and was impressed with her beauty and musical skill, but somewhat shocked at her calling Franklin "Mon cher papa," and by their exchanges of kisses and hugs. Then, a few days later, Franklin took him to the Helvétius home. Adams noted in his diary:

> That She might not be, however, entirely without the Society of Gentlemen, there were three or four handsome Abbys who daily visited the House and one, at least, resided there. These Ecclesiasticks, one or more of whom reside in allmost every Family of Distinction, I suppose have as much power to Pardon a Sin as they have to commit one, or to assist in committing one. Oh Mores! said I to myself. What Absurdities, Inconsistencies, Distractions and Horrors would these Manners introduce into our Republican Governments in America; No Kind of Republican Government can ever exist with such national manners as these. Cavete Americani.

His wife, Abigail, wrote of Madame Helvétius:

> She entered the room with a careless, jaunty air; upon seeing the ladies who were strangers to her, she bawled out: "Ah, Mon Dieu, where is Franklin? Why did you not tell me there were ladies here?" You must

suppose her speaking all of this in French. "How I look," said she, taking hold of a chemise of tiffany, which she had on over a blue lutestring, and which looked as much upon the decay of her beauty, for she was once a handsome woman.

Her hair was frizzled; over it she had a small straw hat, with a dirty gauze half-handkerchief behind. She had a black gauze scarf thrown over her shoulders.

She ran out of the room; when she returned, the Doctor entered at one door, she at the other; upon which she ran forward to him, caught him by the hand, "Helas, Franklin!," then gave him a double kiss, one upon each cheek, and another upon his forehead. When we went to dine, she was placed between the Doctor and Mr. Adams. She carried on the chief of conversation at dinner, frequently locking her hand into the Doctor's, and sometimes spreading her arms upon the backs of both the gentlemen's chairs, then throwing her arm carelessly upon the Doctor's neck.

I should have been greatly astonished at this conduct, if the good Doctor had not told me that in this lady I should see a genuine Frenchwoman, wholly free from affectation or stiffness of behaviour, and one of the best women in the world. I own I was highly disgusted, and never wish for an acquaintance with ladies of this cast.

After dinner, she threw herself on a settee, where she showed more than her feet. She had a little lap-dog, who was, next to the Doctor, her favorite. This she kissed, and when he wet the floor she wiped it up with her chemise. This is one of the Doctor's most intimate friends, with whom he dines once every week, and she with him.

Abigail Adams could not possibly comprehend Franklin's love of the informality, the total lack of artificial manners, the warmth and naturalness of a woman like Madame Helvétius—but what a relief it was for Franklin to escape the formality of Versailles, the vexatious labors at his office, the bills and contracts, the political sniping and intrigues that plagued his working hours. With Madame Helvétius and her coterie, Franklin could discuss the latest plays, scientific experiments, anecdotes and scandals, while carrying on a flirtation most flattering for an old man.

To judge by Franklin's letters to Madame Helvétius, his courtship was getting no nearer final consummation than that with Madame Brillon. He accepted a dinner invitation with a note that said:

"Of course I shall not fail to come next Wednesday. I get too much pleasure from seeing you, hearing you, too much happiness from holding you in my arms, to forget such a precious invitation." In another note, he wrote: "If Notre Dame is pleased to spend her days with Franklin, he would be just as pleased to spend his nights with her; and since he has already given her so many of his days, although he has so few left to give, she seems very ungrateful in never giving him one of her nights."

At first the flirtation ran parallel to his "affair" with Madame Brillon, almost always in a light vein, never to be taken quite seriously. She could not have thought he was preparing to propose when he sent her a fantasy about the flies in his house carrying a mysterious message to hers: "Bizz izzz ouizz a ouizzzz izzzzzzzz etc.," which he then translated as their desire "to see both of you forming at last but one Menage." The proposals would continue. "A bachelor," he told her, "resembles the odd half of a pair of scissors." Finally, he proposed marriage, without subtlety or joking. He genuinely loved her, and wanted to spend the rest of his days with her.

At one point he sent her a very curious "Bagatelle" called "The Elysian Fields." It referred to her "barbarous decision" never to marry again. On hearing her say this, Franklin returned home and had a dream. In it he found himself in the Elysian fields talking with Socrates and M. Helvétius. Franklin was surprised to hear Helvétius ask many questions about politics on earth but not a question about his wife. Helvétius explained to Franklin that to be happy in Paradise one must forget the past. He had, therefore, taken another wife. Franklin remarked that Helvétius' former wife was more faithful than he, for she shunned all suitors, including himself.

Helvétius' new wife in Paradise came along and astonished Franklin, for it was his own dead wife, Deborah. She said to him: "I was a good wife to you for nearly fifty years—be satisfied with that. I have now found a new connection that will last throughout eternity."

Franklin left Heaven, returned to earth and went to look for Madame Helvétius to tell her what had happened in Heaven. He ended the tale with the words: "Here I am. Let us avenge ourselves."

It is the strangest and most disturbing piece Franklin ever wrote, almost completely out of character. His writings are either moralistic or sentimental, lighthearted and genial in their wit; occasionally, as in the "Sale of the Hessians," savage satire, in the style of Swift. Never is he mordant, bitter, spiteful, as he seemed to be in "The Elysian Fields." He must have written it in a low moment of fatigue, pain or frustration in both his negotiations and his love affairs.

Madame Helvétius for her part gave his proposal serious thought. He was old, in his mid-seventies, but she was approaching sixty. He was the most famous and respected man in the Western world; she was tempted. She even asked the advice of Turgot, whom she had twice turned down, angering him by the thought that she might marry Franklin rather than himself, a much younger, handsomer man. But she loved best of all the freedom of her life, the young men who worshiped at her altar, the many famous men who came to her, for herself alone. This she would not share with Franklin, though he be the most famous of all. All of this seemed to the Adamses to be a case of second childhood, lacking in decorum and in dignity. Franklin, they thought, had more important things to do than pursue the frivolous women of France.

Franklin did have a lot to do, more than he could handle, much more than he was competent to assume. From Jonathan Williams he kept receiving samples of arms, munitions and cloth which only a military specialist could properly evaluate. He was also far out of his depth in the field of naval tactics and strategy, yet was forced by events to plunge into it.

John Paul Jones had come to France in the *Ranger,* a fast, well-armed raider, and soon became the terror of the English and Scottish coasts. He captured a British Navy sloop in hand-to-hand combat, plus seven prizes. His exploits impressed Sartine, French Minister of the Navy. Sartine had been reluctant to help the Americans, and had made Captain Wickes's life difficult until war with

England was declared. Then he was glad to cooperate with daring American raiders. He decided to give Jones the command of a frigate, the *Indien,* originally built for the Americans, then transferred to the French fleet. Congress commissioned Jones for the command and Sartine gave him a French crew, but the plan did not work out, for the crew had difficulty taking orders from the Americans. In addition, the French admirals, at war with England, were demanding more ships, which Sartine did not have. Eventually, he took back the *Indien* and gave Jones an old, rusty French man-of-war, with forty guns, the *Duras.* Jones worked hard to refurbish the ship, and, in honor of Franklin, rechristened it the *Bonhomme Richard*—"Poor Richard."

Franklin, involved with all these plans, was playing a game whose rules he did not quite understand, and he admitted that he was at a loss when dealing with naval questions. "I have not enough knowledge in such matters to presume upon advising it, and I am so troublesome to the Ministers on other accounts." The "other accounts" were his constant pleas for money and more money. Congress kept sending Franklin drafts to honor, not only for his own mission, but for the activities of other men, in Holland and Madrid. Whoever needed money wrote to Congress and Congress wrote to Franklin. Franklin continually begged money from Vergennes, from Chaumont, from the banker Sir George Grand and his associates.

At the same time, he was functioning as the United States Consul General, handling commercial and personal affairs and pleas from French and American citizens. He had to sit as a judge in the Admiralty when American privateers brought back prizes to be evaluated in condemnation and sales procedures. He had neither competence nor appetite nor time for all these affairs.

Not only was he overwhelmed by political and money problems, but he lacked the authority, despite his personal prestige, to impose his own policies. He was of equal rank with the other commissioners, and they would often challenge him, particularly the Lee brothers and Izard. John Adams, despite his disapproval of Franklin's poor administration, understood that the overlapping of assignments and the number of "equal" commissioners compounded the errors. A clear-thinking man, he wrote to Congress that the divisions of authority and lines of command were injurious to the American mission. He recommended that one man be made Chief of Mission. Unlike Arthur Lee, who recommended himself for that post, Adams, eminently qualified, stated that Franklin alone had the stature in France to be the American Minister. Adams' views reached the Congress at about the same time that Conrad Alexandre Gérard, the new French Minister to America, took up his duties. Gérard promptly told the Congress that France trusted and loved Franklin and no one else and wished to work through him alone.

Franklin had himself written to James Lovell complaining about the presence in Paris of no less than four energetic American commissioners, with a fifth due to arrive. "The necessary expense of maintaining us all is, I assure you, enormously great. I wish that the utility may equal it." He appealed to Congress "to separate us." In September Congress finally decided to revoke the joint commissions and rename Franklin as the sole Minister Plenipotentiary to France. This did not end his problems, but it did at last stop all the time-consuming and nerve-straining consultations and conferences he had been obliged to hold with his sensitive colleagues. And, although his prestige needed no strengthening, it simplified matters for Vergennes, who could not bear Lee and had come also to dislike Adams.

Meanwhile, the war itself had degenerated into a series of misfortunes and failures on both sides. Washington had just barely survived the brutal winter at Valley Forge. Sir William Howe, fat, warm and comfortable in Philadelphia, fortunately did nothing to capitalize on Washington's weaknesses. London, disappointed in his performance, recalled him in the spring of '78 and named Sir Henry Clinton in his stead. Franklin had been proved right: Philadelphia had taken and swallowed up Howe.

Clinton had decided to evacuate Philadelphia, concentrate his forces on New York and prepare a new summer campaign. Washington, despite his weakened forces, attacked the rear guard of Clinton's army in the Battle of Monmouth Court House, in New Jersey. It was a confused battle, with Washington just averting disaster by dismissing General Charles Lee, who had lost control, and taking command of the troops personally. The only purpose the battle served was to hide Washington's desperate condition from Clinton, who could not believe Washington would have attacked if his forces were as depleted and weakened as his spies reported.

Fortunately for Washington, the British Navy was at a low point in morale, suffering inefficiency of command, particularly at the very top level in London. The First Lord of the Admiralty was Lord Sandwich, who earlier had violently attacked Franklin in Parliament. He was corrupt, inefficient and probably the worst First Lord in British naval history.

Although the French Navy's efficiency and morale were of a much higher order, it ran into bad luck in its very first sorties in America. Franklin's friend, the Comte d'Estaing, sailed into the waters off Sandy Hook on July 11, 1778. The British saw him coming and strengthened their fortifications around the Narrows. Although d'Estaing's men-of-war were mightily armed ships, he lost his nerve and decided not to run the gantlet of the Narrows. He sailed away from New York to explore the British defenses at Newport, and landed an expeditionary force to join the New England militia for an assault upon the base. At that moment, a gale from the northeast burst upon his fleet, blowing it out to sea. He put into Boston to refit his damaged vessels. John Hancock made him welcome, but on the docks French officers and men clashed with the Americans. Duels were fought, bloody riots broke out, and d'Estaing retreated to the West Indies.

The alliance, despite all Franklin's efforts in Paris, got off to a poor start in America.

CHAPTER

15

Peace Feelers and Voltaire

During the early months of 1778, when the conclusion of the alliance was in its final stages, Franklin received a stream of visitors from London—some old friends in the Opposition seeking honorable reconciliation, and some indirect emissaries of Lord North to sound Franklin out, still thinking, on the basis of the spy Bancroft's inaccurate reports, that Franklin would make a deal. The most important of those visitors, a wealthy Whig, William Pulteney, member of Parliament from Shrewsbury, came in March, after the alliance had been signed and publicly affirmed.

Pulteney had had a slight acquaintanceship with Franklin in London. His European agent, William Alexander, a Scotsman, of whom Franklin was fond, was then living in Dijon, France. Pulteney got Alexander to write Franklin to recommend that he see him and listen to his proposals. Then Pulteney, before leaving London, conferred with the Prime Minister, Lord North, and Lord George Germain, the Colonial Secretary. To Germain he had said: "Dr. Franklin knows that I have always respected him when it was the fashion to entertain other opinions. He knows that I have wished always the most perfect freedom of America with respect to taxation and charters; but he knows, too, that I wish the indissoluble union of Great Britain and America as being in the interest of America as well as Britain." This declaration allayed government fears that Pulteney might be entertaining ideas about independence. At that point Lord North and George III were ready to give America just about everything except independence—including a generous dominion status that was already out of date.

William Alexander wrote to Pulteney to tell him of a visit Franklin had already received from another emissary, the Moravian pacifist, James Hutton, who had told Franklin that the ministry was ready to offer everything except "the word, independence." Franklin had said he was not empowered to entertain peace feelers. Alexander added that the Americans would make no move toward a truce while the North ministry was still in power. American passions, he reported, "are roused to the utmost pitch of resentment, and . . . no obstinacy is equal to that of a republic." In Alexander's opinion the only move was to offer concrete peace proposals, including substantial, if not absolute independence. And there was no time to lose, he added. Feelings were running high in Paris, not only among the Americans but among the French. His son had been there, had read the press and made the rounds of the theaters, which were featuring a series of military reviews and battle scenes. "You know the footing on which the spectacles are in Paris, and that they are employed to direct the voice of the people."

Early in March, Pulteney arrived in Paris, registered at a hotel under a false name and sent Franklin a note asking him for a meeting. To impress Franklin, he sent him a copy of a pamphlet he had written, entitled *Thoughts on the Present State of Affairs with America and the Means of Conciliation.* It expressed generous and liberal views, similar to those Franklin had put forward in his negotiations with Lord Howe four years earlier. Franklin felt it showed little appreciation of the march of events.

At his first meeting with Pulteney in mid-March, Franklin told him that "Every Proposition which implied our voluntarily agreeing to return to a dependence on Britain was now become intolerable." He said, however, that "A peace on equal terms undoubtedly might be made" and that the commissioners in France had sufficient powers to make such a peace. In fact, the instructions from the Congress to the commissioners related only to the negotiating of treaties of alliance, and not to the power to negotiate peace with Britain.

Pulteney was impressed by this statement and by Franklin's cordiality. He was somewhat disappointed by his firm insistence on independence, knowing that London would not accept it, but he told Franklin he was ready to return to England and seek out concrete peace proposals to bring back to Paris.

On his return to London he received a letter from Alexander, who had seen Franklin in Paris just after Pulteney. He reported that Franklin had just received copies of the conciliatory acts that Parliament had passed on March 9. He told Pulteney that not a moment should be lost in sending commissioners authorized to negotiate with the Americans in Paris, adding this line: "I write with Confidence and under the eye of a very wise Man."

Encouraged by letters from Alexander and by Lord North, Pulteney returned to Paris, carrying with him a set of eighteen proposals for peace that had been officially approved by the ministry. They included: maintenance of the American government, plus a Royal Governor; America's right to name all judges and civil officers; no veto on the laws of the American Assembly; Congress to remain in existence, but with a President named by the King; no taxes, no military forces, except with the consent of the Assemblies of the States; no Royal Customs; free trade except for existing exclusive companies; Americans to be represented in the British Parliament; mutual amnesty and compensation for wanton damage; the King to be the only Supreme Governor and to have the powers of war and peace and foreign alliances; all hostile resolutions to be annulled and British subsidies to be granted for the development and growth of the colonies.

Pulteney, certain that he had the right answers, called on Franklin in secret. Before revealing his peace proposals he asked Franklin for his word as a gentleman that, should the proposals prove not to be satisfactory, he would never mention them to anyone and would "bury the whole transaction." He then handed over his "protocols of peace." He paced the room nervously as Franklin read and was sharply disappointed to note his cold, unsmiling face. Franklin finished reading, put the papers down and said: "I do not approve of these, nor do I think they would be approved in America." He then added: "But, there are two other Commissioners here; I will, if you please, show your Propositions to them, and you will hear their Opinion. I will also show them to the Ministry here, without whose knowledge and concurrence we can take no step in such affairs."

Pulteney shook his head sadly. "No, Dr. Franklin, as you do not approve of them, it can answer no purpose to show them to anyone else; the reasons that weigh with you will also weigh with them."

Franklin, despite his promise, did show the papers to Silas Deane, who was packing to return to America, and asked him to show them to Gérard, who was sailing with him to take over his new post as French Minister there. Later, Franklin regretted breaking his word to Pulteney and sent a letter to Deane asking him to burn the papers.

Franklin's handling of this affair was consistent with his method of listening to all peace proposals from London and keeping the French informed. It served a subtle, dual purpose: it showed the French how determined the Americans were to maintain their independence; it also showed Vergennes that London was making very seductive offers and that American determination might well succumb unless, of course, the French provided adequate monies and supplies. Finally, if London were to consider serious peace proposals on the basis of independence, the door would have been kept open.

Pulteney went home discouraged but determined to keep trying. He asked Alexander to leave Dijon and take up residence in Passy and keep in touch with Franklin—in effect, to become Pulteney's spy at American headquarters, where there were already more spies than commissioners. Alexander agreed, but on unusual terms. He wrote that he would serve the ministry and the cause of peace, but he would not betray any confidence of his old friend Dr. Franklin. He would tell Franklin that he was staying close to him just in case circumstances might change, "with a view to be able to communicate with any such alteration, without engaging him further than he chooses." Alexander stayed so close to Franklin, indeed, that his daughter Marianne later married Franklin's nephew, Jonathan Williams.

To make sure that there be no misunderstanding of what he had said in conversation, Franklin drafted a letter to Pulteney on the thirtieth of March to confirm his views. He reiterated his eagerness to discuss peace terms, but only on the basis of recognition of the independence of the United States. He proposed a treaty of "Peace, Amity and Commerce" between two sovereign nations. He concluded: "May God at last grant that Wisdom to your national Councils, which he seems long to have deny'd them, and which only sincere, just and humane Intentions can merit or expect."

Despite Franklin's letter, Pulteney kept telling people in London that a deal could be made with Franklin. George III sent North a note saying he did not believe it, except that "probably the old Doctor may wish to keep a door open." More letters came all through April, along with the visit of Franklin's friend David Hartley, who also wanted to talk of the possibility of peace. Franklin told him what he had told Pulteney and, once again, sent a note to Vergennes about the meeting, knowing full well that Vergennes's spies, who stalked his every step, would have informed him of it.

> Mr. Hartley, Member of the British Parliament, an old acquaintance of mine, arrived here from London on Sunday last. He is generally in the opposition, especially on American questions, but has some respect for Lord North. In conversation, he expressed the strongest anxiety for peace with America and appeared extremely desirous to know my sentiments of the terms.

Franklin went on to say that he had no terms at all to propose to Hartley. Britain must end an unjust war and make reparations for injuries. Then one could talk of treaties and mutual trade advantages but nothing exclusive or even superior for Britain over other nations. Britain must understand that peace with America must also include peace with France. A separate peace while Britain fought

France was "impossible." Franklin said he had told Hartley that America now had "common cause with France."

In this letter, Franklin also informed Vergennes of the visit of a Mr. Chapman, who had introduced himself as a member of the Parliament of Ireland, visiting France for his health, yet had immediately entered into questions about peace with England. Franklin ended the letter with information that he had learned of the imminent departure of ships for Quebec, with a precious cargo of goods valued at a half-million pounds sterling. It would sail at the end of April, under convoy of only one thirty-gun frigate. He did not say so in so many words, but he was clearly hinting that Vergennes should arrange for a French intercept of so valuable a prize. Franklin was doing whatever he could to get France more actively into the war, and to keep Vergennes nervous about peace offers.

In June Franklin received the most unusual of all the "peace feelers," one that provoked an exceptionally violent response. It happened one morning when he was at breakfast, reveling in a rich brioche buried under jam while he savored the gossip in the Paris papers. His servant had run in bearing an envelope, marked "Secret and Confidential," which had been thrown through the grille of the gate and found lying in the entranceway to the estate. Intrigued, Franklin slit it open. It began with an entreaty for secrecy, the writer identifying himself as an Englishman who did not think that everything done by the government and the King was holy and infallible. In purple prose, it described the wicked acts of Britain against America and extolled the philosophical wisdom of Franklin. It went on, in lurid fashion, to denounce France and warn Franklin of the pitfalls of the alliance. It claimed that he would get many promises in Paris but few deliveries to America.

Franklin looked for the writer's name; it was a Charles de Weissenstein, unknown to him. As he read on, particularly passages that explained why America's claim to independence was vain and illusory, Franklin became convinced that Charles de Weissenstein was none other than George III.

Franklin was irritated, then angered by long passages proclaiming British might and American weakness. He did not appreciate suggestions that Britain would entertain reasonable terms for peace. His suspicions strengthened when he read a passage that said one could not trust official peace commissioners but rather "undertake, through a most eligible mediator, to transmit into the King's own hands, any proposals on your part, which are not couched in offensive terms." Then the writer advised Franklin not to try to find out who he was. He was more useful "invisible," but, if he succeeded, he might "reveal myself." He proposed that Franklin write out his thoughts on the matter and then

> carry them, yourself, to the Cathedral Church of Notre Dame, between the hours of twelve at noon and one; either on Monday, the 6th of July inst., or on Thursday, the 9th of July. If the iron gates on either side of the choir are open, you will enter and there find a gentleman who has no idea of the nature of this commission, so do not give him any suspicions by taking extraordinary notice of him. . . . For more certain guidance, I have desired him to stick a Rose either in his hat, which he will hold in his hand or up to his face, or else in the buttonhole of his waistcoast.

The letter was datelined Brussels, June 16, 1778. Included in the envelope was an eighteen-point project for "allaying the present ferments in America," and a thirteen-point outline of the "Future Government of North America." It also contained an offer of full amnesty, lifetime pensions and peerages for Franklin, Washington, Hancock, Adams and others.

His suspicions that the writer was the King were confirmed by the vulgar, insulting bribes habitually offered by the government in London. Expecting that the King would read his reply, Franklin wrote a harsh, abusive letter, for he despised George III and held him responsible for all the terrible losses in the war.

He rejected favors and honors at the outset:

> As to my future fame, I am content to rest it on my past and present Conduct, without seeking an addition to it in the crooked, dark Paths you propose to me, where I should most certainly lose it. This, your solemn Address, would therefore have been more properly made to your Sovereign and his venal Parliament. He and They who wickedly began and

madly continue a War for the Desolation of America are alone accountable for the Consequences.

Franklin rejected charges of French inconstancy and pointed to the two-hundred-year friendship between France and the "thirteen United States of Suitzerland." He said France would not cheat America, but that "you are endeavouring to cheat us by your conciliatory bills." All Europe would despise America "if we were weak enough to accept your insidious Propositions." Franklin warned that "there is nothing to be got by attacking us, we have reason to hope that no other power will judge it prudent to quarrel with us, lest they divert us from our own quiet industry and turn us into Corsairs preying upon theirs." As for cheating, "We can govern ourselves a year for the sums you pay in a single Department, or for what one jobbing Contractor, by the favour of a Minister, can cheat you out of in a single article." Franklin reaffirmed American independence: "We can tell you, that you can have no Treaty with us but as an independent State. And you may please yourselves and your Children with the Rattle of your Right to govern us. . . . Your Parliament never had a Right to govern us. And your King has forfeited it by his bloody Tyranny."

Franklin referred to the suggestion that his letter be passed on to the King by someone who would pick it up at the Church of Notre Dame. He wrote: "You, yourself, Sir, are quite unknown to me; you have not trusted me with your true name. Our taking the least step towards a Treaty with England thro' you, might, if you are an enemy, be made use of to ruin us with our new and good friends." In any case, were he to make proposals, "I should never think of delivering them to the Lord knows who, to be carried to Lord knows where, to serve no one knows what purpose."

Franklin said he was answering because "I would let you know our sense of your Procedure, which appears as insidious as your conciliatory Bills. Your true way to obtain a Peace, if your Ministers desire it, is to propose openly to the Congress fair and equal terms." At the suggestion that it could all be arranged by act of Parliament he scoffed: "Good God! an Act of your Parliament! this demonstrates that you do not yet know us, and that you fancy we do not know you. . . . This offer, Sir, to corrupt us is with me your Credential; it convinces me that you are not a private Volunteer in this Negotiation. It bears the stamp of your King." Franklin ended the letter by ridiculing the offer of pensions, which would be paid for out of revenues extracted from America, disgracing their recipients, and laughing at the offer of peerages, a title for which he had no respect. "We consider it a sort of Tar-and-Feather Honour, a Mixture of foulness and folly, which every man among us, who should accept from you, would be obliged to renounce or exchange for that conferred by the Mobs in his own Country, or wear it with everlasting Infamy."

Franklin showed the "Weissenstein" letter and his own reply to Vergennes, who ordered police surveillance of Notre Dame on the day of the proposed mail drop. Police shadows reported seeing a gentleman wandering about the church, "never losing sight, however, of the spot appointed, and often returning to it, looking earnestly about, at times, as if he expected somebody." The police trailed the man back to his lodgings and discovered that he was a "Colonel Fitzsomething, an Irish name." He was not interrogated, under orders from Vergennes, who asked Franklin not to send his letter. The original might have been sent by an intriguer, or an agent provocateur. He doubted that it came from George III and felt that even if it did, there was no point in answering it. This should have occurred to Franklin, of course. Perhaps he was just playing games with Vergennes during a particularly delicate period, when the alliance with France had been signed, without follow-up action, and with no positive word yet from Madrid.

Madrid was playing games, too, games dangerous for both France and the United States. Floridablanca, as cunning and devious as Vergennes, had been sounding out London on the price of Spanish neutrality in the war, suggesting that a cession of Gibraltar might arrange everything. London guessed that he was not anxious to get involved and did not have to be paid off by so big a reward as the rock guarding the entrance to the Mediterranean.

Floridablanca knew he could not get Gibraltar without a war, but he did not want to go to war as a result of signing a treaty with American rebels. Nor did he wish to enter into the same arrangements that Vergennes had made. But he wanted Gibraltar as much as Vergennes wanted vengeance on England, so he hit upon a subtle scheme for forcing the issue. He offered Spain as a mediator in the war, under terms he knew would be rejected by England, thereby making Spain the peacemaker and England the war criminal. He could then make his own secret arrangements with Vergennes to extract from him a promise to help Spain conquer Gibraltar. On those terms he could eventually enter the war.

Floridablanca began to put this scheme into operation as soon as the French-American treaties were official. His chargé d'affaires in London made the neutrality offer, with the request for Gibraltar, in April. The British, as expected, rejected it, saying that Gibraltar was a vital bastion of the British Empire. Floridablanca then transferred his Ambassador in Lisbon to London to warn the British that if peace were not soon made, Spain might be obliged to fulfill her obligations to France. He wrote to his Ambassador: "They must know that what we do not get by negotiations we know how to get with a club."

These intricate maneuvers, in addition to the intrigues going on in the contest over Bavaria, occupied the attention of the European powers throughout the remaining months of 1778. No one, not even France, which had taken the fatal step of provoking war with England over America, would do much more than husband all efforts and resources for purely national interests and purposes. Vergennes had gone very far without Spain, and he would go further, but he would go slowly. It was a frustrating time for Franklin, who had hoped for so much once the treaties were signed, and even more disappointing for the Congress and for General Washington, needing and expecting a flood of arms, munitions and clothing. Riots in Boston, between French and Americans, and excuses in Paris marked the first year of the alliance.

Franklin was patient, knowing there was little he could do directly with Vergennes. Unlike the other commissioners, who saw everything from the American viewpoint, Franklin was fully informed on the intrigues and complexities of European politics. He realized that Vergennes was dealing with a reluctant King, and that the powerful Turgot kept a sharp eye and tongue at work to defend French finances. He could play only two cards with Vergennes: the potential British peacemakers and the force of French public opinion, most particularly the opinion of the noblemen and great merchants and their ladies who had influence at the court at Versailles.

The greatest of all French personalities of the day was the philosopher Voltaire, whom Franklin had long wanted to meet. He had hoped to meet him on his first visit to Paris in 1767, when he had received news that Voltaire extended his respects to Franklin through a mutual friend in London. In 1764 Franklin had been most surprised and delighted to read the Frenchman's praise of Pennsylvania Quakers in his treatise on religious tolerance. He had written that some of the ways and manners of the Quakers were perhaps slightly ridiculous but that they were virtuous men who preached the doctrine of brotherhood among men. "Discord, Controversy are not known in their happy land and the very name of their city, Philadelphia, reminds us that all men are brothers; it is an example for the shame of people who do not yet know tolerance."

Franklin's chance to meet the great philosopher finally came when Voltaire, then eighty-four, in the last year of his life, returned to Paris after an absence of almost thirty years, on February 10, 1778. Franklin sent him a note, and he promptly invited the American, whose fame equaled his own, agreeing that Franklin might bring his grandson Temple with him.

The writer Condorcet, biographer of Voltaire, described the meeting and its context:

> In Paris at this time was the celebrated Franklin, who, in another hemisphere, had been, like Voltaire, the apostle of liberty and toleration. Like him, he had often used the weapon of pleasantry for the correction of human folly, and had learned to regard human perversity as a folly, more terrible, indeed, but still to be pitied. He had honored philosophy

in the realm of physics, as had Voltaire that of poetry. Franklin had delivered the immense legions of America from the yoke of Europe, and Voltaire had delivered Europe from the yoke of the ancient theocracies of Asia. Franklin was desirous to see a man whose glory had for so long a time filled both worlds, and, fortunately, Voltaire expressed a wish to see him. Voltaire, although he had lost the habit of speaking English, tried to maintain the conversation in that language, but, soon, resuming his own, said: "I could not resist the desire of speaking for a moment in Mr. Franklin's language." The American philosopher then presented his grandson, and asked Voltaire's benediction for him. "God and Liberty," said Voltaire, "this is the only benediction which is fit for a grandson of Mr. Franklin."

The two men met again briefly when Franklin escorted Voltaire to an induction ceremony at the Masonic Lodge of the Nine Sisters.

Their final meeting took place at the end of April at the Academy of Science. There are many contemporary descriptions of the event, but the best and most interesting for Americans was the scene noted in his diary by John Adams, in his own tart style:

> Voltaire and Franklin were both present, and there presently arose a general cry that M. Voltaire and Mr. Franklin should be introduced to each other. This was done and they bowed and spoke to each other. This was no satisfaction; there must be something more. Neither of our philosophers seemed to divine what was wished or expected; they however took each other by the hand. But this was not enough. The clamour continued until the explanation came out: Il faut s'embrasser à la française. The two aged actors upon this great theatre of philosophy and frivolity then embraced each other by hugging one another in their arms and kissing each other's cheeks, and then the tumult subsided. And the cry immediately spread throughout the kingdom, and I suppose all over Europe: Qu'il est charmant de voir embrasser Solon et Sophoclé. Solon and Sophocles should embrace, but it must be in the manner of the French.

Adams could not quite make up his mind about Franklin. He knew he was a great man and that his stature was America's most valuable asset in France and Europe. But he still could not abide Franklin's "dissipated" style of life, nor his negligence—if that was all it was—in the financial affairs of the American mission.

CHAPTER

16

Tension Inside the Alliance

On his arrival in Paris in April, 1778, John Adams was distressed to discover serious strife inside the American mission, between Lee, the instigator, and Deane and Franklin, principally over the issue of whether the aid supplied by Beaumarchais was free or reimbursable. In his diary, Adams called the links among the Americans "A Rope of Sand."

"I am, at present, wholly untainted with these Prejudices, and will endeavour to keep myself so. . . . Mr. D. seems to have made himself agreeable to Persons of Importance and Influence, and has gone home in such Splendour that I fear there will be Altercations in America about him." Adams noted that he had heard that Deane had speculated on the London market and had been using his public office to make personal profit on trade and in outfitting privateers, to the amount of at least fifty thousand pounds, adding that "Dr. B. too had made a fortune." He also noted that Lee was disliked by the French and had been indiscreet in conversations, cursing and despising the French people and nation. All of this was causing considerable bad blood all around. As for himself, "I must do my duty to the Public; let it give offence to whom it will." He concluded this section of his diary with the notation that Franklin had not conducted the public business methodically, that there were no minutes, no letter files, no account books, and that everyone lived extravagantly.

Reports by Lee, later reaffirmed in part by Adams, had alienated Congress before Deane arrived to defend himself. Arthur Lee's brother, Richard Henry, was determined to punish Deane severely and had made common cause with the radical Sam Adams, in the Boston-Virginia bloc seeking control of the Congress.

Deane came home to a hostile Philadelphia. Conrad Alexandre Gérard, who sailed with him, received a most cordial welcome. He was met at Chester by a delegation of four members of Congress, headed by John Hancock. He sent a description of the reception to Vergennes, in a letter on July 15:

> Nothing can equal the eagerness of members of Congress and other leading men to call on me and express their sentiments in relation to the alliance and the steps taken by the King. I fear that I should be charged with exaggeration were I to state the terms which the most phlegmatic employ in their daily conversations with me. They style the King "Protector of the Rights of Humanity," which is always the toast in his honor.

Gérard's early enthusiasm was heightened when Congress helped him find excellent lodgings right next to the State House, where Congress met. He was then offered a formal reception and asked what court etiquette might require. He wisely replied that he was accredited to a republican government, not a royal court, and wished only the plainest and most democratic procedures. Congress, pleased with his answer, conferred upon him a rare privilege, denied even to the American press of the day: a pass granting him the right to attend sessions when Congress met as a committee of the whole and when French affairs were being discussed. Thanks to this grant, we can read today, in the dispatches of Gérard and his successor, the Chevalier de La Luzerne, eyewitness reports on these debates and on the behavior of the Congress.

His first report to Vergennes, on July 25, began on a quick note. He was just getting the feel.

> Party spirit exists in Congress as in all similar bodies. Questions seem to arise, however, only through the diversity of principles, or rather out of the different degrees of ambition of a few preponderating members. Some want a constant rotation in the leading offices, especially in Congressional membership; others, on the contrary, aim at securing a negative

vote which would render the choice of the different States subject to their will, ensure them their own places and thereby give the government an aristocratic air.

Several leading men have assured me that Congress is not divided on the great objects of interest to France, nor on any subject which comprises the interests of the United States. A faction did exist in Congress, before our treaty was received, all the more dangerous because treachery could not be imputed to it. It consisted of ambitious men, but of little influence. It was their aim to maintain a sort of balance of power, so that in case of a capitulation to England, they would be ready to profit by it. A Scotch minister, named Witherspoon, the only one of his cloth in the Congress, was the soul of this party. . . . Mr. Samuel Adams, who figured prominently at the outbreak of the Revolution, belonged to it.

Gérard ended with a report on the high prices of vegetables, flour and wood in the colonies, despite the fact that these commodities were plentiful. He attributed it to the fact that there were many speculators in the markets of America. "This science is pushed farther here than anywhere in Europe."

In a follow-up report, Gérard talked of American customs and politics:

The Philadelphia papers contain two resolutions passed by Congress. . . . The second is a renewal of the request made by certain States to interdict dances, spectacles and races. The very day this resolution appeared a public (theatrical) performance, given by Army officers and Whig citizens, was to take place. The following day the Governor of Pennsylvania gave a ball, numerously attended. Congress, finding that its simple recommendation was not regarded as a law, prepared a resolution to enforce it, which rendered incapable of employment every officer who should take part in or attend any spectacle. On the other hand, Maryland, Virginia, and Carolina regarded horse-racing as a national affair. It is the northern members, called the Presbyterian Party, that delight in passing moral laws so as to keep their credit and rigor in full exercise. Such contests interfere with important business.

Referring to Congress, Gérard wrote:

In general the pay of its members is not in accordance with the dignity of the post. Some States give their representatives very little, and always energetically dispute their accounts. No one member lives becomingly, and none can give a dinner except at a tavern. One result of this poor pay is, whenever a member finds that his business suffers, he leaves, and his State has no representative. The principle of rotation in office has the same effect. . . .

Everybody, almost, refuses to testify (against the insolence of the Tories). . . . Scarcely one-quarter of the ordinary inhabitants of Philadelphia now here favor the cause of independence. Commercial and family ties, together with the aversion to popular government, seem to account for this. The same feeling exists in New York and Boston, which is not the case in the rural districts, where the people are cultivators rather than merchants.

Vergennes, receiving these reports in Paris, became increasingly nervous about the cohesiveness and determination of his American ally. One report particularly alarmed him; it came in the fall when Franklin was pressing him for money and he was becoming involved in the Deane affair:

I have thus far [wrote Gérard] depicted the good side of Congress, because I have taken the point of view of its attachment to independence and to the alliance, which is the most important point for us. But it is now time that you should know it as well on its feeble side, so as to appreciate it as a whole. Most of the members who sit in Congress owe their places to their zeal for the American cause, as it is now commonly called. But little attention, however, has been paid to the talents that are requisite for the enormous labor which every branch of the Administration demands, and which Congress manages exclusively. In some departments there is not a member who is familiar with their details. If one member happens to be more conspicuous than another, on account of his intelligence, private jealousy and the principle of anticipating personal ascendancy throw him in the background. A competent merchant on the Committee of Commerce is transferred to Foreign Affairs, and again displaced because he is suspected of making money out of secret information. There are many colonels and generals in Congress but none are employed on the war committees. The result is, Monseigneur, the Administration is extremely backward at all points wherever a fixed system and regularity in details are essential. The arrangements for the organization, recruiting, and regular service of Continental troops remain in suspence. . . . The finances, especially, suffer a great deal. . . . Congress is the universal merchant and provider. You can appreciate the effect of a lack of order in such an immensely important detail, the accompanying loss and inconvenience, especially when you consider that, by this course, it enters into competition with private merchants, who cannot be forced to provide the state with the goods it needs.

I am sorry to be obliged to add, Monseigneur, that personal disinterestedness and pecuniary integrity have shed no lustre on the birth of the American Republic. All its agents have derived exorbitant profits from manufactures. A selfish and calculating spirit is widespread in this land, and, although I can well see that limits are put to its extension, there is no condemnation of the sentiment. Mercantile cupidity forms, perhaps, one of the distinctive traits of the Americans, especially of the northern people, and it will undoubtedly exercise an important influence on the future destiny of the Republic.

The Deane-Lee controversy kept heating up all through the summer, and by early fall Franklin had received requests to try to clear up the clouded affair of Roderigue, Hortalez et cie, the trading house that Caron de Beaumarchais had set up on the recommendation of Vergennes as a front for money and supplies. Everybody in the diplomatic missions in Paris knew what was going on, but they all, particularly Vergennes, had to pretend that there was no government involvement, which is what he had been telling Lord Stormont all through the preceding year. Vergennes could not admit involvement now without branding himself a liar a year ago. Franklin did not want to admit any knowledge for much the same reason, and he particularly wanted to keep as far removed from the imbroglio as possible. Arthur Lee, however, wanted the whole truth to come out to prove that Deane, and possibly Franklin, had been cheating Congress by selling goods and arms that had been granted free.

On September 10, Franklin was forced to send a note to Vergennes on this vexing affair. He informed him that Congress had resolved:

That the Commissioners of the United States in France be authorized to determine and settle with the House of Roderigue, Hortalez the compen-

> sation, if any, which should be allowed them on all merchandise and warlike stores shipped by them for the use of the United States, previous to the 14th day of April, 1778, over and above the Commission allowed them in the 6th article of the proposed contract between the Committee of Commerce and Jean Baptiste Lazarus Theveneau de Francy [Beaumarchais's agent in America].
>
> We are under the necessity of applying to your Excellency upon this occasion, and of requesting your advice. With regard to what is passed, we know not who the persons are who constitute the House of Roderigue, Hortalez; but we have understood, and Congress has ever understood, and so have the people in America in general, that they were under obligations to His Majesty's good will for the greatest part of the merchandise and warlike stores heretofore furnished under the firm of Roderigue, Hortalez. We cannot discover that any written contract was ever made between Congress or any agents of theirs and the House of Roderigue, Hortalez; nor do we know of any living witness, or any other evidence, whose testimony can ascertain to us who the persons are that constitute the House of Roderigue, Hortalez; or what were the terms upon which the merchandise and munitions of war were supplied, neither as to the price, nor the time, or conditions of payment. As we said before, we apprehend that the United States hold themselves under obligations to His Majesty as soon as Providence shall put it in their power. In the meantime, we are ready to settle and liquidate the accounts according to our instructions at any time and in any manner which His Majesty and your Excellency shall point out to us.

The entire letter was a tissue of diplomatic lies. Franklin and the others all knew that Beaumarchais was the principal party in Roderigue, Hortalez. They knew of the many contracts entered into by Silas Deane, as the accredited representative of Robert Morris of the Committee of Commerce, who had not only authorized the deals but had used his own private trading agents and partners to profit from them, just as Gérard had reported to Vergennes. As for the last sentence of the note, it simply and badly passed the buck to Vergennes.

Vergennes was infuriated at being put on the spot. Rarely had he been so angry with Franklin. He suspected that the latter's hand had been forced by Arthur Lee and by John Adams, but he felt that

Franklin, as senior man, could have used his authority to prevent this embarrassment. To show his displeasure, he sent his answer first, not to the commissioners in Paris, but to his own Minister Plenipotentiary in Philadelphia, Gérard. He did this also for reasons that went beyond pique. He knew that Franklin was caught in a Lee-Adams factional pincer and could not be very helpful, whereas Gérard, in Philadelphia, with excellent contacts and influence in Congress, could do a better job. Moreover, Gérard had been involved in the entire affair and had, presumably, been thoroughly briefed by Deane during the voyage to America.

Accordingly, on September 10, 1778, Vergennes sent the following very subtly and carefully worded reply to Gérard:

> These plenipotentiaries have just made a new demand on me, embracing two subjects, one concerning the endorsement of M. de Beaumarchais' accounts under the name of Roderigue, Hortalez and Co., and the other a ratification of the contract which Congress, or the Committee of Commerce, in its name, has made with the Sieur Theveneau de Francy, agent of the Sieur Caron de Beaumarchais. Mr. Franklin and his colleagues would like to know what articles have been supplied by the King, and those that have been supplied by M. de Beaumarchais on his own account, and they insinuate that Congress is persuaded that all, or at least a large portion, of what has been sent is on account of His Majesty. I am about to reply that the King has not furnished anything; that he has simply allowed M. de Beaumarchais to provide himself with what he wanted in the arsenals on condition of replacing what he took; and that, for the rest, I will gladly interpose an order that they may not be pressed for the payment of the military supplies.
>
> As to the contract made with the Sieur de Francy, the Commissioners are empowered to ratify it or reject it, and they ask my advice as to what to do. As I do not know the House of Roderigue, Hortalez, and cannot vouch for it, it is impossible to give any opinion on its standing or its responsibility. Please communicate these two replies to the Congress.

At first glance, this would seem to be a disavowal of Roderigue, Hortalez, but the letter did contain a clear endorsement of Beaumarchais as having been authorized by the King. To anyone who did not know all the details, it could be read as a disavowal of

French aid to the rebels, which is the effect Vergennes wanted to give the British. But, with Gérard there to explain the background, it became clear that Beaumarchais did have to resupply the royal arsenals and therefore had to be paid for what he had sent. However, certain other material would not have to be repaid, Gérard explained.

One side of the affair was finally settled when, at the close of 1778, after studying the entire case, John Jay, then President of the Congress under the rotation system Gérard deplored, sent the following note to Vergennes:

> The Congress of the United States, sensible of your exertions in their favor, present you with their thanks and assure you of their regard. They lament the inconvenience you have suffered by the great advances made in support of these States. Circumstances have prevented a compliance with their wishes; but they will take the most effectual measures in their power to discharge the debt due you.
>
> The liberal sentiments and extensive views which could alone dictate a conduct like yours are conspicuous in your actions and adorn your character. While with great talents you served your Prince, you have gained the esteem of this infant Republic and will receive the united applause of the New World.

Vergennes was briefly mollified by the letter, but other events and other men would increase his difficulties and strain his temper.

Dr. Dubourg, Franklin's fellow scientist, and Leray de Chaumont, his landlord, both of whom Vergennes had used in his dealings with the Americans, and who had become close friends of Franklin, were in serious financial difficulties because of monies they had spent and advanced out of their own pockets for contracts negotiated by Deane but not settled by the Congress. Dr. Dubourg had given up his practice, his teaching, his writings and experiments to devote himself entirely to the American cause, with the warmest encouragement of Vergennes. He was rapidly exhausting his last personal reserves and could only be saved by a royal pension. Chaumont had just been removed from his post as Superintendent of Les Invalides, which paid him thirty thousand livres a year, and retired at a much smaller pension of twelve thousand livres. His estate, on which the Americans lived free, cost him great sums to maintain. He had been giving lavish diplomatic parties in honor of the Americans, without receiving a sou of expenses from the government. He was, or had been, a very rich man, but his resources were being seriously depleted. In a poignant note to Vergennes, Chaumont wrote:

> In short, Monseigneur, I am very far from enriching my family by serving my Prince. Allow me to beg you to tell the Comte de Maurepas that I am the son of a father he loved much, because he was a good servant to the King, and I beg him for the same reason to love me also, and when he thinks me of any use, that he can employ me in all safety. If, Messeigneurs, you have nothing to give me, I shall not have time to get wearied, by continuing my present occupation as long as I can. But when the hour of rest shall have come, I much fear that my children, and I have five, will find my purse empty.

The Prime Minister and Comptroller, very worried about the drain on the Treasury due to the war with England, were not inclined to spend monies for American agents or friends of the Americans. They were angry about Congress' not paying its bills and not honoring drafts by accredited agents. Franklin, as Minister, could well pay Chaumont a handsome rental, and Chaumont should tell Franklin, not the government, his troubles. All of this pained Vergennes, who knew his own responsibility in the state of affairs.

Immediately after these vexations came another appeal from Franklin on December 7, in a note that reviewed at length America's monetary as well as financial dealings. It explained that, at the outbreak of the war, there was very little real money in the country, for it had been drawn out in payments of British imports, and by royal customs. The Congress had issued paper bills in lieu of money. But the costs of building an army and merchant fleet had prompted too great an issuance of this paper money, so that its value fell to seven Continental dollars against one silver, and people were beginning to use the expression "not worth a Continental." Congress, during this monetary crisis, had contracted loans which had to be paid in France "in real money," totaling forty-two million livres tournois, at 6 percent interest, amounting to another two and a half millions. It had hoped to repay these loans, Franklin explained, "by American Produce, or by Loans of Money to be procured in Europe from Private Persons on the Credit of the States, or finally by a Subsidy or Loan from their great and good Friend and Ally, His Most Christian Majesty." Unfortunately, the war in Europe had made both commerce and loans difficult to achieve. The only remaining hope was "the Wisdom and Goodness of His Most Christian Majesty."

Franklin assured Vergennes that "Such is the Fertility of the Lands and Industry of the People in America, that being no longer impoverished by the British Monopoly, there is not the least doubt to be made of their future Ability of repaying with Interest and Thankfulness such Aids of Money as his Majesty in his Goodness shall think fit to afford them."

Vergennes, despite his impatience, knew the situation was serious if not desperate. He sent urgent memos to the Comte de Maurepas and began a campaign inside the government to obtain new funds from both France and Spain.

Within a few days of Franklin's appeal for money, there came more news of political factionalism in America over the Deane affair. The Lee-Adams "Junto," angered by Franklin's elevation to sole Minister Plenipotentiary and by Gérard's support for Deane, enlisted the powerful pen of Tom Paine on their side. Paine, one of the greatest of all pamphleteers, delivered vitriolic attacks on Deane in the press and in the Congress, where Paine held the post of secretary to the Committee on Foreign Affairs. Gérard, who knew that Paine was a protégé of Franklin's, felt it was an act of betrayal that seriously endangered the French mission. He went to work to stop Paine, and sent his report to Vergennes:

> The disadvantages of the freedom of the press beginning to be apparent here, as in all countries where it is recognized. M. Paine, secretary to the Committee on Foreign Affairs, has been led by his animosity to Silas Deane to publish a scandalous assertion that the assistance furnished by

M. de Beaumarchais had been promised as a gift, and that he had the written evidence of it in his possession. I was too sensible of the effect of this falsehood not to take measures to forestall it.

As I had always been on good terms with M. Paine I resolved to call on him and try to have him correct his statement in such a way as not to leave any imputation against France. I had a great deal of trouble in convincing him of his error, and especially to make him promise to retract it. But, to my great surprise and dissatisfaction, nothing has been published by him calculated to remove the impression produced by his false assertion.

I then thought it necessary to refer what he wrote to the Congress. Congress, however, did not wait for this to show me its indignation. It no longer entertains the slightest doubt on this affair as it really is; the very day the paper appeared it took steps to rectify this claim by leaving His Majesty free to offset any portion of it by his indebtedness to the States for subsistences furnished to his forces. Moreover, Monseigneur, all assure me that Messr. Lee and Samuel Adams prevented Paine from giving me the satisfaction demanded.

As a result of this intervention by Gérard, whom Jefferson, Hancock and other cooler heads knew to be a key man for further aid, Tom Paine was told that he would be fired from his job in the Congress. Paine, without funds and in disfavor, with no help from Richard Henry Lee or Sam Adams, went to see Gérard to apologize and seek assistance, arguing that Gérard had had him fired from his job and was responsible for his distress. Gérard was delighted to have the opportunity to buy Paine off, and promptly did so, as he reported a week later to Vergennes:

The only remedy that occurred to me to overcome this difficulty, and even profit by it, was to have an offer made to M. Paine to secure him a salary by the King, in place of that he lost. He called and thanked me for this. I stipulated that he should not make any publication on political affairs nor in relation to Congress, without first consulting me, and that he should employ his pen chiefly in inspiring the people with sentiments favorable to France and the alliance, and in such a way as to maintain hatred and distrust of the English. He seemed to accept this task with pleasure. It promised him the same salary of a thousand dollars per annum as soon as Congress dismissed him. He has already entered on his duties by declaring in the Gazette of the 16th inst. that the matter of assistance did not concern the Court, and was not a political affair.

At this point, Silas Deane, driven almost out of his mind by the attacks upon him and by his precarious finances, decided to take his case to the public. He wrote a violent attack on the Congress, alienating not only his enemies in the Lee-Adams faction but practically all the other members as well.

Copies of Deane's article, "An Address to the American People," reached France. The accusations against the Adamses and the Lees, and the disrespect for the Congress, provoked a fit of temper in John Adams. He rushed to complain to Franklin, as he noted in his diary:

> In conversation with Dr. Franklin, in the Morning, I gave him my Opinion of Mr. Deane's Address to the People of America with great freedom and perhaps too much warmth. I told him that it was one of the most wicked, abominable Productions that ever sprung from a human heart. That there was no Safety in Integrity against such a Man. That I should wait upon the Comte de Vergennes, and the other Ministers, and see in what light they considered this Conduct of Mr. Deane. That, if they and their Representatives in America were determined to countenance and support by their Influence such Men and Measures in America, it was no matter how soon the Alliance was broke.

Franklin was appalled. He wondered whether Adams was losing his mind. To be angry with Deane was one thing; to risk breaking the alliance, without which America might lose the war, was insanity. But Adams would not pay any attention to Franklin's warnings and pleadings. He insisted that he would challenge Vergennes on this affair. In his anger, he also vented his spleen, in diary entries, against his fellow Americans in Paris: "There are two Men in the World, who are Men of Honour and Integrity, I believe, but whose prejudices and violent Tempers would raise Quarrels in the Elysian Fields, if not in Heaven." Here, he was referring to Arthur Lee and Ralph Izard. Then he added: "On the other hand, there is another, whose love of Ease and Dissipation, will prevent any thorough Reformation of anything—and his Cunning and Silence and Reserve render it very difficult to do anything with him." He went on to complain that everybody in France and Europe doted on Franklin and had little regard for John Adams. He had been humiliated, since arriving in France, by a question frequently put to him:

> Whether I was the famous Adams. Le fameux Adams? I found great Pains taken, much more than the Question was worth to settle the Point that I was not the famous Adams. . . . It being settled that he was not the famous Adams, the Consequence was plain—he was some Man that nobody had ever heard of before—and therefore a Man of no Consequence—a Cypher . . . a Man who did not understand a Word of French—awkward in his Figure—awkward in his Dress—no Abilities—a perfect Bigot—and fanatic.

After this exercise in self-pity—which had the virtue of being a not entirely inaccurate picture of himself—John Adams then sat down and did the unforgivable: he drafted a violent, incoherent letter to the French Foreign Minister, attacking his own American colleagues, displaying all the dirty American linen before the court of Versailles:

> When I consider the honourable Testimonies of Confidence which Mr. Deane carried with him to America—when I consider the Friendship which I have heard there was in France between Mr. Deane and the Plenipotentiary, and the Consul of France, I confess I am afraid that even the Honourable Testimonies from your Excellency, and even, I dread to say it, from his Majesty, I hope, I sincerely hope, that the Veneration which is due to the Plenipotentiary and the Consul of France has not been so employed, have emboldened Mr. Deane to this Measure—It may end in a division of the States . . . a total subversion of our Constitution. . . . The Reason of my presuming to address myself to your Excellency, separately, is because Mr. Franklin has unhappily attached himself to Mr. Deane and set himself against Mr. Lee.

A final draft of the letter, somewhat moderated, was delivered to Vergennes in the morning of February 12, 1779. As he brooded over it, wondering what to do about the intolerable strife among the Americans, a messenger arrived with dispatches from America, brought by the sloop *Alliance.* They announced that Congress had decided that there were too many American commissioners in Paris, overlapping their duties, and that therefore Dr. Franklin had been appointed sole Minister Plenipotentiary for France. Vergennes sighed with relief and smiled broadly. He planned to give Lee and Adams a sumptuous farewell sendoff, just as soon as passage could be arranged.

The departure of John Adams was as fraught with difficulties and complaints as his stay had been. By then he and the French detested each other, an unhappy situation that would create trouble for Franklin later, when peace negotiations began in Paris. Franklin was already under fire back in the Congress, as Gérard reported to Vergennes. Franklin had backed Deane against Lee, but, in addition, had been almost unbelievably negligent in correspondence with the Congress. It had not been his fault in 1777, when the British Navy intercepted his letters, but from the fall of 1778 on, Franklin rarely bothered to send a report to Philadelphia. His failure to correspond was considered by many, including his friends and admirers, to be close to a contempt of Congress.

John Adams took his resentments home with him, to fuel the "Junto" in their complaints. He was convinced that he was being harassed by Franklin and Vergennes when his departure plans were delayed. He had made his official farewells in mid-March, and been told that passage had been obtained for him on the *Alliance,* leaving at the end of April. He arrived on board the sloop, installed himself in his cabin, on April 22, expecting to set sail the next day, but the captain told him that he was not yet ready. There were stores to be loaded and he was expecting important mail pouches and some crew replacements. Adams went into town to meet with local personalities and reported, in his diary: "The Zeal, the Ardor, the Enthusiasm, the Rage for the new American Connection, I find is much damped among the Merchants since the Loss of so many of the East and West India ships."

After waiting impatiently for a week, Adams, on the morning of Wednesday, April 28, received a letter from Franklin, enclosing another letter from the Minister of the Navy. Sartine informed him that the *Alliance* had been transferred to Lorient, to join a naval squadron commanded by John Paul Jones. Adams would have to change ships and sail on one of the King's frigates. However, Sartine added, this would be an advantage since the Chevalier de La Luzerne would be aboard to take up his new duties as a replacement for Gérard, who was ill and had to return home. Franklin, in his letter, told Adams that the bigger, better-armed royal frigate was a safer ship than the *Alliance,* and that Luzerne would be an important and amiable fellow passenger.

Adams grumbled at the inconvenience and then grew angrier as time passed without Luzerne's arrival in port. He scribbled furiously in his diary, mainly diatribes against Franklin. He even included attacks delivered by others, such as the clergyman Hezekiah Ford: "I came to France with the highest opinions of Dr. F.," Ford had said, "as a Philosopher, a Statesman and as even the Pater Patriae. But, I assure you, Tempora Mutantur. He has very moderate abilities. He knows nothing of Philosophy, but his few experiments in electricity. He is an Atheist, he don't believe any future State. Yet he is terribly afraid of dying." Adams commented that this judgment was somewhat exaggerated. Franklin, he thought, was perhaps not an Atheist, but that some things he said might give rise to the suspicion. Moreover, Adams had never heard him say that there was a God. "It is too rank to say that he understands nothing of Philosophy but his own electrical experiments, altho' I don't think him so deeply read in Philosophy as his name impute." Spitefully, Adams added that Franklin devoted his time and thoughts to winning admirers, both men and women, and had an "insinuating way of charming the Women. . . . It is the most silly and ridiculous way imaginable in the sight of an American."

By May 12 Adams had become convinced that everyone was plotting against him. "It is decreed that I shall endure all Sorts of Mortifications. There is so much Insolence and Contempt in the Appearance of this. Do I see that these People despize me, or do I see that they dread me? Can I bear Contempt—to know that I am despized?"

At last, after over a month, the Chevalier de La Luzerne arrived and, on June 12, invited Adams and his son, John Quincy, to dine with him. (To Adams' chagrin, young John Quincy was a devotee of Franklin's. The old man loved children and knew how to relate to them. He had seen John Quincy off, and the boy wrote him letters, calling him "My dear friend.") Luzerne, noting Adams' temper, well informed by Vergennes of all the jealousies and enmities inside the American camp, went out of his way to flatter and cajole Adams, with whom he knew he would have to deal in Philadelphia. Adams sopped up the flattery and was overjoyed when he heard Luzerne say, in a dinner conversation, that Franklin spoke French badly, with an abominable accent. Another dinner guest, according to Adams, said that there was something of the charlatan in Franklin, that he was not a great statesman and that Congress might recall him at any moment. He added that Adams, not having been officially recalled, should not have returned. Adams said he could not stay without a portfolio, since Franklin had been named sole Minister Plenipotentiary.

Franklin could easily have guessed what Adams was saying and writing about him, but he was too relieved to be rid of him to worry about it. Besides, he still had on his hands the brothers William and Arthur Lee, commissioned to Berlin and Madrid but unable to leave, for those courts would not recognize American independence; also Ralph Izard of South Carolina, uninvited to the court of Tuscany. As Adams himself had noted, they were hot-tempered men who could raise quarrels in Heaven.

On receiving his appointment as sole envoy to France, Franklin had asked Arthur Lee to give him the public papers in his file. Lee insolently replied that he had no papers belonging to Franklin—what he had were the papers of the Joint Commission. Franklin patiently pointed out that the Joint Commission had been dissolved. No matter, said Lee, these were his papers and he would need them to prove to Congress his own rectitude in these affairs. He haughtily offered to provide Franklin with copies if he insisted. Franklin politely agreed to accept copies. He went even further and offered to give Lee any papers he thought necessary for his defense. Lee said he would let Franklin know.

It was a full year before Congress finally gave up on the missions of the Lees and Izard and recalled them, in March, 1780. Franklin noted: "No soul regrets their departure." He wrote a confidential letter to his friend Joseph Reed, in Philadelphia, warning him about Lee: "I caution you to beware of him; for, in sowing suspicions and jealousies, in creating misunderstandings and quarrels, in malice, subtility, and indefatigable industry, he has, I think, no equal."

For the moment, Franklin was on his own, with his grandson Temple as his sole trusted aide.

CHAPTER

17

Intrigues in Europe

While Vergennes was trying to deal with his difficult American allies, he was nervously watching events in Central Europe, and trying still to cajole Spain into an alliance against England. Spain was the main target of his diplomacy, but it was vitally necessary to have peace and quiet on the European Continent to be able to devote France's energies to the war with England.

The armies of Joseph II and Frederick the Great had gone through an intricate series of maneuvers all through the fall, like two fighters testing each other and sparring for an opening. No battles were fought as they marched, wheeled, threatened, bluffed and then pulled away on each side. They had then gone into winter quarters, giving Vergennes a chance for diplomacy to end the war.

Vergennes did not want either side to win, for both were dangerous neighbors. He therefore proposed that France mediate the dispute. At the same time, he instructed his envoy in Turkey to help arrange a truce with Russia, which freed Catherine for a role in Europe. She promptly mobilized 25,000 troops in Poland, sending a demand to Vienna that Austria accept the French proposal for mediation before the war spread through all Europe. Joseph II capitulated and agreed to a mediation based upon his holding only a small part of Bavaria, near his own frontiers. The war ended with the Peace of Teschen, in May, 1779, a triumph for Vergennes's diplomacy.

The treaty removed both the Austrian and Prussian menace and restored France's traditional role as arbiter of European affairs. It laid the foundation of a new rapprochement for France with Russia and Prussia, and enabled Vergennes to pursue his aim of creating a bloc of neutral nations to combine in demanding freedom of the seas, under an Armed Neutrality Pact, thus reducing Britain's power to blockade or interfere with European shipping. It had the disadvantage of angering Joseph II, who would await his opportunity to pay France back with a mediation maneuver of his own in the war with England. At the moment, however, France had averted serious threats and had won the continental peace she needed.

Throughout these complex negotiations, Vergennes was carrying on his campaign to win over Spain. He told Floridablanca that if he joined in a successful war on England, he could assure the security of the seas for the Spanish fleet and also secure the future of Spain's colonies in North America, which might be endangered by an Anglo-American reconciliation or even by the United States alone, if victorious over England. Floridablanca's interests still centered on Gibraltar and Minorca. He thought that he might persuade England to return those territories to Spain as the price of Spanish neutrality in the war. They loomed more important in his view than the colony in Florida. He would first try to get his way by diplomacy, and, if that failed, there would be time enough to join the war and exact a promise from France to help conquer Gibraltar and Minorca, as the price of his alliance. One way or the other, he meant to win back what he called "that pile of stones." By March of 1779 Floridablanca learned that peace was being arranged between Prussia and Austria. At the same time, his merchant ships and treasure fleet had safely crossed the Atlantic and were in Spanish ports. All his flanks were secured, so he sent an ultimatum to London to accept his offer of mediation. Meanwhile he was busily negotiating with Vergennes the terms of an alliance against England that would reconfirm and strengthen the Bourbon Family Compact.

The Spanish ultimatum was delivered to the British Ambassador in Madrid on April 3, 1779. The terms included: a truce between France and Britain to last indefinitely, which could be ended only on one year's notice by either side; mutual disarmament, within one month in Europe, within four months in America, within a year in Africa and Asia; a peace conference to be held in Madrid, under the mediation of Spain. There would be an armed truce with the American colonies which could not be broken without a one-year advance notice to the King of Spain. The American colonies were to be recognized de facto as independent during the course of the negotiations.

Floridablanca was not the least concerned about American independence; indeed, he opposed it. But the granting of temporary independence on a de facto basis did not commit him in the long run, and served mainly to make it impossible for England to accept his mediation. If England was willing to grant independence to America, it could do so directly and on far better terms than through Madrid. His proposal did offer England some real advantages. It would end a costly, unpopular war, leaving George III in possession of New York, Long Island, Rhode Island, parts of the northwest territories and most of the colony of Georgia; and the rest of America in an uncertain truce, its future to be decided at a peace conference presided over by an unfriendly Spain. If George III had accepted, he would have put America and France in a painful dilemma. France could not refuse to go along with a Spanish mediation without weakening, perhaps severing, the Family Compact. If France went along, America in turn could not refuse without breaking the French alliance. England could use Spain's intrigue and exploit it with diplomatic skill to the discomfiture of its enemies.

A Pitt could have exploited to the full all the opportunities of the Spanish maneuver. A North and a Weymouth lacked the subtlety or authority to persuade the proud, obstinate British King. Weymouth, the Foreign Secretary, told the Spanish Ambassador that Britain would not accept the ultimatum, and would never give up Gibraltar. By clinging to his rock, George III assured the permanent loss of America.

Expecting the British rejection, Floridablanca had concluded a new, secret convention with France. It was signed at Aranjuez, Spain's summer court, on April 12, only nine days after the ultimatum had been issued, and before Britain had even rejected it. It was ratified at Versailles on April 28. Anticipating England's rejection, it provided that Spain would enter the war on the side of France. It agreed to coordinate military and naval operations, including plans for a joint invasion of England. Neither side would enter into separate peace talks without consultation with the other and no treaty or agreement with England could be concluded except by mutual consent. In a clause whose absolute secrecy was particularly underlined, France promised to fight along with Spain to conquer Gibraltar. This indirectly involved the Americans without their even being informed.

Vergennes tried to insert a clause that would prohibit the end of hostilities unless American independence was realized. He had already signed such a clause in the American alliance, but Floridablanca would have none of it. He accepted only an innocuous, ambiguous reference to American independence that was not binding on Spain. Vergennes was so anxious to get Spain into the war that he backed down on this vital clause, a concession clearly incompatible with his promises to America. He had seriously altered and extended the alliance's war and peace terms, not only without America's consent, but without even its knowledge. He certainly did not intend to betray the United States, as his subsequent actions proved, but he was a desperate man, convinced that Spain was needed to beat England. Still, he was bartering away pledges made to America and involving America in European politics. This act and other European intrigues that would follow provoked an American determination to avoid in the future all entangling alliances. American isolationism was rooted deeply in European politics of the Revolutionary period.

Spanish ships began joint operations in the Atlantic in May, and on June 21, 1779, Spain formally declared war on Great Britain. In the period from spring, 1778, to summer, 1779, America had won two of the most powerful nations in the world as allies. Unaware of the intrigues behind the scene, Americans rejoiced. If

Britain could not defeat America alone, how could she hope to defeat America, France and Spain together?

During the period of maneuvers, Spain had been advancing modest credits to the United States through Arthur Lee. Although Lee was accredited as envoy to Spain by the Congress, Madrid refused to receive him, preferring to deal with him through private correspondents. This obviated the need to recognize America. From 1776 through 1779, Spain had given the United States, in secret subsidies, something under a half-million dollars. Loans would be arranged later, but in very small amounts. France remained virtually the sole backer of the United States.

Although Spain's main interest was Gibraltar, Floridablanca never took his eye off another important Spanish concern: the Mississippi River and the territories to the west, from Louisiana to Mexico, a source of vast and potential treasure. The question of navigation on the Mississippi had been settled in the Peace of 1763, imposed by England, granting Britain the right to use the river. But Spain kept putting up legal and physical barriers by refusing landing rights and mooring rights on Spanish colonial territory there. Spain used the outbreak of war between America and England as a further pretext to impede navigation on the Mississippi.

Although refusing diplomatic relations with the United States, Madrid needed eyes and ears in the American capital. A Cuban merchant, Don Juan de Miralles, was sent as an "observer" to Philadelphia and to the headquarters of General Washington, who tolerated him in the hope of receiving more Spanish aid. Miralles reported that Congress was talking about a number of schemes for settling the Ohio and Mississippi valleys. Navigation of the river was becoming an important issue. Spain opposed any American territorial expansion to or beyond the Mississippi. Thus the question of navigation and the issue of boundaries were interlaced and would prove to be of paramount importance when the peace negotiations began in earnest.

Vergennes sent messages to Madrid pledging that he would instruct Gérard, then still in Philadelphia, to defend Spanish interests in the United States but at the same time told Gérard to convince the Americans that France was unqualifiedly supportive of American independence and would make no peace with England until that independence had been recognized by the British. When Spain first proposed mediation, Vergennes had sent an urgent note to Gérard asking him to get the Congress to appoint a peace commissioner to cooperate with him in the event that Britain accepted Spanish overtures. Gérard presented this proposal to the Congress on February 15 and set off a factional debate, involving the principal personalities of Congress, that would last through most of 1779.

Meanwhile, the tides of battle in America were swirling over the entire Eastern half of the continent, like small whirlpools in a vast sea. No conclusive major battles were fought anywhere, but dozens of clashes took place from Maine to Georgia and inland to the posts and forts in the Illinois territory. Nor did relations between American and French soldiers and sailors improve after the signing of the alliance in the spring of 1778.

The British under Clinton evacuated Philadelphia in June, and Washington harassed the retreating troops. Lafayette, in an earlier action, had had his unit almost surrounded by ten thousand British troops, but by keeping his head managed to escape from the trap. Washington congratulated him, but he felt humiliated, for a successful evasion is hardly a victory. The French had as yet provided no victories on land or at sea.

George Rogers Clark, with a small force of only 175 men, set out in May from Kentucky territory for an expedition into Illinois, where there were French outposts. By July he had learned that the French were at war with England and he persuaded the French officers at Kaskaskia to join his command. A French priest, Father Pierre Gibault, said he could also win over his parish, at Vincennes, Illinois. A British expeditionary force left Detroit to attack Vincennes, which had, as the priest promised, joined the American side. But, when the British attacked, the French failed to fight and ran up the white flag of surrender. Learning of this, Clark sent his troops on a surprise attack, overrunning the garrison and recapturing the fort surrendered by the French.

Units of the British fleet loaded 3,500 troops in New York to carry an expeditionary force to Savannah, for an invasion of Georgia. As the year 1778 drew to a close, they captured Savannah and then, in January, 1779, Augusta. Washington sent General Benjamin Lincoln to Savannah to counterattack, with about 2,500 men. Units of Lincoln's forces caught British units in an island off South Carolina and defeated them, while others attacked at Kettle Creek, Georgia, inflicting heavy casualties on a British force. Then Lincoln attacked and recaptured Augusta. The British routed the Americans and reoccupied the city. Similar actions were taking place in Maine, around Penobscot Bay, each side taking, losing, retaking its objectives. Washington's meager forces were being slowly eroded, their arms expended. They were short of everything and most particularly clothing and blankets.

Franklin tried time and time again to get action from Vergennes, but the Foreign Minister was so involved with his maneuvers in the War of the Bavarian Succession and his diplomatic ploys with Floridablanca of Spain that he did little to answer Franklin's pleas. Franklin got new and important help later in 1779, when the Marquis de Lafayette returned to France.

Lafayette had been recalled at the time that Sartine was working on his plan for an amphibious invasion of England, with John Paul Jones to lead the naval task force and Lafayette the assault troops. Lafayette and Jones were both disappointed when the King canceled the plan and decided to assign Jones alone to naval raids. Franklin, in the middle of all the planning, was particularly concerned about the behavior of commando forces. He sent Jones a warning: "Although the British have wantonly burned many defenceless towns in America, you are not to follow this example, unless when reasonable ransom is refused; in which case your own generous feelings, as well as this instruction, will induce you to give timely notice of your intention, that sick and ancient persons, women and children, may be first removed." Jones replied: "The letter that I had the honour to receive from you today, would make a coward brave."

Franklin was besieged with problems involving American

crews. On June 2, 1779, he sent a letter to the Marine Committee of Congress, apprising them of the contentious nature of naval operations.

I received the honour of yours by the Marquis de Lafayette, who arrived safe and well in the Alliance frégatte which you were pleased to put under my orders. There had been a conspiracy on board to seize and run away with the ship to England. Thirty-eight of the crew concerned in the plot were brought in under confinement, and the captain was much embarrassed with them and suspicious of many more. We could not try them here for want of officers sufficient to make a court-martial. The French Admiralty could not take cognizance of their offence. The captain objected to carrying them back, as both troublesome and dangerous. In fine, we got leave to land and confine them in a French prison, where they continue till further orders. . . .

As our ships-of-war that arrive here require an amazing expense to outfit them, and the prizes they bring in often occasion law suits and all the embarrassment and solicitation and vexation attending suits in this country, I must beg the Committee would be so good as to order the several Navy Boards to send no more to be outfitted here without sending effects to defray the expense; add that, if our armed ships should be still ordered to cruise in these seas, a consul or consuls may be appointed in the several seaports, who will thereby be more on hand to transact maritime business expeditiously, will understand it better, relieve your Minister at this Court from a great deal of trouble, and leave him at liberty to attend affairs of more general importance.

Congress, always ready to criticize Franklin for not writing more reports, paid little attention to those he did send, particularly his supplications for more aid. It was more prone to send over high-level, proud and temperamental men than the workaday consuls and naval administration experts that Franklin pleaded for. And, instead of sending him money for these extraordinary naval expenses, it sent him drafts on his accounts and pleas for more loans, subsidies and supplies.

Lafayette stayed on in France, before returning to America, to lobby at court for more aid. Franklin also had help from Leray de Chaumont and the chemist Lavoisier. They were all involved in complex and elaborate arrangements for purchases of clothing, saltpeter, naval stores, munitions and money to pay for these supplies. Franklin succeeded in obtaining another advance of three million livres, although Congress had asked him for the vast sum of fourteen million. The French Treasury was being drained by American loans and the costs of expanding the French Army and Navy for the war with England.

Franklin had first met Lavoisier, the father of modern chemistry, in the summer of 1778. Lavoisier had been appointed Director of the Gunpowder Arsenal, and was also a member of the Farmers-General, thus a very important man for Franklin to win over. A mutual friend had mentioned to him that Franklin might be willing to help in designing new blastproof and fireproof warehouses for the royal gunpowder and saltpeter stores. In August, 1778, Lavoisier sent Franklin a most friendly letter, thanking him for his willingness to take time from so many other duties to help him with his designs. He invited Franklin and his grandson to dine with the Lavoisiers, and a new and valuable friendship flowered for Franklin.

All through the difficult, frustrating first year of the alliance, Vergennes kept Franklin generally informed of the course of diplomatic events, although he did conceal from him the secret clauses in the arrangements with Spain. Franklin was by then completely attuned to European politics and intrigues. But he had set himself the principle of not nagging at Vergennes. Vergennes was his trump card at Versailles. He could not risk losing it.

In the meantime he dined frequently with the Duc de Croy and other noblemen. He maintained and strengthened his contacts with the Freemasons' lodge, over which he now presided. He went frequently to meetings of the Academy of Science and the Royal Academy of Medicine. He kept up a constant correspondence with French men and women throughout the nation. At one point, he received an appeal, addressed to "the Apostle of Liberty," from a French galley slave who volunteered to fight in America if he could win his freedom. Franklin sent the letter to Vergennes, who passed it, through channels, on up to the King. The King, receiving a report that the prisoner had toiled in the galleys for fourteen years with an unblemished record of good behavior, set him free, in honor of Dr. Franklin. Franklin also received letters from a young student of chemistry, who appealed for his help in presenting his ideas to the Academy of Science. Franklin intervened for him. The student's name was Marat. Many years later, Franklin heard from a young lawyer who had tried a case against the community of Saint-Omer, which had promulgated an ordinance prohibiting the use of lightning rods. The young lawyer was Robespierre.

Nothing escaped Franklin's attention and interest. In November, 1778, he attended a party given by a man named Parmentier, who had become obsessed with the idea that the potato would wipe out all danger of famine in the land and be the salvation of French agriculture. French farmers, who had become convinced that potatoes caused leprosy, would not plant them. Parmentier thought that if he could get famous men to eat potatoes it would dispel the ignorant superstition. He ground flour out of potatoes and baked it into bread, inviting Franklin to his potato party. Franklin came, loved the bread and spread the word. Franklin later attended a full-course banquet, with every dish and drink made of potatoes. Served at dinners given by Franklin's noble friends, the potato soon became chic. Peasants began stealing potatoes from Parmentier's experimental fields and the potato was launched in France. (Parmentier, himself, has lived on in immortality in two French dishes: potage Parmentier, France's staple potato soup, and hachis Parmentier, a hash of chopped, leftover meats, covered with a layer of mashed potatoes and baked in a clay dish.)

At the close of the first year of the alliance, a year of indecision on all fronts, on December 20, 1778, a cannon boomed over Paris. Queen Marie Antoinette had given birth to a girl at 11:30 in the morning. The King ordered a free distribution of wine and bread. The Corps de Ville paraded around a bonfire. All public buildings were illuminated at night, and then, at the Place de l'Hôtel de Ville, a second distribution was made, of wine, bread and headcheese sausage. The people rejoiced while whispering it was a pity it was not a boy. At Passy and Auteuil Franklin's friends gave a series of receptions and planned great parties for the Christmas and New Year's holidays.

Franklin knew how bad the American situation was, but he had his duties to perform. He was carrying on his own political intrigues in that year of intrigue in Europe, 1779. He tried hard to make influential contacts with those close to Marie Antoinette, whose brother, Joseph II, having been frustrated in his attempt to seize Bavaria, launched a new intrigue to avenge himself and Austria. Shortly after the Peace of Teschen, Joseph proposed that he mediate in the war between France and England, ostensibly to express his "gratitude" to France for having arranged peace in Europe. In fact, he meant to pay France back and to forestall moves in the same direction by Frederick of Prussia and Catherine of Russia.

France and Spain told the Austrian Emperor that his proposal was inopportune. Vergennes, who had worked hard to establish himself as the arbiter of Europe, would not let the Austrian reverse roles. He also feared that Joseph would try to reduce French power in Europe by favoring the British. Britain did not reject the Austrian offer, but it became a dead letter when Paris and Madrid responded negatively. Britain never placed much trust in Vienna, preferring instead to seek an alliance with Russia. The British Ambassador worked hard to persuade Catherine of the advantages of an Anglo-Russian alliance.

The Czarina, at the height of her reign, a handsome, lusty woman Franklin would have enjoyed, had had a taste of the heady wine of peacemaking in her intervention that had resulted in the Treaty of Teschen. If she could extend her influence beyond Central Europe by mediating between France and England, she might pose as the protector of all Europe. When Sir James Harris, the British Ambassador, proposed an alliance, she countered with her own proposals to mediate peace. She also instructed the Russian Ambassador in Versailles to make the same proposals to Vergennes.

All the belligerents were suspicious of Catherine's moves. They had other plans in 1779. Britain still hoped to bring Catherine over to its side. Spain and France had only just concluded their own alliance. What they sought then was to persuade Catherine to join a bloc of armed neutrals to protect themselves against the British fleet. Every power in Europe was maneuvering for special advantage; none was yet ready for mediation. That would come later.

CHAPTER

18

Bad News on All Fronts

Franklin had foreseen a long period of bad news for the year 1779. He made his forecast on the basis of a manifesto promulgated by the British government toward the end of 1778, announcing "a change in the whole nature and future conduct of the war." To forewarn the French and put pressure upon them to pursue the war more vigorously, he sent a New Year's Day memorial to Vergennes:

> A change for the worse must be horrible indeed! . . . there seems to be no room for doubt that they mean to threaten something more cruel, greater extremes of war, measures that shall distress the people and lay waste the country more than anything they have yet done. The object of the war is now entirely changed. Heretofore, their massacres and conflagrations were to divide us and reclaim us to Great Britain. Now, despairing of that end, and perceiving that we shall be faithful to our treaties, their principle is, by destroying us, to make us useless to France. This principle ought to be held in abhorrence, not only by all Christians, but by all civilized nations. If it is once admitted that powers at war have a right to do whatever will weaken or terrify an enemy, it is not possible to foresee where it will end.

Franklin asked Vergennes to persuade the King to protest publicly in the name of humanity against Britain's cruelties and threats to wage total war against the people as well as against their armies. Then he came to the true purpose of his memorial:

> There is another measure, however, more effectual to control their designs and to bring the war to a speedy conclusion; that of sending a powerful fleet, sufficient to secure a naval superiority over them in the American seas. Such a naval force, acting in concert with the armies of the United States, would, in all human probability, take and destroy the whole British power in that part of the world. . . . It is obvious to all Europe that nothing less is at stake than the dominion of the sea, at least the superiority of naval power, and we cannot expect Great Britain will ever give it up, without some decisive effort on the part of France.

Franklin had hit upon the theme expounded by General Washington: the vital importance of sea power. Washington had become convinced that the war would be lost if the British maintained their absolute mastery of American waters. Franklin, no expert in military strategy, had come independently to the same conclusion. Vergennes would not fail to notice that Franklin made no reference to the fleet commanded by Admiral d'Estaing, already in American waters. Franklin's words "a powerful fleet, sufficient to secure a naval superiority" were a diplomatic way of saying that the d'Estaing fleet was not enough.

The French Admiral, after the fiasco of his failure at Newport, had sailed south to seek easier game in the West Indies. He raided small islands but could not challenge a large British force which had seized St. Lucia. He took to safe harbor in Cape François and decided to lay up there for the winter of 1778–79. But by late February he was surprised to receive instructions to leave Cape François and sail for Northern waters, to act in concert with the American land forces—exactly as Franklin had petitioned Vergennes.

D'Estaing was delighted with his orders. He was a brave and proud man. One of his officers later told superiors in Paris that it was a pity that d'Estaing's seamanship did not match his courage. He set about preparing his ships for war, strengthening every weak seam, training his men in action maneuvers, studying charts and maps of the American coast. He had twenty sail of the line, two battleships of fifty guns each, and eleven frigates—not the superior force Franklin had called for, but a considerable fleet which could give a good account of itself if skillfully commanded. Unfortunately, his preparations took much longer than they should have and he did not sail for American waters until the summer of 1779.

The war was accelerating in the spring and summer of that year. The British raided and burned villages throughout northern New England, in the vicious total-war campaign that Franklin had predicted. Washington diverted troops and sent General Sullivan on punitive attacks against the Six Nations Indian territory to retaliate for Indian atrocities. Sullivan razed some forty villages, destroying fields and orchards and a harvest of some 160,000 bushels of corn, and the American troops committed some of the same cruelties for which they castigated the British. It was an unwise action, for the Indians fled into the forests and then, when Sullivan had completed his campaign, returned to avenge their losses.

In June the Americans were encouraged by Spain's declaration of war against Britain, followed by a Spanish blockade of Gibraltar. Spain's help proved to be only indirect—Spain would never take a fully active role in the war except for purely Spanish interests—by drawing off some British strength to the Mediterranean. The siege of Gibraltar would last three years, draining all Spain's strength without ever breaching the British defenses. It ended finally with a crushing defeat of the Spanish fleet by the British. Spain broke her back on the rocks of Gibraltar and never recovered world power.

July of '79 saw two events that would prove to have an important effect upon the outcome of the war. In New York, Lord Cornwallis returned from a mission to England to become second-in-command to Sir Henry Clinton, and brought with him a plan for a decisive campaign to recapture the Southern colonies and split them off from the rest of the United States. In the North, out of one encounter in a series of battles—mostly defeats—a new-found confidence of American men in their own military valor and capability emerged.

On July 5, General William Tryon's raiders invaded and plundered New Haven. Then, in rapid succession, British troops raided, looted and burned Fairfield, East Haven and Norwalk, which was virtually burned to the ground on July 11. Four days later, infuriated and inspired American forces struck back in an assault on Stony Point, a fortification on the west bank of the Hudson which the British had occupied without resistance on the first of June. General Anthony Wayne won himself the nickname of "Mad Anthony" when he led a series of "suicide squads" and offered cash prizes to the first men to break into the fort. The battle was furious and swift, lasting less than an hour. Fifteen Americans were killed, and 80 wounded, against 63 British killed, 75 wounded and 543 taken prisoner. It was a rare and bloody triumph in a direct assault on a British fortified position, featuring repeated bayonet charges by the Americans against British regulars, reputed to be the world's fiercest cold-steel fighters. The psychological effect of this hand-to-hand victory over the world's best soldiers boosted American morale in one of the darkest periods of the war. "Mad Anthony's" feat was rivaled a month later, on August 19, by another brave, almost foolhardy young American officer, Major Henry "Light-Horse Harry" Lee. Lee led a force of 350 men in a surprise attack on the British garrison at Paulus Hook, opposite New York. He overran the garrison, killed 50 and captured 158 British prisoners.

But these were brief flashes of American lightning in a stormy British sky. Just two days after Light-Horse Harry's triumph, an American naval expedition, carrying commando troops, sailed from Boston headed for an assault on a British fort commanding Penobscot Bay, in Maine. The commander of the joint operation decided to land his men near the British positions and build a fort for a central base of operations. Army and navy officers bickered over tactics and strategy and held endless councils of war, thus giving the British all the time they needed to prepare for the battle. When the time came, it was the British who held the initiative, with a well-planned land and sea attack upon the divided American forces. It was a slaughter and a fiasco. As many as 500 Americans were lost in the battle. Almost 20 of the 37-ship American fleet were destroyed by Admiral Sir George Collier, and the remaining American forces had to flee overland. Two American officers accused of negligence, Dudley Saltonstall and Paul Revere, were subsequently court-martialed.

When the bad news arrived in Paris in the fall, things already were worsening on the American battle fronts. Franklin had troubles enough within his own sphere of responsibilities, particularly money. He wrote that he felt as though he were drawing water for all the tribes of Israel. Congress sent him drafts upon the French which it spent before he even had time to get them honored. Frequently they were not answered at all and debts accumulated, seriously affecting American credit. The value of paper money deteriorated so rapidly that it was impossible to know what the next campaign would cost and Washington's staff could not begin to estimate military budgets.

As Americans were bloodied on land and sea, they were being bankrupted in the marketplace. Congress decided, in an act of desperation, to stop issuing money altogether. On September 3, 1779, it set a limit of $200 million beyond which all circulation emissions would cease. On that date $160 million had already been issued, leaving only the narrowest of margins for federal money. At the current rate of expenditure it would last at most for a few weeks; then there would be no means left to support the war.

The crisis brought about a drastic solution that would have long-range consequences for American history. The issuance of paper money by a central federal authority had given Congress the power to assume the main burdens of the war and all national life as it then existed. Now, with the decline of paper money, power and responsibility would devolve upon the states, strengthening the doctrine of states' rights and the sovereignty of the individual states within the federal system.

Ben Franklin understood the use of paper currency and the devices of various devaluations better than most men of his time. He wrote to Samuel Cooper of the Congress at the moment of currency crisis, to note, with some irony: "This Currency, as we manage it, is a wonderful Machine. It performs its Office when we issue it; it pays and clothes Troops, and provides Victuals and Ammunition; and when we are obliged to issue a Quantity excessive, it pays itself off by Depreciation." But there were limits to such manipulations, particularly outside national boundaries, where paper money did not have the magic properties it possessed within the country. More and more, European bankers and traders demanded merchandise, and would accept no form of payment except gold, which America did not have. Franklin could not cope with the demands either of Congress or of his fellow American commissioners. He had constant difficulties with Arthur Lee and Ralph Izard, later with John Adams and John Jay.

Very early in 1779, he wrote to Izard to refuse him funds he had requested to pay his living expenses:

> Your intimation that you expect more money from us obliges us to expose to you our circumstances. Upon the supposition that Congress had borrowed in America but five millions of dollars, or twenty-five millions of livres, and relying on the remittances intended to be sent to us for answering other demands, we gave expectations that we should be able to pay here the interest of that sum, as a means of supporting the credit of the currency. The Congress have borrowed near twice that sum, and are now actually drawing upon us for the interest, the bills appear here daily for acceptance. Their distress for money in America has been so great, from the enormous expense of the war, that they have also been induced to draw on us for very large sums to stop other pressing demands.

Franklin continued in a tone rare for him, bordering on tartness:

> In this situation of our affairs we hope you will not insist on our giving you a further credit with our banker, with whom we are daily in danger of having no further credit ourselves. It is not a year since you received from us the sum of two thousand guineas, which you thought necessary on account of your being [about] to set out immediately for Florence. You have not incurred the expense of that journey. You are a gentleman of fortune. You did not come to France with any dependence on being

maintained here with your family at the expense of the United States in the time of their distress, and without rendering them the equivalent service they expected. On all these considerations, we should rather hope that you would be willing to reimburse us the sum we have advanced you, if it may be done with any possible convenience to your affairs. Such a supply would at least enable us to relieve more liberally our unfortunate countrymen, who have long been prisoners, stripped of everything, of whom we daily expect to have near three hundred upon our hands by the exchange.

The exchange to which Franklin referred was a matter of great satisfaction and pride to him. He had been working diligently and patiently for more than a year, from his first letter to Lord Stormont, to effect exchanges of American and British prisoners. His efforts had finally paid off.

Izard, already furious with Franklin for having excluded him from the negotiations on the French alliance—which were none of his concern or responsibility—promptly went to see Arthur Lee and John Adams, who agreed that he ought to have his money. With that backing, he then wrote to Congress to protest Franklin's refusal, attributing it meanly and incorrectly to the personal quarrels he had had with Franklin. He called this "an evil that requires an immediate remedy," and stated that disagreements inside the commission were lamentable and endangered the American cause. Izard's design, which to some extent succeeded, was to feed the opposition to Franklin in Congress and to effect his recall; the letter was circulated throughout the opposition clique.

Izard's complaint came at the wrong time for him, in a Congress on the verge of losing its principal money-issuing powers. Congress finally exceeded the limit it had set itself and was obliged to ask the states to provide what they could in the way of the actual goods, food and services needed by the armed forces. This new system had many advantages. Government purchasing agents had created severe inflation of prices. The states now had the power to bypass the marketplace by direct commodity requisitions in the form of produce taxes rather than currency levies. This served to reduce Continental currency in circulation and tended toward increasing its value, in addition to eliminating a great deal of the waste, corruption and fraud inherent in any large-scale central purchasing system. Later, in 1780, Congress extended the system by asking the states to take over the payrolls of the soldiers recruited from their territories. This helped reduce federal debt but further weakened the authority of the federal government, and gave strength to the advocates of states' rights and a confederal rather than a federal system.

In Paris, Franklin maintained his social round. He saw Madame Brillon and Madame Helvétius twice a week, sometimes more frequently. He gave and accepted invitations to dinner. He held a big party in Passy to celebrate the Fourth of July. Adrienne Lafayette, wife of the Marquis, came to the party, bringing greetings from him along with a proposal he was making to the government to put George Washington's portrait on display throughout France on every Fourth of July.

With the news of military setbacks that reached Paris came news of some minor yet welcome successes. Admiral d'Estaing had captured the island of Grenada. To celebrate the victory, Paris hairdressers had created a coiffure called "L'Amiral," featuring a frigate in full sail, in miniature, atop the hair, and another, called "Grenada," a concoction of pomegranates and imitation tropical flowers. One of the leading coiffeurs warned that these extravagant hairdresses, requiring many metal hairpins, were destructive of the hair. He proposed more braiding, and created the first tiny, lace-and-flower hats to be placed on the very top of the coiffure and kept in place by silk ribbons tied under the chin. The hat became the rage of Paris. Franklin pronounced it charming and told his lady friends that the hairdresser was right: metal pins did split and break the hair. They all agreed to do as he counseled.

Franklin became very fond of the French people. Not that he would have approved their way of life for America; when his daughter Sally wrote to ask him for lace and feathers for a new ball dress, he sharply rebuked her, saying that lace and feathers might be fine at the court in Paris but not in America at war. If you want lace, he wrote Sally, wear your cotton until it tatters and it will look lacy; if you want feathers, there are plenty of chickens in the barnyard—pluck them yourself. Franklin, a libertine abroad, was always a prude with his own family.

He wrote his friend Josiah Quincy in April of 1779, to tell him how happy he was among the French.

> The Spaniards are, by common opinion, supposed to be cruel, the English proud, the Scotch insolent, the Dutch avaricious, etc., but I think the French have no national vice ascribed to them. They have some frivolities, but they are harmless. . . . They are only the effects of the tyranny of custom. In short, there is nothing wanting in the character of a Frenchman that belongs to that of an agreeable and worthy man.

In October of that year he wrote to Elizabeth Partridge, his stepniece in Boston, to answer a sly note in her earlier letter about the French ladies being very "kind" to her Uncle Ben:

> I must explain that matter. This is the civilist nation upon earth. Your first acquaintances endeavour to find out what you like, and they tell others. If 'tis understood that you like mutton, dine where you will you find mutton. Somebody, it seems, gave it out that I loved ladies; and then everybody presented me their ladies (or the ladies presented themselves) to be embraced; that is, have their necks kissed. As for the kissing of lips or cheeks, it is not the mode here; the first is reckoned rude, and the other may rub off the paint. The French ladies have, however, a thousand other ways of rendering themselves agreeable by their various attentions and civilities and their sensible conversation.

Franklin's France was not representative of the nation, living unwittingly in the last years of the monarchy. His world was the artificial world of Versailles and the high society of Paris, a world of princes, dukes, great merchants, scientists and musicians. The old aristocracy of bloodlines and the new aristocracy of merchants and landowners lived in luxury, while workers and peasants lived in filth and misery. Franklin saw none of this, for it was not his business to see it. He never forgot that America's survival depended upon the ruling classes, not the masses. A dedicated democrat and republican, Franklin played the royal game because he had to—just as his friend Vergennes, a dedicated royalist, supported the world's most radical republic.

Americans who did not live under the imperatives that governed Franklin saw the other France. One, who became a good friend, was an intelligent, keen-eyed young observer, Elkanah Watson, a young entrepreneur who came to France in September, 1779, to make his fortune as a trader.

After landing, Watson rode a mule from dockside to the office of the American Consul and was astonished to hear a large crowd cheer "les Bostonès." For the French, all Americans were Bostonians. He was surprised by the narrow, dirty streets of the ancient city of La Rochelle, but delighted by his first feather bed, in the inn: "It was not without an effort that I reached the soft summit."

On September 12, Elkanah Watson arrived at the gates of Paris, "the capital of the world, as the Parisians assert." The roads on the way, he found, were excellent, ornamented near the towns by vistas of trees. "From Dreux to Paris, a distance of fifty miles, the roads are paved. The country is beautiful and luxuriant. Venerable Roman towers—Gothic cathedrals—noblemen's seats—and flourishing towns and villages, all conspired to give animation and interest to our journey." But entering the capital region of one of the world's richest and most powerful nations, Watson was shocked by what he saw: "Every village and town swarmed with vociferous beggars. Every hill seemed occupied with its droves of paupers and vagrants, ready to assault the traveler as he ascends it."

In a small village near Paris, Watson had seen "a little host of dwarf beggars, in rags, and most loathsome in appearance, all demanding, in a vociferous chorus, 'La Charité! La Charité!,' and, with tattered hats and capes, pressing up to my very face. The labor of the field was performed by a degraded and ignorant peasantry, the tenants of the nobles and the clergy who held two-thirds of the soil of France."

Watson called immediately upon Dr. Franklin to inform him that he was carrying dispatches for the Comte de Vergennes. Franklin gave him a letter to Vergennes and Watson was off to Versailles. Vergennes's secretary thanked him for the dispatches and escorted the young American to the Royal Chapel, where the King and Queen were coming to prayer. "The King's person was somewhat robust, with a full face, Roman nose and placid countenance. The

Queen had an elegant person, a fine figure, and imposing aspect, and florid complexion, with bright, gray eyes, full of expression."

Young Watson was then invited to dinner the next day, with Franklin.

This was the first occasion of my dining in a private circle in Europe, and, being still in my American style of dress, and ignorant of the French language, and prepared for extreme ceremony, I felt exceedingly embarrassed.

We entered a spacious room, I following the Doctor, where several well-dressed persons (to my unsophisticated American eyes, gentlemen) bowed to us profoundly. These were servants. A folding-door opened at our approach, and presented to my view a brilliant assembly who all greeted the wise, old man in the most cordial and affectionate manner. He introduced me as a young American just arrived. One of the young ladies approached him with the familiarity of a daughter, tapped him kindly on the cheek, and called him "Pa-Pa Franklin."

At the table, the ladies and gentlemen were mingled together, and joined in cheerful conversation, each selecting the delicacies of various courses, and drinking of delicious light wines, but with neither toasts nor healths.

The lady of the house, instead of bearing the burden and inconvenience of superintending the duties of the table, here participates alike with others in its enjoyment. No gentleman, I was told, would be tolerated in France in monopolizing the conversation of the table, in discussions of politics or religion, as is frequently the case in America.

Watson was enraptured by the charm of the French, the beauty of Paris and the extraordinary fame and regard the French accorded Franklin.

In a gallery of paintings in the Louvre, I was much gratified in perceiving the portrait of Franklin near those of the King and the Queen, placed there as a mark of distinguished respect, in conformity with royal directions. Few foreigners have been presented in the Court of St. Cloud who have acquired so much popularity and influence as Dr. Franklin. I have seen the populace attending his carriage in the manner they followed the King's. His venerable figure, the ease of his manners, formed in an intercourse of fifty years with the world, his benevolent countenance, and his fame as a philosopher, all tended to excite love and to command influence and respect. He had attained by the exercise of these qualities a powerful interest in the feelings of the beautiful Queen of France. She, at that time, held a strong political influence. The exercise of that influence, adroitly directed by Franklin, tended to produce the acknowledgement of our Independence, and the subsequent efficient measures pursued by France in its support. . . .

The public mind was highly elated by the belief that a combined French and Spanish fleet of seventy-six sail, under d'Orvillier, was blockading the British fleet in Plymouth, and that sixty thousand troops had assembled in the vicinity of Havre to cooperate with the fleet in the invasion of England. Under all these favorable aspects, no one doubted but that the British fleet, at least, would be annihilated. But, alas!, the Ardent, of sixty-four guns, was captured and the combined fleet returned into Brest, with eight thousand of their crews sick. I confess my spirit of retaliation was gratified, in noticing, in the English papers, accounts of the alarm excited by these movements on the coast of England, and of the inhabitants seeking security in the interior. Such spectacles of distress I had often witnessed in America, when the people were fleeing from the violence and cruelty of England's hireling armies.

While Paris was learning about the defeat of the Franco-Spanish combined fleet in English waters, another disaster was in the making for the French and the Americans in America. The only good news in that black period was the encounter, on September 23, of Captain John Paul Jones's squadron with an armed convoy off Flamborough Head. In his flagship, the *Bonhomme Richard,* Jones attacked the British flagship, the battleship *Serapis.* It was a prolonged, violent duel, each ship scoring direct hits on the other. When the *Serapis'* commander saw flames sweep Jones's ship fore and aft, he called upon Jones to strike his colors, to which John Paul replied: "I have not yet begun to fight." The duel lasted three and a half hours. The *Serapis,* badly hit, most of her crew dead or wounded, signaled surrender, just in time, for the *Bonhomme Richard* was sinking, and the victor, John Paul Jones, just barely managed to get his crew aboard the *Serapis,* leaving his ship to sink in triumph, more than half its crew dead or wounded. It was the one great American naval victory of the war, coinciding with a series of disastrous defeats that followed early in October.

Admiral d'Estaing's raiding operations in the West Indies, and the presence there of his large fleet, had worried the British and prevented their plan for major operations in the Southern colonies. Governor John Rutledge of South Carolina persuaded General Benjamin Lincoln that there was an opportunity for a surprise sea and land attack to regain Georgia. They convinced Washington, who approved the operation and sent a request to the French to have d'Estaing cooperate with Lincoln in an assault on the British garrison in Savannah.

D'Estaing's fleet arrived off the approaches to Savannah on September 8, 1779. The combined total of his troops, plus Lincoln's, in addition to a legion of 500 commanded by General Pulaski, was about 5,000 men. The British garrison numbered 3,200 defenders, under General Sir George Prevost.

D'Estaing arrayed his ships in battle formation, his flagship in the center, surrounded by six battleships and more than a hundred transport and supply ships under cover of the armed frigates, the whole moving slowly, with fast scouting sloops on the perimeters, outside the port of Savannah. On the evening of the eleventh of September, the Admiral dropped anchor at the mouth of the Savannah River. No British fleet was in sight. Fifteen hundred assault troops landed, each with three days' provisions and water. Across the river, on the bank opposite the port, were the forces of General Lincoln.

D'Estaing, of senior rank and commander of the joint operation, sent a delegation to Savannah to inform Prevost of his situation, demanding his surrender. Prevost, hoping to send out scouts to ascertain the enemy's true strength and dispositions, and to rally loyalists to his side, stalled for time. He told the delegation to inform d'Estaing that he would answer as soon as he had consulted his senior officers and the political authorities.

High winds, driving rain, then thick fog halted the disembarkation of more troops and made operations impossible, giving Prevost the time he sought. The weather continued foul for a week.

The vessels that had moored off the coast had to lift anchor and sail back to sea to avoid destruction. The assault troops were cut off from the fleet and their supplies. Just as the weather had wrecked d'Estaing's operations off Newport, it seemed as though it might do the same in Georgia.

The sky finally cleared and the troop and supply ships returned to the coast to complete the landings. Once his siege forces were in place and their strength clear to Prevost, d'Estaing sent another delegation with an ultimatum to surrender. An immediate attack would have won the day, but the Admiral was fighting a gentleman's war, trying to avoid casualties by a show of strength. The luckless d'Estaing had exaggerated his strength to Prevost—all his men and supplies had not been disembarked. The British were well entrenched just below Savannah and an assault would be bloody and risky.

Prevost sent back word that he was willing to surrender but that he had to put up at least token resistance for a show of face, and he wanted a bit more time to arrange it. But an American advance detachment, under Colonel Maitland, with seven hundred men, seeing an opening to exploit, jumped off on an attack at St. Augustine Creek. Prevost had to make an instant decision—resistance. D'Estaing learned of this and knew he had been stalled. He began to make his own plans to lift the siege and go on the attack.

The attack began on the morning of October 9. A battlefield account was kept by one of the officers, Major Thomas Pinckney of the South Carolina militia:

> The French troops were to be divided into three columns, the Americans two . . . and at 4 o'clock in the morning, a little before daylight, the whole was, on a signal being given, to rush forward and attack the redoubts and batteries opposed to their front. The American column of the right, which adjoined the French, were to be preceded by Pulaski, with his cavalry, and the cavalry of South Carolina, and were to follow the French until they approached the edge of the wood, when they were to break off and take their position. . . .
>
> But by the time the first French column had arrived at the open space, the day had fairly broke, when Count d'Estaing, without waiting until the

other two columns had arrived at their position, placed himself at the head of his first column and rushed forward to the attack. But this body was so severely galled by the grapeshot from the batteries as they advanced, and by both grapeshot and musketry when they reached the Abbatis, that, in spite of the effort of the officers, the column got into confusion, and broke away to their left towards the wood in that direction; the second and third French columns shared successively in the same fate, having the additional discouragement of seeing, as they marched to the attack, the repulse and loss of their comrades who had preceded them.

Everything in the planning had gone awry. A number of units that d'Estaing had expected on his flank had gotten lost in a swamp; others—Americans—had been betrayed by deserters; still others had been caught in a cross-fire from an armed British cutter in the river and British guns behind earthworks on the right flank. The Admiral showed more courage than sense in attacking with his lead column without the flanking support columns. The risks of delay were far less than an exposed, unsupported assault on entrenched positions. Worst of all, Count Pulaski, an inspiring and valuable leader, had been hit by a cannonball as he advanced to breach the British rear. He was mortally wounded and died on the field. Admiral d'Estaing suffered a slight shrapnel wound.

The combined allied forces lost 224 killed, 584 wounded. The siege of Savannah was lifted by October 18. Two days later a humiliated d'Estaing, his entire American campaign a dismal failure from the time of his arrival, lifted anchor and set sail, with no idea of what he would try next. Georgia, held more firmly than ever by the British, virtually ceased to exist as an American state. The morale of Southern patriots, particularly the embattled Carolinians, who feared they were next for British occupation, sank to its lowest point. It marked the end for that year of any American or allied plan to break the British grip on the Southern colonies.

Although the British did not hold any other colony in thrall, there was a general stalemate in the Jerseys, New York and New England. Washington, with depleted, exhausted forces and no fresh money from Congress, was forced again into winter quarters under miserable conditions at Morristown, another Valley Forge. His paper strength, counting militiamen, was 27,000, his effective strength more like 13,000. General Sullivan had fallen ill and resigned his commission. The weather turned bitter cold, as it had the previous year. Washington was again short of fuel, food and clothing. The paper money in his treasury was worthless and no one would take it.

Washington divided the State of New Jersey into military districts, assigned each district a quota to supply him with food, grain and blankets, and sent out his troops to make the collections. Enlistments were expiring and there were daily desertions. The great victory at Saratoga was long forgotten; it had not been the turning point all had hoped. Nor had France and Spain's joining the war helped turn the tide. At the very best, it had helped stem the tide, at low-tide levels for the Americans.

Meanwhile, Lord Cornwallis, in New York, was studying dispatches from the Southern front, confirming his view that it would be possible to launch a major campaign in 1780 to slice the South off from the United States. The Franco-American defeat at Savannah strengthened his determination. He presented the Commander in Chief, Sir Henry Clinton, with his plan. It was based upon an amphibious assault upon Charleston, South Carolina.

Charleston had fought hard and well to repulse Cornwallis when he had tried to capture it in 1776. He felt he could now take it if Clinton permitted him a sustained attack instead of the hit-and-run raiding tactics that Clinton had been using. He argued that he could invest Charleston, win over Americans loyal to the British cause, or wavering, and then, with that nucleus, conquer all of the Carolinas. Once he had taken them, he would proceed to another combined land and sea attack on Virginia, and, with that accomplished, take all the coastline of Chesapeake Bay. His plan was comprehensive, and looked a certain success. The British Navy ruled American waters, with no fear of the French. Clinton gave his approval of the plan for the spring of 1780. With the South cut off, he could then direct all his might against New England and destroy the American rebellion.

Everything that could go wrong in that dismal year 1779, did. Military crises, monetary crises, political crises and diplomatic skulduggery—each one paralleled the next, sowing the seeds of even worse misfortunes, divisions and deceptions for 1780. Franklin had told Lee that the American Revolution was not to be understood except as a miracle. To survive the next two years would require even more miracles.

All year long, Congress had been debating in sessions and in the corridors and taverns whether or not to accept Vergennes's suggestion that it appoint a commissioner empowered to negotiate peace should the conditions be obtained. This was part of the game being played by Vergennes, Joseph II, Catherine of Russia and Frederick of Prussia, all more concerned about European power politics than the fate of the Americans. Finally, those who favored naming a commissioner, on the grounds that "the absent are always wrong," prevailed. It was decided in September to name a man authorized not only to participate with the European continental powers in peace negotiations but also to make a treaty of commerce with England if peace materialized.

From the start it had been the nature of Congress first to debate whether something be done, then to debate, sometimes more heatedly, about who should do it. So was the case with the decision to name a Peace Commissioner. At the opening session, Henry Laurens of South Carolina nominated John Adams, just returned from Paris, for the post. Meriwether Smith of Virginia promptly proposed his own favorite candidate, John Jay. The factions went into caucus, came out and voted: no decision. Adams was in first place, but short of the absolute majority needed for the appointment. They caucused again, vote-traders buttonholing congressmen, offering support on pet projects for votes for their candidate. Second ballot: no decision among several candidates, Adams still top of the list. Another move to smoky corners for palaver. Partisans of Deane tried to break the deadlock by extending the field: they proposed that a Minister Plenipotentiary to Spain be named. Henry Laurens, John Adams' champion, sought support from the Lee-Adams faction by proposing Arthur Lee. Anti-Lee forces, to cross him up, proposed John Adams for the Spanish post. The pro-French faction proposed John Jay, the man they wanted all along. Vote on that issue: John Jay won by one vote, including his own. The New England group, which voted for Jay, asked Jay's faction to throw support now to Adams for Peace Commissioner. The deal made, Adams got the nomination by an absolute majority.

Instructions for Adams were voted by Congress on August 14, 1779. The most important point was an absolute interdiction to enter into any peace negotiations unless England first agreed to recognize the sovereignty, freedom and unqualified independence of the United States. This had to be "assured and confirmed by the Treaty or treaties of peace, according to the form and effect of the Treaty of Alliance with his Most Christian Majesty." Independence and the French alliance were the prerequisites laid down by Congress. Equally indispensable as a peace condition was a definition of the boundaries of the United States: the present northern boundary of New York and New England to the St. Lawrence at 45° north latitude; across to Lake Nipissing to the source of the Mississippi River (not then known); the Mississippi on the west; southward to the Chattahoochee at its junction with the Flint, east to the St. Marys and the Atlantic. A Joint Commission could be empowered to discuss the location of the eastern boundary, somewhere between Massachusetts and Nova Scotia.

Congress instructed Adams to work for the cession of Canada and Nova Scotia and to insist on equal, common rights to the fisheries, but not to make it an ultimatum or prerequisite. He might accept an armistice, but only with the consent of France, and only if "all the forces of the enemy shall be immediately withdrawn from the United States." In all matters other than those stipulated as unconditional, Adams was to coordinate all negotiations with the French. Finally, in view of the difficulty of communications, he was "to govern yourself by your own discretion, in which we repose the fullest confidence." Jay, now Minister to Spain, left America on the same ship that took Gérard home. The French Minister had suffered for months from fevers of unknown origin and had asked to be recalled to Paris.

By the time that Adams had been instructed and was preparing to leave, the Spanish mediation and the Austrian mediation, which had prompted his appointment, had already been rejected. He would arrive in Paris without a mission, other than his second portfolio, to negotiate a commercial treaty with Britain, which was not intended for action unless a peace could first be negotiated. This was not the way Adams would see it, and he would, almost on arrival, plunge himself into sharp controversy with Vergennes, who, with Franklin, rued the day Adams had been appointed.

On the diplomatic front, obscured by the high-level maneuvers, there took place a meeting between two almost unknown men who would play an intriguing role in a series of peace moves, both real and phony, the two sometimes overlapping so that it was impossible to know what was real, what a feint, what an outright deception.

One of the men, Thomas Hussey, was one of those strange characters who live in between the outer and inner worlds of international politics, moving deftly in the shadows of both. Hussey was an Irish priest who had been educated in Spain. He had become chaplain of the Spanish Embassy in London. He was also a spy in the Spanish intelligence service and became chief of that service in London, his cloth and collar serving as cover for his espionage activities. The British knew what he was doing but did not want to move against a priest, particularly an Irish priest in the Spanish service. Both countries were important to Whitehall. Hussey became friendly with a London playwright, Richard Cumberland, an agent in the British intelligence service, and a protégé of Lord George Germain, the Colonial Secretary. Germain thought that Cumberland's friendship with Hussey might permit him to accompany the priest to Madrid on a confidential mission to sound out Foreign Minister Floridablanca's terms for peace, but ordered him not to mention the American colonies or Gibraltar. Privately he told him he might listen if Floridablanca had any specific proposals to make on his terms for getting Gibraltar back. George III was determined not to yield Gibraltar, but all the diplomats thought some kind of deal might be found, and Hussey told the Spanish he was sure he could work it out. Their negotiations, at first secret, became known when they were seen publicly in Madrid, and affected Vergennes's decision, later, to move toward a Russian proposal and away from the tricky, self-seeking Floridablanca.

As the year 1799 wound down, Franklin was saddened to learn, on December 13, of the death of his dear friend and fervent supporter, Dr. Barbeu Dubourg. Dubourg, who ruined himself in the service of the American cause, died miserable and penniless. On Christmas eve there was a bit of good news: the Marquise de Lafayette gave birth to a son. A messenger from the Marquis woke Franklin in the middle of the night to bring him the good news and to tell him that the boy would be christened George Washington Lafayette.

CHAPTER

19

From Bad to Worse

The new year, 1780, started with another allied defeat. Admiral Sir George Rodney, en route to the West Indies with a new fleet, caught a Spanish squadron off Cape St. Vincent, on January 11, and, in what became known as the "Moonlight Battle," scored a decisive victory. The news determined the Conde de Floridablanca more than ever to concentrate his nation's strength in and around Gibraltar and Minorca, and to renew his secret negotiations with the British with the view of obtaining his terms in a peace treaty rather than in battle.

Floridablanca felt pressed to sound out the British, for the new American envoy to Spain, John Jay, had arrived on January 10 in Cádiz. Jay had immediately sent a dispatch to the pro-American Conde de Aranda, soliciting Aranda's help in launching his diplomatic mission. Jay had also asked Franklin to assign William Carmichael, of the American mission in Paris, to work for him in Spain, and had asked Carmichael to leave at once for Madrid to sound out the climate and set up offices.

Floridablanca moved to forestall anticipated American pressures. He drafted a secret policy memorandum outlining Spain's basic terms for peace: Gibraltar, always at the top of his list, the Floridas and Honduras. He stated that a settlement with England should be negotiated swiftly before Jay could open his own negotiations, to present him with an accomplished fact. He stipulated that a peace treaty "need not include the point of independence" for the American colonies. Although Spain was now in the war as an ally of France, Spain was not officially an ally of the United States and had never committed its government to recognition of American independence. Jay would run into the same kind of resistance and duplicity from Floridablanca that had aborted Arthur Lee's mission.

Floridablanca briefed his Irish priest-spy, Thomas Hussey, on his new policy and sent him back to London at the end of January to confer with Lord George Germain. Hussey told Germain that Spain would hold off on the recognition of America until it had received a reply from London and negotiations were under way. He did not admit that Spain had no intention of recognizing the United States, and sought to present recognition as a part of the price it was paying England for the return of Gibraltar. He stipulated that the reply had to be in Madrid by the end of February. Floridablanca's machinations were serious violations of his treaty with France, but, despite that treaty, he felt justified in unilateral action since Vergennes had concluded the alliance with America and recognized the United States without the consent of Spain, indeed against Spanish advice.

Vergennes, in Paris, knew about Hussey, and suspected that Floridablanca was renewing in secret the negotiations he had undertaken with Britain before the signing of the French-Spanish treaty. There was nothing much he could do to counter Floridablanca without a confrontation that would have weakened the alliance. He knew how stubborn Floridablanca was, how inward-looking on Spanish interests; Floridablanca's basic policy was to keep the United States embroiled and weak, so that it could not endanger Spanish interests in the Gulf of Mexico, from Florida to Louisiana to Mexico. The Spaniard was also vitally interested in holding and extending Spanish territories and forts along the Mississippi, from New Orleans to St. Louis. When the time came, Ben Franklin would be adamant in defending American prior interests and rights to the great river and its territories.

Franklin was kept informed, by diplomatic friends, of Spanish secret negotiations. He himself maintained correspondence with friends in London, who kept trying to win him over to new British schemes for peace with America—always short of absolute independence—and also to undermine his faith in the alliance with France. One such friend was David Hartley, who had played an important role in helping Franklin arrange the exchange of prisoners.

Early in February, Franklin wrote to Hartley to answer questions the latter had posed in an earlier letter about America's policy on continuing the war beyond reasonable and special interests if France were to apply pressure. Franklin had always answered every letter of this kind by restating forcefully his loyalty to the alliance and his refusal to contemplate a separate peace for special American advantage. He wrote Hartley that he was

> as much for Peace as ever I was, and as heartily desirous of seeing the War ended, as I was to prevent its Beginning; of which your Ministers know I have strong proof before I left England, when, in order to effect an accommodation, I offered at my own Risque, without orders for so doing, and without knowing whether I should be own'd in doing it, to pay the whole Damage of destroying the tea at Boston, provided the Acts made against the Province were repealed. This offer was refused. I still think it would have been wise to have accepted it. If the Congress have, therefore, entrusted to others rather than to me, the Negotiations for Peace, when such shall be set on foot, as has been reported, it is perhaps because they may have heard of a very singular opinion of mine, that there hardly ever existed such a thing as a bad Peace or a good War.

Franklin would use that maxim on war and peace many times, particularly at the time of the conclusion of the peace with England in 1783. He knew that peacemakers were more often cursed than blessed, for the making of peace requires the acceptance of compromise, and compromise always infuriates those who believe in the exclusive justice of their own cause.

Franklin referred to Congress' entrusting others with a peace mission because he knew about John Adams' new assignment. He was hurt, not only because Adams had been chosen, but that the whole affair had been kept secret and that Congress had not informed its Minister to France; Franklin learned of it through friends. It was clearly a snub to him, an indication that his detractors and enemies, particularly the Arthur Lee faction, had successfully undermined congressional trust and respect for its most eminent representative. The old man, wearied by his labors, weakened by gout, began to think of offering his resignation.

Franklin never had had any illusions about the behavior of his colleagues or about human nature in general. He was profoundly humanitarian while deeply mistrusting human beings.

On February 6, 1780, he wrote to his friend Richard Price in London to present his affectionate respects to all his old friends in the Society of Honest Whigs meeting in Franklin's favorite haunt, the London Coffee House. It was much in character for Franklin to keep up warm correspondence all through the war with his friends, though they were nationals of the enemy power. Franklin wrote:

> We make daily great improvements in *Natural,* there is one I wish to see in *Moral* Philosophy; the discovery of a Plan that would induce and oblige Nations to settle their Disputes without first Cutting one another's throats. When will human Reason be sufficiently improved to see the Advantage of this! When will Men be convinc'd that even successful Wars at length become Misfortunes to those who unjustly commenc'd them and who triumph'd blindly in their Success, not seeing all its Consequences. Your great comfort and mine in this War is that we honestly and faithfully did every thing in our Power to prevent it.

To his old scientist-friend Dr. Joseph Priestley, Franklin then wrote with remarkable prescience as well as deep humanitarian feeling.

> The rapid progress true Science now makes occasions my regretting sometimes that I was born so soon. It is impossible to imagine the Height to which may be carried, in a thousand years, the Power of Man over Matter. We may perhaps learn to deprive large Masses of their Gravity and give them absolute Levity, for the sake of very easy transport. Agriculture may diminish its Labour and double its Produce; all Diseases may, by sure means, be prevented or cured, not even excepting that of Old Age,

and our Lives lengthened at pleasure even beyond the antediluvian Standard. O that moral Science were in as fair a way of Improvement, that men would cease to be wolves to one another, and that human Beings would at length learn what they now improperly call Humanity!

On February 5, John Adams, cocky in his new role as unique Peace Commissioner, had returned to Paris. He had not distinguished himself as Franklin's co-commissioner for the alliance; now he was on his own, under none of the restraints of a diplomat accredited to a court. He was, nevertheless, diplomatically courteous in his first communication with Foreign Minister Vergennes, on February 12:

I am persuaded that it is the intention of my constituents and of all America, and I am sure it is my own determination, to take no steps of consequence in pursuance of my commissions, without consulting his Majesty's Ministers. And as various conjectures have been and may be made concerning the nature of my appointment and powers, and as it may be expected by some that I should take some measures for announcing these to the public or at least to the Court of London, I beg the favor of your Excellency's opinion and advice upon these questions:

(1) Whether in the present state of things, it is prudent in me to acquaint the British ministry that I am arrived here, and that I shall be ready to treat whenever the belligerent powers shall be inclined to treat.
(2) Whether it is prudent in me to publish in any manner more than the Journals of Congress may already have done, the nature of my mission.
(3) Or whether to remain on the reserve, as I have hitherto, since my arrival in Europe.

Vergennes, a shrewd old hand at this game, noted the arrogance between the lines and the subtlety of some of the phrases. Adams had declared it his "intention" to consult the French, not his commitment to do so. Consultation means no more than just that; it does not carry with it any obligation to comply with the advice sought. And by posing the three questions, Adams was, from the outset, setting the limits and defining the areas of his consultation.

Vergennes knew he would have trouble with Adams and decided to put him sharply in his place. He replied coldly on February 15:

> I have received the letter which you did me the honor to write me on the 12th of this month. I think before I reply to different points on which you consult me, that it is proper to wait for the arrival of M. Gérard, because he is the bearer of your instructions, and will certainly be able to make me better acquainted with the nature and extent of your commission. But in the meantime I am of opinion that it will be prudent to conceal your eventual character, and above all to take the necessary precautions that the object of your commission may remain unknown to the Court of London.

This was not merely a snub but a major putdown, almost insulting. Indeed, Adams did consider it a grievous injury that the French Minister should not accept his word on his appointment and the nature of the mission before hearing it from Gérard, the French Minister to Philadelphia, returning home carrying copies of his "instructions." Adams merited the treatment by his own high-handed letter, coming as it did at a time when his mission had been aborted before he had arrived.

As Peace Commissioner, without a peace conference Adams had nothing to do. And Vergennes thought he had already quietly exaggerated his role by talking, in the opening line, of his commission to negotiate peace as well as a treaty of commerce with England. According to earlier dispatches from Gérard, Congress intended Adams to seek out a commercial treaty only after a peace had been obtained, so if there were no peace negotiations, it followed that a treaty of commerce was not to be considered. The worst blow to Adams was Vergennes's admonition to "conceal" his mission. He was eager to publish it officially and to take first steps, but he was now temporarily halted.

Vergennes finally relented when he read a copy of Adams' instructions, which conformed exactly to what Adams had stated. On February 24, he wrote and told him that he might feel free to announce his mission publicly in France and in Holland, for the *Royal Gazette* was preparing to publish it and the King would formally receive Adams and confirm his mission. However, he enjoined him from saying a word about the commission to negotiate a commercial treaty with Britain as unnecessary and premature. Adams would brood on this and other snubs for weeks.

While Vergennes and Adams were fencing futilely about hypothetical peace negotiations, more important events were taking place on the diplomatic and military fronts that winter of 1780. Sir Henry Clinton, acting on the Cornwallis plan for an offensive in the South, had landed his troops on Johns Island, near Charleston, South Carolina. The landings were preparatory to the planned capture of the Southern capital city later in the spring.

Other events were taking place in Madrid and in St. Petersburg which would affect the course of the war. Hussey, in London, sent a cipher dispatch by a personal servant to Floridablanca on February 16 informing him that England would not agree to evacuate Gibraltar as a first, indispensable article of negotiations. Once those negotiations did begin to show some progress in good faith, exchanges of territory would then be considered, Hussey reported. Hussey consistently exaggerated, or simply misunderstood, England's willingness to treat on Gibraltar and kept Floridablanca negotiating hopefully without knowing he had no chance to get his way. Floridablanca created a minor crisis between Paris and Madrid when he refused to receive Gérard, who had just arrived from America, in his capacity of French Minister Plenipotentiary to the United States. French Ambassador Montmorin wrote to Vergennes describing the incident as an official rebuff. It put new strains on relationships within the Family Compact.

Not content with merely snubbing the French, Floridablanca then put off John Jay in Cádiz by sending him word on February 24 that he might come to Madrid if he wished but that it was not opportune to welcome him in any "formal character." That must await a "public acknowledgment and future treaty." Poor Jay would go to Madrid as a private citizen with no diplomatic status.

Four days later, the Spanish Council of Ministers met with Floridablanca. The Navy Minister, González de Castejón, suggested that negotiations might be undertaken in the strictest secrecy. "We can, then, always break them off," he told the Council. He insisted that Spain must be "the last country in Europe to recognize any sovereign and independent state in North America." He also proposed that Spain's ally, France, be told nothing about any negotiations until they had succeeded. This was precisely the policy of Floridablanca, who emerged from the meeting strengthened by the proposals of the powerful Minister of the Navy.

Naval affairs then brought about a most important change in the nature of relations among the European powers, adversely affecting British interests. The British, by far the greatest sea power in the world, had instituted, at the outbreak of the war in 1778, a severe policy of restrictions against neutral shipping. The Admiralty had drawn up a long list of what it claimed was contraband and ordered the Royal Navy to intercept and search neutral ships sailing to belligerent ports. If contraband—by British definition—was found, neutral vessels and cargoes were to be seized and confiscated. Many Danish, Swedish and Prussian merchants ships were seized and a number of Russian ships hauled into British ports and released only after long delays.

Spain instituted an even harsher policy when she entered the war. Spanish armed cruisers seized all vessels heading for Mediterranean ports, and if they were carrying provisions that the Spanish captains considered to be materials of war—for example, bolts of cloth that might be used for uniforms—they would be escorted to Cádiz and sold, ship and cargo, at public auction.

Late in 1779 a Dutch ship with Russian cargo was seized and sold. While the Russians were preparing a diplomatic protest to Madrid, they received word of another, graver incident: a Russian ship had been seized by the Spaniards. These Spanish moves, sure to provoke European powers, were motivated by the obsession of Floridablanca and the Spanish Admiralty: the blockade of Gibraltar. They were determined to starve out the island garrison, forcing it to use up its supplies, so that the Spaniards might launch an invasion of the rock.

Catherine of Russia had been trying for more than a year to

organize the neutrals into a concerted defense against belligerent naval raids on neutral shipping. At the same time, the British were wooing her, seeking an alliance between London and St. Petersburg. Britain's most dashing and brilliant diplomat, Sir James Harris, had been sent to seduce the Empress. He was a great favorite at court and became a close friend of Prince Potemkin, Catherine's current adviser and lover. But, her ex-favorite, old Count Panin, whom she still trusted, was a prudent man. He saw no gain for Russia by any involvement in the British–French-Spanish war, and even less interest in far-off, revolutionary America. He persuaded her to resist all alliances with belligerents and move, instead, toward organizing a neutral Europe.

Catherine was infuriated by the Spanish confiscations and immediately gave orders for naval armament of Russian shipping. Potemkin told Harris that it would be used only against Spain, in retaliation. But Catherine astonished all the diplomats when she instructed Count Panin to draw up a code of neutral rights, announcing to the world that Russia would defend her shipping against *all* belligerents. Proposals were sent to Denmark-Norway, Sweden, Austria, Holland and Portugal to join with Russia in a League of Armed Neutrality to protect commerce and all neutral rights, signaling the end of British hopes for a Russian alliance. It was just what Vergennes had been hoping for. He had made tentative proposals for such neutral action almost two years earlier. Although this might prohibit French and Spanish action, and cut off American privateers in European waters, it would ultimately hit Britain hardest, for the British had the largest, most efficient and far-ranging fleets.

Panin drew up the plans for Catherine's Armed Neutrality and sent them to the courts at London, Versailles and Madrid. The French and Spanish, under pressure from Vergennes, promptly informed St. Petersburg that they would abide by the new rules laid down by the Empress. The British, refusing to accept her new principles and prohibitions, coolly informed the Russians that Britain would, as always, live up to her treaty obligations and naval traditions.

Denmark-Norway, Sweden, Austria and Prussia all agreed to join the Armed Neutrality League, with some reservations about certain clauses, particularly the definition of contraband. Only Holland, with the most to fear, hesitated. Holland was geographically nearest to British power, and had far greater ocean trade than the other neutrals. The Dutch were concerned about their overseas colonies and wanted a guarantee of their colonial possessions written into the new convention. They also faced a serious dilemma in their relationship with the British, because of conflicts between two existent treaties. Under one maritime treaty, Holland had the right to trade with France and Spain without British interference. But another treaty between the British and Dutch provided that if either party was threatened or attacked the other must come to its aid. If the Dutch took recourse in the first treaty, the British could counter by invoking the second. All this was, in any case, somewhat theoretical, since the reality was British power. The Dutch were afraid that the British Navy might invoke the second treaty as a pretext for war, and the British confirmed these fears by warning the Dutch sternly not to join the Armed Neutrality. This was one of the reasons for the long negotiations between The Hague and St. Petersburg.

Franklin followed all these developments closely, thanks to the excellent work of his close friend and representative in The Hague, Charles Dumas. Dumas conducted business transactions, public relations and propaganda for the American cause, on Franklin's directives, and also received guidelines from Vergennes through the French Ambassador, one of the most influential diplomats in The Hague. In order to get the neutrals to pressure London, France had offered all European powers the traditional guarantee of "free ships, free goods" for a six-month period if Britain would do the same. By 1779 the Dutch were convoying their merchants ships with armed vessels and Britain was threatening hostile action.

Hoping that the Armed Neutrality might induce England to be more reasonable in seeking peace with Spain, Floridablanca sent a dispatch to Hussey in London, telling him to inform Whitehall that Charles III wished to pursue peace talks with all haste, in view of the imminent arrival of John Jay in Madrid. He outlined terms relating to America based upon the British peace terms offered back in 1778.

Vergennes and Franklin also conferred on the new opportunity afforded by the Armed Neutrality. They hoped that armed convoys in all European waters would require far greater British patrols and draw off strength from the American battle front. This, Franklin urged Vergennes, was the moment to send a greater fleet and a large expeditionary force of French troops to join General Washington.

Franklin's pleas were strengthened by similar proposals from the Marquis de Lafayette, who was preparing to return to America. Franklin and Lafayette were delighted when they heard that Vergennes agreed, in principle, with their strategy, and would take up the question with his colleagues in the King's Council of Ministers. On March 14, eager to bear the news to Washington and to enter into action again, Lafayette set sail for America.

Just before Lafayette left, he handed Franklin a letter, written by George Washington almost a year before, in commendation of the brave and able service the young Frenchman had performed in the war. Communications between Washington and Franklin were rare, and Franklin's reply, a warm tribute to Washington, is a special jewel in the treasury of American letters. It is dated March 5, 1780.

I have received but lately the Letter your Excellency did me the honor of writing to me in Recommendation of the Marquis de la Fayette. His modesty detained it long in his own Hands. . . .

Should peace arrive after another Campaign or two, and afford us a little Leisure, I should be happy to see your Excellency in Europe, and to accompany you, if my Age and Strength would permit, in visiting some of its ancient and most famous Kingdoms. You would, on this side of the Sea, enjoy the great Reputation you have acquir'd, pure and free from those little Shades that Jealousy and Envy of a Man's Countrymen and Cotemporaries [*sic*] are ever endeavouring to cast over living Merit. Here you would know and enjoy what Posterity will say of Washington. For 1000 Leagues have nearly the same effect as 1000 years. The feeble Voice of those grovelling Passions cannot extend so far either in Time or Distance. At present I enjoy that Pleasure for you, as I frequently hear the old Generals of this martial Country (who study the Maps of America, and mark upon them all your Operations) speak with sincere Approbation and great Applause of your conduct; and join in giving you the Character of one of the greatest Captains of the Age.

I must soon quit the Scene, but you may live to see your Country flourish, as it will amazingly and rapidly after the War is over. Like a Field of young Indian Corn, which long fair weather and Sunshine had enfeebled and discolored, and which, in that weak state, by a Thunder Gust, of violent Wind, Hail, and Rain, seem'd to be threaten'd with absolute Destruction; yet the Storm being past, it recovers fresh Verdure, shoots up with double Vigor, and delights the Eye, not of its Owner only, but of every observing Traveler.

The best Wishes that can be form'd for your Health, Honour, and Happiness, ever attend you from your Excellency's most obedient and humble servant,

B. Franklin.*

Washington needed all the praise and reassurances that he could get. As Franklin himself had noted, he had been the object of a number of criticisms and cabals undermining his authority as Commander in Chief. His operations were gravely endangered by shortages of food, fuel, clothing and ammunition, even pay for his soldiers. And a new monetary crisis would make it worse.

It erupted in March, and would wreck American credit in Europe, making Franklin's task almost impossible, for Congress continued to write drafts on loans that dried up as soon as Europeans learned of the American devaluation of March 18, 1780.

On that day, Congress ordered the recall of all Continental paper currency, to be exchanged for a new issue of paper at the rate of forty old dollars to one new dollar. The states would tax this money out of existence at the rate of fifteen million dollars a month;

*The French, who love Franklin and all he said and did, have preserved this letter in their own literature and history classes. Saint-Beuve referred to the passage on Indian corn and the American Revolution as an inspired comparison, which, in "the breadth of its images recalls the Homeric comparisons of the Odyssey."

as the states delivered the old paper, Congress would emit the new paper, which was to be guaranteed jointly by state and federal governments and to draw 5 percent interest, payable in bills of exchange. The states would make the new paper legal tender. It was a desperate measure, virtually repudiating all the paper currency in existence. For those who had accumulated paper money, or held promissory notes and loans, it meant a forty-to-one loss of their investment. For Franklin, trying to deal with European bankers and businessmen, it was a catastrophe. It meant, in effect, that until it had been proved that the operation was a success, the only way he could make purchases for Washington's needs was by direct barter of American produce. No one would accept American paper of any kind.

It was in this dreary month of March that Franklin wrote a poignant note to the President of the Congress telling him of the terrible conditions of American credit. So bad were all conditions that this letter of March 4 was not dispatched until May 31, for the ship *Alliance,* which was to carry it, was blocked in port by a strike of seamen who had not been paid their prize money for earlier captures of British vessels. Franklin pleaded with Congress, as he had done unsuccessfully so many times, to free him of the responsibilities of dealing with Admiralty Courts and maritime affairs. He also warned that he could not honor money requests from every agent that Congress sent to Europe:

> . . . if every agent of Congress in different parts of the world is permitted to run in debt and draw upon me a pleasure to support his credit, under the idea of its being necessary to do so for the honour of Congress, the difficulty upon me would be too great, and I may, in fine, be obliged to protest the interest bills. I therefore beg that a stop may be put to such irregular proceedings. . . .
>
> A great clamor has lately been made here by some merchants who say they have large sums in their hands of paper money in America, and that they are ruined by some resolution of Congress which reduces its value to one part in forty. As I have had no letter explaining this matter, I have only been able to say that it is probably misunderstood, and that I am confident the Congress have not done, nor will do anything unjust towards

strangers who have given us credit. I have, indeed, been almost ready to complain that I hear so little and so seldom from the committee of correspondence; but I know the difficulty of communication, and the frequent interruption it meets in this time of war. I have not yet received a line this year.

Franklin included a note about the new Armed Neutrality:

It is a critical time with respect to such cases, for whatever may formerly have been the law of nations, all the neutral powers, at the instance of Russia, seem at present disposed to change it, and to enforce the rule that free ships shall make free goods, except in the case of contraband. . . . I have therefore instructed our privateers to bring in no more neutral ships, as such prizes occasion much litigation and create ill blood.

In a later letter to Charles Dumas in The Hague, Franklin stated his views on the freedom of the seas even more strongly and broadly:

I approve much of the principles of the confederacy of the neutral powers, and am not only for respecting the ships as the house of a friend, though containing the goods of any enemy, but I even wish, for the sake of humanity, that the law of nations may be further improved by determining that, even in time of war, all those kinds of people who are employed in procuring subsistence for the species, or in exchanging the necessaries or conveniences of life which are for the common benefit of mankind—such as husbandmen on their lands, fishermen in their barks, and traders in unarmed vessels—shall be permitted to prosecute their several innocent and useful employments without interruption of molestation, and nothing taken from them even when wanted by an enemy, but on paying a fair price for the same.

While these exchanges were taking place, Vergennes was also hearing from his Minister in Philadelphia, the Chevalier de La Luzerne, who had replaced Gérard. Luzerne had moved quickly to establish himself and, in a few months, had personally met and dined with the leading members of Congress. He was a skilled diplomat, personable, elegant, witty and sophisticated, and had become a favorite of congressional leaders. He would, within a year, attain a position of such influence that he was virtually an ex officio member of the American government, wheeling and dealing like a veteran politician. Few diplomats have ever attained such a position of power in a foreign government as Luzerne in Philadelphia.

Luzerne alerted Vergennes to serious trouble in the American government and army early in April, 1780. He wrote about the monetary crisis and the mismanagement of France's aid program:

> It is difficult to form a just conception of the depredations which have been committed in the management of war supplies—foraging, clothing, hospitals, tents, quarters and transportation. About nine thousand men, employed in this service, receive enormous salaries and devour the subsistence of the army, while it was tormented with hunger and the extremes of want. Congress determined to apply a prompt remedy and has just appointed a Committee of Three, invested with the amplest powers ever conferred on a deputation of this kind. This resolution brought on long and warm discussion, in which a large party, jealous of seeing three individuals endowed with such unlimited power, strove to restrict it by instructions. They insisted on the danger of associating the Commander-in-chief with it, whose influence, it was stated, was already too great. His virtues were spoken of as an additional cause of alarm; it was remarked that the enthusiasm of the army, joined to a sort of dictature conferred on him, placed Congress and the thirteen states at its mercy.

Luzerne went on to describe the political machinations that were finally defeated by the efforts of Morris, Hancock and Jefferson in support of drastic reforms and closer coordination with George Washington. The principle of a committee of three men endowed with special powers to clean up the mess was confirmed. It would lead rapidly to a triumph for Robert Morris, who became a kind of commander in chief in the financial and monetary field equivalent to Washington in the military, and who would save the federal government, in extremis, from bankruptcy. Luzerne, like Gérard before him, also informed Vergennes of the high levels of corruption in American politics.

> If this great work is conducted as vigorously as expected, there is no doubt that it will restore Congress to the consideration which this senate

has lost. If I may believe some of its members, it deserves to lose favor through the interested maneuvers to which certain delegates have surrendered themselves, in availing themselves of their knowledge of the secret operations of the administration to ensure the success of their commercial speculations.

The corruption and inefficiency of Congress and the federal bureaucracy, combined with the depreciation of the currency, was creating new crises in supply for General Washington and his officers. Farmers and merchants were reluctant to make sales for paper money. General Ben Lincoln, under new British pressure in the South, was trying unsuccessfully to supply his troops. He wrote frantic letters to Washington and the Congress, as the British, sensing their opportunity, began to move on their plan for a Southern offensive.

General Lincoln, after the failure to recapture Savannah, had fallen back on Charleston. He saw, as Cornwallis had, that Charleston had to be held or the entire South would be open to invasion and occupation. To hold it, Lincoln had a very thin line of only about 1,200 regulars and some 2,000 militiamen. Against him, Sir Henry Clinton, with Cornwallis second-in-command, was amassing a British invasion force of 8,500 troops, about one-third of them Americans loyal to Britain. The South was a mass of contradictions in the American Revolution; some of the bravest, best fighters, patriots and brilliant statesmen were Southerners, just as Southerners counted in their ranks the most bitter opponents of an independent America.

Clinton also had fourteen men-of-war in his invasion fleet, protecting almost a hundred transport ships. Against this naval force, the Continental Navy could count on only three frigates and the sloop-of-war, the *Ranger,* under command of Commodore Abraham Whipple. Washington, with few troops to spare, ordered some additional Virginian and North Carolinian units to make their way swiftly to Charleston. They were few in number and lightly armed.

Whipple sailed his tiny flotilla close to the gates of Charleston, hoping that his ships could shoot down the invasion boats at close range. The British smiled as they watched his futile maneuver. They had no intention of launching frail assault boats in a frontal landing that would expose them to Whipple's guns. British troops were landed on the flank, south of Charleston, without opposition. Lincoln, with small forces, had left the southern land side undefended.

British frigates ran the gantlet of the guns at Fort Moultrie, defending the harbor of Charleston. British guns overwhelmed the fort's cannon. On April 8, the British fleet anchored inside Charleston's harbor, while assault troops moved into position land-side. Clinton sent an emissary to demand the surrender of Charleston. Lincoln, recalling how Britain's General Prevost had stalled the Americans at Savannah, to gain time for a counterattack tried the same tactic at Charleston. Unfortunately, he lacked the trained troops and full supplies that Prevost had had; he was also faced with a nervous City Council, fearing bloodshed and destruction in a lost cause.

Lincoln stalled too long. All the British forces were disembarked and the ring was too deep and tight for him to break through. On May 12, he had to run up a white flag and surrender without condition. The British took nearly five thousand prisoners and captured intact the three Continental frigates which Commodore Whipple had not thought to scuttle. It was a humiliating, disastrous defeat for the Americans.

Sir Henry Clinton quickly found Americans ready to set up a Loyalist government in the state capital. Within a few months, his troops, under Cornwallis—Clinton, confident of success, had sailed back to New York—had swept through almost all of South Carolina. The American militia was overwhelmed by the combined British troops and American Loyalists. Cornwallis strengthened his garrisons at Savannah and Port Royal, increased the permanent force at Charleston and brought back the former Royal Governor. The merchants of Charleston lined up to do business with England, and, by the first day of summer of 1780, South Carolina, like Georgia, was again virtually a colony of Britain. The thirteen united states were now eleven.

While the military front was riddled with this series of setbacks, and the currency situation was verging on bankruptcy, when the friendship and assistance of France were more than ever needed, John Adams chose that moment to launch a campaign to force Vergennes's hand. Nothing was to prove better to the Congress the inestimable value of Franklin's common sense, patience and tact than the hotheadedness and imprudence of John Adams. It was outrageous that Franklin should suffer criticism and mistrust in the Congress, when he alone maintained friendship for America at the European courts.

Adams' pressure campaign began on March 21, in a note that opened with an expression of his appreciation to Vergennes for having arranged his presentation to the King and Queen, but immediately went on to complain that official announcement of his mission, promised by Vergennes to be published in the *Royal Gazette,* had not yet been carried out. Tactlessly, he asked Vergennes whether "the Omission is accidental, or whether it is owing to any alteration in your Excellency's sentiments." No experienced diplomat would ever so much as hint to the other side that it had changed its mind on a promise.

On March 30, Vergennes wrote to apologize and explain that he had been mistaken when he had promised publication in the *Royal Gazette.* He had since learned that the presentations of plenipotentiaries were not customarily announced in the *Gazette.* Instead, he offered to publish the announcement in the *Mercure de France* and to permit Adams to have it reprinted in other foreign gazettes. He included in his note the text of the proposed announcement for Adams' approval: "Mr. Adams, whom the Congress of the United States has designated to assist at the conferences for a peace, when that event shall take place, arrived here some time ago, and has had the honor to be presented to the king and the royal family."

If Vergennes had slapped Adams in the face, he would not have enraged him more. The icy announcement gave Adams no title but "mister." It defined his assignment not as a Peace Commissioner but merely as an assistant to a conference, if and when such a conference took place. One can hardly blame Adams for being angered. But a diplomat, particularly an envoy of a small, weak power under siege, seeking help from the only real ally his country can count on, simply cannot afford anger. Franklin never once forgot this. Adams never understood it.

He sat in Paris with nothing to do, brooding about Vergennes's curt notes. He knew perfectly well that the political maneuvers for peace which had motivated his appointment had all unraveled. If he had nothing to do, it was not because of some French plot against him, but simply because there was nothing to be done. Yet, week after week, he would reread the diplomatic file, confer with Franklin, seek some means of action and generally make a nuisance of himself.

It was just at that time that John Jay, and his pregnant wife, Sally, arrived in Madrid after a long, tiring journey overland from Cádiz. The Spaniards, still in the midst of secret negotiations with the British, gave him as cool a brush-off as the French had given Adams.

In London Lord Hillsborough called in the agent Richard Cumberland and gave him a letter addressed to Floridablanca, accrediting him as an agent and expressing George III's ardent desires for peace. Cumberland was to accompany Thomas Hussey to Lisbon, where he was to await developments, as Hussey went on to Madrid for further instructions. Cumberland was told that he might also proceed to Madrid himself if Hussey learned that Spain was ready seriously to negotiate peace without insisting that Britain turn over Gibraltar and Minorca. Cumberland was authorized to open negotiations and to insist that Spain agree to pledge strict neutrality toward the rebellious colonies in America. This was tantamount to asking Spain to break with France, and too much even for Floridablanca, who was prepared to bend or sidestep his treaty with France but not risk an open break.

Shortly after his arrival John Jay sent a memorandum to Floridablanca stressing the determination of the Americans to fight on for independence. No peace negotiations, no compromises, would be considered that did not recognize America's total independence. In the note, he also requested Spanish aid, in money, ammunition and clothing. He sent the note on April 25, and four days later sent another appeal to Floridablanca to honor a draft of one thousand pounds sterling drawn on his funds as Minister to Spain.

Floridablanca stalled for some two weeks, then finally agreed to see Jay. On May 11, Jay and his secretary, William Carmichael, were received by Floridablanca. The Foreign Minister told them that an official aid program was not opportune at that time, but that King Charles III had graciously decided to advance the Americans forty thousand pounds sterling out of his private purse. In payment, the Americans must send cargoes of tobacco, timber and other products. Jay was told sharply that Spain would never relinquish its right to navigation of the Mississippi River. Jay was left with no illusions as to the kind of "ally" he was dealing with.

Hussey, pushing hard for the peace that he wanted to conclude with England, had received no encouragement from Floridablanca on the terms that Cumberland had given him. Yet he sent a message to Cumberland in Lisbon that "All is well." Late in May, Cumberland set out for Aranjuez, where the court was about to move for the summer. Floridablanca, knowing that Jay would alert Franklin to warn the French of his machinations, called Jay in to explain that Hussey and Cumberland had come to work out some private business dealings. Jay could do nothing but thank the Spaniard for his "courtesy" and repeat the well-known themes of American policy.

Three days later, Floridablanca called Jay in again. The Spaniards had received all the details of the surrender of the Americans at Charleston. The news shocked and dismayed Jay, who also learned of the death of Don Juan de Miralles, the Spanish agent in America, of a heart attack while inspecting the American troops in Morristown. Until a new agent could be dispatched, Floridablanca informed Jay, nothing further could be done. Jay sent back a report to the Congress that "in this conference, not a single nail would drive." His mission was totally stalled.

Floridablanca called him back two days later to say that he had a reply to suggest to Jay's earlier request for one hundred thousand pounds sterling: Spain would pay this amount in installments over a two-year period if Congress would turn over to Spain four "handsome" frigates and other vessels of war, all fully equipped. Jay could just choke back his rage when he asked the Spanish Foreign Minister how he thought that Congress could find the money to build and equip four frigates when it had no cash to defray its own daily expenses. Floridablanca shrugged his shoulders and waved his hands to indicate that that was America's problem, not his.

When he returned to his quarters fuming, Jay found a letter from Carmichael, in Aranjuez, announcing the arrival there of both Hussey and Cumberland. He described Hussey as "a priest with a conscience as pliable as a lady's kid-skin gloves." At that point, Jay also received a disappointing letter from Franklin, in response to a suggestion he had made that they keep in close communication and coordinate their diplomatic missions. Franklin, politely but evasively, wrote:

> I shall endeavour to perform my part with you, as well to have the pleasure of your correspondence as from a sense of duty. But my time is more taken up with matters extraneous to the functions of a minister than you can possibly imagine. I have written often to the Congress to establish consuls in the ports and ease me of what relates to maritime and mercantile affairs, but no notice had yet been taken of my request.

It was clear to Jay that Franklin was not going to get involved in his problems and that he could look for no help from Paris.

Franklin included in his letter a special note for Sally Jay, who had written him asking for a recent portrait of himself. He told her that he was pleased to send her the best of five or six engravings made from different paintings. He added:

> The verses at the bottom are truly extravagant. But you must know that the desire of pleasing by a perpetual rise of compliments in this polite nation has so used up all the common expressions of approbation that they are becoming flat and insipid, and to use them almost implies censure. Hence, music, that formerly might be sufficiently praised when it was called "bonne," to go a little further they called it "excellente," then "superbe," "magnifique," "exquise," "céleste," all which being in their turns worn out, there only remains "divine."

In mid-June, Franklin wrote again to Spain, this time to Carmichael, to share the news that Lafayette had safely arrived in Boston on April 28, and had said that he expected the King to send new naval squadrons and troops as reinforcements for Washington. Franklin also wrote at length about the anti-Catholic riots that had just racked London.

> The beginning of this month a mob of fanatics, joined by a mob of rogues, burnt and destroy'd property to the amount, it is said, of a million sterling. Chapels of foreign ambassadors, houses of members of Parliament, that had promoted the act of favoring Catholics, and the houses of many private persons of that religion were pillaged and consumed, or pulled down to the number of fifty; among the rest, Lord Mansfield's is burnt with all his furniture, pictures, books and papers. Thus, he who approved of the burning of American houses has had fire brought home to him.

The leader of the riots, Lord George Gordon, had been arrested and imprisoned in the Tower of London. In a footnote, Franklin added that Arthur Lee, who had long been waiting in Lorient for passage home on the *Alliance,* had instigated a mutiny aboard but that it had been put down. "That restless genius, wherever he is must either find or make a quarrel."

Franklin sent a note to John Paul Jones telling him that he need not accept Lee as a passenger if he was indeed guilty of instigating the mutiny. There were several other ships due to sail and Jones could, if he wished, transfer Lee to some other captain. Franklin washed his hands of Lee and would make no further arrangements for him.

Troublemaker Lee might be gone, but John Adams was still there to cause Franklin grief. On June 16, Leray de Chaumont wrote to the Foreign Office to report an angry meeting with Adams. He had gone to see him at the urging of several businessmen and bankers who had been burned in the American currency devaluation and were holding paper dollars worth one-fortieth their former value. Chaumont suggested to Adams that Congress make special arrangements to save the European investors from ruinous losses. But Adams had arrogantly waved aside his request.

> Mr. Adams replied that the course taken by Congress was wise and just, and particularly so; that *those who complained of it were emissaries and spies of the English;* that it would be very unjust to treat Europeans differently from the Americans; that the country could get along without the former should they abandon trade with America; that the French had less reason to complain than anybody else, since France derived the greatest advantages, because, without America, to which France would not be under too great obligation, England would be too powerful for the House of Bourbon; that, had it not been for America, Russia, Denmark, Switzerland, Portugal and Holland would not be in league against England. . . . I confess that this answer astonished me.

It also astonished and infuriated Vergennes. France was one of the world's greatest powers; it had given America vital aid and had gone to war as America's ally; yet here was an American minister making light of France and suggesting that France needed America more than America needed France. Vergennes wrote a sharp protest to Adams and got an equally sharp rejoinder, repeating essentially the same arguments that Adams had made with Chaumont. Finally, on the margin of one of his internal memos, Vergennes noted: "An ulterior explanation with M. Adams on the depreciation of money would be superfluous. M. de Luzerne is instructed to treat with Congress on this subject, which better appreciates the alliance between the King and the United States than M. Adams."

In Madrid, on June 19, poor John Jay sent a bill for $333 for services that he could not pay, asking Floridablanca to cover the bill for him. He was broke and humiliated. Floridablanca, the next day, sent him a curt note, saying he would pay this bill but warning Jay that in the future "it will be impossible to show the same complaisance for other bills without consulting the pleasure of the King." Never had American prestige been lower in a European capital.

Adams continued to send his rockets to Vergennes, as though America were the richest and strongest nation on earth. He demanded that Vergennes explain to him why he wanted Adams to refrain from informing the British of his diplomatic mission. He insisted that the relations between America and France and their obligations were "mutual," between equal powers. He refused even to consider any special indemnification of French investors and merchants hurt by devaluation.

Vergennes, thoroughly fed up with Adams, wrote to Franklin on June 30 to say that he and the King were persuaded that Franklin did not share Adams' views on American obligations toward its debtors in Europe. He asked Franklin to take up the affair with Congress. "The King expects you will lay the whole before Congress, and His Majesty flatters himself that this senate, imbued with other principles than those developed by Mr. Adams, will satisfy His Majesty that it judges the French worthy of some consideration on its part, and that it knows how to appreciate the interest which His Majesty does not cease to manifest towards the United States."

Franklin repudiated Adams' letters and promised Vergennes that he would seek an equitable solution. Adams promptly sent an angry letter to Franklin and another long, complaining letter to Vergennes, ending with a most unwise footnote: "There are some remnants of Prejudice against Americans among the French; and, it must be confessed, that there are some in America against France." By July 29 Vergennes decided to end his communications with Adams. He sent him a short, blunt note stating that in the future he would correspond on American affairs only with Dr. Benjamin Franklin, the only American officially accredited to the French government. Adams was clearly branded as persona non grata in Paris.

Franklin, as exasperated with his colleague as Vergennes was, broke with Adams in a note to Vergennes, on August 3. He wrote that Adams

> had given such just cause of Displeasure; and that it is impossible his Conduct should be approved by his Constituents. I am glad that he has not admitted me to any Participation in his Writings, and that he has taken the Resolution he expresses of not communicating with me or making use of my Intervention in his future Correspondence; a resolution that I believe

he will keep, as he has never communicated to me more of his Business in Europe than I have seen in the newspapers. . . . I shall, as you desire, lay before Congress the whole Correspondence which you have sent me for that purpose.

Adams packed up and set off for Holland. He was bitter and convinced that Franklin had conspired with Vergennes to sabotage his mission. He wrote members of Congress that the reason that Vergennes was so fond of Franklin and would deal only with him was that Franklin was completely subservient to the French. Franklin, knowing what Adams was up to, decided to present his own case to the Congress. On August 9, he sent a report to Samuel Huntington, then President of the Congress:

Mr. Adams has given offense to the court here by some sentiments and expressions contained in several of his letters to the Count de Vergennes. . . . Mr. Adams did not show me his letters before he sent them. . . . It is true that Mr. Adams' proper business is elsewhere (England); but, the time not yet being come for that business, and having nothing else herewith to employ himself, he seems to have endeavoured to supply what he may suppose my negotiations defective in. He thinks, as he tells me himself, that America has been too free in expressions of gratitude to France; for that she is more obliged to us than we to her; and that we should show spirit in our applications. I apprehend that he mistakes his ground, and that this court is to be treated with decency and delicacy.

Franklin explained that the French King felt that he was benevolently aiding a poor and oppressed people and that it would be useful to accept this view in good and humble spirit as the best way to get more aid.

Mr. Adams, on the other hand, who at the same time means our welfare and interest as much as I or any man can do, seems to think that a little stoutness and greater air of independence and boldness in our demands will procure us more ample assistance. . . .

Mr. Vergennes, who appears much offended, told me yesterday that he would enter into no further discussions with Mr. Adams, nor answer any more of his letters. He is gone to Holland to try, as he told me, whether something might not be done to render us less dependent on

France. . . . It is my intention, while I stay here, to procure what advantages I can for our country, by endeavouring to please this court; and I wish I could prevent anything being said by our countrymen here that may have a contrary effect.

The diplomatic family quarrels did not prevent Franklin from continuing his many social activities with his French friends. In the midst of the Adams crisis, he received a letter from Georges Cabanis, one of the favorites of Madame Helvétius. Cabanis was visiting his father, who wanted to know exactly how to make a lightning rod to protect his house. Franklin told him, in a letter of June 30: "A simple rod of iron of half an inch in diameter, tapering to a point, and extending nine feet above the highest part of the building, and descending into the earth till four or five feet beneath the surface, will be sufficient." He then went on to give news about "Notre Dame d'Auteuil": "I now and then offend our good lady who cannot retain her displeasure, but, sitting on her sopha, extends graciously her long, handsome arm, and says 'là, baisez ma main: je vous pardonne,' with all the dignity of a sultaness. She is as busy as ever, endeavouring to make every creture about her happy, from the Abbés down thro' all ranks of the family, down to the birds."

Meanwhile, John Paul Jones was quarreling with his fellow officers and crew and with the French authorities over what ships he should command and where he might anchor. Everyone wrote to Franklin to complain about Jones. On July 5, Franklin, who admired Jones, sent him an acid note of reproof:

> Hereafter, if you should observe on occasion to give your Officers and Friends a little more praise than is their Due, and confess more Fault than you can justly be charged with, you will only become the sooner for it, a Great Captain. Criticising and censuring almost every one you had to do with, will diminish Friends, increase Enemies and thereby hurt your affairs.

There was one bright spot in all the stormy clouds in that summer of 1780. Vergennes had made good his promises to Lafayette and to Franklin to send reinforcements to America. He had been planning to ever since he had written Luzerne about it in February, telling him "The King has decided to send a squadron with a troop corps to North America." He asked Luzerne to keep it secret, except for Washington, the President of the Congress and a few reliable, pro-French patriots who might be trusted. Alexander Hamilton was delighted by the news. He had been depressed about the apathy of the public and the Loyalist sentiments of so many Americans. He had concluded that "our countrymen have all the folly of the ass and all the passiveness of sheep. They are determined not to be free and they can neither be frightened, discouraged nor persuaded to change their resolution. If we are saved, France and Spain must save us."

General Washington had hoped that the French might order Admiral d'Estaing to leave his West Indies operations and try his luck again in American waters. He was overjoyed to learn from Lafayette that the King was sending an expeditionary force of some fifteen thousand men, under General Comte Jean-Baptiste de Rochambeau. Washington saw in that large force the chance to turn the tide after the disaster of Charleston. He was certain that he would not now be defeated by the British. He sent a note to Luzerne in Philadelphia to express his gratitude, assuring the French that this "cannot fail to contribute greatly to perpetuate the gratitude of this country."

Vergennes issued secret instructions to Rochambeau, to be read only when the expeditionary force was at sea. Vergennes had learned to have great respect for the British spy network. He did not even give the details to his good friend Franklin, whose carelessness about secret information Vergennes knew all too well. The instructions, preserved today in the French archives, read:

> The Convoy has orders to land the troops on Rhode Island, where they may be at hand to join General Washington's army if he shall think that necessary; but, as it is possible that the English, after having voluntarily evacuated Rhode Island, may return to it and take possession, it is necessary . . . that the Marquis de La Fayette should request General Washing-

ton to send to Rhode Island, even to Block Island, if the inhabitants can be trusted, some of the French officers who are serving with him. Should no French officer appear with a letter from General La Fayette, giving instructions as to the availability of disembarking, and should no signals be seen, the French squadron, with its convoy, will go into Boston harbor and there await advices from General Washington.

The French squadron made its landfall on the evening of July 9. American pilots raced out to board the ships, with the good news that the Americans still occupied Rhode Island with forces strong enough to hold it against anything the British had in the area. Arrangements were made for the squadron to sail into Newport, all standards flying, the seven stately line-of-battle warships in the foreguard, five frigates behind, with the French fleur-de-lis on the mastheads, transports following with drum, bugle and fife corps playing. The procession was designed to make a show of strength and panache that would excite the crowds and send words of glory winging through the embattled states.

But Neptune was still pro-British. He had used every mean trick of weather against the French each time they sailed into an American port. On the morning of the big sea parade, the worst thick, cold, clammy New England fog rolled in to envelop and swallow up the French squadron. Washington's liaison officer, General William Heath, sailing down from Providence to meet the French with a welcoming committee, was becalmed at sea.

It was a disaster. Rochambeau, writing to the Navy Minister on July 16, reported: "There was no one in the streets; only a few, sad and frightened faces in the windows. I talked to some of the principal citizens, informing them that this was the vanguard of a much larger force on the way and that the King had decided to uphold them with all his power and strength." He reported that they seemed unimpressed and indifferent. He ended, however, on a happier note: "This excellent news traveled fast and on the evening of the following day all the houses were illuminated and the bells rang out and there were fireworks."

Difficulties and misunderstandings soon began to put new strains on the alliance despite the magnificent effort the French had made in sending so great an expeditionary force. Not only were the allies at odds with each other but there was dissension inside the French camp, due to tangled lines of command between young Lafayette and the veteran Rochambeau. Lafayette had sent Rochambeau a set of plans, wildly reckless, for an assault on the British main base in New York and Long Island, although there was no French fleet capable of tackling Britain's mighty navy. Rochambeau was astonished to receive such battle proposals from Lafayette—who was, in his view, only a liaison officer with Washington—while receiving not a word from Washington himself. Washington had told Lafayette that his presence as Commander in Chief was essential to maintain order and activity at American headquarters and asked him to explain the situation to General Rochambeau. Instead, Lafayette told Rochambeau nothing, but informed everyone around him that he did not understand Rochambeau's lack of combativity. French infantry, Lafayette declared, was invincible and ought to be sent immediately on the attack.

Rochambeau was swiftly informed of Lafayette's arrogant and indiscreet behavior. He sent him a letter reminding him: "It is always well to think the French invincible, my dear Marquis, but let me tell you a great secret which I have learnt from 40 years' service with them. There are no troops more easily beaten when they have lost confidence in their leaders, and they lose this confidence immediately when they see that they are called upon to suffer because of an individual ambition."

In August Rochambeau wrote Vergennes to report that there was consternation and dismay in every quarter. Paper money had now fallen to a ratio of sixty to one, and Washington could not get a recruit unless he paid him one hundred "hard dollars." Washington's army had fallen to a low of only some three thousand men, while the Americans were saying that the King should have sent twenty thousand men and twenty ships to drive the British from New York.

The war will be an expensive one. We pay even for our quarters and the land occupied by this camp. I shall, of course, use all possible order and economy. Send us troops and money, but do not depend upon these people nor upon their means. They have neither money nor credit. Their means of resistance are only momentary and called forth when they are attacked in their own homes. They then assemble for the moment of immediate danger and defend themselves.

Washington kept pressing Lafayette for more help. "Unless we secure arms and powder from the Count, we certainly can do nothing. With every effort we shall fall short at least four thousand or five thousand arms and two hundred tons of powder." Rochambeau refused to make a move or adopt a plan until he could see Washington face to face. On August 12, he wrote Lafayette, flatly rejecting the younger man's claim to have full powers to represent Washington in all matters.

As the summer and fall went by without any coordinated plan for a joint campaign, a French officer on the headquarters staff wrote a gloomy letter home:

> We are of no possible aid to our allies. We cannot leave our island and our fleet cannot leave port without exposing us to the enemy, who, with superior forces in the way of men and ships, would certainly attack us and cut off our retreat to the mainland.
>
> Instead of helping the Americans, we are a drawback to them. We cannot reinforce their army as we are about a twelve day march from them, separated by arms of the sea which are dangerous to cross in winter because of huge blocks of floating ice. We are, in fact, a burden to our allies because our victualizing makes provisions scarce for them. We are even an expense to them because by paying cash for our provisions we depreciate their paper money and consequently the purveyors refuse to sell provisions for their paper money.

British Admiral Samuel Graves sailed to join squadrons in New York; then the combined fleet, with fifteen warships, appeared off Newport, sealing the French in. If more troops and a large fleet did not challenge the British, Rochambeau's reinforcements for Washington would remain bottled up in Rhode Island. Lafayette wrote furious letters to Luzerne demanding that he stir up Paris to send a fleet and a second division of troops. Washington finally arranged a meeting with Rochambeau and told him that he could make no plans for an offensive because the French had not sent all their expeditionary force at once. Rochambeau replied that naval superiority was essential to any attack and that he could not commit his troops to an offensive without naval cover. He said that New York should be the main target and then startled the American staff by stating that an attack on New York would require an assault force of at least thirty thousand men. He pledged France to supply fifteen thousand if the Americans would supply the same in their own defense. Washington, with only three thousand men, and the state militia about to terminate its service, simply could not give a positive reply to the proposal. That ended all hopes for any major offensive for the winter of 1780–81, and they parted with no plans made at all for the following year. The high hopes of July, when the French expeditionary force had arrived, had melted away, as Washington put it, "like the morning dew."

Washington reported to Congress that he could take no further steps without money to pay troops and buy supplies. Congress had no money. The only hope, as always, was France, a France whose Treasury had already been drained by the cost of paying for Rochambeau's force and all the French costs for their own war effort.

Congress knew it would have to turn to Franklin again for yet another loan, after all the efforts he had already made, but Franklin had been flooding them with a wave of complaints about their many drafts upon him, stressing his impossible situation. Franklin's enemies—the Lees and Adams family and their friends—saw a chance to undercut Franklin. They proposed the nomination of Lieutenant Colonel John Laurens, son of Henry Laurens, as a special envoy with the mission of raising a new loan in Europe. Gouverneur Morris understood what the game was, and he stated it bluntly as "a plan to remove Franklin indirectly, a thing which could not for obvious reasons be accomplished directly." Later, he added caustically, "In a word we have sent a young beggar instead of an old one."

Luzerne, perfectly informed on what Congress was up to, wrote to Vergennes, telling him that a loan would certainly have to be granted if Washington was to be able to raise an army strong enough to combine with Rochambeau in a joint campaign to defeat the British. He strongly urged Vergennes that, if France could afford the loan, it ought to be granted to Franklin before Laurens and his special mission (which included Tom Paine) could arrive in France. Luzerne and Vergennes had no intention of letting Franklin's enemies sabotage him.

While all these diplomatic monetary and interallied crises were exploding, the situation was deteriorating on the military fronts. After the fall of Charleston, Washington sent General de Kalb to try to shore up the Carolinas. He assigned to him the Maryland and Delaware line regiments, veteran outfits that had fought in the Northern campaigns. They made their way to Hillsboro, North Carolina, suffering severe hardships along the route. The states failed to furnish them with supplies. Soldiers went days without food, then gorged themselves on green fruits and vegetables and raw meat. Hundreds of men came down with dysentery and cramps. Congress then appointed its favorite political general, the "hero" of Saratoga, Horatio Gates, to be Commander in the South, over strong objections from Washington, who did not admire Gates.

At that critical moment, Admiral de Guichen, who had brought Rochambeau's forces to America, decided the odds were too great, and, running the British blockade, returned to France with his fifteen warships, dismaying Washington, who had hoped he would try to fight the British off Newport. Rochambeau was stranded in Rhode Island.

When General Gates took command from de Kalb at Hillsboro, he decided to launch an assault on Camden, South Carolina. Instead of taking the wagon road, through rich and patriotic farm country, he decided on a short cut through piny barrens where only a chicken could scratch out a meal—and there were no chickens. His weakened troops suffered new deprivations and hardships. When he arrived at the approaches to Camden, he did not have three thousand men left fit for battle. Less than a thousand were Continental regulars and they were in poor shape.

Lord Cornwallis' scouts had traced every faltering step of Gates's march. The British were a smaller force but perfectly conditioned, fully equipped veteran British troops. Before dawn on August 16, Cornwallis attacked Gates. One of the fiercest, bloodiest battles of the war ensued. The American militia panicked and broke under savage British bayonet attacks. Baron de Kalb, mortally wounded, held his line with the veterans of Maryland and Delaware. But the militia broke ranks and ran for their lives, with General Gates, on his thoroughbred horse, leading the flight. Gates did not stop fleeing until he reached Charlotte, some sixty miles from the battlefield. He disgraced himself, and his military career came to a shameful end. American losses in dead and wounded were heavy.

North Carolina was now open to Cornwallis and he marched his victorious troops into that state. Major Patrick Ferguson, at the head of some four thousand South Carolina Loyalists fighting in the British ranks, sent scouts ahead with word that he would lay waste all the frontier settlements and hang all American militiamen from the nearest tree. His foolish threat aroused the entire countryside, which rose up in arms, just as the men of New England had arisen when Burgoyne had invaded their settlements. They were deadly marksmen with long rifles and as invisible as Indians in the forested lands. They pinned and ambushed the British, killed Ferguson and slaughtered every Carolinian who did not hold up a white flag. Cornwallis was obliged to beat a hasty retreat back to South Carolina. It was just about the first good news Washington would receive in that black year of defeats.

In Madrid, John Jay's troubles were deepened by the death of his new-born daughter and continued coolness from the Spanish. He was distressed, on September 3, to receive a call from Don Diego de Gardoqui, who had been an American purchasing and shipping agent, and seemed highly sympathetic to the American cause. Gardoqui dashed Jay's hopes by telling him that the only way to get aid was for America to yield to Spain all navigation rights on the Mississippi River. He also told Jay that he would be appointed to succeed Miralles in Philadelphia, with such instructions. Jay firmly replied that his proposal was totally unacceptable.

Jay was somewhat cheered when he received a letter from Franklin, answering his urgent plea for aid and confirming his refusal of any concessions on the Mississippi. Franklin had gone to the French to tell them how desperate the situation was and had received a pledge of new credits. He said he could assign twenty-five thousand dollars to Jay's account. He advised Jay to keep a "good, even temper" in Spain, despite his cold reception there. He reminded him, as he had Adams, that America was not in a position to make demands, only to beg most humbly and to present the best argument for the American cause in a determined but polite manner. On the Mississippi, however, Franklin wrote: "Poor as we are, yet as I know we shall be rich, I would rather agree with them to buy at a great price the whole of their right on the Mississippi than sell a drop of its waters. A neighbor might as well ask me to sell my street door." Franklin was not subservient to our allies, as Adams thought. He was pliable, humble, exceedingly polite when seeking aid or funds, always diplomatic in argument, but absolutely unyielding on any issue he felt involved America's security and future growth.

Throughout this period, Franklin was involved in a desperate attempt to buy and ship saltpeter to Washington. He found several sources and made the necessary purchases, but the French Ministry of the Navy would not grant him the necessary export licenses; the French military was trying to hoard that invaluable material for its own forces. It was then that Franklin's friendship with the chemist Lavoisier began to pay off. Lavoisier was in charge of the King's arsenals of explosives. He admired Franklin as a fellow scientist and was grateful to Franklin for having helped design fireproof and lightningproof devices for the arsenals. He managed slowly to procure the permits for Franklin. There were still problems with transport and the British blockade and most of the saltpeter did not get through, but what little did was precious to Washington.

New diplomatic ploys began to spin intrigues in the last three months of 1780. The Russians, having formed the Armed Neutrality League, decided to broaden their diplomatic efforts and began making strong hints about a possible peace mediation. Vergennes wrote his Ambassador in St. Petersburg to say that he was interested in Count Panin's ideas on American independence and wanted to hear more about them. He thought, perhaps, that Catherine herself might act as arbitrator and might consider not only a mediation but a simultaneous armistice. This represented a serious breach of faith with the Americans, and with his good friend Franklin, whom he did not inform of these moves.

The war was becoming increasingly expensive for France. Vergennes felt the Americans were not doing enough in their own cause and were too dependent on France. In addition, he was in a fight for his own political life with a powerful rival, Jacques Necker, Director-General of Finances, who, like his predecessor, Turgot, was resolutely opposed to French support for the American Revolution because it was ruining the kingdom. Vergennes had a difficult time reconvincing Louis XVI to support America. His colleague, Navy Minister Sartine, was less fortunate, and lost his job. The alliance came close to collapse in the last months of 1780, and the French government almost broke up in internal fighting.

On December 16, Holland finally joined the Armed Neutrality. Four days later, England declared war on Holland—another severe blow to America. Holland as a neutral had been most useful, as had been her West Indian colonies. Now they were under British attack, unable to send supplies to the United States.

On December 19, having received encouraging replies from London, Catherine of Russia called in British Ambassador James Harris and advised him to make peace as a means of destroying the American Revolution. She told him: "Deal with your colonies separately. Try to divide them. Then their alliance will fall of itself." Harris reported this conversation back to London and received a reply from the Prime Minister, Lord North, that Britain was now willing to accept mediation and to make peace with France, but only on condition that France repudiate its alliance with the United States.

The day after Christmas, the terrible year almost over, Franklin, approaching the seventy-fifth year of his life, having suffered his most severe attack of gout, confessed to his diary, in a rare moment of weakness and low morale, that he was worn down with fatigue, besieged by his enemies, overwhelmed with financial and monetary problems that seemed insoluble. He began to think that the time had come for him to leave the scene.

CHAPTER

20

The Darkness before the Dawn

The winter of 1780–81 was one of the worst trials for General Washington. His men were again short of blankets, clothes and shoes. Continental money was now worthless and Washington had no hard currency. Bad news was reported from the West Indies. Admiral Rodney, having been informed of Britain's declaration of war on Holland, sailed to attack the rich Dutch trading post at St. Eustatius Island, a vital supply base for the Americans. The garrison did not even know that war had been declared and was totally unprepared for Rodney's swift, powerful assault. He captured some three million pounds sterling worth of booty and a fleet of blockade runners, loading up for the United States. It was a terrible blow for Washington, and the news moved the Congress to redouble its appeal to Franklin for French aid.

On New Year's Day, the President of the Congress, Samuel Huntington, sent Franklin a letter to be presented to the King of France, along with a copy of the instructions being carried to France by John Laurens, the new special envoy. Laurens would bring an urgent plea for at least twenty-five million livres over and above the twenty-five millions that Franklin had already obtained the year before. On January 15, George Washington sent a letter to Franklin, introducing Laurens and explaining his particular qualities as special envoy. Laurens, wrote Washington, had been the General's aide, was a military specialist, knew exactly what Washington needed and could be helpful to Franklin in making the right purchases and explaining the situation to the French court.

> The present infinitely critical posture of our affairs, made it essential in the opinion of Congress to send from hence a person who had been eye-witness to their progress and who was capable of placing them before the Court of France, in a more full and striking point of light, than was proper or even practicable by any written communications. It was also judged of great importance that the person should be able to give a military view of them and to enter into military details and arrangements.

Franklin did not doubt Washington, but he knew it was not the whole story. Laurens could have been sent as a military aide to Franklin, the Minister; he need not have been sent with full ministerial powers of his own. That decision, Franklin knew, had been made by men who were trying to go around him and force his recall or resignation. Franklin, hurt and ill, was of half a mind to quit right away, but he did not want to leave in failure. He decided to make a maximum effort to obtain a new French loan before Laurens could arrive, and then resign with his colors flying high.

Washington gave Franklin no details on how truly desperate his situation was. He was afraid his letter might be intercepted by the British. But he did stress his desperation in a background information paper to Laurens. He wrote that "the patience of the army, from an almost uninterrupted series of complicated distress, is now nearly exhausted, and their discontents matured to an extremity, which has recently had very disagreeable consequences and which demonstrates the absolute necessity of speedy relief, a relief not within the compass of our means." The relief needed included monies to buy clothing and food and pay the soldiers, and, most importantly, "a decided effort of the allied arms on this continent in the ensuing campaign, to effectuate once and for all the great objects of the alliance, the liberty and independence of these states."

Washington appended the minutes of a conference he had held with Rochambeau in which they had agreed on the necessity of an additional fifteen thousand men for a spring and summer campaign. The French had promised two divisions totaling fifteen thousand men, but Rochambeau had arrived with only half that force. The other half had been blockaded at Brest when the British threw a strong cordon around the port to lock in Admiral Comte François de Grasse and his troop transports. Washington said that if a choice had to be made between more men and more money, "it were preferable to diminish the aid in men; for the same sum of money which would transport from France and maintain here a body of troops with all the necessary apparatus, being put into our hands to be employed by us, would serve to give activity to a larger force within ourselves, and its influence would pervade the whole administration."

A few days later, the Marquis de Lafayette, intensely loyal to Washington, wrote to Vergennes telling him how the French had failed their allies, appealing to French pride for new and greater efforts:

> Since the hour of the arrival of the French, their inferiority has never for one moment ceased, and the English and the Tories have dared to say that France wished to kindle, without extinguishing, the flame. This calumny becomes more dangerous at a period when the English detachments are wasting the South, when, under the protection of some frigates, a corps of fifteen hundred men are repairing to Virginia, without our being able to get to them. On the whole continent, with the exception of the islands of Newport, it is physically impossible that we should carry on an offensive without ships, and, even on those islands, the difficulty of transportation, the scarcity of provisions and many other inconveniences render all attempts too precarious to enable us to form any settled plan of campaign. . . . it becomes, in a political and military point of view, necessary to give us, both by vessels sent from France, and by a great movement in the fleet in the islands, a decided naval superiority for the next campaign; and also, Sir, to give us money enough to place the American forces in a state of activity.

Neither Washington nor Lafayette dared tell Vergennes the true extent of their miseries. They made no mention of the six

Pennsylvania regiments that, on January 2, had mutinied, stormed out of their camp and marched for Philadelphia to present their grievances to the Congress. A hastily named special congressional committee had ridden to head off the mutineers in Princeton. The leaders of the revolt were given their chance to complain about their lack of food, clothing and pay, received promises of prompt congressional action, and then agreed to re-enlist and return to camp. A few soldiers deserted, but most of them returned to arms.

Another mutiny broke out on January 20, as Lafayette wrote to Vergennes, when three New Jersey regiments rebelled. Washington had often complained about the lack of discipline and patriotism of the Jersey men, and he sent a crack unit of regulars to put the mutiny down. The regulars quickly subdued the rebels and arrested the ringleaders. Washington called a court-martial and two leaders of the mutiny were hanged.

To try to stem the British tide in the South, Washington, at year end, had appointed one of his favorite commanders, thirty-eight-year-old General Nathanael Greene of Rhode Island. On taking the Southern Command, Greene had reported back to Washington that "The appearance of the troops was wretched beyond description, and their distress, on account of lack of provisions, was little less than their suffering for want of clothing and other necessities." Greene knew, moreover, that his forces were outnumbered by the British. He took the audacious decision to divide his small band into two separate columns. He reasoned that together they could not face a fight with Cornwallis but that separately, using commando tactics, they might confuse the enemy and set up ambushes. He took command of one column and put the other under General Daniel Morgan. Meanwhile, Washington sent him reinforcements, including the elite cavalry of Light-Horse Harry Lee.

Cornwallis' scouts reported the American maneuvers back to him, and, to meet it, he decided to split his own army into three parts, intending to use two columns forward and one in reserve in a lightning attack on the American units. This was exactly what Greene had hoped might happen. Now that the British had split up their own central army, the Americans had a chance against them.

The British column sent after Morgan was the first to make contact. Morgan was expecting them and he had set his men in position on a plain near Kings Mountain, at a site called the Cowpens. When the British charged en masse, Morgan's men were ready and laid down a hail of bullets. They then pulled back, changed positions and fired into the rear of the British ranks. Morgan's smaller force cut and twisted, fired, ran, reloaded and fired again until by the end of the day they had killed or captured 90 percent of the British force. It was a small victory, but a vitally important one for American morale.

Greene continued these tactics for weeks, cutting, twisting and running from Cornwallis, but sweeping in for quick raids, then out again. Cornwallis should have gone back to Charleston and organized for his major campaign to cut off the South. Instead, his pride had been hurt. He chased the elusive Americans through North Carolina instead of conducting a coordinated campaign, and fell right into Greene's trap.

While Cornwallis was chasing Greene, the British had opened up another front in Virginia. Sir Henry Clinton had given the turncoat Benedict Arnold command of a force of almost two thousand American Tories who had volunteered to fight for Britain. The British fleet carried his forces down to the Virginia coast, where they had landed without resistance. Quickly, Arnold, one of the best field commanders in America, marched his troops into Richmond and captured it with hardly a shot being fired. One of the reasons for his success, in addition to his speed and daring, was Governor Thomas Jefferson's failure to prepare his defenses. Jefferson had to flee Richmond as Arnold's troops rushed in.

As soon as Washington heard what had happened, he sent Lafayette, with three divisions, to counterattack in Virginia, with orders to capture the traitor. Meanwhile, Washington at last persuaded the French to take action. Admiral Sochet Destouches, with eight ships of the line, and twelve hundred troops, sailed from Newport. British Admiral Marriott Arbuthnot, learning of this, sailed out of Long Island Sound to try to intercept and engage the French. His ships were faster than the French and he had favorable winds in his sails, with the result that he sailed right past the French without ever seeing them. Unfortunately, a strong fleet of British frigates at Hampton Roads sighted the French and gave chase. The French, outgunned, swung around and raced back to Newport, another of their missions aborted.

The British were also on the move on the diplomatic front. Franklin's old adversary, Lord Stormont, on hearing that Catherine of Russia had proposed a mediation, decided the time had come for a political power play. He drew up a plan to bribe Catherine to support the British side in a peace conference, by offering her the island of Minorca. He also had a tempting bribe to offer Joseph II of Austria—in fact, a double bribe. He would propose to Catherine that she accept Austria as a co-mediator, with Vienna as the site of the conference. This would pay the French back for having turned down earlier Austrian bids for mediation, and bring Joseph to the British side. He also told Joseph that the British would open up the Scheldt to Austrian shipping, from Antwerp to the sea, to strengthen Joseph's Austrian colonies in the Netherlands.

To Stormont's surprise and chagrin, neither imperial ruler would respond to his offer. Catherine told Panin, "Someone is trying to pull my leg." Joseph nervously noted Britain's declaration of war on Holland and decided that it was a little too dangerous to embrace the British bulldog. He did, however, jump at the opportunity to become co-mediator, with the prestige of Vienna's having been proposed as a site for the conference. And he was pleased when Catherine agreed to send her mediator to Vienna.

Vergennes, in Paris, watching all these moves, was worrying about the disastrous war news coming in from America. He was gravely concerned about the monetary disaster in America and the new demands for monies from a French Treasury already seriously drained by war costs. At the same time, he was acutely aware of Floridablanca's ploys with Hussey and Cumberland. He would not let Floridablanca double-cross him and was determined to counter his peace moves with Britain. For the first time, Vergennes began to have serious doubts about America's ability to hold out against the British. He began to rethink his own policies and wrote, for the King's Council, a confidential memorandum that amounted to a sellout of his ally, the United States.

In that memo of February, 1781, Vergennes stated that it would be possible to accept a mediation and a peace based upon the traditional principle of uti possidetis, that is, on boundaries traced by the actual possession of territories at the time of the truce. This would have left the British in possession of almost all of Georgia, most of South and North Carolina, New York City and Long Island, and of fortified posts throughout the Western territories and New England. Spain would keep West Florida and the east bank of the Mississippi up to the Arkansas River and some posts in Illinois and Michigan territory.

A devious but essentially honest man, Vergennes admitted that he was virtually abandoning the American cause. He wrote:

> One may, therefore, presume to say that the King would be lacking in delicacy, that he would be somewhat violating his engagements, that he would be giving the Americans just cause for complaint or at least distrust, if he should propose to Congress to sign a truce leaving the English what they possess on the continent. Therefore, only the mediators, bound by no such ties, could make a proposition so painful to the United States.

Vergennes himself would not deliberately wreck American hopes, but he would let Russia and Austria do so and go along with their proposals.

Vergennes told Russia and Austria that he was prepared to accept their mediation at a conference in Vienna, but that he would first have to consult with his allies, the United States and Spain. By so doing, he was forcing Floridablanca's hand on the side game he was playing with Hussey and Cumberland. Floridablanca could not risk offending the other European powers, so he, too, had to agree to the mediation, while stipulating that Spain insisted on Gibraltar, the Honduras and Florida. He was obliged, however, to repudiate Cumberland and ask him to leave Spain. His private dealings with the British had come to an end.

Having checked Spain, Vergennes then set about plans to control and maneuver the United States. On March 9, he wrote to Luzerne, telling him to make every effort to get John Adams replaced as Peace Commissioner. He knew that Adams would see through his scheme and raise all sorts of objections to the terms of the Vienna conference. Luzerne was to persuade the Congress that there was no practicable way to refuse to participate in the mediation since all the other belligerents had already agreed. If it proved impossible to replace Adams, as Vergennes expected, Luzerne was to get Congress to write Adams a new set of instructions, subordinating him to the supervision and advice of the French. He urged that Congress be reasonable in drafting its peace terms. In the event that diplomacy moved very rapidly in Europe, before Congress could reply, then, although Adams was already in Europe as an accredited peace delegate, Vergennes would take it upon himself to represent the interests of the United States, even in the absence of their permission, and Luzerne was so to inform the Congress, lest "a refusal to do so might bring on disastrous and incalculable results."

Franklin had received the same bad news that Vergennes had from America and was keenly aware of the machinations of the great powers. He was also under pressure from Congress and from George Washington to obtain more aid in men and money. At the same time, he was under the personal pressure of wanting to negotiate a loan before Laurens could arrive, and offer his resignation on a high point rather than at a low moment in his mission. He had already been informed by Carmichael and other friends that his enemies were still trying to get him recalled. He wrote to Carmichael, in Spain, at the end of January, saying:

> I hear that a Motion has been made in Congress by a Caroline Member for recalling me, but without Success; and that A. Lee has printed a Pamphlet against me. If my Enemies would have a little Patience they may soon see me Remov'd without their giving themselves any Trouble, as I am now 75.

He then wrote an eloquent appeal to Vergennes for help, restating reasons he had often used before in his most forceful and positive style. He asserted that "the Misfortunes of the last Campaign, instead of repressing have doubled their [the Americans'] Ardour; that Congress has resolved to employ every Resource in their Power to expel the Enemy from every part of the United States, by the most vigorous and decisive Cooperation with Marine and other forces of their illustrious Ally."

Vergennes did not believe in America as much as Franklin did, but he was feeling guilty about the peace plot that he was conspiring to put over on the Americans, and he felt a personal obligation toward Franklin. He had also written Luzerne that he had been offended by the appointment of Laurens, since it implied lack of confidence in his relationship with Franklin. Accordingly, Vergennes went to the King's Council to plead for new aid for America. He used many of Franklin's arguments, principally that England would become the "Terror of Europe" if it held the principal American ports and controlled American trade. Despite the opposition of the Finance Director, Vergennes persuaded Louis XVI to make a further effort to keep the Americans fighting.

On March 10, Franklin received a copy of a royal proclamation which had just been sent to the President of the Congress:

MY DEAR GREAT FRIENDS AND ALLIES:

We have received your letter of the 22nd of November past, which you directed Dr. Franklin to deliver. We have seen therein, with pain, the picture of the distressed state of your finances, and have been so affected that we have determined to assist you as far as our wants and the extraordinary and enormous expenses of the present war, in which we are engaged for your defence, will permit.

That day Vergennes called in Franklin to ask him to report to Congress the impossibility of France's lending the twenty-five million that Congress sought. The Treasury simply could not provide it. Furthermore, the King felt that an additional loan would be difficult because it would interfere with a public loan drive being launched by the French government itself inside France. However, aware of America's distress, the King of France had generously decided to grant the sum of six million livres, not as a loan but as a free gift, and in addition to the three million that Vergennes had already made available to Franklin for current drafts of interest. The money would be kept in a special account by the Royal Treasurer in the name of George Washington, and Washington alone could draw upon it.

Franklin wrote promptly to the President of Congress, informing him of this grant and of its terms. He explained that the money was destined directly for the army and that the French were fearful that if it were sent to the Congress, it might be diverted for other purposes. Franklin gave it as his opinion that "There was no room to dispute on this point, every donor having the right of qualifying his gifts with such terms as he thinks proper." Having obtained the money he had been hoping for—less than requested but an important free gift—Franklin then offered his resignation as Minister to France:

> I have passed my seventy-fifth year, and I find that the long and severe fit of the gout which I had the last winter has shaken me exceedingly, and I am yet far from having recovered the bodily strength I before enjoyed. I do not know that my mental faculties are impaired; perhaps I shall be the last to discover that; but I am sensible of great diminutions in my activity, a quality I think particularly necessary in your Minister for this court. I am afraid therefore that your affairs may, some way or other, suffer by my deficiency. . . .
>
> I have been engaged in public affairs and enjoyed public confidence, in some shape or other, during the long term of fifty years, and honor sufficient to satisfy any reasonable ambition, and I have no other left but that of repose, which I hope the Congress will grant me by sending some person to supply my place. At the same time, I beg they may be assured that it is not by the least doubt of their success in the glorious cause, nor any disgust received in their last service, that induces me to decline it, but purely and simply the reasons above mentioned. And as I can not at present undergo the fatigues of a sea voyage (the last having been almost too much for me) and would not again expose myself to the hazard of capture and imprisonment in this time of war, I purpose to remain here 'till the peace—perhaps it may be for the remainder of my life; and if any knowledge or experience I have acquired here may be thought of use to my successor, I shall freely communicate it, and assist him with any influence I may be supposed to have, or counsel that may be desired of me.

The old man then went on, poignantly, to ask the Congress, most humbly, to "take under their protection" his grandson, William Temple Franklin. He praised Tempe's abilities, intelligence, background and experience and asserted that he might well fill the post of minister abroad in some capital, but that, perhaps, he needed a bit more experience and might be appointed secretary to a minister, as he had long been secretary to Franklin himself.

As Franklin wrote his resignation to the Congress, its special envoy, John Laurens, arrived in Paris. Instead of congratulating Franklin on obtaining the free gift of six million livres, he complained strongly that the sum was not nearly enough and that America needed the full twenty-five million that Congress had asked him to negotiate. Leaving Franklin, he called on Vergennes and spoke in the same vigorous terms about the desperate need for the full sum.

Vergennes, ever the diplomat, evaded any specific response or pledge. Instead, he asked Laurens to draw up a list of the most urgently needed supplies. Laurens had such a list all ready, as he reported to the President of Congress in a letter of March 20, recounting his interview with Vergennes:

> I extracted a list, in which I confined myself to the artillery, arms, military stores, clothing, tents, cloths, drugs and surgical instruments. . . . The constant language of M. Vergennes is that our demands are excessive; that we throw the burden of war upon our ally; that the support of it in different parts of the world, has cost France exertions and expenses which fully employ her means; that the public credit however well established, has its limits, to exceed which would be fatal to it. . . . My expectations are very moderate.

Franklin, too, had only moderate expectations of more aid, as he wrote to John Jay in Spain, in a letter in which he told Jay that he would like him to succeed as Minister to France, leaving William Carmichael as envoy to Madrid. He told Jay that he would not mail his letter of resignation until he heard whether Jay would agree to replace him.

On the same day, April 12, Franklin wrote Carmichael to thank him again for his friendly tips about Franklin's enemies:

I do not take their Malice so much amiss, as it may farther my Project (of Rest). Lee and Izard are open, and, so far, honorable Enemies; the Adams, if Enemies, are more covered. I never did any of them the least injury, and can conceive no other Source of their Malice but Envy. To be sure, the excessive Respect shown me here by all Ranks of People, and the little notice taken of them, was a mortifying Circumstance; but it was what I could neither prevent nor remedy. Those who feel Pain at seeing others enjoy Pleasure, and are unhappy because others are happy, must meet daily with so many causes of Torment, that I conceive them to be already in a State of Damnation; and, on that account, I ought to drop all Resentment with regard to those two Gentlemen. But I cannot help being concern'd at the Mischief their ill Tempers will be continually doing in our publick Affairs, whenever they have any concern in them.

After he had completed his correspondence and his arrangements for his resignation that day, Franklin ordered his carriage to take him to the estate of the Comte and Comtesse d'Houdetot, at Sannois, some ten miles from Passy. Madame d'Houdetot had become the third woman in Franklin's life, not a rival for his amorous affections, as were Mesdames Brillon and Helvétius, but one of his closest friends. The Comtesse d'Houdetot was no beauty—she was pock-marked and cross-eyed—yet her husband would be devoted for some forty years of marriage, and her lover equally devoted for more than fifty years, and her intermittent passionate adventures included a famous love affair with the philosopher Jean-Jacques Rousseau, who immortalized her as his love "Sophie" in his *Confessions.* She had a host of friends and admirers at court and in the diplomatic set, including Franklin, and, after Franklin, Thomas Jefferson.

On a beautiful April day, Sophie d'Houdetot hosted a "fête champêtre"—a kind of poetical and philosophical picnic in honor of Ben Franklin. When scouts signaled the approach of his carriage, all the distinguished guests ran out into the fields and surrounded him, singing and throwing flowers. He had to descend from the carriage and join them, arm in arm, as they strolled through the fields to the site of the feast. It must have been a torture on his gout-swollen legs.

All day long they drank, sang, toasted Franklin, freedom, the

Magna Carta, William Tell, in verse after verse of extravagant and hyperbolic stanzas of rather dreadful poetry. After the banquet, Franklin planted a Virginia locust tree in Sophie's garden. More verses were expounded. By then an orchestra had appeared and the party went to the château for dancing. There they all sang the chorus of a song honoring the lightning rod. It was frivolous, absurd, charming, gay and, also, extremely useful, for Sophie became one of the most ardent supporters of the American cause.

John Adams, serving that cause in Holland, was finding himself as frustrated there as he had been in France. He wrote to Franklin in April to deny rumors of his success in obtaining a Dutch loan. "I have not one grain of faith nor hope." He said that there were "capitalists" who did trust America and might be willing to risk loans, but that they were afraid of mobs and Dutch soldiers who were blaming America for keeping them at war with England. Adams raged about the duplicity of England, which hired European mercenaries, floated loans in Europe, sought alliances everywhere, while denying that America had the right to do the same. He was equally angry with Europeans for playing up to Britain's double standard. "Let all Europe stand still, neither lend men nor money nor ships to England nor to America, and let them fight it out alone. I would give my share of millions for such a bargain. America is treated unfairly and ungenerously by Europe. But, thus it is, mankind will be servile to tyrannical masters and basely devoted to vile idols."

In Paris, Laurens kept up his pressures on Vergennes for more money and military supplies. By then, Vergennes had received Lafayette's description of America's desperation and his eloquent appeals for more French help. He went back to his colleagues on the Council, but they were adamant—not another sou. Vergennes finally came up with a solution: the Americans could borrow another ten million in Holland, with French security for the loans.

By June Laurens had completed his mission. He knew that the maximum had been obtained. He sailed for America, carrying with him two and a half million in cash, and leaving another two million, two hundred thousand in France for military stores, to be paid for by Franklin. And he sent a million and a half to Holland, to be forwarded from there. It was assumed that the Dutch loan would cover necessary drafts, but it was not so easily negotiated. Week after week it was delayed. Franklin refused to let the monies be dispatched from Holland until new monies had been found.

William Jackson, the American delegate in charge of the shipment of the money, was furious with Franklin and demanded that he approve its release. Franklin wrote Jackson that it was better to hold the money in reserve to meet outstanding bills rather than risk American default on payments: "I cannot suffer the credit of our country to be destroyed." The money had been given in trust to Franklin by the King of France. He would not let others, as they had done in the past, meddle in his difficult affairs. He had already sent his resignation and was not going to be talked into anything that would injure either America or his own reputation, since he intended to spend perhaps the rest of his days in France and Europe. He won all points, for later Jackson wrote to Franklin to apologize and confirm that he had been completely right in his stand. Then, in August, Franklin received a letter from the President of Congress, rejecting his request to resign, praising Franklin's virtues and magnificent services to his country, asserting that America still needed her most illustrious son, no matter how old or tired he might be.

Franklin was delighted. In his heart he had not truly wanted to resign. It was true that he was old and tired, but he had great reserves of energy. He had been more hurt by the attacks on him than he had admitted even to himself, and there was an element of pique in his resignation. Now he felt vindicated and reinvigorated, as he told William Carmichael in a letter of August 24. "I must," he wrote, "buckle again to business and thank God that my health and spirits are of late improved. I fancy it may have been a double mortification to those enemies you have mentioned to me that I should ask as a favor what they hoped to vex me by taking from me and that I should nevertheless be continued." Franklin esteemed his continuance in office as "an honour, and I really esteem it to be greater than my first appointment, when I consider that all the interest of my enemies, united with my own request, were not sufficient to prevent it."

In America fighting was continuing on the Southern front, where General Greene was still playing at fox and hounds with Cornwallis. When Cornwallis, with superior forces, invaded North Carolina, Greene was running just a few miles ahead of him, portaging boats on wagon wheels, so that he might cross the Dan River into Virginia, just ahead of the Cornwallis pursuit. When Greene crossed the river, Cornwallis was triumphant, so he thought, in North Carolina.

But Greene was preparing a counterattack. Under cover of darkness, he recrossed the Dan and led his troops, in early March, to the crossroads town of Guilford Courthouse, where he dug into entrenched positions to await a British attack. The attack came on the Ides of March, at dawn on the fifteenth. Nathanael Greene later reported to the Pennsylvania Assembly:

> The battle was long, obstinate, and bloody. We were obliged to give up the ground and lost our artillery, but the enemy have been so soundly beaten that they dare not move towards us since the action, notwithstanding we lay within ten miles of him for two days. Except the ground and the artillery, they have gained no advantage. On the contrary, they are little short of being ruined. The enemy's losses in killed and wounded cannot be less than between six and seven hundred, perhaps more.

General Greene's estimate proved correct. British battle reports admitted that one out of every three British troops at the battle was a casualty, dead or wounded. It was one of the most serious British losses in a major encounter in the war.

It was not a clear-cut victory from the American point of view, since Greene had finally been forced to retreat before the British. But he had inflicted serious casualties, and Cornwallis, weakened, without supplies and reinforcements, had to pull back and retreat to fixed positions on the coast, at Wilmington, North Carolina. The withdrawal of Cornwallis permitted Greene, a bold officer, to launch a series of raids into South Carolina, keeping the British off balance all through the summer of 1781. It was the first sign of an American dawn, a hope of ultimate victory. Out of black defeat and chaos, the Americans were on the point of turning the tide of battle to a most astonishing, wholly unexpected victory.

CHAPTER

21

Out of the Darkness, Victory

At the height of the Battle of Guilford Courthouse, Lord Cornwallis, sensing a turning of the tide, fearful lest his great plan to cut off the South might be lost by Clinton's failure to mass troops for a decisive campaign, wrote to his colleague, General William Phillips, who was operating in Virginia: "If we mean an offensive war in America, we must abandon New York, and bring our whole force into Virginia; we then have a stake to fight for, and a successful battle may give us America. If our plan is defensive, mixed with desultory expeditions, let us quit the Carolinas (which cannot be held defensively while Virginia can be so easily armed against us) and stick to our salt pork at New York, sending now and then a detachment to steal tobacco, etc." Cornwallis knew exactly what he was saying to Phillips, for that General had been spending his time in Virginia raiding and burning tobacco farms, arguing that it was the principal crop that paid for French and Spanish supplies. Cornwallis had nothing but contempt for this petty strategy. It might annoy the Americans but it would not win the war. Sir Henry Clinton, like his predecessor, Sir William Howe, was quite comfortable in New York, eating a good deal more than salt pork. He had no intention of pulling out and fighting a campaign in Virginia with its thick forests, deep rivers and American riflemen who slunk about and sniped like Indians. Instead, he merely agreed to let

Cornwallis march into Virginia and promised him reinforcements.

Reinforcements arrived within a month by sea, reaching Cornwallis at his headquarters in Wilmington. By April 25 he was ready to go back on the attack. He set off for Petersburg, Virginia, and marched through the land without any American opposition. Benedict Arnold, that elusive tactician, had slipped around Lafayette, sent to Virginia to find him. With only light cavalry, still waiting to meet up with Light-Horse Harry's heavy cavalry, with no naval support at all, Lafayette was lost in the Virginia forests. General Phillips, however, had been contacted by Cornwallis' scouts and had joined up with him in Petersburg, giving him a strong, combined force of almost 7,500 men, including Colonel Banastre Tarleton's redoubtable horse troops, who had raided Charlottesville and captured seven Virginian legislators. Once again, Thomas Jefferson had a very narrow escape, galloping out of town a few hoofbeats ahead of the British.

While Cornwallis was launching his new strategy, the French were preparing for counterattacks of their own. Vergennes had convinced Louis XVI that all they had risked would be lost if they did not send naval forces to America. Admiral de Grasse, France's most daring and able seaman, broke the British blockade at Brest with a powerful fleet of twenty line-of-battle ships. He was fired up to avenge the defeats and fiasco of d'Estaing, to restore French credit and provide the vital support to free Rochambeau's landlocked French Army. Toward the end of March he was in full sail to the West Indies, and from there he would go to American waters.

The American waters were troubled politically as well as militarily. Not yet aware that Franklin had already decided to resign, his enemies kept up a running battle for his recall. French Minister Luzerne countered by organizing his own lobby, headed by General Sullivan, who became all but a French agent, and by a young New Yorker, Robert Livingston, a graduate of King's College (Columbia) who admired both Franklin and the French, and had won a political reputation as one of the drafters of the New York State Constitution.

The personality conflicts took place in the larger context of an important change in congressional operations. Until the spring of 1781, the principal executive business of Congress, in the absence of a federal executive power, was vested in committees, particularly on foreign affairs and finance. At that time, congressional leaders decided there was a need for executive authority, for committees were better at arguing and drawing up reports than acting. It was then that Robert Morris was named Superintendent of Finance, a kind of financial czar. Even more tangled in disputes than finance were foreign affairs, so a debate began to choose a Secretary of Foreign Affairs—America's first Secretary of State.

All the factions agreed this was necessary, but each was determined to name its own man. Luzerne wanted to be sure it would be someone dedicated to the alliance with France—his candidate was Livingston. The Adams-Lee clique, suspicious of the French and sworn enemies of Franklin, lined up behind the terrible-tempered Arthur Lee.

The Adams-Lee faction rapidly rounded up five states for Lee. He needed only two more to have the majority of the thirteen states. Luzerne, alarmed, went into high gear. He arranged a series of luncheons, receptions and dinners at his embassy. He promised more French aid if Livingston was elected and warned the delegates that Arthur Lee was not trusted by the French. If Lee was chosen, it might have serious consequences for more shipments of men and money. Franklin was the only man whom the French admired and trusted enough to handle the aid programs. If his enemies were to triumph, Franklin would leave and the entire alliance would be endangered.

While these political battles were being fought in April and May, the fortunes of war were shifting on the Virginia front. Lafayette, having heard that Arnold had pulled out of Richmond, marched into the Virginia city on April 29, to prepare its defenses against another possible British assault. Two other generals had their eyes on Richmond: George Washington and Charles Cornwallis. Near the end of May, Washington gave urgent orders to Anthony Wayne to take his brigade of one thousand men from

Pennsylvania south to Virginia. Four days later, on May 24, Lord Cornwallis, at the head of his troops, also departed for Richmond.

On the first day of May, Washington had written a gloomy assessment of the situation in his diary:

> Instead of having magazines filled with provisions, we have a scanty pittance scattered here and there in the different States. Instead of having our Arsenals well supplied with military stores, they are poorly provided, and the workmen all leaving them. . . . We are daily and hourly oppressing the people—scouring their tempers—and alienating the affections . . . and instead of having the prospects of a glorious campaign before us, we have a bewildered and gloomy, defensive one—unless we should receive a powerful aid of ships, land troops, and money from our generous allies.

The same week Cornwallis marched for Richmond, Washington met General Rochambeau at Wethersfield, Connecticut, to plan their summer campaign. Washington wanted a joint assault on New York City, but he was worried, as always, about naval support. He wrote Rochambeau: "In any operation, and under all circumstances, a decisive Naval superiority is to be considered as a fundamental principle, and the basis upon which every hope of success must ultimately depend." Washington had by then received word that the powerful fleet of Admiral de Grasse would be committed to the campaign, and that de Grasse would pick up three thousand troops in Santo Domingo. Laurens was about to sail home with fresh money in hand, while Franklin had new money to pay for the list of supplies that Laurens had drawn up. By the time Washington met with Rochambeau much of his gloom had lifted. He was still apprehensive and would not dare to launch the planned campaign until the monies had arrived and the fleet sailed into position, but these now seemed just a matter of waiting a few weeks.

The diplomats were just as busy as the politicians and soldiers that month of May, 1781. On May 21, while Washington and Rochambeau were conferring in Connecticut, Russia's Prince Gallitzin and Austrian Foreign Minister Prince Kaunitz were in Vienna conferring on preliminary proposals for the mediation conference.

They agreed on four principal articles: (1) All proposals put forward by the belligerents would be considered at Vienna. (2) A separate peace between Britain and the colonies would be negotiated and signed at the same time as the general peace among the European powers, the peace to be guaranteed by the mediators, Austria and Russia, and by other neutral powers. (3) There would be a general armistice for a period of one year, during which all boundary questions and other issues would remain in statu quo. (4) Negotiations were to proceed at once, with the plenipotentiaries receiving full powers and instructions. This plan was immediately distributed to all the concerned courts.

As soon as Vergennes received the document from Vienna, he asked Adams to come to Versailles to discuss and coordinate policies. Behind Adams' back he had been encouraging Luzerne to try to get Adams recalled or to name one or more additional negotiators to contain Adams. Vergennes feared, most of all, dealing with the proud, arrogant, unfettered Adams—thus he also asked Luzerne to get Congress to write new instructions, ordering Adams to take the advice of the French.

The congressional committees, meanwhile, had come up with a plan to name a new American Minister to Russia. They thought that Russia would accept the envoy and recognize American independence, putting more pressure on England to make an honorable peace. Vergennes and Luzerne were alarmed by this American illusion. They had to remind Congress what had happened to every envoy they sent over save Franklin: Izard had never been received by the court of Tuscany; Arthur Lee had been rebuffed and humiliated by the Spanish and the Prussians, as had his brother, William; Jay was living miserably, as a beggar, humiliated by Floridablanca in Madrid. Why send yet another American to be shamed by an autocrat like Catherine, who had made it clear that she had no sympathy for a rebellion by serfs?

Nonetheless, a faction in the Congress had elected Francis Dana, and sent him off to Russia. Luzerne asked the Congress to keep his mission secret so as to avoid the embarrassment the others had suffered. When Catherine agreed to be a mediator in Vienna,

Luzerne told Congress that Dana's mission was doomed, for as mediator Catherine could not suddenly step in and take sides on American independence. Congress agreed to hold Dana in the West, instructing him to take his advice on his next move from Vergennes and not to act without agreement from the French.

Having contained Dana, Luzerne now set about to contain John Adams. He also pushed his campaign to get Livingston elected Secretary for Foreign Affairs. In a committee meeting in Congress, Luzerne spoke warmly of John Adams' patriotism and zeal for his nation's cause. He also spoke of his proud and stubborn character and showed the Congress examples of the correspondence that had so enraged Vergennes.

The King of France, Luzerne went on, had pledged to do all he could to help his American allies at Vienna and to support America's plenipotentiary there. The King was the only monarch who had recognized the existence and independence of the United States. If, therefore, Adams became obstinate and quarreled with the French, as he had done so often, and if he made insupportable demands on them, he might force the King to withdraw his support, and America would be totally without friend or ally in Vienna. There was only one way to avert such a disaster: Congress must either give Adams the strictest instructions to take his leads from Vergennes or name at least two additional peace envoys so that Adams could not act alone. Luzerne strongly recommended that one of the new Peace Commissioners should be Benjamin Franklin, who enjoyed the highest trust of the French and was the most admired American in all of Europe.

Luzerne played his hand brilliantly. As soon as he left, the committee chairman began to draft a list of resolutions for the full Congress on the following main points: (a) that the Congress accept the offer of mediation by Austria and Russia; (b) that the American delegation work only through the French Ministry; (c) that the American delegates be empowered to sign a peace, along the lines of previous instructions, and only on condition that American independence be recognized on the same basis that it had been in the treaties with France; and (d) that the American delegates present their instructions to the French ministers and leave it to the French delegates to find the means to work them out.

It was everything that Vergennes had asked Luzerne to accomplish, a stunning diplomatic coup, in which the Frenchman had led the American congressmen by the nose. It was a most unwise move by the Congress, for it delivered the American peace delegation to the French bound and gagged. It can be understood only against the background of fear, even desperation, of a Congress that had lost control of the country's currency, lacked the money to recruit, pay and arm its defense forces, and indeed felt virtually helpless except for the aid that France would furnish.

The congressional committee worked through the week and then, on the weekend, met with Luzerne to see whether its draft satisfied the French Minister. He approved it in general and made some suggestions on the issue of boundaries, to keep it loose until a peace conference might follow the armistice and truce. He thought the instructions to Adams too weak, and asked the committee to set down in simple, clear and unmistakable language the order that Adams was to work through and under the directions of the French Minister, Vergennes, and was to take *no* unilateral action. The members noted the changes, redrafted their resolutions and submitted them to the Congress on Monday, June 12. The resolutions all passed, with majority votes. In effect, there would be no American delegation in Vienna. America would be a junior member of the French delegation.

The Congress then moved to consider the question of appointing additional delegates to the Peace Conference. At first, the resolution had been rejected, but after much lobbying it was reconsidered and passed. Then came the nominations and members proposed, in turn, the names of John Jay, John Laurens, his father Henry Laurens, Thomas Jefferson, Joseph Reed, William Carmichael and Benjamin Franklin. Congress moved to vote on June 13.

On the first ballot, John Jay won a majority and was elected. Congress then adjourned for a day of politicking, since Jay was the only man on whom there was general agreement. Luzerne organized his friends for Franklin while the "Junto" against Franklin, under Arthur Lee, rallied its forces for the test vote. Because of the resolution making the American delegation subservient to the French, they feared Franklin all the more, and thought he would seriously undercut Adams and the other delegates.

When the balloting began, the forces were so split that no one of the candidates could win the majority of seven of the thirteen states. On the first ballot, there were five votes for Tom Jefferson, four for Ben Franklin and one for Henry Laurens. The others by then had withdrawn. A second ballot followed; same result. On the third ballot, the forces held firm: Jefferson, five; Franklin, four; Laurens, one.

Luzerne's "agent," General Sullivan, then rose and proposed that, instead of further balloting, all three be declared elected. The opposition exploded and there nearly was fistfighting on the floor. Opposition spokesmen then moved to accept the proposal but asked for an endorsement vote on each man, with the vote on Franklin to come last. Sullivan saw through the maneuver, and held fast. Eventually, the opposition caved in; the new Peace Commissioners would be John Jay, Thomas Jefferson, Benjamin Franklin and Henry Laurens, all to join with John Adams, all ordered to do nothing without the express knowledge and consent of the French ministers. They were also ordered, independently of the French, to accept no proposal that might leave any part of the thirteen states in British hands and to insist that any peace treaty officially recognize the existence and independence of the United States as a sovereign nation.

As soon as the resolution was passed, Samuel Huntington, President of the Congress, sat down and sent a general message, to which were attached detailed instructions, to the new commissioners and the original envoy, John Adams:

> You are at liberty to secure the interest of the United States in such a manner as circumstances may direct, and as the state of the belligerent and the disposition of the mediating powers may require. For this purpose you are to make the most candid and confidential communications upon all subjects to the ministers of our generous ally the King of France; to

undertake nothing in the negotiations for peace or truce without their knowledge or concurrence, and ultimately to govern yourselves by their advice and opinion, endeavouring in your whole conduct to render them sensible how much we rely upon his Majesty's influence for effectual aid in everything that may be necessary to the peace, security and future prosperity of the United States of America.

The letter was a total capitulation to French demands. It might well have been dictated by Luzerne. To cap his triumph, Luzerne followed up by organizing his lobby for the election of the new Secretary for Foreign Affairs. The campaign was long and fiercely fought among the factions of the Congress. When the voting came, it went to more than a dozen ballots, the lead seesawing between Livingston and Lee. But the victory finally went to Luzerne, whose warnings of a break in the alliance if Lee was selected finally frightened enough votes into Livingston's camp. The French now had an American delegation in Europe subservient to Vergennes and an American Secretary of State in Philadelphia who owed his job to the French Minister. Never again in American history would our country yield so great a measure of its sovereignty to a foreign nation.

While all this was raging on in the United States, Franklin, awaiting news on his letter of resignation, was again overwhelmed with drafts and bills and news of shipping losses. The most heartbreaking news of all was the British interception of *Le Lafayette,* the ship laden with supplies and saltpeter that Franklin had labored so long to purchase and license. He wrote about these travails to President Huntington on July 11, 1781:

The Number of Congress Bills that have been drawn on the Ministers in Spain and Holland, which I am by my Acceptances obliged to pay, as well as those drawn upon myself, the extreme importance of supporting the credit of Congress, which would be disgrac'd in a political as well as pecuniary Light, thro' all the Courts of Europe, if those Bills should go back protested, and the unexpected Delays arising with regard to the intended Loan in Holland—all these considerations have compelled me to stop the 1,500,000 Livres which were to have been sent by way of Amsterdam.

Franklin went on to say that he was now laboring to find and finance clothing, arms, ammunition and stores to replace those lost in the *Lafayette.*

Two weeks later Franklin wrote to Robert Morris, of whose appointment as Superintendent of Finance he had just learned. He congratulated him and thanked him as a patriot for making the sacrifice of his considerable private affairs to give full time to the service of his country, and he warned Morris that he should not expect the gratitude of his fellow countrymen.

The Publick is often niggardly even of its Thanks, while you are sure of being censured by malevolent Criticks and Bug-Writers who will abuse you while you are serving them, and wound your Character in nameless Pamphlets; thereby resembling those little, dirty, stinking insects that attack us only in the dark, disturb our repose, molesting and wounding us, while our Sweat and Blood are contributing to their Subsistence.

With his many burdens, Franklin still did not neglect one of his most important activities: anti-British propaganda. In the spring and summer of 1781 he circulated throughout Britain and Europe a forged "Supplement" to the Boston *Independent Chronicle.* It purported to reprint a message sent by the Seneca Indians to the Governor of Canada, and a special parcel they had sent him as an example of their service to the British. A Captain Gerrish of the New England Militia was represented as having intercepted the letter in a raid on the Indians.

At the request of the Senneca Chiefs, I send herewith to your Excellency, under the care of James Boyd, eight packs of Scalps, cured, dried, hooped and painted. . . .

1. Containing 43 Scalps of Congress soldiers, killed in different skirmishes; these are Stretched on black Hoops, 4 inches diameter; the inside of the Skins painted red with a small black spot to note their being killed with Bullets. Also 62 of Farmers killed in their Houses; the Hoops red, the Skin painted brown and marked with a hoe; a black Circle all around to denote their being surprised in the Night; and a black Hatchet in the Middle, signifying their being killed with that weapon.

The letter went on to catalogue 88 scalps of women, 193 of boys, 211 of little girls, all with grisly details of colored hoops and hieroglyphics signifying the nature and means of their deaths. It ended with greetings to the British Governor: "I do not doubt but that your Excellency will think it proper to give some farther encouragement to those honest people"—that is, Britain's Indian allies.

The letter provoked outraged protests all through Europe and in England, where the Opposition was growing daily stronger, demanding honorable peace terms and an end to the odious war against the Americans. George III responded by instructing his ministers to pursue the war more vigorously than ever. He had high hopes for Cornwallis' spring and summer campaign. The British also sent stiff objections to Vienna about the terms of the mediation and warned several times that the British would not attend if any Americans were officially accredited as delegates.

George III had not yet heard that the tides of battle were beginning to shift against Cornwallis. His "triumphal" march from Carolina to Virginia was far from an unqualified triumph. For the first time Cornwallis was running into serious resistance and was being harassed by the mobility of Greene's hit-and-run strategy.

Colonel Francis "Swamp Fox" Marion had sliced at British forces in the Carolinas. The garrison at Georgetown, South Carolina, feared being overwhelmed and had withdrawn to Charleston. In Florida, the Spaniards, whose only participation in the war was directed toward Spain's own colonies, had sent a strong force to attack Major General Archibald Campbell's garrison at Pensacola. By the end of May Campbell, besieged, with supplies running out, surrendered to the Spanish, breaking Britain's grip on West Florida and opening up Cornwallis' rear doors in Georgia.

Cornwallis, unruffled by what he considered mosquito bites on his flanks and rear, marched from Petersburg to try to cut off and capture the Marquis de Lafayette. It could have been a decisive coup and it almost succeeded. But Lafayette, putting wisdom above pride, pulled his troops back and fled to the north, out of Cornwallis' trap. While the French were falling back on land, they were advancing on the seas. Admiral de Grasse had arrived in the West

Indies and gone immediately into action, attacking and capturing the British island of Tobago in the first days of June. Within days, American partisans and frontiersmen laid siege to the garrison at Augusta and, in a ten-day assault, took the fort. The mosquito bites were getting bigger, redder, more painful. A few days later, Lafayette met up with General Wayne's Pennsylvania brigade and the new combined force began to move back south, ready to meet Cornwallis. Washington was cheered not only by these small successes but by getting news from Rochambeau, on June 13, that Admiral de Grasse, with his powerful fleet, would be sailing north to join them for combined operations in July or August.

Washington and Rochambeau had agreed on a major offensive to be launched against either Clinton's army in New York or Cornwallis' in the south, depending on which target seemed better to de Grasse. While awaiting the final decision, Rochambeau agreed to make a show of strength by taking a strong force to meet Washington at White Plains, either to be ready to attack New York or to fool Clinton by suddenly moving around New York and marching toward the south.

The American troops attempted a surprise attack on British outposts north of the Harlem River on July 2, but British scouts got word in time for the garrison to withdraw across the river, leaving only one strong outpost at King's Bridge. The maneuver by Washington, plus spy reports that Rochambeau was bringing a powerful French force to Washington's support, alarmed Clinton. Just as Washington had hoped, Clinton dispatched urgent orders to Cornwallis to send three thousand of his best troops to help hold off a Franco-American offensive against New York.

The initiative was moving to Washington in July, 1781. Cornwallis, obeying orders, led his forces toward a port for transshipment to New York, sending a dispatch to Clinton that his army was now so depleted that he could not carry out his plans to conquer Virginia. Shortly afterward, on July 8, Cornwallis received new orders from Clinton to send his reinforcements to Philadelphia, to make a diversion there that would draw Washington off from New York. But on July 12, Clinton learned that Rochambeau had arrived in force at White Plains. The confused British commander fired off another urgent order to Cornwallis to shift plans and send his troops, after all, to New York. The British command was beginning to lose its grip on events.

Cornwallis, understanding that Clinton was indecisive and confused, had been taking his time about carrying out his orders, since they changed every three or four days. Finally, on July 20, he received the dispatch from Clinton he had been hoping for: an attack on New York did not seem imminent, the campaign in Virginia was still high-priority and he might keep all his troops if he wished. Clinton suggested that he set up a new naval and land base at Yorktown, to use for operations against Virginia. Cornwallis happily set about obeying this order.

While Clinton was floundering about, Washington and Rochambeau were testing his defense lines. They made a strong demonstration in front of the King's Bridge outpost, found it well manned and heavily gunned. Reconnaissance patrols reported the British dug in, in strength, all along the Harlem River. General Washington began thinking that it might be best, after all, to bypass New York and march to meet Cornwallis in Virginia. Rochambeau agreed, and they sent joint dispatches to Admiral de Grasse asking his urgent counsel.

De Grasse had been advised by American weather experts that his naval actions had to be undertaken and completed before mid-October, for that would be the height of a violent hurricane period. Poring over his charts and the record of the past, de Grasse decided to avoid New York, where d'Estaing had gotten into trouble trying to run the Narrows, and that the best place for his large fleet to move into action was Chesapeake Bay. He so advised Rochambeau. Rochambeau brought his message to Washington in mid-August and Washington concurred.

On August 19, Washington and Rochambeau began to break camp in White Plains. Rochambeau's siege artillery, too heavy to be hauled overland, was sent to Newport to be loaded on ships, which took off to rendezvous with the de Grasse fleet, by then off Cape Hatteras. As the ships began to converge for the coming offensive, Washington and Rochambeau were ferrying some six thousand men across the Hudson to begin the march south.

The British did not seem to understand what was happening or know what to do to counter it. So unaware were they of a major American offensive that Admiral Rodney, one of their best seamen, had set sail for England for a leave of absence, taking four heavy battleships with him. Admiral Sir Samuel Hood had moved his fleet from the West Indies toward New York to reinforce the British there, but had gotten involved in minor fights along the way. It was not until he arrived, in the last days of August, that he could inform Clinton that de Grasse had sailed to Northern waters. Hood was ordered to combine his fleet with the ships of Admiral Graves and go to Chesapeake Bay, not knowing that de Grasse had already reached his destination and was anchored there in full force.

Washington, who had always fought a "gentleman's war," decided the time had finally come to use trickery and deception. He left a strong force of four thousand men at White Plains, with orders to move around and make a show of strength. He even ordered them to construct bakeries and send out information to spies about a major attack.

Washington's trick worked. Clinton, fearing an offensive against New York, did not send a single reinforcement to Cornwallis, thinking Washington was still in full force at White Plains. By the last day of August Washington and Rochambeau were marching past Philadelphia. Cornwallis, meanwhile, not knowing that a large force was heading his way, had taken his troops to Yorktown to begin converting it into his operational base.

While the soldiers were moving into position for the decisive battle of the summer campaign, the diplomats were still sparring evasively all around the rings of the chancellories of Europe. No date had yet been set for the mediation conference at Vienna. All the parties were being diplomatically polite but raising new questions daily—particularly the British, for George III was still suspicious and resentful of other powers' attempting to intervene in what he considered purely a British civil war in America.

John Adams had come to Paris at the request of Vergennes in July, before it was learned that the Congress had appointed Franklin, Jefferson, Jay and Laurens as co-commissioners, and before Vergennes had the advantage of Congress' instructions, still at sea, to put Adams under the French and to make no moves without their consent. On July 13, Vergennes received his first letter from Adams, commenting on the proposed articles of armistice, truce and peace which had been drafted by Gallitzin and Kaunitz. Adams had so many objections to raise that Vergennes knew he was in for another bout with the obstinate man. Adams told him that no truce could be considered unless it provided that all alliances be maintained during and after the truce and that British forces be withdrawn from the United States—conditions the British would never accept. Adams further stated that a truce signed by the British government would be meaningless without an act of Parliament suspending and repealing all the statutes pertaining to the United States, which would not accept a truce as a colony of Britain. Adams told Vergennes that the United States, as an independent nation, "are considered and acknowledged as such by France. They cannot be represented in a Congress of Ministers from the several Powers in Europe, whether their Representative is called Ambassador, Minister or Agent, without an acknowledgement of their independence, of which the very Admission of a Representative from them, is an avowal." Since George III would under no conditions go to Vienna to acknowledge the independence of the United States, Vergennes knew the mission would be hopeless.

Adams considered the whole scheme in Vienna a conspiracy by Vergennes to sell out the Americans as France maneuvered for advantage with the other European powers, and he refused to go to Vienna except as an acknowledged representative of a sovereign state. On July 19, Adams reiterated this assertion even more stringently. He told Vergennes that the American representative in Vienna must have the title of minister plenipotentiary and must exchange letters of mutual accreditation with the British Minister. "This, it is true, would be an implied acknowledgement of his Character and Title, and those of the United States too: but such an acknowledgement is indispensable, because, without it, there would be no treaty at all, in consequence, he would expect to enjoy all the Prerogatives of that Character and the moment it should be refused him, he must quit the Congress, let the consequences be what they might." Adams went on to object to the frequent references to the "American colonies" in the diplomatic exchanges, asserting to Vergennes that there was no longer any such thing as an American colony, but only the sovereign United States. Unless this was stated explicitly in the documents, he would not go to Vienna, nor would Congress be bound by any agreements taken there.

Vergennes held his head as he read Adams' letters. Sometimes he felt that it was almost worse to read Adams' long-winded and arrogant communications than to argue with him face to face. But when they met, he longed to go back to Adams' letters. Vergennes wrote to Luzerne telling him how impossible Adams was and asking Luzerne to arrange some way around him, not knowing yet that this had been done. Luzerne, at that moment, was toying with the idea of getting Washington removed from his command. He told Vergennes that Washington was not a skilled professional soldier, that he failed to discipline his troops, that he delegated the order of battle and planning to his staff and spent most of his time writing political letters to the principal personalities of the Congress and the thirteen states. But Luzerne suspected that there had probably been too many articles written about Washington's greatness to replace him without a serious break in American morale. Luzerne then went on to give Vergennes thumbnail sketches, rarely flattering, about a score of American generals, including Schuyler, Gates, Putnam, Sullivan, Greene and Wayne.

By then Vergennes knew just how difficult an ally America was proving to be. He could not budge Adams, who noted later in his diary that he had "defeated the profound and magnificent project of a Congress at Vienna for the purpose of chicaning the United States out of their independence." Adams had, indeed, served his country well by refusing to be a dupe of Vergennes's disloyal plot to abandon the United States in Vienna. But he alone had not defeated the mediation.

George III, more obstinate and proud even than Adams, had

been brooding about the Vienna project ever since it had been launched. He had permitted his ministers to go through the motions of diplomatic courtesy, not wanting to risk isolation in Europe by acting too hastily. But he never could overcome his suspicion—absolutely unfounded—that Vienna would somehow maneuver him into recognizing American independence. The only ally America would have in Vienna, the only nation with any commitment to American independence, was France, and France was already weakening in its determination to support the American cause in a war that was becoming a serious drain on French resources. George III either did not know this or did not believe it. He finally called in his ministers, listened to their reports, and took the decision to refuse to go on with the Vienna mediation, which he characterized as a foreign intervention in the domestic affairs of Britain.

As he had unwittingly done so many times in the past, George III saved America's neck just as it was about to be chopped off. He might well have prevented the American Revolution at the outset had he only listened to the moderate proposals that Franklin had made to his ministers in London in 1773–74; or, in 1775, had he not obstinately kept the tea tax after canceling all the other Townshend duties. He might have crushed the Americans early in the war had he made a total and immediate commitment of troops and ships rather than a piecemeal one. And he had had many chances to make a deal with the French over Vergennes's head if he had not been so haughty and so ready to defy the French.

The majority of the Americans had been loyal to the Crown, and many still were even after six years of war. Important French ministers had serious doubts about the alliance and the war, and the cause of America was nowhere popular among the European monarchies. With all those trump cards to play, George III might well have won the game. But he was rigid, inflexible, proud and obstinate.

As the mediation of Vienna gradually unraveled, with hopes declining that the war could be settled by negotiation, the belligerent armies were converging on one another for the ultimate military test: a major clash between the principal forces of the two opponents. Before the combined French and American armies could meet the British in a major action, the two commanders had to assure themselves of the most perfect harmony of views and coordination in their tactics and strategy, and to improve the relations among their armed forces, which had been strained by American resentments of the French troops for drawing upon local provisions, for failing to go into action and for the frequent fiascos involving the French Navy.

Rochambeau and Washington had taken great pains to keep their armies separate at White Plains, but to put on a good show of parade discipline and martial spirit among the men while choosing the most diplomatic officers to meet together in staff conferences. Everything had gone well, and the armies were in good spirit and friendly when they marched to Philadelphia. There, the French put on the kind of show at which they are brilliant, parading in full dress, wheeling and reversing formations in perfect rhythm, while drummers and buglers played martial airs. An eyewitness wrote: "Had you seen the French troops march through the Town and exercise, no, you could not have helped feeling Pain as a native of England, and Joy as an American and an Ally of France. The British troops never attained that degree of Perfection. . . . This is not Enthusiasm, it is Truth."

While the allied forces were marching south from Philadelphia to join up with Lafayette's contingent, Baron von Steuben was also on the march with some 1,000 men to meet up with the main bodies of troops. Adding von Steuben's brigade to the forces under Lafayette and Rochambeau, the French forces came to almost 7,000 men. Washington had some 6,500 American regulars and 3,000 Virginia militiamen in his command, so the combined armies totaled somewhere around 16,000 men, the greatest force by far that he had ever been able to field against the British. Cornwallis had no more than 8,000 men in his Yorktown operational base. He badly needed the reinforcements that Clinton did not dare send him, fooled as he was by Washington's fake attack on New York. For once everything worked right in the French and American planning, and everything went wrong for the British.

Washington did have some anxious moments as he marched south. On September 2, he wrote to Lafayette asking for news of Admiral de Grasse and the fleet. "I am distressed beyond expression, to know what has become of the Count de Grasse, and for fear the English Fleet, by occupying the Chesapeake, should frustrate all our flattering prospects in that quarter." But, three days later, in Chester, Pennsylvania, the dispatch he was longing for arrived: de Grasse was anchored in Lynnhaven Bay and had gotten there before the British. The French officer who delivered the message later wrote that he had never seen a man so overjoyed: "Washington acted like a child whose every wish had been gratified."

On that very day, as Washington was reading about de Grasse, one of the most strategic battles of the war was already under way off the Chesapeake Capes. A French scout frigate, off Cape Charles, signaled to the Admiral that it had sighted nineteen ships, the fleet of Admiral Graves. It was bad news for Admiral de Grasse, for, anticipating that the British were still one or two days' sail away, he was engaged in disembarking assault troops, near Jamestown. Some two thousand of his sailors were absent, convoying the infantry in landing craft. The tide was high, the winds contrary, and de Grasse's huge battleships hard to handle in sudden action.

Admiral Graves had an excellent opportunity, with the winds in his sails, his ships in full speed, to cut right into the middle of the French while they were trying to form a line of battle. But Graves was no John Paul Jones. Instead of a daring attack, he elected to move in traditional formations. He tacked his ships, waited for the French to move into battle, then sailed at a classic diagonal course to encounter the enemy. By then Admiral de Grasse had his ships well in line. The winds had died down and both fleets were moving slowly, which favored the heavier French. The British flag communications broke down and the captains had to shout orders from ship to ship. The French performed with drill perfection, so that when the two fleets finally met late in the afternoon, de Grasse had sixteen battleships bearing down on eleven of the British, the other eight British having sheered off in confusion.

For more than two hours the ships fired at each other at stone-throwing range, until darkness set in, obliging them to pull apart. The French ships had outgunned the British and inflicted heavy casualties on all the crews, while two of the British warships had been so hard hit that they were sinking. French casualties were light, all ships afloat in good condition. The French had won their very first naval victory. The triumph off the Chesapeake Capes was, perhaps, even more important psychologically, for it boosted the morale of the armies, so long landlocked, and demonstrated that the British were no longer sole masters of the seas.

Admiral de Grasse, one of the most subtle, intuitively brilliant of all the French commanders in the Revolutionary War, then pretended to give chase to the British. He did not really want another battle, for his men were tired and shocked by the eyeball-to-eyeball cannonades, and his ships could stand repair. But he wanted the British to keep away from the Capes so that his colleague, Admiral de Barras, could land siege artillery without resistance. Graves, not wanting to risk his badly battered ships and crews in another clash, fell in with the de Grasse maneuvers. De Grasse deliberately let Graves wheel off to his flank, and when he saw the British bows pointed to the north, he let them go their way to naval shipyards in New York, feeling sure the main battle would be over before Graves would return.

Washington, the day after the sea battle, reached the Head of Elk, the northernmost navigation point on Chesapeake Bay. There he began disembarking about two thousand men, while he dispatched the rest of the army overland toward Baltimore and Annapolis, where they would be picked up by French ships.

Meanwhile, on September 6, Benedict Arnold was making an amphibious landing of British, German and Loyalist American troops at New London, Connecticut. His objective was to lure off Washington's army from Yorktown, to give Cornwallis more time to set his defenses and for reinforcements to reach him. There were only about 160 Americans in the garrison at New London and they were rapidly overwhelmed by Arnold's large force. When, on surrendering, the American commander offered his sword to the Tory officer, the sword was seized, reversed and run through his body. The British troops went mad, burning the village to the ground, slaughtering the American troops. Eighty-five of the men who had surrendered were butchered on the spot, another sixty-nine wounded, many mortally. Covered with blood and shame, Benedict Arnold, now a murderer as well as a traitor, reimbarked. He did not even bother to stay and do the job of luring off part of Washington's army. This once fervent patriot and brilliant officer had sunk to the morality of a blood-crazed animal.

Washington, still on the march, came to his home in Mount Vernon, where he paused briefly to confer with and entertain Rochambeau and senior French officers. Their cooperation was proceeding to everyone's satisfaction. They went on from Mount Vernon to Williamsburg, where, to his delight, Washington saw Lafayette march in. They embraced and danced with joy as Lafayette gave Washington the news of de Grasse's victory off the Chesapeake Capes. Washington set off at once to visit the French fleet. By then, de Grasse had been joined by de Barras, who had sailed down from Newport. Washington cried as he looked out into the harbor and saw a mighty force of thirty-two French ships, guaranteeing him the control of the seas that he had yearned for, begged for, dreamed of ever since the first shots at Lexington and Concord six years before.

Washington and Rochambeau were rowed out to de Grasse's flagship, the huge 110-gun *Ville de Paris.* Washington, now restored to the dignified posture of a Commander in Chief, did not dance or cry, but could not resist striding up and down the decks, examining the huge French cannon, with its royal fleur-de-lis medallions, and congratulating the gunners, many of them still swathed in bandages from wounds suffered in the battle. He gave de Grasse a bear hug and got a kiss on both cheeks in return.

The allied sea and land commanders went into conference to draw up plans for the investment of Yorktown (then known as York, on the York River). De Grasse assigned all his light craft as ferrying boats to move the land armies from Elkton and Annapolis. He also committed the fleet to sail to positions opposite Yorktown and deliver naval artillery fire in response to appeals from land commanders. They worked out a series of signals and secure communications for maximum coordination of the land and sea forces. It was the best, most professional planning of the entire war. Nothing, this time, would be left to chance or emotional gallantry.

Ben Franklin, wallowing in a flood of unpaid bills in Paris, worn down by complaints from Adams about Vergennes and from Vergennes about Adams, interspersed with begging letters for money from John Jay, still being shunned and snubbed by Floridablanca, would have given much to have been with Washington in that planning session on the *Ville de Paris.* He would have given much even to have known of it. Instead, he was writing to the Superintendent of Finance, Robert Morris, to report that Henry Laurens, his co-Commissioner for Peace, who had been captured on his way to France and was now in the Tower of London, had signed bills on the credit of John Adams, who had forwarded Laurens' bills to Franklin for payment. Franklin found this proceeding "extraordinary." He had received other drafts from The Hague and Madrid, in addition to those upon his mission in France. Franklin told Morris: "In the situation you will see I am in, by the letters of Vergennes, [this] terrifies me."

The bright news for Franklin that summer came in the letters that informed him his resignation was unacceptable to Congress. On the contrary, his services were needed not only to continue to seek aid to pursue the war, but as a Peace Commissioner should the happy event of peace materialize. He also learned that his arch-enemy, Arthur Lee, had been defeated, and his admirer, Robert Livingston, elected Secretary of State. He wrote a most satisfied letter to William Carmichael about these developments, including a better atmosphere in Paris now that Colonel John Laurens had left.

> He was indefatigable while he staid, and took true Pains, but he brusqu'd the Ministers too much, and I found after he was gone that he had thereby given more Offence than I could have imagin'd. . . . The Offence he gave

will, I hope, have no durable Effects, tho' it produced me some Mortifications. Good humor and a kind Disposition towards us seems again to prevail. I had, before his Arrival, got the grant of 6,000,000, and have since obtained more, or I could not have paid Mr. Jay's bills.

The "more" to which Franklin referred was a new advance of two million livres which his friend Vergennes had obtained for pressing bills.

John Jay, in Madrid, was still pursuing the elusive Floridablanca, who kept pleading that he was "too busy" or "too ill" to confer with him about Spain's joining the Franco-American alliance. In desperation, Jay offered him important concessions, including the point on which the United States had always refused to yield: navigation on the Mississippi. Countering Franklin's warnings not to "sell a drop of its waters," Jay proposed relinquishing to Spain navigation on the river south of 31° north latitude; he further offered a U.S. guarantee to the Spanish King of "all his dominions in America." He restricted this only by stating that the offer would be withdrawn if Spain did not accept it before a general peace was under way.

It was a more than generous offer and could have caused the United States great difficulty had Floridablanca accepted it. But the Spanish Foreign Minister wanted no part of an alliance with the United States. He turned Jay's proposals over to his undersecretary, Bernardo del Campo, and resisted all the pressures brought upon him by his Ambassador in Paris, Franklin's friend, the Conde de Aranda. Floridablanca would fight the war without America as an ally and worry about boundary questions later. He felt that the Spanish fleet and expeditionary corps could hold Florida and other territories without American help in the war and resist American pressures afterward.

The war was then heading for a tremendous climax. De Grasse had told Washington, in their battleship conference, that the hurricane season was approaching and that he could not long keep his fleet in these dangerous waters. Washington and Rochambeau agreed to launch the assault on Yorktown on September 28, thanking de Grasse for his sacrifice in holding out long enough to support the assault. He promised that his land attack would be far enough advanced for de Grasse to get his fleet out of the way of the hurricanes.

The day the investment of Yorktown began, Cornwallis, the defender, had about eight thousand men, well dug in. They were also, however, blocked in by the French fleet with little chance of escaping or receiving reinforcements if the battle turned against him.

Washington began cautiously, throwing a ring around Cornwallis, making no attempt, at first, to enter into combat. Some of his officers, eager for action, asked permission to test the defenses, and Washington gave the nod to a dashing young Lieutenant Colonel, Alexander Hamilton, who led his men in sorties to draw Cornwallis out. Heavy shelling of the British positions was to begin on October 9. For the first time, Washington had all the siege guns he needed and could outgun the British, just as, for the first time, he had naval control of the waters around the battlefield. For the first time, too, Washington had adequate supplies of food and ammunition and his troops were in good health. But he was worried about a possible smallpox epidemic. On September 29, the day after the battle began, he issued an order to counter this threat: "Our ungenerous enemy, having, as usual, propagated the smallpox in this part of the country, the Commander in Chief forbids the officers and men of the Army having any communication with houses or inhabitants in the neighborhood or borrowing any utensils from them."

Cornwallis had used a number of "dirty tricks" to harass his attacking enemy. A French officer noted in his battle log:

> To stop the advance on York, Lord Cornwallis, instead of attacking our column as a soldier would have done, had recourse to ruses, such as only savage Indians are capable of employing. He had thrown into the wells heads of steers, dead horses, and even the bodies of dead Negroes. The result was the French Army was short of water; it could have been molested in a more worthy manner.

The investment of Yorktown began in earnest on the night of the seventh of October. One of Rochambeau's aides kept a diary of action on the French front: "At eight o'clock in the evening we opened a trench at three hundred fathoms from the works. The ground, which is very much cut up by little ravines, greatly facilitated our approach and enabled us to reach our trenches under cover without being obliged to dig a tunnel." The chaplain noted in his diary: "The night was the most favorable in the world. Providence seemed evidentally to have drawn the curtain of darkness around us on purpose to conceal us from the enemy until the time of our greatest danger had passed. Not a man killed or wounded in the American camp, and but a few in the camp of the French."

The American unit given the command to attack a vital British strongpoint, Redoubt 10, was Alexander Hamilton's. He had French Lieutenant Colonel Gimat, a veteran of two years' fighting in Virginia, on his right, and Lieutenant Colonel John Laurens on his left. The attack was swift and overran the British position, with Gimat breaking through first, the Americans following close up to overwhelm the outnumbered British defenders, opening a large breach in Cornwallis' defense works.

As his men advanced, Washington kept up a withering destructive fire of big siege artillery, pounding Yorktown and setting it afire. As soon as a redoubt was taken, the American and French engineers dashed forward, under artillery fire, and extended the assault trenches by five hundred yards on either side, creeping closer and closer to the final defense lines, while the big guns continued to hammer and blast the walls and the garrison inside. It was a perfectly coordinated, irresistible attack.

Cornwallis simply did not have a chance. He was hopelessly outnumbered and outgunned, and trapped inside Yorktown. Later he would say that he would never have taken a stand there if he had not counted on strong reinforcements from Clinton and the certainty that the all-powerful British fleet would command the waters. He had had no warning of the approach and strength of the French fleet, no knowledge that Washington had tricked Clinton to keep his main forces in New York.

A professional soldier, Cornwallis knew when he was beaten and would not sacrifice his men uselessly. On October 17, he sent out a unit carrying white flags. On the nineteenth he surrendered his entire force. His surrender came close to the anniversary of the surrender of Burgoyne at Saratoga. Twice the Americans had met the British in a major battle and twice the Americans, this time with their allies, the French, had won a great victory. Legend has it that the British and Hessian bands led the troops into prison camps playing the traditional British Army march, "The World Turned Upside Down."

The victory at Yorktown did turn the world upside down, although not immediately. Saratoga had brought about the successful negotiation by Franklin of the alliance with France. Yorktown would lead, in the months ahead, to the beginnings of a genuine peace conference, not the phony mediation of Vienna.

But it did not happen overnight. Nor did the war end at once. The British still had a powerful army in New York and a powerful fleet in Atlantic waters. De Grasse set sail for the West Indies, running ahead of the hurricanes, and not anxious for a head-on naval battle with the British. He had done his job and would keep himself in reserve.

Yorktown did not end the capability of the British Army and Navy. But it did demonstrate that royal authority could not be restored in America without a very long and devastating war, galvanizing all the men, monies and energies of the Empire. And there was no will for such an effort in England. The war was unpopular and, after Yorktown, impossible. The doves would, at long last, triumph over the hawks. Even the obstinate George III would be forced to yield.

Benjamin Franklin had played the key role in forging the alliance that had enabled America to fight on after Saratoga. After Yorktown, Franklin would play the major role in writing the peace and establishing, beyond further doubt, the existence and independence of the United States.

PART IV

PARIS: *The Peace*

CHAPTER

22

The Dawn of Peace

It was four or five weeks before Paris and London learned the news of Cornwallis' surrender. They were trying weeks for Franklin, who was tired in body and soul, tormented by consular duties he abhorred and financial woes he abominated, constantly chivied by whining Americans who brought all their troubles to him—from Jay in Madrid to John Adams, still trying to arrange a Dutch loan and a treaty in The Hague, continually sending Franklin warnings to beware of the French. It was almost the last straw for Franklin, then, to hear of the uncouth appearance and behavior of his protégé, Tom Paine, who had become a scandal in Nantes and the subject of controversy in the Foreign Office.

Paine had come to France earlier in the year as secretary to Colonel John Laurens. He had stopped off in Nantes, where Franklin's young friend Elkanah Watson had set himself up as a merchant. Paine had a letter of introduction to Watson and rented rooms in his lodging house. The name "Tom Paine" was a magic one in Europe, second perhaps only to Ben Franklin, for his *Common Sense* had been translated and flashed like a current of electricity through the Continent, particularly among French intellectuals, who hailed him as another American apostle of liberty.

On his arrival in Nantes, the mayor and most distinguished citizens all came to call upon him to pay their respects. Watson, deeply embarrassed by what happened, described the event in his diary.

> He was coarse and uncouth in his manners, loathsome in his appearance, and a disgusting egotist; rejoicing most in talking of himself, and reading the effusions of his own mind. . . .
>
> I often officiated as interpreter, although humbled and mortified by his filthy appearance and awkward and unseemly address . . . he was absolutely offensive and "perfumed" the whole apartment. He was soon rid of his respectable visitors, who left the room with marks of astonishment and disgust. I took the liberty, on his asking for the loan of a clean shirt, of speaking to him frankly of his dirty appearance and brimstone odor, and prevailed upon him to stew for an hour in a hot bath. This, however, was not done without much entreaty, and I did not succeed until, receiving a file of English newspapers, I promised that after he was in the bath, he should have the reading of them, and not before. He, at once, consented, and accompanied me to the bath, where I instructed the keeper in French (which Paine did not understand) to gradually increase the heat of the water, until "Monsieur était bien bouilli." He became so much absorbed in his reading that he was nearly parboiled before leaving the bath, much to his improvement and my satisfaction.

Franklin, for once without his sense of humor, was furious with Paine. The French set great store on style and Franklin did not want one of America's greatest revolutionary voices to give the image of a dirty, coarse radical. At the same time, there was gossip in Vergennes's office about Gérard's earlier letter stating that he had put Paine on the King's payroll as a propaganda agent of France. When Luzerne arrived in America, he reported that he did not trust Paine and would keep him at a distance. Paine heatedly denied reports that Gérard had paid him. Luzerne gave him nothing, but his assistant, François Barbé-Marbois, wrote that Paine kept coming to the French Embassy seeking to win Luzerne's confidence. He said that Paine submitted all his articles in advance of publication to Luzerne, giving rise to the suspicion that he wanted to get back on the French payroll.

In December, 1781, Luzerne had asked Paine to write articles refuting letters that Silas Deane, now back in France auditing his accounts, was sending to America. It is not clear from the official dispatches whether or not Luzerne paid Paine fees or a salary for this work; Paine's name does not appear in Luzerne's accounts for this period, but his name does crop up in 1782 and again in 1783 as having received money from the French Embassy for commissioned articles. It is sad and difficult to accept one of our great Revolutionary patriots as a paid foreign agent. One can judge how afflicted Franklin was to hear these rumors, for he never mentioned one word about them in any of his letters or his diaries, although it was freely discussed in the Foreign Ministry, which he frequented.

John Adams, low in spirit, down with a fever, wrote and complained to Franklin and to the President of the Congress that there was little point in his staying in Europe. He told the President on October 15 that the Congress of Vienna was a dead issue and that "upon the whole, according to the best judgment I can form, it will not be worth while for Congress to be at the expense of continuing me in Europe with a view to my assisting at any conference for peace, especially as Dr. Franklin has given me intimations that I cannot depend upon him for my subsistence in the future." He made it sound as though Franklin were personally cutting him off from funds, whereas Franklin was insisting that Congress provide monies for its envoys in Europe and not dump everyone's bills on the French mission.

Franklin received a torrent of reports from friends about vicious attacks upon him being spread by his enemies, who would never give up, even though Congress had just renewed and extended his mandate. The old man had to comfort his friends, who were concerned about his welfare. He never seemed unduly anxious about the attacks. His generous views were expressed in a letter to Francis Hopkinson in September:

> As to the Friends and Enemies you just mention, I have, hitherto, Thanks to God, had Plenty of the former kind; they have been my Treasure; and it has perhaps been of no Disadvantage to me that I have had a few of the latter. They serve to put us upon correcting the Faults we

have, and avoiding those we are in danger of having. They counteract the Mischief Flattery might do us, and their Malicious Attacks make our Friends more zealous in serving us and promoting our interest. At present, I do not know of more than two such Enemies that I enjoy, viz. Lee and Izard. I deserved the enmity of the latter because I might have avoided it by paying him a compliment which I neglected. That of the former I owe to the people of France who happen'd to respect me too much and him too little; which I could bear and he could not. They are unhappy that they cannot make everybody hate me as much as they do; and I should be so, if my Friends did not love me much more than those Gentlemen can possibly love one another.

Early in October, when the siege of Yorktown was under way, Franklin was writing to friends about the treachery of Benedict Arnold, which had dismayed European supporters of the American cause. To his friend Jan Ingenhousz, he had apologized for not answering his queries sooner, for he had been suffering from a three-months "fit of the Gout," but went on to say this of Arnold:

He tried to draw others after him, but in vain, not a Man follow'd him. We discover'd his Motive by an intercepted Letter, a copy of which I enclose, which shows it was a Bribe of five thousand pounds sterling. . . . Never were Wars more unjustly and causelessly begun than those England is now engaged in with your country and mine. If she persists in them she is ruined; as she deserves to be.*

Franklin was lonely as well as tired in the October days before he learned the news of Yorktown. His dear friend Madame Brillon was prone not only to physical diseases but to bouts of mental and spiritual depression; she had been ailing. Her doctor had recommended a change of scenery, and she had left for Nice on the Riviera. Franklin missed her and wrote her so in some of the most tender, charming and witty love letters he had ever penned.

Long ago, when I was young, I sometimes loved powerfully at a distance of a thousand leagues. But a few years ago . . . I did not deem

*Benedict Arnold, after the British defeat, sailed to England, where he lived to the end of his days. Silas Deane also went to England when Congress refused to clear him. He died en route to Canada, where he had hoped to start a new life.

myself capable of loving further than a league away. Now, I discover that I was wrong, for you go every day further and further away from me, and I don't see that my feeling diminishes. That is because you are always present in my mind.

Franklin said that he had heard that in the provinces the ladies were somewhat more "libertine" than in Paris, and he hoped that some of this attitude would rub off on her, so that she might return to Passy "with more vigor and less rigor."

In return, Madame Brillon paid Franklin a beautiful compliment, based on her real insight into this remarkable man who loved her:

I found in your letter, besides tokens of friendship, a tinge of that gaiety and that gallantry that cause all women to love you, because you love them all. You combine with the kindest heart the soundest moral teaching, a lively imagination, and that droll roguishness which shows that the wisest of men allows his wisdom to be perpetually broken against the rocks of femininity.

As the fall advanced, the weather in Paris stayed springlike and Franklin began to throw off all the ill effects of his gout. He threw open the windows of his house—he was a fresh-air fiend—and went on outings to his friends, the Le Veillard family, and to Madame Helvétius. He felt so spry that when he heard the news that Marie Antoinette had given birth to another son, he rushed over to Versailles, when the baby was just one day old, to pay his respects to the Dauphin, further endearing himself to the royal family.

Then, late in November, came the great news of Yorktown. Vergennes had the first word and Franklin was the first man he told, so that he might join him in a victory toast. It was virtually a last-minute reprieve for Vergennes, whose ministry was under criticism, his recommendations having drained the French Treasury, with no apparent progress in the conflict. After months of setbacks and disappointments came the greatest victory of the war, the first victory for the French-American alliance that Vergennes and Franklin had together created, at a moment when the Prime Minister,

Comte de Maurepas, was on his deathbed. He was said to have died with a smile, saying, "Now I die content." As for Lord North, when he received the news, he blanched, staggered and groaned, "O God! It is all over."

Franklin knew it was not yet all over. The shrewd old sage, who never permitted himself to despair in adversity, was never complaisant in victory either. He had received a letter from Madame Brillon, who told him, teasingly, that she was sulking, for he had not written to her about the great victory at Yorktown. He replied in a letter on Christmas Day, one of the most revealing of Franklin's communications with her.

> You are sulking, my dear friend, because I did not send you at once the story of our great victory. I am well aware of the magnitude of our advantage and of its possible consequences, but I do not exult over it. Knowing that war is full of changes and uncertainty, in bad fortune I hope for good, and in good I fear bad. I play this game with almost the same equanimity as when you see me playing chess. You know that I never give up a game before it is finished, always hoping to win, or at least to get a move, and when I have a good game, I guard against presumption.

Events proved Franklin right. Yorktown did not bring about an immediate collapse of the British. What it did was to submerge the Congress in a wave of euphoria. Considering the war won, Congress turned inward to concentrate on internal, financial and political affairs, forgetting that Washington, in his major effort, had expended much ammunition, still lacked food, clothing and medicine for his men, and was now virtually abandoned, an empty-handed conqueror. He retired again into winter quarters, in far better condition than in previous years, but disillusioned and worried about the future. It was then, at the urging of Alexander Hamilton, that he began to write down his ideas on American defense, a defense he never again wanted to place in the hands of other peoples. He was grateful to the French, but wanted never again to have to depend upon the goodwill of an ally. His writings were eventually published under the title "Sentiments upon a Peace Establishment," and were the basis, much later, in his Farewell Address, of his warnings to the American people to avoid entanglement in foreign alliances.

In this last month of 1781, George III fired Sir Henry Clinton as Commander in Chief and sent Sir Guy Carleton to replace him. Fighting was still going on in the South, where General Nathanael Greene set about mopping up the British detachments after the defeat of the main body of troops. He swept down from the Carolinas all the way to Savannah, Georgia. There he threw a blockade around the city, confident that he could starve it out without a bloody assault that would cost him too many men. He no longer feared British counterattacks, for there no longer was a British Army of the South. He sat there for months, until the British evacuated by sea, and Georgia once again returned to the fold. By the end of 1782 the United States were again thirteen.

Franklin, well informed by friends in London, was patiently waiting for the first signs that the British were genuinely ready to talk peace with an independent United States. His fellow commissioners were all absent. Thomas Jefferson had written to say that his wife was seriously ill, probably dying, and that he could not leave her side. It would be three years before Jefferson finally came to Paris. John Jay was still trying to get help from Madrid. He was not happy with his assignment as Peace Commissioner and particularly unhappy with Congress' instructions that the American envoys were to be subject to the French Foreign Ministry. He had written back asking to be released from the assignment. Adams was still brooding in The Hague, feeling much the same as Jay, asking to come home. Henry Laurens had been, at last, released from the Tower of London, but was still in the city, on parole, trying to arrange his exchange with Lord Cornwallis, so that he could go on to Europe. Franklin was the sole Peace Commissioner in place and in function.

He received an early sign of shifting political winds when the great libertarian Edmund Burke wrote to him at the end of February to say that the House of Commons had voted a motion condemning the war and calling for direct peace negotiations. Burke wrote:

I congratulate you, as the friend of America, I trust, as not the enemy of England; I am sure, as the friend of mankind; on the resolution of the House of Commons, carried by a majority of nineteen at two o'clock this morning, in a very full house. . . . I trust it will lead to a speedy peace between the two branches of the British nation, perhaps to a general peace; and that our happiness may be an introduction to that of the world at large. I most sincerely congratulate you on the event.

In addition to Edmund Burke, many powerful voices were being heard in London in full cry against the war: Charles James Fox and John Dunning condemned Lord North, calling for his resignation. Even Lord Shelburne, a most cautious man, always supportive of the Crown, began to talk about the moment to be seized, the moment of peace. He still would not commit himself to any word about American independence, and, like Burke, talked of the "two branches of the British nation." But the doves were obliged to use such cautious language; any hint of support for American independence and George III would have turned down all peace proposals. The brooding King was so furious over his defeats, so angry with his American subjects that he even wrote notes indicating his preference for abdication rather than capitulation. He felt he would rather give up his crown than his colonies. The King's most loyal supporter was Franklin's old adversary in Paris, Lord Stormont, now in charge of foreign affairs, who announced that the French would have to take the Tower of London before he would recognize American independence.

It was early in February that Franklin received an innocent note from Madame Brillon that was to have important consequences, as he later noted in his diary. In it she told him that she had written a letter of introduction to Franklin at the request of Lord Cholmondeley, whom she had met in Nice. She wanted to warn Franklin that he might be "a British spy." It would be some weeks before Franklin heard from Cholmondeley, on March 21, and by then great events were shaking London.

At the end of February, under severe pressure from the parliamentary Opposition, George III wrote to his Prime Minister, Lord

North, to say that he was now prepared to negotiate peace on the principle of the ground possessed, but to treat only with the separate provinces, to detach them from the continental alliance with France. He would not deal with an entity called the United States of America. His position was still rigid, but for the first time he was talking of peace negotiations. The King was weakening.

A few days later, on March 4, Parliament adopted a resolution that all but called for the end of the war and the recognition of the independence of "the revolted colonies." In a desperate move, the King sent an envoy to Paris to see Vergennes and formally propose peace "on the grounds possessed." Vergennes stiffly replied that Louis XVI would consider an honorable peace only if the British dealt on an equal basis with the ally of France, America.

Vergennes's reply left Lord North and the King with no more room for maneuver. On March 20, with the Opposition raising a storm in the Commons, North held a last, painful meeting with the King and told him that he had no choice left but to resign. His Ministry had lost all credit, as well as control of the House. He then went to the House and announced that he would resign in a few days, just as soon as the King could put a new government together.

It was the very next day that Lord Cholmondeley wrote to Franklin, asking for a meeting at Passy the following morning. Cholmondeley arrived and chatted pleasantly with Franklin about mutual friends. Franklin did not yet know that North had resigned and that an old friend, Lord Shelburne, was about to play the key role in London. Cholmondeley casually mentioned to Franklin that Shelburne had a high regard for him and would certainly be pleased to hear from him after such a long time. He offered to carry a letter to Shelburne, since he was immediately returning to London.

Franklin, ever pleased to keep his connections with London open, at once sat down to write a friendly note to Shelburne. He told him that Shelburne's French friends, the Abbé André Morellet and Madame Helvétius, were well, and that the lady was very happy with a present of gooseberry bushes that Shelburne had sent over from London.

Franklin could have no idea of the confusion reigning in London at that moment. The King, still toying with the idea of abdication, would not replace Lord North with a member of the Opposition, who had publicly spoken in favor of independence, and so ruled out men like the Duke of Richmond or Fox for the Prime Minister's post. He decided to turn to Shelburne, who had always opposed independence, though he had moderated his views under the pressure of the news of British defeats and the growing unpopularity of the war. Shelburne hoped that diplomacy might be able to work out a compromise that would keep Britain and America united, under one king, in one empire, but each with its own sovereign parliament. This would offer America the "Irish solution," which was being negotiated at that very moment, March, 1782. By April Ireland received the cession of parliamentary sovereignty by the British and established its own legislative body while remaining in the Empire.

But Shelburne hesitated about accepting the King's offer to head the ministry. He was not a party leader and had no strong following of his own. It would be almost impossible for him to be Prime Minister, he explained to the monarch. Instead of himself, he nominated the Marquess of Rockingham. Rockingham had many friends among the Opposition as well as in the court party. He was the man who, back in 1766, had led the ministry which repealed the Stamp Act, and might so be remembered by the Americans. George III was suspicious of Rockingham, but he finally yielded, on condition that Shelburne would accept the portfolio of Secretary of State for Colonial Affairs, the key post for dealing with the Americans. The post of Secretary of State for Foreign (i.e., European) Affairs was given to one of the leaders of the Opposition, Charles James Fox, who had supported Franklin in his efforts to negotiate a compromise in 1774–75.

George III continued to consult regularly with Shelburne, instead of his Prime Minister, giving Shelburne tremendous power without the burden of being the chief executive of the government. Shelburne lost no time in answering Franklin's friendly letter. He had been waiting for it and was ready to respond by sending an agent to talk to Franklin. He also selected another agent to meet with John Adams in Holland, for British spies had reported that

Adams, reported to be angry with the French, was willing to talk confidentially with the British about a separate peace. Thus Adams, it was believed, would not balk at breaking the terms of the alliance ruling out a separate treaty.

To meet with Franklin, Shelburne chose a Scottish merchant, Richard Oswald, who had a good reputation as a man of peace and common sense, although he had made a fortune in the slave trade. Oswald had had an American agent for that trade, to whom he paid a 10 percent commission on each cargo of slaves: none other than Henry Laurens. Oswald was also a friend of the economist Adam Smith, was familiar with Smith's work and with the writings of the physiocrats of Paris, and was felt to be the ideal man to sound out Franklin. As his envoy to Adams, Shelburne did not choose an Englishman. He sold the idea to Henry Laurens, who, as a commissioner, could publicly meet with Adams frequently without provoking any questions. Shelburne had become friendly with Laurens and knew that he, like Adams, was anti-French and anxious to be released from the parole that kept him in London. Early in April, Oswald and Laurens crossed the Channel together, Laurens then heading for The Hague and Oswald to see Franklin at Passy.

Before his arrival, Franklin had, on April 6 and 7, received letters recommending the Scot as a man of the highest integrity and goodwill, from both Lord Shelburne and Henry Laurens. The two men met at Passy on April 15. Franklin noted in his diary:

> All I could learn was that the new ministry sincerely wished for a peace; that they considered the object of the war, to France and America, as obtained; that if the independence of the United States was agreed to, there was no other point in dispute, and therefore nothing to hinder a pacification; that they were ready to treat of peace, but he intimated that if France should insist upon terms too humiliating to England, they would still continue the war, having yet great strength and many resources left. I let him know that America would not treat but in concert with France, and that, my colleagues not being here, I could do nothing of importance in the affair; but that, if he pleased, I would present him to M. de Vergennes, Secretary of State for Foreign Affairs. He consenting, I wrote and sent the following letter.

In that letter to Vergennes on April 16, Franklin recounted the earlier visit of Lord Cholmondeley, then the letters from Shelburne and Laurens. He loyally and fully summarized his entire talk with Oswald. Franklin was convinced, both morally and practically, that at this moment of opportunity it was imperative to keep strictly to the letter and law of the treaty with France. Any move toward a separate peace or any division would sabotage the alliance and risk losing all that had been won. Franklin was the only one of the American commissioners who felt so strongly about loyalty to the alliance. He would again have a difficult time handling his colleagues. Franklin never had full and frank cooperation from any other American envoy until his good friend Thomas Jefferson arrived three years later.

On April 18, Oswald came to Passy to join Franklin for a trip to Versailles to open conversations with Vergennes. Vergennes told Oswald exactly what Franklin had told him, that the allies would not deal separately and would not negotiate anything but a general peace for all parties, not for any one belligerent. Oswald explained that he was not an official negotiator and could do nothing but listen, and asked Vergennes to give him specific terms that he might take back to Shelburne. Vergennes replied that Britain had no allies to consult, had only to read its own mind and was better placed to present its terms first—a shrewd move on Vergennes's part, forcing Britain to be the first to reveal its hand.

Oswald, a skillful trader in his own right, saw the ploy and tried to counter it on the way back from Versailles by telling Franklin again that if France was unreasonable, England would be unanimous in pursuing the war. Franklin, as cunning a negotiator as any, used his favorite trick of setting his face in stone and simply not replying. He told his diary that he recalled the old adage "that they who threaten are afraid." On his arrival home Franklin penned a letter to Shelburne which he asked Oswald to deliver. He simply informed Shelburne that the Americans were officially accredited to talk of peace and that Oswald should be so accredited by the British government to enter into specific negotiations.

Franklin had not forgotten the American prisoners in British and Irish jails. For years he had endeavored to effect exchanges against British prisoners in American hands. He closed his letter to Shelburne with another appeal for an exchange under flags of truce. He had another favorite project which had been in his mind for decades and which he put back on the table at every opportunity: the cession by Britain of Canada and Nova Scotia to the United States. When he came to Oswald to bid him farewell, he engaged him in a conversation on that issue.

Franklin noted in his diary that, as he told Oswald, peace must be founded on genuine reconciliation, which, in turn, should be based on fair and just reparations for injuries and losses suffered. It would be best if the offers were voluntary. He reminded Oswald of a previous conversation in which Oswald had remarked that it had been politic of France to cede Canada to Britain in the peace after the Seven Years' War. Would it not now, asked Franklin, be politic of Britain to return this favor to America? Franklin felt that Oswald had been "much struck with my discourse."

Pleased with the way things were going, Franklin then sat down and loyally wrote a full report on the Oswald mission to John Adams. He asked Adams to come to Paris to be there when Oswald returned. He also suggested that Laurens come and informed Adams that he was making the same suggestion to Jay in Madrid. Franklin had no intention of acting alone; he was scrupulous about observing and respecting the prerogatives of his colleagues—who were considerably less scrupulous with him. Franklin was also pleased with Vergennes, who had never once brought up the question of Canada. For a time Franklin had feared that the French might demand the return of territory to which they had more claim than did the United States. But Vergennes had long ago given up any hope and lost any desire for the recreation of the French colonial empire.

John Adams also had Canada on his mind when he met with Henry Laurens on April 15. He wanted Canada to be ceded, but, failing that, he would settle for a British agreement to dismantle their border garrisons and create a demilitarized frontier between Canada and America. He disabused Laurens about British notions that he would treat separately with England. He said he would work closely with Franklin and would respect the treaty with France. Whatever his private thoughts on the matter, Adams was not going to be used as a tool by the British to break up the alliance. He told Laurens firmly to tell Shelburne that an acknowledgment of American independence must be a preliminary to any negotiation and that there would be no proceeding without France. He won Laurens over to his thinking and Laurens carried that message back to Shelburne.

Shelburne still had not given up hope for some kind of federal union between America and Britain under the imperial flag. To get around Franklin, Adams and Vergennes, he sent instructions to Sir Guy Carleton, his Commander in Chief in America, and to Admiral Robert Digby, his naval commander, to try their luck in direct negotiations with George Washington, Congress and the governors of the thirteen states. They received their instructions on April 4, within days of Oswald's memorandum to Shelburne underlining the purposes of these moves: "I always supposed we must satisfy the Americans in such a manner as to have a chance of soothing them into neutrality." He felt that his first order of business was to sound out the American commissioners in Paris on a separate peace. This was also what Carleton and Digby were to do in America.

General Carleton sent a messenger to Washington, bearing copies of the resolution of the House of Commons in favor of peace and independence. He proposed a simple armistice on land warfare along the Atlantic coast settlements. This would, of course, leave the British free to conduct naval warfare, to seek out and destroy the French fleet and to remain in control of American waters. Washington saw through the ploy. In addition, he was intensely grateful to the French for the aid they had sent, which had helped him win the first, great campaign against Burgoyne, and then his latest great victory over Cornwallis. Washington would not hear of any separate British-American deals of any kind, let alone what Carleton was proposing. He refused to send the British dispatch on to the Congress, refused also to engage in a one-sided truce.

Congress was no more taken in than Washington. It met and

passed a resolution condemning the "insidious steps which the Court of London is proposing."

Carleton came back to Washington again, raising the ante by promising that American independence would be recognized by Britain "in the first instance," and informing him that negotiations for peace with France were already under way. The idea still was to split the allies apart. The British felt that if the Americans had their precious independence guaranteed, they would have won their major goal and have no reason to fight on in support of French and Spanish terms for peace. But Washington and Congress saw through this as completely as they had the first time. They let it be known, without ambiguity, that all negotiations would be carried on in Paris, with the American Peace Commissioners working loyally, hand in hand, with the French.

It was at that moment that another great battle was fought on the sea that would have an important impact on Paris. Admiral Sir George Rodney, Britain's finest seaman, had returned from leave in England with a powerful fleet of twelve new ships-of-the-line, joining up with Admiral Hood's twenty-two ships. The combined British fleet set sail for the West Indies to intercept Admiral de Grasse and his own big fleet of twenty-nine ships. The British caught up with the French on April 12 off the Saints, an island group lying between Guadeloupe and Santo Domingo. One of the greatest naval battles in a century raged throughout the day. As the sun set, the British had won a smashing victory, paying de Grasse back for the British defeat off the Chesapeake Capes. Seven French battleships were captured. The single greatest French loss was the capture of Admiral de Grasse himself and his 110-gun flagship, the *Ville de Paris,* on whose decks Washington had admired and cheered French power.

Although it was a terrible blow to the French, their spirits were still high from the victory at Yorktown. Louis XVI, hearing of Rodney's victory over de Grasse, defiantly declared: "I have lost five ships. I will build fifteen to take their place and one will not find me more tractable at the peace."

Despite these brave words, the defeat did make France a good deal more tractable in the peace talks and made Franklin's negotiating position easier, for Vergennes had had the idea of using this peace treaty to undo some of the losses sustained to Britain in the Treaty of 1763, particularly in Africa and Asia. After the Battle of the Saints, Vergennes abandoned that idea and laid down no more demands that it would have been difficult for Franklin to support.

Franklin now faced the Paris peace negotiations alone as he advanced into the seventy-sixth year of his life. Laurens, released from parole at his request, decided, for personal reasons, that he was not ready to serve as commissioner in Paris. Adams was in the middle of important negotiations with the Dutch for a loan and a treaty. Jay did decide to wind up his affairs in Madrid, but it was not until the end of June that he arrived in Paris.

Sensing that every move he made, every word he spoke, would later be subject to the closest scrutiny, Franklin kept a detailed diary, which became the main source for historians of this period. Franklin had told Adams many months before, on October 12, 1781, that he expected severe criticism of any peace efforts. "I have never known a peace made, even the most advantageous, that was not censured as inadequate, and all the makers condemned as injudicious or corrupt. 'Blessed are the Peacemakers' is, I suppose, to be understood in the other world, for in this they are frequently cursed." Franklin meant at least to get his own version on the record.

Oswald returned to Paris to meet again with Franklin on May 4. He brought with him a letter written by Shelburne, expressing his confidence in all the parties and thanking Vergennes for his "candour." He said that Oswald was authorized to settle "with you the preliminaries of time and place" of the peace talks. He added that his colleague, Secretary Fox, a bitter rival who did not intend to leave the field open for Shelburne, had also decided to send a foreign agent, Thomas Grenville, to participate in the negotiations. He delighted Franklin by informing him that transports were being arranged to convey American prisoners back to America, as a sign of goodwill.

Oswald told Franklin that the British Cabinet had met and had agreed upon the need to treat for a general peace. Then he added a note which Franklin instantly recognized as a major tactic to separate the French and the Americans. He said that the peace would be based on "the allowing of American independence, on condition that England be put into the same situation that she was left by the peace of 1763." In other words, Britain would give America her principal aim, but the French and Spanish—nothing. The British hoped that the Americans would not delay signing the peace if France demanded territory or reparations or pushed to get Gibraltar for Spain, that the Americans would not want to go on fighting for purely European political goals.

Franklin proceeded cautiously. He was determined to be loyal to the alliance, but he did not want to reveal all the cards to Vergennes at once. He might need some for a side game with his ally. He had not told Vergennes about his suggestions to Oswald that Britain cede Canada and Nova Scotia. This amounted to a separate American negotiation not quite faithful to the spirit of the alliance. Nor did he tell Vergennes of the latest British ploy involving the Treaty of 1763. Franklin had general overall confidence in Vergennes, but knew that his friend was tricky and subject to great political pressure. He had to be cautious, particularly since he was acting alone.

Franklin told Vergennes about the return of Oswald and the imminent arrival of Grenville, son of the famous George Grenville, former Chancellor of the Exchequer. Vergennes sent a note thanking Franklin and setting an appointment for Oswald.

They met at Versailles on May 6, for a generally pleasant conversation to set the mood and tone of the talks, while waiting for Grenville to arrive. On the way back from Versailles, Oswald, still busy inserting wedges between the allies, told Franklin "the affair of Canada would be settled to our satisfaction, and his wish that it might not be mentioned till towards the end of the treaty." Oswald warned Franklin particularly that the British anticipated the greatest trouble in the talks with Spain, but hinted darkly that Spain could be brought "to reason." He underlined the hint by saying that

Russia, "a friend to England," had made great discoveries "on the back of North America, and had made establishments there, and might easily transport an army from Kamchatka to the coast of Mexico and conquer all those countries."

Franklin was not for a moment impressed by these remarks. He knew that Catherine of Russia was not a true friend of England's, and doubted that she had the means or desire to engage in imperial conquests in America. He noted dryly in his diary: "This appeared to me a little visionary." He also wrote to Adams what Oswald had said, particularly about independence and the Treaty of 1763. "This seems to me a proposition of selling to us a thing that was already our own and making France pay the price they are pleased to ask for it."

As soon as Franklin had dispatched his letter to Adams on May 8, Oswald arrived at Passy, bringing with him Thomas Grenville. Franklin was surprised to learn that Grenville, there on a French visa, had not yet reported in to Vergennes but had come first to see him. Another wedge. Franklin, refusing to be distracted, immediately sent a message to Vergennes telling him that Grenville had arrived and asking for an audience. He then began questioning Grenville on the terms of his mission as laid down by Fox. Franklin was not sure whether Fox and Shelburne were playing games, with himself as the pawn between them.

Grenville said that "the idea of subjugating America was given up," and that America and France, having obtained what they had fought for, should be ready to treat at once of a general peace with all the belligerents, and that the site of the peace conference should be Paris. Franklin was favorably impressed by Grenville, whom he found to be "a sensible, judicious, intelligent, good-tempered and well-instructed young man"—high praise indeed.

Grenville and Oswald stayed on to dine with Franklin but left before Vergennes's messenger returned with word that the requested audience was granted for the following morning. Franklin sent his own messenger to Grenville asking him to be back at Passy for breakfast at eight, after which all the envoys would go together to Versailles. Franklin did not want to lose a moment. Delays could be fatal in the early stages of peace talks.

The bargaining began immediately in Vergennes's office. Grenville said that, with England giving America independence, France was expected to restore the conquests she had made of British islands and receive back her own islands of St. Pierre and Miquelon, two tiny fishing islands off the coast of Canada. Vergennes smiled at Grenville and told him that he was giving America what America already had: independence, a fact that Dr. Franklin would be glad to confirm, as Franklin promptly did. Independence, said Franklin, was something that had been won "at the expense of much blood and treasure, and which we are in full possession of." Vergennes then pointed out to Grenville that England had not been content with accepting a status quo ante in the Seven Years' War but had grabbed all Canada, all Louisiana, all Florida, Grenada and other islands and fisheries, in addition to establishments in Africa and the East Indies. How could England make an unprovoked war on America and France and then "have everything restored which she had lost in such a war"? Grenville promptly retorted that the war had not been provoked by England but by France, which had given encouragement to the Americans to revolt against the motherland. Vergennes exploded indignantly, asserting that America had declared its independence long before France had given the least encouragement and that Franklin would testify to that. Franklin, knowing that Vergennes was lying, remembering his early conversations with the secret French agent Bonvouloir in Philadelphia long before the Declaration of Independence, sat quietly, letting his silence be taken for assent. He would not contradict his ally, but he did not want to lie for Vergennes.

Not wanting to abort the talks before they had really begun, Vergennes quickly cooled off, told Grenville that the French King sought only "justice and dignity" and would deal fairly at the conference table. He also advised Grenville to communicate at once with Spain and Holland and said he hoped Grenville would find means of amusing himself in Paris while these preliminaries were being arranged.

Franklin found Grenville "thoughtful" and troubled on the

ride back from Versailles. He had not liked what Vergennes had said and was beginning to see how difficult the negotiations would be with a diplomat of Vergennes's experience, shrewdness and toughness. Grenville planned to see Vergennes again, the next day, but this time did not ask Franklin to accompany him. He had not liked the tandem play of Franklin and Vergennes against him. It must have been very painful for a young envoy to have to deal with either Vergennes or Franklin, let alone the two of them together.

Franklin then received the visit of his dear young friend Lafayette, now not only a hero of America but also an American citizen, an honor conferred upon him by the Congress. Congress had written Franklin to keep in close touch with Lafayette after his return home and Franklin was eager to do so. He knew how valuable Lafayette would be, how faithful to American as well as to French interests. Lafayette proposed that he remain in Paris to act as a useful intermediary in the peace talks. Franklin accepted at once, with great pleasure.

Receiving a message from Grenville offering to send letters by courier to England, Franklin immediately wrote friendly notes to Fox and Shelburne, praising their envoys, thanking them for the efforts being made, particularly the humane release of American prisoners. Oswald returned to England while Grenville continued private talks with Franklin, going over much the same ground already covered.

During this lull Franklin was much amused by a Russian diplomatic error. Catherine's son, the Comte du Nord, was visiting Paris, and her Ambassador, Prince Bariatinski, had told his servant to send out visiting cards to all the foreign ministers. According to etiquette, Franklin had to respond in writing, which he did by going by the Russian Embassy and putting his name on the acknowledgment list there. The next day the Russian servant came to Passy to say that a mistake had been made, pleading with Franklin to return the visiting card. He explained that it had been sent in error, for Russia had not recognized the United States, therefore Franklin could not be received as a Foreign Minister. Franklin laughed and said that he would burn the card and advised the servant to erase his name from the embassy list. Franklin added, in his diary, that other Northern nations seemed much less worried than Russia. The King of Denmark had sent Franklin a note inviting him to dinner. The Ambassador of the King of Sweden had inquired whether Franklin was desirous of negotiating a treaty of commerce. Too bad then for the Russians! America did not need them in 1782.

Toward the end of May the pace began to quicken again when Grenville called upon Franklin to say that he had received full powers to deal on peace with France and her allies. France, however, would have to agree to send a minister with the same powers to London. Vergennes had said he would put the proposal favorably to the King.

That afternoon, Lafayette came to Passy. Franklin told him what Grenville had said, and the two men agreed that Lafayette would be the ideal man to serve as French Minister. Lafayette said that he was on his way to see Vergennes and would put the proposal to him.

Franklin dined that night with the unfortunate Comte d'Estaing and noted that everyone was dejected by the news of Rodney's defeat of de Grasse. To cheer the party up, Franklin told them what had happened when the Turkish bashaw had been taken with his fleet at Lepanto by the Venetians. "Ships," he said, "are like my master's beard; you may cut it, but it will grow again. He has cut off from your government all the Morea, which is like a limb, which you will never recover." Franklin told his French friends: "And his words proved true."

The next day Franklin dined at Versailles with friends at court and thus missed Lafayette, who had gone to see him at Passy with confusing news, which he left in a note: according to Vergennes, Grenville had presented his official powers and they had related only to France, with no mention of the United States. Vergennes had coldly informed Grenville that France would not treat for the United States and that the Briton must have official powers to negotiate with Franklin or there would be no negotiations. Vergennes had been anxious to get Congress to instruct the American envoys to work under his advice and guidance, but he would not tolerate America being insulted by having no official position of its own at a peace conference. He also knew that the Americans would not accept such a secondary role.

Grenville came to see Franklin on Saturday, June 1. Franklin told him that Vergennes had advised him of the dispute over his powers. Grenville said it must be an error by the Foreign Office, which had used an old form. To show his good faith, he revealed to Franklin secret instructions he had received to acknowledge the independence of America unconditionally before the commencement of a peace conference. He argued that, France being America's only treaty ally, America was under no obligation to coordinate its peace aims with those of Spain or Holland, the other belligerents. He pointed out that it would make things very difficult for England if it had to satisfy in turn each of four belligerents, each of them holding out until all four got the terms they wanted. Franklin coolly suggested that if England made generous proposals to each of them, each would have good reason "to prevail with the others to accept those offered to them."

Franklin waited patiently for London to correct Grenville's credentials before the preliminaries could proceed. On the fourteenth of June, Grenville called upon him to report that full powers had been granted to him to deal with all the belligerents, including the United States. He also had been instructed to "declare the independence of America previous to the treaty as a voluntary act," separated from the request for using the Treaty of 1763 as the basis for peace between England and France. It was an important, a vital concession by London.

On Sunday, June 23, John Jay arrived from Madrid and Franklin, at last, did not have to handle all the details of the talks alone. He wrote at once to Secretary of State Robert Livingston and Superintendent of Finance Robert Morris, to bring them up to date on the talks and to complain, as always, about their continued requests for money. Franklin pointed out that he had already received a promise for another six million livres, "together with the clearest and most positive assurance that it was all the King could spare to us," and that he could not, in the face of that, go back to the King and suggest he had not been telling the truth. Franklin said he was sure that Adams would find the money in Holland, where he was on the verge of concluding a loan for three million florins, which would "supply the deficiency."

He informed them that Ireland had been granted home rule and that the Irish were most grateful to the Americans, whose revolution had forced England to yield to Irish demands or suffer another revolution. The Ambassador of Sweden had again approached Franklin at Versailles and asked him whether he was authorized to enter into talks for a treaty with his country and Franklin had told him he did have such powers. He asked Livingston to confirm this power specifically for Sweden and let him know whether such a treaty was desired. Despite a severe bout of influenza, painful headaches and chest pains, despite his regular references to his approaching death, Franklin showed every sign of a vigorous life. He would not wait for death to come upon him; he would work his way to the ultimate rendezvous.

At the end of June, Franklin broke off his journal, as negotiations for a preliminary peace accord entered a climactic stage.

CHAPTER

23

The Peace Conference Begins

The nature of the peace talks changed when Prime Minister Rockingham died in the influenza epidemic, on July 1, 1782. This time there was no argument about who should head the government. George III ordered Lord Shelburne to accept the post of Prime Minister. By then, Shelburne was ready. His bitter rivalry with Fox, the Foreign Secretary, had badly divided the Cabinet and made it impossible for Britain to deal with its four enemies in any consistent, cohesive manner. Shelburne took over and Fox resigned. Now one hand guided British policy. Shelburne named William Pitt the Younger as Chancellor of the Exchequer, Thomas Townshend as Home and Colonial Secretary and Thomas Robinson to replace Fox in the Foreign Office, but he kept all power of decision on the peace talks in his own hands. A new envoy to replace Grenville, Alleyne Fitzherbert, was sent to Paris, under strict instructions to refer every substantive issue back to London. Not only did Shelburne mean to keep personal control, but George III was watching over Shelburne's shoulder, reading every document he received or sent. The King was still not reconciled to American independence, despite all the assurances that had been given to Franklin.

Franklin felt the time had come to get genuine talks started. As a means of provoking some movement, he drew up a confidential memorandum, the same tactic he had used back in London in

1774–75. In this memorandum, which he read to Oswald, who had been kept on in Paris, Franklin listed four "necessary" and four "advisable" points of peace:

NECESSARY

1. Independence, full and complete, and all British troops to be withdrawn from the United States.
2. A settlement of the boundaries of the colonies of each side.
3. A confinement of the boundaries of Canada.
4. Freedom of fishing on the Banks of Newfoundland, for both fish and whales.

ADVISABLE

1. Voluntary offer of reparations to those ruined by war, to a total of some 600,000 pounds.
2. A public statement by Parliament acknowledging the injuries done by Britain. A few kind words would go far.
3. Ships and trade to be on equal footing with British ships and trade.
4. Giving up every part of Canada.

Oswald reported these "thoughts" to London, recommending that the "necessary" articles be accepted, after which, he thought, the Americans might well drop the "advisable" proposals.

Shortly after Franklin had read these suggestions to Oswald he learned that Shelburne had succeeded Rockingham and that the King had warned him against the grant of independence. Franklin immediately warned Oswald that there could be no consideration of the terms of peace until Shelburne had explained himself clearly on independence. He also told him that Jay was now down with the flu and no talks could be held until Jay was better.

Later Jay, Adams and their friends would say that they had influenced the terms of peace more than Franklin, who they claimed was totally committed to the French and would not act without them. But Franklin had proposed the cession of Canada very early on in the talks, without even informing Vergennes; from the first he had demanded American independence as the preliminary prerequisite of peace; and he had made his proposals to Oswald without consulting or informing Vergennes. He read the proposals instead of submitting them in writing because he knew that he was acting behind his ally's back and did not want any written proof of his actions. Franklin was as devoted to American interests as Adams or Jay, but expressed himself in more diplomatic terms and always sought a way around confrontation, whereas his colleagues were disputatious men, inexperienced in the art of gentle manipulation.

John Jay recovered from the flu and promptly gave a series of headaches to Franklin. After his two frustrating years in Spain, getting nowhere on a treaty or a sizable loan, Jay was convinced that the French had not used their influence on Madrid as they might have. He simply did not know that Floridablanca had given Vergennes as hard a time as he had had. He was certain that Spain and France were united to defend their own interests, without regard for America, and that America must defend *her* interests and not worry so much about the allies. He suspected that Franklin was too "soft" on the French, too subservient to them. Franklin mildly pointed out to him what he had already done, and reminded him of the instructions from Congress to coordinate with the French and do nothing without the consent of Vergennes. This merely strengthened Jay's conviction that Franklin was too easygoing. He would fight him on every point.

Early in August, Shelburne sent word to Franklin that England was now ready to recognize American independence without qualifications or conditions. He asked that Franklin's four "necessary" terms be considered as the basis for a treaty to be negotiated rapidly, but that the four "advisables" be dropped.

Jay, having read the definition of Oswald's power to treat with the Americans, objected to the language "to treat with commissioners named by the said colonies or plantations." There were no colonies in America, only free states, and he would not deal with Oswald under this colonial designation. Adams had already written from The Hague to back up Jay on this point. Franklin thought they were needlessly legalistic. If Britain acknowledged independence, what did it matter what Oswald called them? Franklin was no lawyer and he would not get involved in such disputes. Vergennes backed him up, telling Jay the term "colonies" in Oswald's credentials signified nothing. He pointed out that the British, in communicating with the French, used an ancient form of address when referring to George III as King of England and King of France. By treating with him, Vergennes said, he was not acknowledging George III as King of France. He told Jay that the very act of exchanging documents of powers between the British and American envoys was already a tacit British acceptance of independence for the Americans.

Far from being won over, Jay was now more than ever convinced that Vergennes did not care about American independence so long as he could use it as leverage for his own interests. Franklin argued that Jay's suspicions were unfounded. The French had already recognized American independence, had supplied men and monies most generously, without which the war would not have been won, had always treated the Americans fairly, and, furthermore, he reminded Jay, the Americans were under instructions to take Vergennes's advice on matters like this. Jay was not impressed. He felt he must follow his own judgment and not the instructions of distant Philadelphia, drafted by men who were not close to events in Europe. Like Adams, Jay was self-confident, self-righteous and highhanded. Franklin believed them more difficult to deal with than the British. And yet their obstinacy was useful, served the American cause well and acted as a brake upon Vergennes and the easygoing Franklin. The "good guy–bad guy" tactic of negotiations worked well and naturally for the Americans, mainly because it was not a ploy but a reality.

Oswald had been disturbed to hear Franklin and Jay talk of a "lasting peace." He wondered whether they had in mind siding with the continental powers of Europe against England in any future conflicts, and went to see Franklin to ask him to clarify this point. The old sage gave him an historical and philosophical answer. During the peace talks between Rome and the state of Tarentum, the Tarentines had asked the Senate how long the peace would last. The reply was precise: "If conditions were reasonable, the peace would last long; if not, it would be short." Oswald was relieved to realize that there were no ulterior motives in Franklin's mind.

At the end of August, the British Cabinet met and voted an irrevocable commitment to American independence if Franklin would agree to treat on the basis of his first four points, although Oswald was cautioned not to reveal the decision on independence but to use it as bait and lure. Above all, he was to work on Franklin and Jay to accept independence as a clause of the peace treaty to be negotiated rather than as the prerequisite to the talks they had been demanding.

At this point, early in September, Franklin fell ill again, with a painful kidney stone, the disease that would cause him much suffering, and, a few years later, finally kill him. The responsibility for negotiations fell on Jay, who was torn by suspicions and mistrust of almost everyone. He was not sure even of his own ground. When Oswald satisfied him that he would deal with them as commissioners of the United States, he weakened in his determination—and Franklin's—that independence must precede and not be a clause of the treaty. He did not know the British had already decided to grant it in advance if they had to. He could have gotten what he originally asked for if he had stood firm. While he wavered, in September a combined French-Spanish armada made a last, desperate assault on Gibraltar. But the British held out and the allied assault failed, strengthening Britain's hand in the peace talks and making the Spanish even more difficult to deal with.

On September 4, the British made Jay a firm offer of peace on the basis of independence and the acceptance of Franklin's four necessary points. But first Oswald tried again to make independence an article of the treaty. Jay hesitated and an excellent opportunity began to fade in the light of developments. It was a fluid, four-way action, involving America, France, Spain and Holland, and difficult for the various envoys to manipulate successfully.

With Franklin ill, Adams busy and Laurens refusing to take up his duties, Jay was all alone and very nervous. He had had a hard time with European diplomats from the day he had arrived in Spain. Even on the way over from America, on the same ship with France's sophisticated and wily Conrad Alexandre Gérard, returning to take up his old job as principal secretary to Vergennes for the peace talks, Jay had reacted uneasily to Gérard's lively curiosity about his plans and instructions. This was followed by Floridablanca's tricks, twists and snubs in Madrid and his secret treaty with France. On his arrival in Paris, Jay had immediately gotten in touch with Floridablanca's Ambassador, the Conde de Aranda, who began going through similar maneuvers that deepened Jay's suspicions. Aranda would not receive him in his capacity as Ambassador, for Spain still did not recognize American independence. He told Jay they could meet as private citizens—a most unfavorable atmosphere for serious peace talks—for Aranda said he had no powers to be a peace negotiator. All through August and early September, Jay tried to get Aranda to ask for such powers, but he always refused. On September 10, angry and fed up with the runaround, Jay broke off the conversations with him.

It was the position that Aranda was taking in private, on future boundaries, that led Jay to decide it would be no good talking further, even if proper accreditations were arranged. Sitting down with Jay, with a huge, detailed map of America on the table between them, Aranda had traced out Spanish demands that Jay would not accept. First, he claimed West Florida, by right of conquest; the Spanish had beaten the British and seized the territory. Then he laid claim to the east bank of the Mississippi all the way north to Ohio, even to the Great Lakes. Congress and Jay had wavered a bit on the great river when he was desperately seeking a treaty in Madrid, but now that Spain had turned him down and been niggardly on aid, he had no intention of conceding anything much on the Mississippi. Aranda's outline of postwar boundaries was totally in conflict with Jay's version, Franklin's views and anything the Congress would accept.

Aranda then appealed to Vergennes for help, under the terms of the secret treaty between France and Spain. Vergennes suggested that the Wabash might be a proper boundary for the territory north of Ohio, perhaps an Indian buffer state could be created between the United States and the Mississippi. This was not just a diplomatic skirmish. The stakes for America's future were tremendous, and Jay was quite right to be careful and obstinate about such imperial proposals. He went to Franklin to fill him in on what was happening, and Franklin, an advocate of firmness on the Mississippi, wrote to Foreign Secretary Livingston, on September 12, warning him that Spain was trying to "coop us up within the Allegheny Mountains." Franklin recommended that Congress insist upon the Mississippi "as a boundary, and the free navigation of the river." Jay, despite his suspicions, admired Franklin and was pleased at his reaction. He argued a lot with Franklin in the course of the peace talks, made common cause with Adams, but never hated Franklin nor tried to discredit him as Adams did.

Anyone who has covered complex peace talks knows how difficult they are and how, at times, all parties have a good deal of right on their side. It is rarely a case of good against evil, of justice versus injustice, of nationalism versus humanism. Most often, it is a case of each delegation's being under instructions to defend the national interest, with strong reasons for their actions. Such was the case in the Paris talks of 1782–83.

Vergennes obviously had strong interests and rational grounds for being concerned about his relations with Spain—his King, Louis, did not want to break with his Spanish uncle, Charles. The western and southern boundaries of America were important to Charles of Spain, not to Vergennes. Charles was also obsessed about Gibraltar. On the other hand, Jay and Franklin cared nothing about Gibraltar and had no reason to prolong the war to get the rock for Spain. And the Americans had more reason than any power to be concerned about their western boundaries and navigation on the great river that was the key to future expansion.

Gérard put his bright head together with Aranda's and worked out proposals that would startle Jay and deepen his mistrust. Jay did not understand the twists of diplomacy as Franklin did and had a low level of tolerance for the interests of others. Gérard went to Jay with a new map. It kept America away from the Mississippi south of Ohio, granting that to Spain, and also excluded America from the territory north of Ohio, leaving that in British hands. The area he blithely proposed to cede to Britain comprised present-day Ohio, Indiana, Illinois, Michigan, Wisconsin and Minnesota. This would have reduced America to a small, East Coast nation with no opening at all to the West.

Jay was appalled, and even more distraught when he learned that Gérard, after delivering this proposal, had set off for London following a morning conference with both Vergennes and Aranda. The news convinced him that the French and Spanish were plotting against America, trying to make a deal with Britain behind his back. In fact, Vergennes had sent Gérard to open discussions on the terms of the treaty with France and Spain, not particularly to make an anti-American deal, but Jay could not know that.

Some of his suspicions were, however, justified. Gérard told Shelburne that France was not committed to all the American terms, and he added that there was no pressing reason for Shelburne to inform the Americans about the French and Spanish talks with him. Franklin had done much the same thing in his own talks with Oswald and Grenville and in his letters to Shelburne. None of the allies was totally open with the others, and this gave the British, adept at power games, a chance to play one against the other. They leaked to the Americans a copy of a letter intercepted on the seas from the French Consul General in Philadelphia, Barbé-Marbois, to Vergennes. Barbé-Marbois wrote that the members of Congress were not in full agreement on the issue of fishing rights and that perhaps America might be excluded from the lucrative Newfoundland fisheries in the treaty. This, of course, heightened Jay's suspicion that Vergennes was ready to sell out his American allies.

Jay decided that he must foil the conspirators. He ignored his instructions to work with the French and failed to inform Franklin of his next move, which was to send Franklin's young friend Benjamin Vaughan, in Paris keeping an eye on the peace moves, back to London with new proposals which Jay had no right to make on his own. Vaughan was then a secret agent of Shelburne's, and Jay told him to tell the British Prime Minister that independence could be an article of the treaty, and that America was willing to work separately and secretly with the British on peace terms. This was a clear violation of the French-American treaty, and a most unwise move.

The Cabinet accordingly made out Oswald's new instructions to deal with the American envoys separately, as delegates of an entity called "The United States of America" and as secretly as possible. On October 5, in Paris, he exchanged powers formally with the Americans. Jay gave him the American terms, based on Franklin's four points plus a new proposal: that England and America should share freedom of navigation on the Mississippi. Just as Gérard had suggested that Britain and Spain share these rights and territories without mentioning America, so now did Jay reverse the ploy, leaving out the French and Spanish. Franklin went along with this, from his sickbed, although he did not like granting any rights to England. Jay had dropped Franklin's cherished proposal to annex Canada, but he insisted on fishing rights and, in addition, the right to dry fish on the Newfoundland shores.

Jay's proposals, with Oswald's favorable comments, were delivered to the Cabinet in London on October 11. During that week the British learned that Sir George Elliot had successfully held Gibraltar against the French-Spanish attack force. It stiffened their attitude on the peace talks, and the ministers decided to draft objections to Jay's proposals. No longer trusting Oswald completely, feeling he had come under the influence of Franklin, the Cabinet chose Henry Strachey, who had been secretary to Lord Howe during the abortive peace talks with Franklin on Staten Island, as a member of the Paris delegation, to keep an eye on Oswald and hold him in line. They also gave him counterproposals to make. He was to insist on compensation for American Tory Loyalists, whose properties had been either destroyed or confiscated. He was also to insist upon payment of debts due British merchants in "hard money," not valueless Continental paper. They rejected the request to dry fish as likely to cause conflict with British fishermen who used the shores. They proposed changes, favorable to Britain, in the boundaries of Canada, and ignored any notion of ceding Canada to the United States. Strachey set off for Paris and arrived there just about the time that John Adams arrived from Holland. Talks were firming up on specifics and all the envoys were getting into place.

Adams arrived bristling with energy and suspicion of everybody, a gallant American knight prepared to give battle to all. He went immediately to Jay's house but did not find him in. He did not call on Franklin right away—he wanted to find out first what had been going on, not believing Franklin's full and frank reports to him. He went to see an American friend, Matthew Ridley, who told him that Franklin had been ill, had canceled his dinner parties to take his meals in bed, but was now out of his bed again, although confined to his estate. Ridley said that Franklin worked closely with the French and adhered strictly to the letter of congressional instructions, which was no more than Adams had suspected.

The next day he saw Jay, who told him what had transpired. Adams endorsed all Jay's actions and proposals, including his failure to keep Franklin fully informed. Jay reported that Gérard had recently dined with him and Franklin and had been outspoken in his criticisms of American demands on boundaries and fishing rights. This did not surprise Adams, who exploded about Franklin; Jay noted in his diary that Adams "spoke freely what he thought."

Adams knew he had to call on Franklin, and he finally swallowed his aversion and went to see him on the twenty-ninth, after first meeting with Jay, Oswald and Strachey. He told Franklin how much he mistrusted the French and how much he trusted Jay. He said frankly that he and Jay would work hand in hand, omitting the same offer to Franklin. It was clear to Franklin that henceforth he would be in a minority of one. After another meeting the next day, the old man, weak from his bout with the stone, never one for head-on confrontations if they could be avoided, philosophical about the fact that circumstances would ultimately dictate their roles, told Adams and Jay: "I am of your opinion, and will go on with these gentleman [Oswald and Strachey] without consulting this court." Franklin was prepared, under the pressure of Adams and Jay, to ignore the strict instructions of Congress. At least, that is what Franklin told them.

Adams, having received his commission to negotiate peace long before the others had been named, was the senior man and chairman of the U.S. delegation. It was he who had received detailed instructions from Congress. Franklin had been informed in a summary letter from Secretary of State Robert Livingston sent early in January of that year, 1782. Livingston instructed Franklin that the boundary between the United States and Canada had been pretty well defined by earlier "grants, charters, proclamations," etc., and therefore need not become a difficult issue. He anticipated far more trouble on "our western and northwestern extent," and felt that America's claim to extend to the Mississippi "is founded in justice," as well as the practical effects of the tides of war. He said that fishery rights might be hotly disputed, "not because our rights are doubtful, but because Great Britain has never paid much attention to rights which interfere with her views." He expected this to be a difficult point of litigation. He suggested to Franklin that he argue that America, having long been a part of the British Empire, had long exercised fishery rights, so that they had become part of the American economy; that, in addition, there was a natural human right to use the waters that belong to all mankind and not to one nation. He also reminded Franklin that Americans had fought on the side of the British in imperial wars to assure Britain's rights to the fisheries. Americans had died for those fisheries and so had a right to live by them.

Livingston then brought up the subject of Americans who had remained loyal to the British cause, including the many who were either banished from America or who had voluntarily returned to Britain. He anticipated the issue of reparations, and argued that it would be inconvenient and unfair to let the Loyalists return or to compensate them unless suitable reparations were also made for American properties burned or looted by those same pro-British partisans in the course of the war.

He added a note about granting Spanish demands for the Floridas, cautioning that great care must be taken to define the boundaries of the Florida territories, while conceding the principle. Livingston ended the letter by saying that Charleston had been invested and would be back in American hands and that the French had brilliantly recaptured the Dutch trading post of St. Eustatius. He closed in good spirit and with confidence in the future.

By early October the Marquis de Lafayette had been appointed, as he and Franklin had proposed, to be an intermediary among the allies. John Adams immediately protested the decision, referring quite disagreeably to his "mongrel character of French Patriot and American Patriot." Adams agreed there ought to be a "go-between," but he did not like Lafayette, mainly because he felt him to be too thick with Franklin. He feared that Franklin would pass on to Lafayette all the Americans' confidential talks, a nasty and inaccurate reading of Franklin's character. Adams and Jay agreed to keep some things from Franklin.

Franklin, unperturbed, kept up his close, friendly relations with Lafayette, wittily congratulating him on the birth of a daughter and suggesting that he have thirteen children, each named for one of the American states. Franklin added that he would think it well if Connecticut and Massachusetts changed their names before the new Lafayette children were born. Meanwhile, back in America, Morris learned that Jay had sent proposals to the British without consulting Franklin, and that he had completely dropped from his terms Franklin's suggestion for the cession of Canada. Morris and others were quite displeased.

Adams, Jay and Franklin began daily meetings among themselves and with the British. Although Franklin had promised not to consult the French at that time, Adams worriedly noted in his diary in reference to Franklin and Jay: "Between two as subtle spirits as any in this world, the one malicious, the other, I think, honest, I shall have a delicate, nice, critical part to act. F's cunning will be to divide us. To this end, he will provoke, he will insinuate, he will intrigue, he will manoeuvre."

From October 30, negotiations went into round-the-clock sessions. Every preliminary point was examined through the magnifying glasses of national interest and the personal pride and temperament of the negotiators. Adams resented everyone and everything. He was even angry that Franklin maintained his grandson Temple as secretary to the U.S. commission, although Temple had been secretary to the American mission for six years, ever since Franklin had arrived in France in December, 1776. Adams was paranoiacally convinced that Franklin was maneuvering to get Temple named as American Minister to France, while Franklin, after the peace, would move on to become American Ambassador to England, a post Adams wanted for himself. It never seemed to occur to him that by January, 1783, just a few months away, Franklin would be seventy-seven years old, and that he was suffering from gout and kidney stones—hardly ready to set about a new and difficult assignment, especially one he could not hold for long. But Adams was not rational about Franklin.

Although the negotiators haggled over every point, the will to prevail was there, and by November 5 they had agreed on a draft of the preliminary basis of peace, to serve as the basic document for the peace conference.

The agreement included acknowledgment of unconditional independence for the United States. It confirmed all four of Franklin's "necessary" points—a triumph for America's first and premier diplomat. The British accepted freedom of navigation and commerce on the Mississippi, the river whose waters Franklin would never sell. Boundaries were laid down for the United States: on the east, the Atlantic and the St. Croix River; on the north, the Canadian line, from the St. Lawrence to the Lake of the Woods; on the south, the boundary would run along latitude 31° east from the Mississippi to the Chattahoochee and then, by the northern boundary of Florida, back to the Atlantic; in the west, the Mississippi would be America's boundary line. Agreement was reached on fishery rights and debts, on reparations and condemnations and amnesty for Loyalists to be left to the discretion of the individual states.

On the whole, the terms were what the Americans wanted and needed. Only one potentially bad mistake was made, by Jay. He insisted on working out a secret clause with the British on West Florida in the event they managed to keep it from Spain. Jay preferred Britain to Spain as a neighbor because of his personal animus against the Spanish, but his judgment was poor. Spain was a declining power, Britain still a vigorous, imperialist, expansionist power. Britain would have been a dangerous neighbor and rival in the opening of the American South and West, along the Gulf of Mexico and northward toward the great plains. With strong positions also in Canada and the Northwest, Britain could have held America in a vise.

After much finger-chewing, there were some clauses left open that would cause irritation for a long time. The principal one was the issue of reciprocity of trade, which ran contrary to British navigation laws and would provoke great difficulties in the Parliament. The Americans did not press for it, for they were only too happy to get the British to agree to free navigation on the Mississippi. For their part, the British felt that the American Loyalists were being left to the doubtful mercies of the individual states and would have no legal recourse for damages, a small point in the greater picture but looming large in politics, for the Loyalists had a strong lobby in Parliament. One of the strongest, most strident voices in favor of compensation for the Tories was a man "more royalist than the King," the ex-Governor of New Jersey, William Franklin, Ben's now truly illegitimate son.

In the final round of talks, after London had approved the drafts, with small amendments, Franklin was the one who fought hardest against his son's demands. He had compiled a long list of damages to Americans inflicted by the Loyalists and said there could be no talk about compensation unless both sides were repaid. Adams finally yielded a point on the fisheries, permitting the British to substitute the word "liberty" for "rights" in reference to American participation in the fisheries. They were "free" to do so, but had no treaty right to—a weakening of the American position, for a general freedom to do something can be more easily restricted than the legal right to do it. This seemingly small point would spawn a hundred years of controversy. Lastly, the negotiators agreed that once the peace treaty was signed, British armies would withdraw from America "with all convenient speed," a most unhappily ambiguous phrase, certain to stir up trouble later.

During the last day of the preliminary talks, Henry Laurens

finally arrived. He was still ill, and grieving at the news of the loss of his son John, Washington's former aide and envoy for the loan. He had been killed in a minor skirmish, leading his men in a foolhardy cavalry charge. All the negotiators mourned his loss and expressed condolences to Laurens. Laurens, the former slave trader, made an undistinguished and ultimately futile plea to add a clause to the treaty forbidding evacuating British armies from carrying away slave property—all he could think of at the moment when America was on the verge of winning peace and independence.

The negotiators finally finished nit-picking every clause and all signed the preliminary articles on November 30, 1782. The articles were described, in the preamble, as the treaty of peace "proposed to be concluded." The British-American treaty could not be promulgated until a similar treaty was agreed upon with France. But the Americans did sign without prior consultation with the French, a clear violation of their specific instructions from Congress and of the spirit of the alliance.

Franklin did what he could to prevent a breach with the French without going back on his word to his colleagues. The night before signing he sent a note to Vergennes telling him that the preliminaries would be signed the next day. Then, after the signing ceremony, Franklin sent Vergennes a copy of the agreements, lacking the secret clause on West Florida. Vergennes was not happy about the procedure, but he did not scold Franklin; he knew the pressures that Adams and Jay had put upon him. But Vergennes became annoyed when, later, Franklin told him that the British had given him a safe-conduct pass for a ship to carry "important papers" to America. Franklin added it might be a good idea to use that ship for new financial aid that he had been pressing for.

Vergennes immediately understood that the ship was being used to send Congress copies of the peace agreements, and was irritated, because it meant that the agreements were not being held in Paris pending developments in parallel French and British talks, but were taking on the appearance of a separate British-American peace without regard for the French. This time, Vergennes did remonstrate with Franklin. In answer to Franklin's request for more money, at the very moment that he seemed to be acting behind France's back, Vergennes wrote him a sharp note:

> You perfectly understand what is due propriety; you have all your life performed your duties. I pray you to consider how you propose to fulfill those which are due to the king. I am not desirous of enlarging these reflections; I commit them to your own integrity. When you shall be pleased to relieve my uncertainty I will entreat the king to enable me to answer your demands.

Vergennes's words could not have been more to the point: either satisfy me about your behavior or no money. Franklin then set about penning a reply which has become famous in diplomatic history, a masterpiece of explanation to clear up an awkward incident. No other American could have written this note.

He began by pointing out that he had informed Vergennes about the sailing partly as a convenience to Vergennes but mainly because it was vital that Congress hear about the agreement from its own envoys before the British could get their version to Philadelphia first. The agreement, he pointed out, was made conditional upon the French's successfully negotiating the basis for their own treaty and would not come into effect until the French had concluded their talks. How could this be construed as failing in duty to the King? Then, in a brilliant move, Franklin did what few diplomats ever learn to do: he admitted to having breached propriety by signing before consulting Vergennes. He simply confessed his error and apologized. Further, anticipating Vergennes's fears, he added a sentence which he underlined in his letter: *"The English, I just now learn, flatter themselves they have already divided us."* The appositional words "I just now learn" were a disarming stroke of diplomatic genius. Franklin, of course, had not just learned it, but he disposed of the accusation by this casual suggestion that the report had just come to his attention, and went on to assure Vergennes that the British were "totally mistaken" in their belief.

Vergennes was charmed. Franklin, the chess player, had beaten the brilliant, veteran French diplomat at his own game. Vergennes, with good grace though still apprehensive about America, yielded on the loan, and gave Franklin an installment of six hundred thousand livres, with a promise eventually to make it a full six million. The French Treasury was at that moment so strained that it had called a moratorium on payment of its own bills. Until France had won a satisfactory peace settlement, Vergennes did not want to risk leaving the Americans to their own devices. Money was the bond he meant to use to hold them in line, and he would dole it out as long as possible to protect France's position.

The negotiations among Vergennes, Aranda and Fitzherbert were proceeding in Paris. French demands were moderate, but Spain was holding everything up by insisting there would be no peace until Britain yielded Gibraltar. At that moment there arrived in Paris the Comte de Grasse, who had been exchanged as a war prisoner but who had conferred in London with Prime Minister Shelburne before the exchange. De Grasse startled everyone by reporting that Shelburne was ready to return Gibraltar to Spain. Vergennes was overjoyed and dispatched Gérard to London to arrange the deal, since Fitzherbert professed no knowledge of such an intention and would not agree to it on his own.

In London, Gérard discovered that de Grasse was wrong. Shelburne had not committed himself on Gibraltar, indeed was still firmly opposed to any cession, particularly since the French-Spanish armada had been defeated, and since America had weakened Spain's position by signing the preliminaries. America was not an ally of Spain and would not continue the war for Gibraltar. Vergennes was in the middle, for France was committed by treaty not to make peace until Spain had received its cherished rock. Vergennes, however, had no intention of supporting Spain's obsessive demand and he let Shelburne know this. What he sought was an exchange to buy Spain off. He also suggested to Aranda that if Spain really wanted Gibraltar, which it could not win by war, Spain ought to offer territory to Britain in exchange.

Floridablanca, understanding that his chances were all but impossible, told Aranda to inform the British that he might yield on Gibraltar on condition that Britain make territorial concessions. Instead of offering Spanish territory, he wanted British territory to pay him for dropping his demand. He even tried to get the French to give him Corsica as inducement to drop his claim. Vergennes told him that was out of the question. He then sent Gérard back to London to sound out Britain on a deal for Gibraltar.

The British told Gérard they might make an exchange for either Puerto Rico, Martinique, Guadeloupe or Santo Domingo, on condition that Spain also agree to indemnify Britain fully for all the fortifications, ammunition and stores on Gibraltar, plus the return of all Spanish conquests in the war, including West Florida. Britain had asked for a mountain of diamonds for the rock.

These proposals were debated back and forth between Paris and London all through November, while the Americans were negotiating with the British. There was great pressure on Shelburne's government, and mounting unrest as rumors reached the Opposition, some attesting to British obstinacy, some asserting that Shelburne was giving away the Empire. When the Opposition learned that Shelburne had offered an exchange for Gibraltar, there was an uproar. Vergennes and Aranda began to fear that Shelburne might be overthrown on this issue, bringing about a political crisis that might kill the peace negotiations.

Shelburne, frightened by the opposition on Gibraltar, withdrew his proposal and came up with a new deal: Britain would keep Gibraltar but give Spain Minorca and both East and West Florida. Aranda, by now alarmed at the deterioration of the political situation, decided to accept the latest offer. He preferred that the French hold their islands in the West Indies, since France was no danger to Spain's American colonies. He knew, too, that Vergennes would have a difficult time trading off Martinique and Guadeloupe to appease Spain, and Vergennes might come tumbling down. Vergennes was delighted and grateful for Aranda's daring decision to risk the wrath of Floridablanca, who had long suspected that Aranda was too sympathetic to the French and the Americans.

But Floridablanca knew, at least, that he had been checkmated in Paris and London. Spain was in no position to fight on alone for long. He gave up and told Aranda to accept Minorca and the Floridas and sign the preliminary peace agreements. The agreements were signed on January 20, 1783, at Versailles. A new year had dawned. It was time to conclude the definitive peace treaty.

CHAPTER

24

Peace, at Last!

As soon as the preliminary peace accords had been signed, all hostilities ceased, even between Britain and Holland, although they had not completed their talks. The Anglo-American-French-Spanish accords amounted to a general peace; the specifics with Holland would be worked out. No one would prolong the war to support Dutch demands for the return of colonies captured by the British, but the French told Holland that they would turn over those territories they had captured and had been holding for the Dutch.

Meanwhile, politics had taken a sudden, unexpected turn in London. As soon as Parliament had received copies of the peace accords for ratification, different pressure groups began to decry some of the clauses. There was widespread criticism of Lord Shelburne, although he had done the best he could in the circumstances. The war was highly unpopular in England and there had been a clamor to end it. Now that it had been ended, everyone looked for a scapegoat to blame for Britain's misfortunes and humiliations. Shelburne was through as Prime Minister.

This came as no surprise to Franklin. The old philosopher was a humanitarian, with a deep commitment to his fellow man, but he knew just how mean and mischievous men could be. He had expressed his feelings most eloquently in a letter to his dearest friend and fellow scientist, Dr. Joseph Priestley, during the anxious days of the previous summer when peace still hung in the balance:

I should rejoice much, if I could once more recover the Leisure to search with you into the works of Nature; I mean the *inanimate,* not the *animate* or moral part of them. . . . Men I find to be a sort of Being very badly constructed, as they are generally more easily provok'd than reconcil'd, more dispos'd to do Mischief to each other than to make Reparation, much more easily deceiv'd than undeceiv'd, and having more Pride and even Pleasure in killing than begetting one another; for, without a Blush, they assemble in great Armies at Noon Day to destroy, and when they have kill'd as many as they can, they exaggerate the Number to augment the fancied Glory; but they creep into corners or cover themselves with the Darkness of night, when they mean to beget, as being asham'd of a virtuous action. A virtuous Action it would be, and a vicious one the killing of them, if the Species were really worth producing or preserving; but of this I begin to doubt.

Franklin then went on to tell Priestley a Swiftian story of an angel who had a mission on earth and was guided down by a "courier-spirit." They arrived in the West Indies just at the moment of the fierce naval battle between de Grasse and Rodney.

When, thro' the clouds of smoke, he saw the Fire of the Guns, the Decks cover'd with mangled Limbs, and Bodies dead or dying, the ships sinking, burning or blown into the Air; and the Quantity of Pain, Misery and Destruction, the Crews yet alive were thus with such eagerness dealing rounds to one another; he turn'd angrily to his Guide, and said "You blundering Blockhead, you are ignorant of your Business, you undertook to conduct me to Earth and you have brought me to hell!" "No, Sir," says the Guide, "I have made no mistake, this is really the Earth, and these are men. Devils never treat one another in this cruel manner; they have more Sense, and more of what Men (vainly) call Humanity."

Franklin was living in a minor hell of his own, his feet tender and painful with the gout, his body racked by cramps and pains from his kidney stone. But, as always, he maintained his outward good humor, ate and drank his favorite foods and wines, although in less quantity than formerly. He kept examining his urine and saw the hand of death in the rusty gravel and occasional clots of blood. He complained to no one and went about his business. He knew that the peacemakers would be cursed, not blessed, as had just befallen Shelburne, but he passionately desired peace and a chance, at long last, to return home to spend his last days with his family and friends in his native land.

One of his old British friends, David Hartley, with whom he had corresponded all through the war, surprised him by turning up as the new British envoy to the peace talks. Oswald had resigned when Lord Shelburne's Cabinet had fallen. The British, with perversity, had replaced Shelburne, the man of peace, with Lord North, who had been Prime Minister through the war. And Shelburne's rival, Fox, had again been called back as Foreign Secretary. The North-Fox government was an anomaly. North had opposed American independence and pursued the war; Fox had opposed the war and supported American independence. The government made no sense, except in the parochial politics and rivalries inside London.

Like all new brooms, Hartley came in with sweeping plans for new amendments and a new commercial treaty. All the envoys, exhausted by their long, detailed labors on the preliminaries, were impatient with new suggestions that threatened to undo all their work. They dragged their heels and led Hartley into interminable discussions of his projects. The peace talks dragged on for weeks and then for months. The Americans countered Hartley's proposals with new proposals of their own. It soon became evident that the only peace treaty that could be agreed upon was virtually the same document that had been thrashed out and signed the previous November, the document based upon Franklin's four "necessary" points plus the additional clauses that had been so painstakingly negotiated.

While the Americans were going through the motions with Hartley, other British envoys were talking with the other belligerents. Aranda and Vergennes were immovable on their terms. No one would support the Dutch, by far the weakest power, so they had to capitulate on their demand for the return of their colonies and settle for whatever crumbs the French would brush off the conference table. At last the final terms were agreed upon. Except for the Dutch, each side was satisfied with the outcome. France got back some islands—St. Pierre, Miquelon, Tobago—and Britain got

back the Grenadines, Santo Domingo, St. Christopher. Spain got Minorca and the Floridas, but Britain kept control of Gibraltar, guarding the entrance to the Mediterranean, a lifeline of the British Empire. On the whole, Britain got everything except America, and that had been lost many feckless years before.

America got almost everything it sought: freedom of navigation on the Mississippi, a reasonable frontier with Canada, fishery rights and, the most precious victory of all: freedom and independence for the United States of America. Almost everyone had contributed to the victory: the farmers of Lexington and Concord, the brave militiamen in all thirteen states, General Washington and Superintendent Morris providing the military and financial leaderships to stave off defeat in desperate moments. The commissioners in Paris had had the courage and daring to break with their instructions and free themselves of subservience to the French, strengthening the American hand at the conference table. Franklin, participating in the breaking of the rules, nonetheless had the wit and diplomatic skill to prevent a rupture with the French.

If many had contributed to the great moment of victory and independence, no one man had done as much as Benjamin Franklin. He had been the architect and mechanic of the alliance that had provided, with infinite pains and complexities, the supplies and the monies that had made Washington's final triumph possible. He had been the very heart and soul of the peace talks, the one man to whom all turned. It was not to Adams or to Jay that Shelburne had written. Nor had they drafted the four points on which peace was built. It was Franklin, old, ill, but steady and wise.

The treaty of peace was signed in Paris on September 3, 1783. The King declared a holiday and prayers of thanksgiving for peace. Wine and sausages were distributed to the people and there was dancing in the streets of Paris, as thousands of toasts were drunk to the great apostle of liberty, Benjamin Franklin, warrior and peacemaker, premier agent of the Revolution. The King and Queen did not know they were celebrating the approaching end of their regime. The French Treasury had been drained. What Jefferson would call "the infectious disease of freedom" had already deeply infected the French. The American Revolution would lead directly to the French Revolution, as an important contributing factor. But few suspected this on that happy night of peace in September, 1783.

CHAPTER

25

Home, to Rest at Last

Franklin was eager to go home, but there was still work to be done. He would, before completing his mission, negotiate a treaty of amity and commerce with Prussia. There were wondrous new developments in science that fascinated him, particularly the latest innovation: man's first flight through the air. The Montgolfier brothers, pioneers in the new science of aeronautics, had built a balloon that would take men into space. They had launched it one week before the signing of the peace treaty, in August, in the village of Annonay, near Lyons.

A physicist named Jacques-Alexandre Charles had followed their lead and built a balloon to be launched in Paris. It was covered in silk and filled with hydrogen gas, made by pouring oil of vitriol over iron filings. Franklin wanted very much to see it. He was too ill to walk to the balloon site, in the Champs de Mars, where today the Eiffel Tower stands, across the river from Franklin's statue, near his house in Passy. But he went in his carriage and got as close as he could. He also had a small telescope so he could watch the balloon in flight. When someone asked him what good a balloon could be, he quipped in reply: "What good is a new-born baby?"

The ascension was a huge success. The balloon rose to a height of some two thousand feet. The astronauts waved white pennants aloft, as the crowds cheered the advent of a new age. Later, a balloon would make the flight from London to Paris, carrying, for Franklin's grandson, the world's first airmail letter—a welcome event for a man who had long been a postmaster.

Franklin, with the imagination of a Jules Verne, foresaw the future importance in warfare of flight through the air. In January, 1784, he wrote to his friend Jan Ingenhousz about this. He felt that leaders might be convinced of the folly of war if they knew how destructive it could become. He speculated: "Where is the prince who can afford so to cover his country with troops for defence as that ten thousand men descending from the clouds might not in many places do an infinite deal of mischief before a force could be brought together to repel them?"

When, in 1944, war correspondents entered the office of America's Lieutenant Colonel Lewis Brereton, commander of the First Allied Airborne Army, about to launch 35,000 paratroopers and glider-borne infantry over Holland, they saw on his desk the words Franklin wrote in 1784. Brereton, pointing to the quotation, said: "Even after 160 years, the idea remains the same."

Franklin hated war. He also hated the injustices of society. In March, 1785, he wrote about the cruel penal laws of the time and blamed them on surplus wealth. "Superfluous property is the creature of society. . . . When, by virtue of the first laws, part of the society accumulated wealth and grew powerful, they enacted others more severe, and would protect their property at the expense of mankind."

Thomas Jefferson, finally arriving in Paris, noted that he found there "more respect and veneration attached to the character of Dr. Franklin in France than to that of any other person, foreign or native." International honors were bestowed upon Franklin, who was more amused than inflated by them.

Franklin sent a cool letter of reconciliation to his son William and sent William's son, Temple, to London to visit with his father. He was lonely in Passy without Temple, whom he adored, but his dearest friends and loves, Mesdames Brillon and Helvétius, rallied him and warmed his heart with their attentions. He would miss them and all his other friends when he left France.

In May, 1785, Congress wrote accepting his request to resign his post and return home. He left France in July, good sailing weather on the Atlantic. Franklin was worried about the trip, unsure he could survive another Atlantic crossing but determined to try to reach his native shores to end his days. He was now seventy-nine years old, his legs swollen, his body tormented. Madame Brillon and Madame Helvétius wept as he said goodbye to them. They had never granted him the ultimate favors he had sought, but they loved him deeply, as he loved them.

His journey to Le Havre to board his ship was a triumphal parade. His carriage was cheered, his path strewn with flowers, great parties and receptions held for him at almost every stop of the stage. His ship crossed the Channel on the twenty-second and twenty-third, landing on the morning of the twenty-fourth in Southampton. William Franklin came down from London to see his father for the last time. Bishop Shipley came with his wife and daughter to pay respects to his old friend. Franklin kept hoping that Polly Hewson would come and sail with him to America, but she could not prepare herself to leave England at that point.

Franklin had a wonderful crossing. The sea air braced him and he felt well and free from all the long years of work and worry. He renewed his experiments on the temperature of the waters and filled his journal with a number of scientific treatises, ranging from Eskimo kayaks to the cause and utility of the Gulf Stream, diets for sailors, lifesaving devices and drills on shipboard and a host of other "Maritime Observations."

On Wednesday, September 14, his ship cast anchor opposite Philadelphia and, after health inspection, he was taken to shore and landed at Market Street Wharf. He wrote in his journal: "God be praised and thanked for all His mercies." Ben Franklin was home again, free, he thought, to spend his last days in the study and exposition of science.

The entire city of Philadelphia turned out to welcome him. He was overwhelmed by his reception, "far beyond my expectation." Just as he had thought he was home to rest on his return in 1775, only to find new calls for his services, so again did public affairs put their grip on the sick, old man. A committee of citizens called upon him to be their candidate in the elections to the Executive Council of the state. Both the Constitutionalists and the Anti-Constitutionalists, engaged in a fight over the state's constitution, wanted him.

On October 11 Franklin was elected President of the Council. Then he was elected President of Pennsylvania. He would have no time for science or leisure. Probably he wanted none, despite his protestations. He could have pleaded age and infirmity. Instead, he once more seized upon his duties with zest.

In March of 1786, now aged eighty, Franklin was elected delegate to the Constitutional Convention of the United States. He had feared his stone would grow worse, but he exercised with dumbbells every day, abstained from drinking wine and felt well enough to attend the sessions.

The Constitution was drafted with only minor contributions by Franklin. He was called upon to make a closing address on September 17, the final day of the Convention. He said that there were parts of the Constitution that he did not approve of but that "the older I grow the more apt I am to doubt my own judgment and to pay attention to the judgment of others. . . . Thus I consent, Sir, to this Constitution, because I expect no better and because I am not sure that it is not the best." No statement could better illustrate the modesty, wisdom, common sense and flexibility of this greatest of all Americans of his day.

Franklin continued to work through 1786–89, but his willing body was being destroyed by his diseases. He was taking opium for his pains and the drug had killed his appetite—he lost weight and looked skeletal. It was then, in his dying days, that he wrote his thoughts on God in a letter to Ezra Stiles, the president of Yale.

> Here is my creed. I believe in one God, Creator of the universe. That He governs it by his providence. That He ought to be worshipped. That the most acceptable service we render Him is doing good to His other children. That the soul of man is immortal, and will be treated with justice in another life, respecting its conduct in this. These I take to be the fundamental principles of all sound religion, and I regard them as you do in whatever sect I meet with them.

Franklin added that he had the highest respect for the system of morals of Jesus but said that it had received various "corrupt changes," and that he had some "doubts as to his divinity, though it is a question I do not dogmatize on." He added wryly that soon enough he would be able to find out.

Franklin's time came on April 17, 1790, eighty-four years and three months after his birth. His last words, uttered as he was uncomfortably shifting his position in bed, were: "A dying man can do nothing easy."

Nothing Franklin had ever done had been easy. He had lived always in the eye of a storm. But he loved every minute of his life, bad and good alike. He was so alive, so universal in his thoughts, that he is the most permanently contemporary of all Americans. Not only does he live on in our memory and in the memory of the British and the French, but somehow he lives on as one of us today.

If Washington or Jefferson were to be resurrected and walk into the Congress today, that garrulous body would be struck silent in awe. If Ben Franklin were to come alive and walk in, why, he would wave his favorite gold-tipped crabapple stick at his colleagues, slide into a seat easily, chat with them, show up later for dinner and flirt with their wives.

Franklin was different from our other Founding Fathers in many ways, but, perhaps, principally, in that Jefferson and Washington were plantation owners, the early aristocrats of America, members of the rural ruling classes, whereas Franklin was a member of the urban lower classes, a working man, a printer, one of the pre-proletariat of America. As a poor boy and school dropout who became wealthy, learned in many fields and respected throughout the world, his life is the almost perfect illustration of the American dream. Franklin was, at one and the same time, a common and a most uncommon man. In this sense he is not only one of our Founding Fathers, he is the quintessential American, what we would like all Americans to be.

Bibliography

Franklin's fifteen years in England as a colonial agent are well documented, his nine years in France somewhat less so. Through 1771, the definitive source is the Yale edition of the *Franklin Papers* (19 volumes thus far, New Haven: 1959–74), which includes not only everything extant that Franklin wrote but also every letter written to him, often with voluminous notes. For succeeding years, the ten volumes of Franklin's *Writings* edited by Albert H. Smyth (New York: Macmillan, 1905–7) make up the fullest selection. The *Complete Works* edited by John Bigelow (12 volumes, New York: Putnam, 1904) contain useful notes and some letters to Franklin not reprinted by Smyth. The *Autobiographical Writings* edited by Carl Van Doren (New York: Viking, 1948) include a number of pieces not found in any other collection, and the notes are extensive and valuable. Van Doren's *Benjamin Franklin* (New York: Viking, 1938) is still the indispensable biography. Less comprehensive but more up to date is Alfred Owen Aldridge's excellent *Benjamin Franklin, Philosopher and Man* (Philadelphia: Lippincott, 1965). Many fascinating and hitherto undisclosed details of Franklin's personal life, with shrewd insights into his character, make *The Private Franklin: The Man and His Family,* by Claude-Anne Lopez and Eugenia W. Herbert (New York: Norton, 1975), of first importance for any student of Franklin. The same qualities distinguish Mme Lopez' *Mon Cher Papa: Franklin and the Ladies of France* (New Haven: Yale University Press, 1966), the first full-length study of Franklin's relations with Mesdames Helvétius and Brillon, among others, and it is a mine of bibliographical information. Aldridge's *Franklin and His French Contemporaries* (New York: New York University Press, 1956) is similarly valuable for its leads to often obscure sources. *Franklin in France,* by Edward Everett Hale and Edward Everett Hale, Jr. (2 volumes, Boston: Roberts Bros., 1888), though outdated in some respects, is still a major work, thoughtful and scholarly, with extensive quotations from Franklin's correspondents during his stay in France.

As a guide to Franklin's official career in France, the most useful single work is Samuel Flagg Bemis, *The Diplomacy of the American Revolution* (Bloomington: Indiana University Press, reprinted 1967). Gerald Stourzh, *Benjamin Franklin and American Foreign Policy* (Chicago: University of Chicago Press, 1954), is balanced and scholarly, with extremely useful bibliographical notes. On negotiations leading to the peace treaty of 1783, Richard B. Morris, *The Peacemakers: The Great Powers and American Independence* (New York: Harper & Row, 1965), stands alone; massively detailed and minutely documented, it draws on some hitherto unexamined materials in European archives and elsewhere. Henri Doniol, *Histoire de la participation de la France à l'établissement des États-Unis d'Amérique* (5 volumes, Paris: Imprimerie Nationale, 1886–92), reprints many documents, in both French and English, from French archives. The twenty-five volumes of B. F. Stevens, *Facsimiles of Manuscripts in European Archives Relating to America, 1773–1783* (London: 1889–98), make available many documents in the Public Records Office, London, the Auckland collection at King's College, Cambridge, and the Archives des Affaires Étrangères in Paris (those in French with parallel translations into English); on some of the murkier periods, especially that before the Franco-American alliance of 1778 became official, there is almost nowhere to go but to the not always easily decipherable contents of these huge, handsome folios. On the American side, the most useful collection is the six-volume *Revolutionary Diplomatic Correspondence of the United States,* edited by Francis Wharton (Washington: Government Printing Office, 1889), with an introduction and notes that remain of great interest though occasionally tendentious and somewhat out of date. More recent, and also useful, are the *Letters of Members of the Continental Congress,* edited by Edmund C. Burnett (Washington: Carnegie Institution, 1921–36).

Other publications drawn upon in the research for this book include:

Abernethy, Thomas Perkins. *Western Lands and the American Revolution.* New York: D. Appleton-Century, 1937. Useful on the wrangling in Congress and financial speculation in Paris.

———. "The Origin of the Franklin-Lee Imbroglio," *North Carolina Historical Review,* XV (1938):41–45. On Silas Deane, Robert and Thomas Morris, and Franklin, about whom the author is inclined to revive the questions raised by Arthur Lee.

Adams, John. *Diary and Autobiography,* edited by L. H. Butterfield. 5 volumes, Cambridge: Harvard University Press, 1961–66. The great patriot and peppery colleague in whom Franklin somehow always brought out the worst left a vivacious record, flattering to neither man but valuable for that very reason.

Aldridge, Alfred Owen. "Jacques Barbeu Dubourg, A French Disciple of Benjamin Franklin," *Proceedings of the American Philosophical Society,* 95(1951):331–92. Some hitherto unpublished material on French secret aid and on one of Franklin's close friends in Paris.

Andrews, Charles M. "A Note on the Franklin-Deane Mission to France," *Yale University Library Gazette,* II (1928):53–68. An important footnote on the Pulteney mission of 1778, reprinting letters of Franklin and Deane.

Augur, Helen. *The Secret War of Independence.* New York: Duell, Sloan & Pearce, 1955. Useful on the arms trade in the early years of the Revolution, and Franklin's role in it.

Bell, Whitfield J. " 'All Clear Sunshine': New Letters of Franklin and Mary Stevenson Hewson," *Proceedings of the American Philosophical Society,* 100 (1965): 521–36. Correspondence with the English friend who may have been, of all the women in Franklin's life, the one he loved most.

Bemis, Samuel Flagg. "British Secret Service and the French-American Alliance," *American Historical Review,* XXIX (1924):474–95. On Edward Bancroft as spy and double agent. A few historians still aren't convinced; for most, Bemis settled the matter.

Bernardy, Amy A. "La Missione di Beniamino Franklin a Parigi nei dispacci degli Ambasciatori Veneziani in Francia 1776–1786," *Archivio storico italiano,* LXXVII (1920):237–62. What the Venetian ambassadors wrote home about Franklin—mainly concerning diplomatic snubs to an envoy whose country nobody but the French had recognized.

Bigelow, John. "Franklin's Home and Host in France," *Century Illustrated Monthly Magazine,* 35(1888):741–54. On Donatien Leray de Chaumont, Franklin's landlord at Passy, with a description of the house and its setting.

Bonsal, Stephen. *When the French Were Here.* Garden City: Doubleday, Doran, 1945. An illuminating record of what French officers saw and did in America, based on letters in French archives, some not previously translated.

Bowen, Catherine Drinker. *The Most Dangerous Man in America: Scenes from the Life of Benjamin Franklin.* Boston: Little, Brown, 1974. An affectionate tribute—her last book—by the noted biographer of John Adams. The final scene is the one at the Cockpit in London.

Boyd, Julian P. "Silas Deane: Death by a Kindly Teacher of Treason?" *William and Mary Quarterly,* Ser. 3, XVI(1959):165–87, 319–42, 515–50. The controversy over whether Silas Deane was or was not a traitor to the United States goes on and on, with no sign of being finally resolved. Here is one scholarly case against him, with a good deal on Edward Bancroft as well.

Capefigue, Jean-Baptiste Honoré. *Louis XVI, ses Relations Diplomatiques.* 4 volumes, Paris: 1844. See Volume I for a royalist view of Franklin.

Carroll, Charles. *Journal.* New York: New York Times, 1969. A firsthand account of the ill-fated journey to Canada in 1776, in which Franklin took part.

Chinard, Gilbert. "Music Enjoyed by Franklin," *Proceedings of the American Philosophical Society,* 100(1956):331–37. On Scottish airs, drinking songs, the armonica, Handel—whose music Franklin didn't enjoy—and Mme Brillon.

Clark, William Bell. *Lambert Wickes: Sea Raider and Diplomat.* New Haven: Yale University Press, 1932. Details on Franklin's embarkation for France in 1776 and the cat-and-mouse game played by American privateers, minutely documented.

Cohen, I. Bernard. *Franklin and Newton.* Philadelphia: American Philosophical Society, 1956. An account of Franklin's contribution to physics, which the author believes is generally underrated.

Commager, Henry Steele, and Richard B. Morris, eds. *The Spirit of 'Seventy-Six: The Story of the American Revolution as Told by the Participants.* Indianapolis and New York: Bobbs-Merrill, 1958. Firsthand records giving the human dimension of military events.

Conner, Paul W. *Poor Richard's Politicks: Benjamin Franklin and His New American Order.* New York: Oxford University Press, 1965. On Franklin's political ideas, notably his vision of a British commonwealth.

Correspondance secrète, politique et littéraire. Londres: chez John Adams, 1787. The eighteenth-century underground press, with lively vignettes on what opinion-makers in France were talking about—including several Franklin anecdotes.

Corwin, Edward S. *French Policy and the American Alliance of 1778.* Princeton: Princeton University Press, 1970. A standard work, with a useful bibliography.

Crane, Verner W. *Benjamin Franklin and a Rising People.* Boston: Little, Brown, 1954. An entertaining and reliable short biography.

———, ed. *Benjamin Franklin's Letters to the Press, 1758–1775.* Chapel Hill: University of North Carolina Press, 1950. Documenting one of Franklin's main activities during his stay in England, with useful commentary.

———. "The Club of Honest Whigs: Friends of Science and Liberty," *William and Mary Quarterly,* Ser. 3, XXIII (1966):210–33. Some of Franklin's closest associates in England figure here.

Currey, Cecil B. *Code Number 72: Ben Franklin, Patriot or Spy?* Englewood Cliffs, N.J.: Prentice-Hall, 1972. Deliberately controversial, even provocative, this revisionary antidote to the partisan tone of earlier biographers (including Van Doren) is finally unpersuasive but worth consulting as a bracer as well as for its bibliographical notes.

———. *Road to Revolution: Benjamin Franklin in England, 1765–1775.* Garden City: Anchor Books, 1968. Ditto the above.

Davidson, Philip. *Propaganda and the American Revolution.* Chapel Hill: University of North Carolina Press, 1941. Excellent background material, with some observations on Franklin and Paine.

Deane, Silas. *Papers,* ed. Charles Isham. 5 volumes, New York: New-York Historical Society, 1887–89. The letters of this unhappy figure are an important source on American relations with France during the early years of the American Revolution.

Deffand, Marquise du. *Lettres . . . à Horace Walpole (1766–1780),* edited by Mrs. Paget Toynbee. London: Methuen, 1912. More anti-American than Walpole was, the aged Mme du Deffand entertained both Franklin and the British Ambassador at her salon, and passed along the latest about them.

Dupuy, R. Ernest, and Trevor Dupuy. *The Compact History of the Revolutionary War.* New York: Hawthorn, 1963. Military engagements crisply recorded; the most useful single book on the subject.

Durand, John, ed. *New Materials for the History of the American Revolution.* New York: Henry Holt & Co., 1889. Documents from French archives, translated and annotated, including a letter written by the French agent Bonvouloir from Philadelphia and an account of the attempt to bribe Tom Paine.

Duveen, Denis I., and Herbert S. Klickstein. "Benjamin Franklin and Antoine Laurent Lavoisier," *Annals of Science,* 11(1955):103–28, 271–308. A carefully documented study of Franklin's association with the great chemist, and with other scientists of his age.

Eddy, George Simpson. "Ramble Through the Mason-Franklin Collection," *Yale University Library Gazette,* X(1936):65–90. Quotes some previously unpublished letters to and from Franklin.

Fay, Bernard. *Franklin, the Apostle of Modern Times.* Boston: Little, Brown, 1929. Enthusiastic and not always accurate, this biography by a French-born author does shed light on Franklin's associations in France.

Fennelly, Catherine. "William Franklin of New Jersey," *William and Mary Quarterly,* Ser. 3, VI(1949):361–82. A sympathetic account of Benjamin Franklin's Loyalist son.

Ferguson, E. James. "Business, Government, and Congressional Investigation in the Revolution," *William and Mary Quarterly,* Ser. 3, XVI(1959):293–318. On graft and profiteering, Robert Morris and the politics of the Lee-Deane controversy.

______. *The Power of the Purse.* Chapel Hill: University of North Carolina Press, 1961. Details on the French loans to the U.S. and the currency devaluation of 1780.

Force, Peter, ed. *American Archives,* 4th and 5th Ser. Washington: 1837–46, 1848–53. Contains some documents not in other collections, e.g., a letter of Dubourg to Franklin dated June–July, 1776.

Franklin, William Temple, ed. *The Works of Dr. Benjamin Franklin.* 6 volumes, Philadelphia: 1808–18. The editor of this collection, Franklin's grandson, traveled with him to France and served as his secretary. There is less here than might be hoped for in the way of firsthand annotation, however.

Franklin, Benjamin. *Satires and Bagatelles,* ed. by Paul McPharlin. Detroit: Fine Book Circle, 1937. Along with the more widely reprinted of the "Bagatelles," this collection includes such things as the "Petition of the Letter Z" (written to let off steam over the importunities of Ralph Izard) and "The Flies in Mr. Franklin's House Address Madame Helvétius," which must rank as the zaniest proposal (or proposition?) on record.

Gershoy, Leo. *From Despotism to Revolution.* New York: Harper & Row, 1947. Good on the personalities of European rulers of the eighteenth century.

Gleason, J. Philip. "A Scurrilous Colonial Election and Franklin's Reputation," *William and Mary Quarterly,* Ser. 3, XVIII(1961):68–84. On the events of 1764, when Franklin lost an election to the Pennsylvania Assembly.

Greene, William. "Journal of a Visit to Paris," *Massachusetts Historical Society Proceedings,* 54(1922):84–138. Includes an entertaining account of several visits to Passy.

Hall, Max. *Benjamin Franklin and Polly Baker: The History of a Literary Deception.* Chapel Hill: University of North Carolina Press, 1960. Documenting the most durable of Franklin's hoaxes, a feminist tract ahead of its time.

Hanna, William S. *Benjamin Franklin and Pennsylvania Politics.* Stanford: Stanford University Press, 1964. Political maneuverings, elections won and lost, and a not altogether savory picture of Franklin.

Hans, Nicholas. "Franklin, Jefferson, and the English Radicals at the End of the Eighteenth Century," *Proceedings of the American Philosophical Society,* 98(1954):406–26. On cross-Channel correspondence during the Revolution, the use of ciphers and the Enlightenment.

Hart, Albert B., ed. *American History Told by Contemporaries.* 2 volumes, New York: Macmillan, 1924. Volume 2 contains firsthand material from the Revolutionary period.

Hawke, David Freeman. *Paine.* New York: Harper & Row, 1974. Good on Paine's visit to France with John Laurens in 1781, and on his relations with Gérard and Luzerne, the French envoys to America.

Hays, I. Minis, ed. *Calendar of the Papers of Benjamin Franklin in the Library of the American Philosophical Society.* 5 volumes, Philadelphia: American Philosophical Society, 1908. Brief summaries of most items, chronologically arranged. A mine of information on the where, when and who of Franklin's correspondents.

Henderson, H. James. "Congressional Factionalism and the Attempt to Recall Franklin," *William and Mary Quarterly,* Ser. 3, XXVII(1970):245–67. An analysis applying statistical methods to a murky episode.

Hindle, Brooke. *The Pursuit of Science in Revolutionary America, 1735–1789.* Durham: Duke University Press, 1956. Useful on Franklin's relations with Joseph Priestley.

Jay, John. *Correspondence and Public Papers,* ed. H. P. Johnston. 4 volumes, New York: G. P. Putnam's Sons, 1890–93. Volumes I and II contain firsthand information on the peace negotiations of 1782–83.

Jay, William. *The Life of John Jay.* New York: J. & J. Harper, 1833. Contains an interesting passage on Jay's recollection of the visit of Bonvouloir, the French secret agent, to Philadelphia in 1775.

Jorgensen, Chester, and Frank L. Mott, eds. *Benjamin Franklin: Representative Selections.* New York: Hill & Wang, 2nd ed., 1962. The long biographical introduction and extensive bibliography are both useful.

Kammen, Michael G. *A Rope of Sand: The Colonial Agents, British Politics, and the American Revolution.* New York: Random House Vintage Books, 1974. Informative on Franklin's career as a colonial agent, and the events leading him to side with the rebels.

Kite, Elizabeth S. "Benjamin Franklin—Diplomat," *Catholic World,* CXLII(1935):28–37. Depicts Franklin as a prisoner of the French Foreign Ministry.

Labaree, Leonard W. "Benjamin Franklin's British Friendships," *Proceedings of the American Philosophical Society,* 108(1964):423–28. The several circles in which Franklin, ever the joiner, was at home in London—and also in Scotland.

Labaree, Leonard W., and Whitfield J. Bell, eds. *Mr. Franklin: A Selection from His Personal Letters.* New Haven: Yale University Press, 1956. Some of

Franklin's best letters, beautifully presented and illustrated.

Lee, Richard Henry. *Life of Arthur Lee.* 2 volumes, Boston: Wells & Lilley, 1829. An adversary view of Franklin, but nonetheless a valuable one, emerges from the diaries that make up a good part of this memoir.

Lopez, Claude-Anne. "Saltpeter, Tin and Gunpowder: Addenda to the Correspondence of Lavoisier and Franklin," *Annals of Science,* 16(1960):83–84. Contains some hitherto unpublished letters, along with details of one of the irksome negotiations Franklin was involved in during his stay in France.

Lutnick, Solomon. *The American Revolution and the British Press, 1775–1783.* Columbia: University of Missouri Press, 1967. Including an account of the speculation, most of it abusive, on what that dangerous man Franklin was really up to in France.

Madariaga, Isabel de. *Britain, Russia, and the Armed Neutrality of 1780.* New Haven: Yale University Press, 1962. On the role of Catherine the Great in European policy at the time of the American Revolution.

Marshall, Christopher. *Diary,* edited by William Duane. Albany: Joel Munsell, 1877. A Philadelphia druggist's account of events during the Revolution.

Mémoires secrets et inédits sur les cours de France aux XV, XVI, XVII et XVIII siècles. 8 volumes, Paris: 1829. Containing many Franklin anecdotes.

Meng, John Joseph. *Despatches and Instructions of Conrad Alexandre Gérard, 1778–1780.* Baltimore: Johns Hopkins Press, 1939. Documents from the French archives, consisting mainly of the correspondence (in French) between Vergennes, the French Foreign Minister, and Gérard, the first French envoy to the United States.

______. "French Diplomacy in Philadelphia, 1778–79." *Catholic Historical Review,* 24(1938):39–57. Summarizing Gérard's career in America, with attention to the Lee-Deane imbroglio.

Moore, Frank, ed. *Diary of the American Revolution.* 2 volumes, New York: New York Times & Arno Press, 1969. Background material culled from contemporary newspapers.

Morison, Samuel Eliot. *The Oxford History of the American People.* New York: Oxford University Press, 1965. The chapters on the Boston Massacre and other events leading to Lexington and Concord are especially vivid and circumstantial.

Morris, Richard B. "The Revolution's Caine Mutiny," *American Heritage,* XI (April, 1960). John Paul Jones, Arthur Lee, and Franklin were all involved in this disagreeable episode surrounding the half-mad Captain Landais.

Newcomb, Benjamin H. *Franklin and Galloway: A Political Partnership.* New Haven: Yale University Press, 1972. On the friend, deputy and political heir who eventually sided with the Loyalists. This book mainly concerns Pennsylvania politics before the Revolution.

O'Donnell, William Emmet. *The Chevalier de la Luzerne.* Louvain: Bibliothèque de l'Université; Bruges: Desalée de Brouwer, 1938. The successor to Gérard as French Minister to the United States, who wielded even greater power over the Congress. See Chapter V for the best available account of the manipulations that led to Franklin's nomination as one of five commissioners to negotiate peace with Britain.

Pennsylvania Magazine of History and Biography. Many issues contain memoirs and letters nowhere else in print. See, e.g., Volume XIII(1888):97–115, for the journals of Manasseh Cutler, recalling Franklin in his old age; and Volume XXVII(1903):151–75, for letters of Franklin's correspondents, including William Strahan, Joseph Priestley and his son William.

Parton, James. *Life and Times of Benjamin Franklin.* 2 volumes, New York: Mason Brothers, 1865. An old-fashioned, full-scale biography, out of date in some particulars but immensely good reading.

Plumb, J. H. "Ravaged by Common Sense," *New York Review of Books,* April 19, 1973. A thoughtful assessment of Franklin's character and place in history.

"The Price Letters," *Massachusetts Historical Society Proceedings,* XVII(1903):262–317. Correspondence of an English Unitarian Minister with Franklin, Arthur Lee, and others on both sides of the Atlantic.

Priestley, Joseph. *Memoirs* . . . London: J. Johnson, 1806. A close friend and disciple who recorded Franklin's last hours in London in 1775, with comments on his attachment to Britain.

Quincy, Josiah. *Memoir of the Life of Josiah Quincy Jun. of Massachusetts.* Boston: Cummings, Hilliard, & Company, 1825. Includes a firsthand record of meetings with Franklin in London during the latter part of 1774 and early in 1775.

Ramsey, David. *The History of the American Revolution.* New York: Russell and Russell, 1789. A contemporary account, especially good on the Southern campaign.

Roelker, William Greene, ed. *Benjamin Franklin and Catharine Ray Greene: Their Correspondence 1755–1790.* Philadelphia: American Philosophical Society, 1949. The record of a flirtation that became a lifelong friendship, somewhat primly annotated.

Sainte-Beuve, C. A. *Portraits of the Eighteenth Century.* New York: G. P. Putnam's Sons, 1905. See Volume I, pp. 211–75, for a French assessment of Franklin.

Sellers, Charles Coleman. *Benjamin Franklin in Portraiture.* New Haven: Yale University Press, 1962. Learned, fascinating and full of details on Franklin's social life in England and France.

Smith, Paul H. "Benjamin Franklin: Gun Runner," *Pennsylvania Magazine of History and Biography,* 95(1971):526–29. A critical review of *Road to Revolution* by Cecil Currey.

Smyth, Albert H. "Franklin's Social Life in France: With Hitherto Unpublished Letters," *Putnam's Monthly,* I(1906):30–41, 167–73, 310–16, 431–38. Letters to and from Mme Brillon, with Franklin at his most winsome and entertaining.

Sosin, Jack M. *Agents and Merchants: British Colonial Policy and the Origins of the American Revolution.* Lincoln: University of Nebraska Press, 1965. Useful on the episode of the Hutchinson letters.

Steell, Willis. *Benjamin Franklin of Paris, 1776–1785.* New York: Minton, Balch & Co., 1928. Quasi-fictional portrayals of Franklin and his associates in Paris, based on authentic material but with some inaccuracies, as in the spelling of names.

Stinchcombe, William. *The American Revolution and the French Alliance.* Syracuse: Syracuse University Press, 1969. Good on peace instructions of 1781, and on congressional politics generally.

Tolles, Frederick B. "Franklin and the Pulteney Mission," *Huntington Library Quarterly,* XVII(1953):37–58. Based on previously unpublished material in the Huntington Library.

U.S. Continental Congress. *Journals.* 34 volumes, Washington: Government Printing Office, 1904–37. Since there was no official transcript of debates, not everything one could wish to know is recorded here, although official resolutions are.

Van Alstyne, Richard W. "Great Britain, the War for Independence, and the 'Gathering Storm' in Europe, 1775–1778." *Huntington Library Quarterly,* XXVII(1964):311–46. On gunpowder from Holland, with a dissenting view of Edward Bancroft.

Van Doren, Carl. *Jane Mecom: The Favorite Sister of Benjamin Franklin.* New York: Viking, 1950. Sheds light on Franklin's family and social life.

______. *The Letters of Benjamin Franklin and Jane Mecom.* Princeton: Princeton University Press for the American Philosophical Society, 1950. Includes some previously unpublished Franklin letters.

______. *The Secret War of Independence.* New York: Viking, 1941. An account of secret aid, treason and spying, with detailed bibliographical notes.

Van Tyne, Claude H. "Influences which Determined the French Government to Make the Treaty with America, 1778," *American Historical Review,* XXI(1915–16):528–41. Arguing that Vergennes found it "the better policy to join with America and thus win her support . . . than to wait for England to make peace with America"—a notion shrewdly exploited by Franklin and his colleagues.

Watson, W. C., ed. *Men and Times of the Revolution, or Memoirs of Elkanah Watson.* New York: Dana, 2nd. ed., 1857. An arresting account of social life at Passy and elsewhere in France, full of charm but including a malodorous portrait of Tom Paine.

Wright, Esmond. *Fabric of Freedom, 1763–1800.* New York: Hill & Wang, 1961. A survey of British policy in America, with particular attention to the Stamp Act and the Continental Congress.

Index

The abbreviation F is used for Franklin. Letters to or from Franklin are indexed under names of correspondents. Subentries are in chronological order according to the first appearance of a subject in the text.

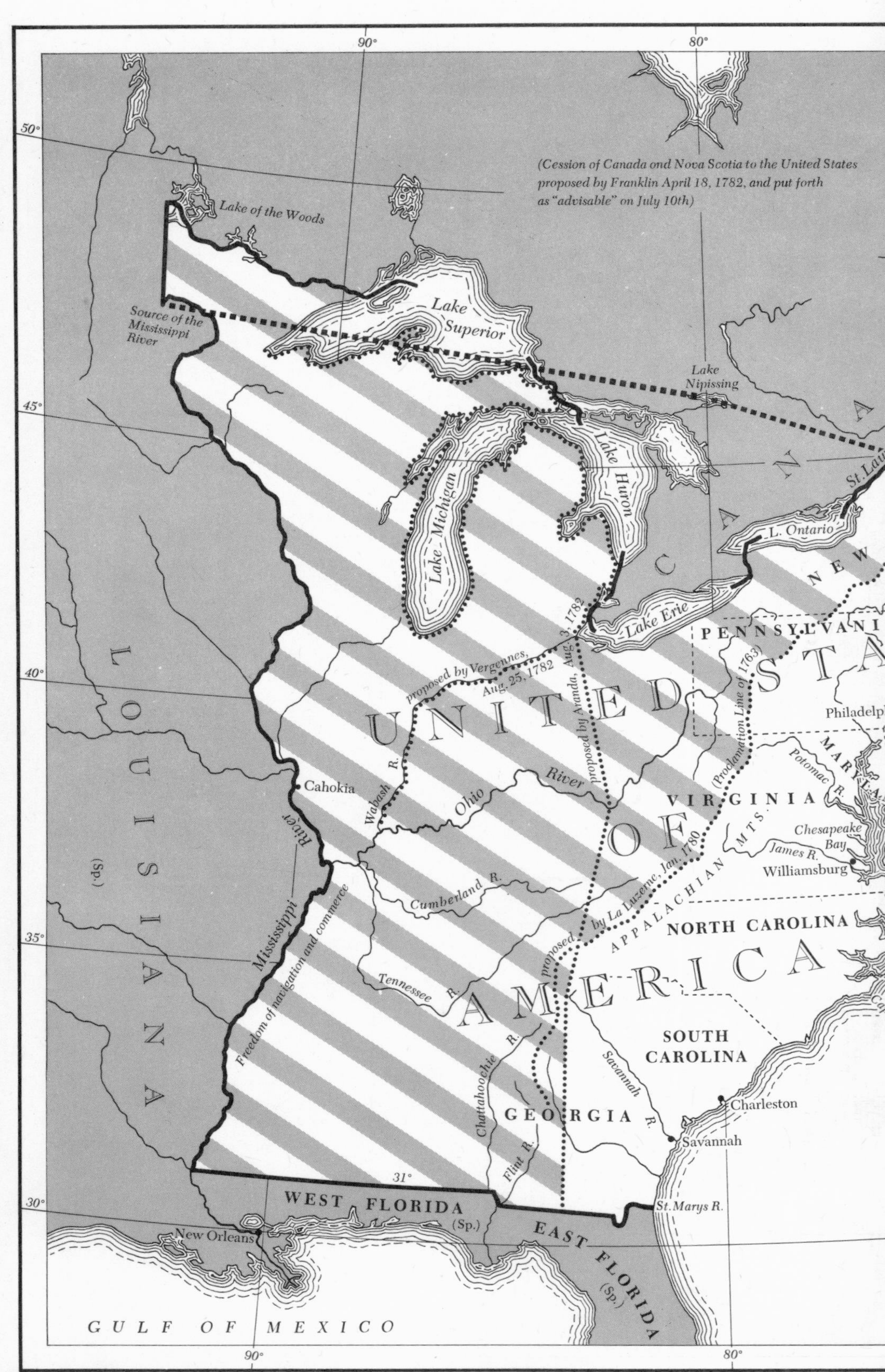
(Cession of Canada and Nova Scotia to the United States proposed by Franklin April 18, 1782, and put forth as "advisable" on July 10th)
Lake of the Woods
Source of the Mississippi River
Lake Superior
Lake Nipissing
Lake Michigan
Lake Huron
L. Ontario
Lake Erie
St. Law
C A N A D A
L O U I S I A N A
(Sp.)
PENNSYLVANI
VIRGINIA
MARYLA
NORTH CAROLINA
SOUTH CAROLINA
GEORGIA
UNITED STATES OF AMERICA
NEW
proposed by Vergennes, Aug. 25, 1782
proposed by Aranda, Aug. 3, 1782
proposed by La Luzerne, Jan. 1780
(Proclamation Line of 1763)
APPALACHIAN MTS.
Cahokia
Wabash R.
Ohio River
Cumberland R.
Tennessee R.
Mississippi River
Freedom of navigation and commerce
Chattahoochie R.
Flint R.
Savannah R.
Potomac R.
Chesapeake Bay
James R.
Williamsburg
Philadelph
Charleston
Savannah
St. Marys R.
New Orleans
WEST FLORIDA (Sp.)
EAST FLORIDA (Sp.)
GULF OF MEXICO
31°
90°
80°
50°
45°
40°
35°
30°